A Materialist Reading
of the Gospel of Mark

List of Symbols

AA	adversaries (actants)
ACT	actantial code
ANAL	analytic code
BAS	basileic code
c→b	passage from "curse" to "blessing"
C	crowd (actant)
CHR	chronological code
DD	disciples (actants)
GEO	geographical code
Gr	Greek text of Mark
J	Jesus (actant)
I, II	individual actant(s)
Ib, IIb	individual(s) who is (are) blessed (cured)
Ic, IIc	individual(s) who is (are) cursed (sick, defective)
MYTH	mythological code
Q1, etc.	question(s) in the ANAL code
SOC	social code
STR	strategic code
STR AA	strategy of the adversaries
STR J	strategy of Jesus
STR Z	strategy of the Zealots
SYMB	symbolic code
TOP	topographical code

A Materialist Reading
of the Gospel of Mark

FERNANDO BELO

Translated from the French by
Matthew J. O'Connell

ORBIS BOOKS
Maryknoll, New York 10545

In order to adhere more closely to the numbering of footnotes in the original French edition, the English translation utilizes a system that includes some *a* and *b* notes (e.g., 59, 59a, 59b, 60).

First published as *Lecture matérialiste de l'évangile de Marc: Récit-Pratique-Idéologie*, 2nd edition revised, 1975, copyright © 1974 by Les Editions du Cerf, 29, bd Latour-Maubourg, Paris

English translation copyright © 1981 by Orbis Books, Maryknoll, NY 10545

Library of Congress Cataloging in Publication Data

Belo, Fernando, 1933-
  A materialist reading of the Gospel of Mark.

  Translation of Lecture matérialiste de l'évangile de Marc.
  Bibliography: p.
  1. Bible. N.T. Mark—Commentaries. 2. Sociology, Biblical. 3. Marxian economics.
I. Title
BS2585.5.B4413   226'.306   80-24756
ISBN 0-88344-323-6 (pbk.)

For Nuno Teotonio Pereira
and the other companions.

To the brothers and sisters in Brazil and Chile.
The Gospel of Mark was written,
nineteen centuries ago,
amid the same savage and bloody repression.

In memory, too, of the blacks massacred in South Africa.

According to the good old western tradition,
repression and massacres
are the work of people who often call themselves Christians.
Supreme misreading of the Gospel,
incurable blindness.

> But greater than all this
> is Jesus Christ,
> who knew nothing of finances,
> nor are we told he had a library.
>
> *Fernando Pessoa*

Recollection

of my father and mother
who learned to be brother and sister to me,
of the evening of life

of the old teacher
with the clear eyes
under his gray hair,
who was killed by Stupidity
a few months before the feast day

of my sister, named after a prophet,
who, through death and madness,
sought only life.

Then
there is the Daughter of the forest,
there is Clara,
there is André.

Summary Table of Contents

Publisher's Preface

Seldom does a publisher feel the need to write a Preface. That exercise is usually best left to someone whose authority in the book's field would serve to commend the book to readers interested in that field.

Belo's *A Materialist Reading of the Gospel of Mark* is, however, a quite unusual book which, in turn, calls for the unusual practice of a Publisher's Preface. If nothing else, it makes it easier for an irate reader or reviewer to ask, "Why did you ever publish it?" rather than try to reach a rather inaccessible author to ask, "Why did you ever write it?"

In this case, the book was published for basically the same reason it was written, viz., that the text, in Belo's words, "is the fruit of passion and naiveté."

The passion may well seem evanescent to the reader who is asked to painstakingly plod through a detailed exegesis of the Gospel of Mark in which references to social scientists and scripture scholars shuttle back and forth like threads on a loom—and often with the same eye-blurring speed.

The naiveté (the author is naïve enough to admit he is naïve) may seem to many readers amply confirmed on page after page as the author, with few academic credentials, struggles to bring the vari-colored lights of many disciplines to focus brightly on a question every socially concerned Christian must eventually confront: "How can I, attempting to witness to Christ in this most savage and inhuman of modern centuries, find new ways to relate to my ancient Gospel heritage?"

At base, *A Materialist Reading of the Gospel of Mark* is, despite its heavy technical apparatus, autobiographical; it tells how Belo attempted to find answers to the above question. The reader willing to share his search will be surprised by what surprised Belo, will feel within the agonies that often beset him, and will, hopefully, at journey's end, find Belo's exultant freedom upon entering into the *ekklesia*—not simply a Christian community as a gathering, but an *ekklesia* with a specific practice on three levels, economic, political, and ideological. The practice, that is, of faith, hope, and charity.

Preface to the English Translation

I am very happy to see an English translation of my book being published, and I am deeply grateful to Matthew O'Connell, who had the courage to undertake so thankless a task. At the same time, I feel a certain dread. Even French readers have suffered from the jargon of the Parisian theories I was forced to use and from the maze of references to Althusser, Barthes, Kristeva, Bataille, Derrida, and others. English-speaking readers are said to be more empirical and pragmatic; will they not feel smothered by all this foreign and massive theorizing?

This swarm of concepts, without which, however, I could not have written a single line, creates several kinds of obstacles. But these are due less to any inability to understand than to misapprehensions. I shall mention two such obstacles, one connected with exegesis, the other with Marxism.

In most cases, the exegetes have regarded my book as insulting to their science, inasmuch as a number of polemical notes dealing with the ideology at work in exegetical discourse have been taken as casting doubt on the exegetes' competency. But, as a matter of fact, since I am not a specialist in exegesis, I would indeed have been a hypocrite if I did not recognize and acknowledge my substantial debt to the exegetical sciences.

Of course, when I level accusations of idealism against exegetes in the name of "my" materialism, I open myself to the same accusation in reverse: I too am an ideologue. This is precisely why I attempt to define the theoretical place from which I do my reading—something that is not a usual practice in texts in which readings of the Bible are offered.

In addition, for reasons having to do with my method and its Barthesian inspiration, exegetes here and there have concluded that I am reviving the classical problem of the life of Jesus. But this is not at all my intention; on the contrary, I pay no attention at all to "the history of Jesus." On the other hand, I am profoundly interested in the "narrative of Jesus"—but then I situate myself *within the text.*

The other misapprehension is one to which I myself succumbed: I thought that, given the situation at the beginning of the seventies, the gospel could help us in the Revolution. But Chile and especially the Portuguese experience into which I plunged immediately after the publication of the French original of this book showed me that this myth had had its day. We must rather learn the difficult analyses and strategies of subversion and transformation if we are to make the earth a habitable place that can satisfy human beings and enable them to live in social relationships better adapted to the materiality of the body (hands, feet, eyes) in which the power of our bodies plays the decisive role.* This implies that, without abandoning my analyses I would now be more alert to certain impasses in contemporary Marxism (but I do not see that this would make much difference in the analyses of biblical Palestine) and more disposed to accentuate the aspect of "messianic power" as the most interesting result yielded by my reading.

Turning back now to the reception of my book in France and Italy, I must note that the difficult theoretical jargon I use led many to *read* the book *in a group*. The result I least anticipated has doubtless been the network of militant readers that sprang up in many places. The linking of these readers has been effected in part by the periodical *La Lettre* and my friend M. Clévenot, who has already organized some international meetings and has been endeavoring for some time to carry my thinking further, applying it to other texts of the Bible and to the marginal areas of Christian history (for example, heresies and the Christian forms of utopian socialism). Exegesis and Christian history are emerging from the universities and being taken up by those who regard Christianity as important in their lives and their faith.

This advance toward a materialist Christianity—"materialist" in the sense that the issue will no longer be "grace for souls" but "the power *(puissance)* of bodies"—has hardly begun. There is something tragic and profoundly equivocal in the monopolizing of the gospel by churches, theological discourse, and the universities. This book will fulfill its destiny only when it is itself forgotten (it is, after all, highly theoretical), and something new has come to pass. How describe this "something new"? It will be present when the gospel—with, of course, texts from other horizons—becomes a grill for the reading and valuation (in Nietzsche's sense of the word) of our practices, of our bodies, and of the power that is at work in our bodies and that can be called by the beautiful name "Spirit." In other words: in everyday personal, bodily relationships, on the edges and in the interstices of the capitalism that is suffocating and killing us, things will happen that may be unobtrusive but that can also be unreservedly affirmed and shouted abroad: things which the first Christians grasped and of which Paul said that eyes had never seen them, ears never heard them. All this will be connected with what we are looking for under the name "liberation." It will be connected as well with the ancient promise of resurrection.

---

*[Throughout the book the author uses three French words, each of which has its distinct reference and connotation: *pouvoir*, the power of one class over another; *autorité*, authority, or "power" where there are no social classes; and *puissance* (Mark's *dynamis*), as in *la puissance du corps*, "the 'power' of the body." The limitations of English vocabulary at this point forced me to translate both *pouvoir* and *puissance* (and even *autorité*, at times) by "power" and to let the context indicate the reference. Where *puissance* and *pouvoir* occur together or are contrasted, *pouvoir* may even be translated by, e.g., "authority." —Tr.]

Introduction

K/X OR THE PROBLEMATIC

This text is the fruit of both passion and naiveté.

My writing itself surely gives evidence of the passion: of a body-to-body struggle with the text of the bourgeois-Christian ideology that for a number of years marked out the limits of my field of speech, and a text-to-text struggle with my body that was thus imprisoned.

Where I was naive was in believing that someone with nothing but a licentiate in theology, someone who was a foreigner to boot, could, in independence of the university and the exchanges it makes possible, play an intertextual game that is full of pitfalls, and attempt to cross concepts from highly differentiated epistemological fields: exegesis of the Old and New Testaments, history, semiotics, historical materialism, and philosophy. The "specialists" in these various disciplines will surely cry "Scandal!" or even accuse me of lacking in intellectual perceptiveness.

Yet the risks involved seemed worth it in view of what was at stake, namely, to make possible a confrontation between a political practice that aims to be revolutionary, and a Christian practice that no longer aims at being religious. In any event, the possible criticisms, however severe, cannot take from me the pleasure that was mine during the five or six years it took to write this book.

In a church that is becoming more and more synonymous with crisis,[1] the important new fact of recent years has been the appearance, in Latin America and Latin Europe, of a generation of Christians who are determined to be Marxist in their language and analyses, their political commitments, and the polemics that are their strategies. I give the word "new" its fullest possible meaning, for it is in these Christians alone, and not in the neoreligious associations of the young, that we can discern the possibility of new ways of relating to the Gospel tradition.

Such new ways bring their own difficulties, however, the clearest being the danger that the reference to the Gospel will disappear because it cannot find an embodiment in concrete practices and in the discourse that sustains them. A question often raised shows what is at stake: is not the faith an ideology that contradicts the practices aimed at liberation, in which Christians are now striving to take part?

1

On what epistemological terrain can such a question be raised? On that of historical materialism, where the concept of *ideology* is at home, or on that of theology where the concept of *faith* is situated?

It seems that after thirty or forty years of great productivity, theological discourse has gotten winded. The intensification of the crisis through which Christianity is passing only accentuates the theological *void* the crisis has created (a void that is discernible in the area of publication).

It is a commonplace in various circles that the void is a symptom of a crisis in the language of faith, and that we must find "another" language in which faith can recover "its" meaning. An odd diagnosis, indeed, that finds the specifically Christian to reside at the level of language alone! Isn't the traditional triad faith, hope, and charity? By what right are the latter two left out of the picture? It could easily be shown, I believe, that the exclusion is a symptom of the grip traditional theology has on the discourse of the professionals, a grip that theology maintains by means of ancient dichotomies such as soul/body, transcendence/immanence, or God/world. On the other hand, the reduction of the problem to one of language alone also manages, does it not, to leave out of consideration a number of phenomena that can be rather embarrassing, such as those relating to economics and politics?

The real need, then, is to change terrain. This is the direction taken by the "political theologies" of the Germans and by the Latin American "theologies of liberation," both of which seek to fill the void mentioned above. It then becomes possible to speak of an *epistemological crisis* in theology, which is simply the result of a political crisis, that is, of the impact of the class struggle on the Christian scene.

If we go back now to the question of faith/ideology, our detour, brief though it has been, opens the way for an essay on "faith" in political terms and in terms specifically of an analysis conducted in the epistemological field of historical materialism. Since a key concept in this field is *practice* ("praxis," as they liked to call it a short time ago), an answer may be found to the faith/ideology question if we can define the specifically Christian "something" in terms of practice. Now, as it happens, among the texts dealing with Christian origins, the Gospels are structured as a *narrative* (*récit*); since every narrative is a discourse about/of a practice, perhaps it is the place where the necessary inquiry should be undertaken. Then, shifting to the terrain of the concrete political practices proper to the class struggle, it will be possible to confront these *in a verifiable way* with the "Christian practice" that has been defined through a study of the Gospels, and to ask: is there convergence, or conflict, or contradiction?

If I were to tell the story of how this text came to be written, I would have to recall, first of all, a sketch of it that was presented as a thesis for the licentiate in theology at the Catholic Institute of Paris in 1968. All that has survived of that essay is the choice of Mark's Gospel as the object of analysis. Why this document? The reasons will become clear later in the book; for the moment, I shall say only that it is no accident that Mark is the poor relative among the Gospels and neglected to the profit of the others, which are richer in discourses and teachings and show a higher degree of theological elaboration.

It is likewise no accident that the theologians and "spiritual" writers prefer Paul or John to the Synoptics, whereas the Synoptics have won the favor of a series of readers who have cut their ties to the bourgeoisie and endeavored to regain contact with the proletarian classes. I am thinking of the movements inspired by Charles de Foucauld, the "revision of life" groups within the Young Christian Workers and other organizations, the priest-workers, and so on. This reading has remained marginal; it has not managed to escape the influence of the dominant religious ideology and, in any case, has not won favor with the more "scientific" exegetes. Yet it is from such a reading that I myself have long drawn inspiration; in it I found my initial questions as well as the thread that has guided me in my approach.

Inasmuch as I was thrust by circumstances into an isolation that has only recently been broken, chance determined the reference works I read and the books I came across in the bookshops. Chance thus played no little part in deciding the texts that gradually were brought together and interrelated in my reading and writing.

The reading of Mark raised two initial questions for me: how should I read the text? How should I interpret it? The two questions gave rise to two quite distinct procedures; I passed from the one to the other according to mood, but made sure that each retained a certain autonomy. As a guide in the reading process I took Roland Barthes (to whom I later added Julia Kristeva). The slow passage from a structural analysis of narrative in general to a textual analysis of *this* narrative will be discussed in its proper place.

Much more marked by groping and chance was my search for a set of Marxist concepts that would enable me to relate what is "represented" in the narration to the social formation in which the events are said to have taken place, namely, Palestine in the first century of our era. Part I of this book, on the concept of "mode of production," raises difficult epistemological problems; the brevity of the section does not permit me to take these difficulties fully into account, and for that reason I think I should dwell briefly here on the way the pages came into existence.

After having worked through a certain number of texts of the Althusserian school (why Louis Althusser? Because he put some philosophical order into the confused mass of Marxist texts), I came to see that, apart from a few references to noncapitalist social formations, these works gave the lion's share of their attention to the capitalist mode of production and that, within that area, they were interested chiefly in the economic instance and, to some extent, the political. I would have to look elsewhere for materials for a theory of ideology. I moved from the linguistic theories of Emile Benveniste to the philosophical works of Jacques Derrida by way of Freud's *Interpretation of Dreams* and some texts by and on Jacques Lacan. But how to harmonize these various contributions remained an open question. There was another question likewise unresolved: since I was not interested in exegesis for exegesis's sake or in history for history's sake, what relation was I to establish between the subasiatic formation of ancient Palestine and the monopolistic state capitalism within which we carry on our struggle?

The first clue came to me from the Althusserians and their epistemological theory. On the one hand, the distinction between dialectical materialism and historical materialism[2] and, on the other, Etienne Balibar's references to the "absolute invariance in the elements which are found in *every social structure* (an economic base, legal and political forms, and ideological forms)"[3] and to the possibility of drawing up "*a comparative* table of the forms of different modes of production"[4]—these led me to take a position squarely on the level of dialectical materialism and to attempt a kind of *formal theory* of the unvarying elements. I made this decision despite the danger of methodological confusion and despite the resistances such a procedure must inevitably arouse.

The other decisive contribution came from Jean Jacques Goux's essay "Numismatiques," which brings out in a striking way the *isomorphism* to be seen in the genesis of the forms of exchange. Marx came to this isomorphism in the first chapters of *Capital* for economic exchanges, Freud in his *Three Essays on Sexuality* for sexual impulses, and Lacan for the genesis of the ego; Marx again in some notes on monarchy; and, finally, Derrida for logocentrism in western metaphysics. I may have taken some liberties in making use of Goux's work, but the homology I propose for the modes of circulation depends basically on him. I had little difficulty, moreover, in extending the homology to production and consumption, thus maintaining a single framework for the concepts to be applied.

There was still an area of obscurity; it seemed minor, but proved to have unexpected consequences. The several references in Mark to the matter of *uncleanness* led me to read Mary Douglas's book, and this in turn introduced me to a world whose existence I hardly suspected. Her method, however, left me somewhat unsatisfied, but a remark of Luc de Heusch in his introduction to the French translation of her book led me to Georges Bataille's two great essays on eroticism and on general economics. (I was naively unaware of the distrust most Marxists have for these essays.) Bataille's books enabled me, first of all, to make a bold sally into the legislative texts of the Old Testament and to find therein the broad lines of the *symbolic order* that still plays a part in the Gospel texts. His books enabled me, further, to recast my essay on the mode of production so as to take account of the two levels which I call infrastructure and superstructure. I thus eliminated another lacuna in the texts of the Althusserians, who do not deal with "primitive" societies. (Emmanuel Terray does deal with them, of course, but he uses only ready-made concepts.)

After this short description, the reader will perhaps find it easier to understand how certain questions played a part in the proposed formalization of the concept of mode of production. I refer to the question of the *site of a reading* (this is decisive in Mark); the question of the conditions for the possibility of a revolution in a subasiatic social formation, thus enabling us to compare Jesus with the Zealots and encouraging greater precision in the concepts of *determination* and *closure*; the question of the relations between messianism and the Jewish and Christian religions, which leads to a *theory of religion*; finally, the question of the articulation of the *desires* and the *utopia* of the "actants" of the narrative with their *general equivalents* in the subasiatic social formation.

There were thus two theoretical procedures that remained independent for a time but later intermingled at the writing stage. The latter stage was one of surprises for me; in a way, I became a spectator watching the work of theoretical production as it evolved. It was as though, in the writing process, the concepts worked on their own and produced other concepts.

First came the production of the concept of the subasiatic mode of production that characterized Palestine in the first century of our era. The production of this concept "verified" the validity of the theoretical model that I had applied to the more or less disorganized materials provided by the professional historians. Thus I discovered the overdetermined role of the Jerusalem temple as the focal point in which the contradictions of the social formation were concentrated; this discovery had an important influence on the reading of Mark.

Next, the interpretation of this reading turned into an *essay in materialist ecclesiology,* that is, an ordering of concepts that might yield an explanation of the complicated transformations which the early *ekklesiai* underwent, and of the churches that suppressed and replaced them. In a sense, the essay is a contribution to the history of early Christianity from a materialist standpoint. (The importance of the concept of *invariance* in the constitution of such an ecclesiology is evident.)

Finally, in this work, a specific theoretical problematic is to be read, in the form of a rough sketch of a theory of the relations between *narrative, practice, and ideology.* The last section of the essay on the mode of production (Part I) raises this question, which is then developed throughout the essay in ecclesiology. Have I the right to claim that this contribution sheds light on the highly controverted question of Althusser's theoreticism? If so, then the relation between theory and practice is to be approached from the side of a *theory of narrative.* The criticism leveled at Althusser's antihumanism could likewise be refuted along similar lines: the only humanism is that of people in revolt (as Camus would say); the factor in the practices of people and classes in times past that can provide us with a key to our own destiny would then be their *subversiveness.* By this last I mean the subversiveness that yielded fruits of liberation in terms of bread, of bodies, and of speech (reading and strategy); the subversiveness that created a way out of the everyday world of repression, a window opening on "the singing tomorrows."

To sum up: A *reading of Mark,* which forms the textual core of the book, is the focal point of a threefold problematic: (1) of biblical exegesis and biblical history; (2) of the theoretical articulation of *narrative, practice,* and *ideology*; and (3) of *materialist ecclesiology,* which makes it possible to change the terms in the initial question of the relations between revolutionary political practice and Christian practice. In each of these problematics, my aim, I might say, is always to read Mark with the help of Marx: K/X, then, if I may so put it and render my homage of Roland Barthes's splendid book, S/Z.

I shall end my outline of this ambitious program by saying that the reading of the book will not always be easy—unfortunately!—because many readers will very likely come here and there on areas of theory with which they will be insufficiently familiar.

Let me end where I began. There is nothing neutral about this text, and my bias (even if this does not mean a taking of sides) is clearly stated. When I had reached the field of a materialist ecclesiology and a revolutionary problematic, I could have done what so many others have done, that is, let fall away the whole religious ideological structure to which I was such a passionate adherent in my youth. But when people thus put a stone on the grave of the past, do they not risk seeing the past rise up again in another form, or even allowing it to be active still but in a different guise? I have preferred to plunge ahead and attack the decisive text, the Gospel itself, and to try to determine just where I stand in relation to it. A period of psychoanalysis enabled me to see that I was not on the wrong track; the convergence between the work of speech on the couch and this work of textual analysis through writing soon became evident. Here I am proposing another grill for reading: this text is to be read as a halting effort to move from the familiar surroundings where one lived for so long, to move out like a child who is learning to walk and is experiencing spaces hitherto forbidden, or like a pupil who, with great difficulty but prodded by a naive passion, is learning to read and write.

PART I

THE CONCEPT OF "MODE OF PRODUCTION" (AN ESSAY IN FORMAL THEORY)

PRACTICE, INSTANCE, SOCIAL FORMATION

Practice: "Any process of *transformation* of a determinate given raw material into a determinate *product,* a transformation effected by a determinate human labour, using determinate means (of 'production')."[1]

Hypothesis 1. If we accept that there are three general kinds of "products," namely, "economic goods," the systems whereby the agents of the social formation have their places determined, and texts,[2] then we can define *three.*

Instances: structured aggregates of practices relating to the same general kind of product; the instances therefore are *economic, political,* and *ideological.*[3] Each instance comprises more or less complex regions and fields.[4] The fact that each instance is structured[5] implies that it follows its own specific *logic;* this is why Althusser maintains that each instance is autonomous.

Hypothesis 2. Within each of the three instances, we can distinguish three *modes:* production, circulation, and consumption.[6]

Social formation: the complex aggregate, forming a structured whole, of the various distinct and relatively autonomous instances, the latter being interrelated according to specific modes of determination that are established, in the last analysis, by the economic instance.[7] In an historical social formation several modes of production coexist, one of them being dominant in relation to the others; historical transformations imply torsions, dislocations, and survivals among the forms belonging to the various instances.[8]

N.B. Readers who are put off by Part I, which is highly technical, will perhaps do better to begin immediately with Part II. As they read on, they will find whether, and to what extent, they should go back and look more closely at the section they passed over.

INFRASTRUCTURE AND SUPERSTRUCTURE

Hypothesis 3. On the basis of the following analysis by Bataille of the function of *taboos*:

> There is in nature and there subsists in man a movement which always *exceeds*[9] the bounds, that can never be anything but partially reduced to order. . . .
> In the domain of our life excess manifests itself insofar as violence wins over reason. Work demands the sort of conduct where effort is in constant ratio with productive efficiency. It demands rational behaviour where the wild impulses worked out on feast days and usually in games are frowned upon. If we were unable to repress these impulses we should not be able to work, but work introduces the very reason for repressing them. These impulses confer an *immediate satisfaction*[10] on those who yield to them. Work, on the other hand, promises to those who overcome them a reward *later on*[10]. . . . Most of the time work is the concern of men acting collectively and during the time reserved for work the collective has to oppose those contagious impulses to excess in which nothing is left but the *immediate*[10] surrender to excess, to violence, that is. Hence the human collective, partly dedicated to work, is defined by *taboos*[11] without which it would not have become the *world of work*[11] that it essentially is.[12]

—on the basis of this analysis we can define an *infrastructural level* of articulation for the three instances:

Infraeconomic: the structure of a process of production that implies the *postponement* of consumption.

Infrapolitical or symbolic[13]: the concrete field of the relations among the *bodies* of the agents of the social formation, as articulated with *the symbolic order:* the text of the taboos that put order into this field, the text being one region of the ideological instance.

Hypothesis 4: The *symbolic* (field and order) is the domain especially of *relations of kinship,* that is, of the physical reproduction of the agents of the social formation. On the basis of Lacan's definition of *identification* ("the transformation *produced* in a subject when the latter assumes an image,"[14] or an "imago" as psychoanalytical theory calls it[15]), we can say that the basic process proper to the symbolic is the *production,* by way of the imago of the father in the subject-son, of a specific father/son relationship.

Infraideological: constituted by an oral language[16] that is articulated as a system of differentiated meaningful elements, which system is set up as *different* from the "reality" of the social formation and makes it possible to *read* this reality, that is, to organize it according to specific semantic classifications; and constituted, in addition, by the *function,* exercised in this language, of discovering the *violence* of death for the sake of preserving life, that is, of distinguishing life/death.[17]

Hypothesis 5: The *superstructural,* which in every case already overdetermines the infrastructural, is the level of the organized concrete forms of the various instances which we shall be discussing.

Hypothesis 6: The life/death contradiction, which is connected either with the eating of corpses or with the birth/death cycle in the physical reproduction of the agents of the social formation, is specific to the infrastructural level; that is why the discovery of it is a function belonging to the infraideological.

ECONOMIC, POLITICAL, AND IDEOLOGICAL MODES OF PRODUCTION

Hypothesis 7: Using Althusser's definition of *practice,* we can define as homologues the *modes of production* for each instance.[18]

Productive forces: the relation between the productive agents *(labor power)* and the means of production, including raw materials.[19]

Hypothesis 8:[20] In labor power we must consider a textual element, the *program,* which is the effect of earlier readings of the work process by the productive agents; the reading of this program by the producers is intrinsic to labor power and is an element in the superstructural articulation of the economic and ideological instances.

Relation of production: the relation of economic ownership[21] between the appropriators of the surplus economic products and the means of production.
Means of economic production: the specific combination of the two relations just named, as defining the type of mode of production (in the strict sense of the term).

Hypothesis 9: If the appropriators of the surplus are the workers themselves or all the agents of the social formation together, we will speak of an *autoproductive* economic mode of production (a classless social formation). If the appropriators are the nonproducers, who form a *class* distinct from the class of producers, we will have a class economic mode of production, permeated by a superstructural economic contradiction.

Autonomy: political force intrinsic to the agents,[22] which causes them to occupy the *places* they do on the checkerboard that is the social formation.

Means of political order or political production: on the one hand, the collection of two-sided commands (prohibition of certain places/assignment of other places) that create the concrete political order of the social formation (the commands may either by direct *imperatives*—"do this"—or the result of the reading, by the agents, of the *legislative texts*[23]); on the other hand, *weapons.*

Ordering forces: relation between autonomy and the means of order.

Relation of (political) production: relation between the appropriation of the order of the social formation and the means of order.

Mode of political production: the specific combination of the two foregoing relations.

Hypothesis 10: If the appropriators of the order are all the agents involved, we will have an *autogestional* (classless) political mode of production; the political relations will be relations of authority.[24] If the appropriators form a *class* distinct from the other agents, we will have a *state-administered* political mode of production (with classes), that is permeated by a superstructural political contradiction: the political relations will be relations of *power.* The state is possible only if *weapons,* appropriated by the dominant class, can gain control over the autonomy of the agents of the dominated class.

Hypothesis 11: There can be no autogestion without autoproduction.[25] Historically, autoproductive and autogestional social formations[26] are characterized by the dominance of the symbolic field; the relations of economic and political production exist within the kinship system.[27]

Ideological raw material: the texts already produced, the *reading* of which gives the agent the *competence* (in Chomsky's terminology) to produce a new text as an ideological product.

Means of ideological production: the linguistic structures,[28] possession of which defines the competence of the agent; these structures are *semantic* (structures interrelating the elements that are significant, according to semantic regions) and *syntactic* (structures interrelating the functions or sites occupied by the significant elements in the phrase).

Inscriptive forces: relation between the producers of texts (writing power) and the means of production.

Ideological relation: relation between the ideological appropriators and the linguistic structures. It is established through specific mechanisms, namely, *ideologies.*

Mode of ideological production: the specific combination of the two foregoing relations.

Hypothesis 12: The function of ideologies is to organize semantic regions in accordance with fixed codes[29] (which I shall call *parametric codes*) so as to permit the *reading* (necessary if the structures of the social formation are to be reproduced) of the texts produced in the various practices.[30] The parametric codes always produce in advance the (ideo) logic that determines the classification of signifying elements in semantic regions.

Hypothesis 13: The dominant code always deals with the specific region of the ideological instance, that is, the region of the discernment of life and death.

Hypothesis 14: When the appropriating elements in the ideological relation are the totality of the agents of the social formation, we will speak of a (classless) *autogrammatic* ideological mode of production.[31] When there exists a caste of specialists in language (oral and/or written), viz., scribes, scholars, intellectuals, who appropriate the ideologies and produce, to the advantage of the dominant class, a certain *deformation* of the reading which the other agents have made of the social formation, then we will speak of a *logocentric* ideological mode of production (a class social formation) that is prey to a superstructural ideological *contradiction*.

Hypothesis 15: There can be no autogrammatism without auto-production and autogestion.

ECONOMIC, POLITICAL, AND IDEOLOGICAL MODES OF CIRCULATION

Hypothesis 16: On the basis of J. J. Goux's analysis of the isomorphism of the forms of exchange, we can assert two principal kinds of modes of circulation: *barter (troc),* which corresponds to the first three phases of the form "value" (simple, developed, general), and *systematic circulation (circulation à l'appareil).*

Economic mode of circulation: the process of shifting economic goods from the sphere of production to the sphere of consumption.[32]

Economic barter: in order for product A to become *merchandise,* that is, exchangeable for product B, another piece of merchandise, a relation of comparison is established between A and B. The "body of A," its *use value,* is ignored, and its equivalence to the "body of B" gives it an *exchange value.* The equivalence is established in terms of the work time required by each piece of merchandise (abstract or social work), so that $xA=yB$ (x and y being the quantities of the two pieces of merchandise). This is the *simple form* of value.

If we consider merchandise A, B, C . . . , A is compared with all the others, so that $xA=yB=zC$. . . . Here we have the *developed form* of exchange value.

Finally, when merchandise X is given a privileged place as the standard by which the value of all the other merchandise is determined, then

$xA=yB=zC=\ldots=aX$, and we have the *general form* of exchange value.

Each piece of merchandise thus acquires a fixed value depending on the amount of work time required for its production, according to the formula $\frac{x}{a}$ for A, $\frac{y}{a}$ for B, $\frac{z}{a}$ for C, etc. In the barter system, the producers are in principle all equal; the value of all the products is calculated according to the same unit of time.[33] Barter in itself is, then, a process of circulation proper to an autoproductive social formation.

The monetary system: constituted by a *system of coinage* that circulates parallel to the merchandise. Historically, the monetary system has come to use *gold* as the *general equivalent* of all merchandise; that is, gold has been given the privileged place of merchandise X. The monetary system has a threefold function: imaginary, symbolic, and real.

1. An *imaginary* relation (a kind of identification) is established between gold and each product; this relation turns the product into merchandise by giving it an exchange value in the form of a *price* ("something of the ideal order," says Marx). The set of imaginary relations then establishes gold as the general equivalent, abstraction being made from the gold's use value, for its preciousness from this point of view is irrelevant for consumption. The gold is withdrawn from circulation, and its "body" becomes the standard for exchange values, a standard erected into a *law* governing circulation by reason of gold's functioning as the *measure* of prices (these last being expressed in pounds of gold).

2. In the process of circulation, money functions as a *symbol* (representative) of gold. In barter, circulation takes place according to the formula $M-(x)-M1$, where x is an ideal, nonmaterialized calculation of the value of the pieces of merchandise, M and M1, that are being exchanged. In the monetary system, money, A, not only causes circulation but itself circulates; it is an *instrument of circulation*. $M-A-M1$ entails $M1-A-M2$, which in turn entails $M2-A-M3$, and so on. That is, money is in constant circulation as representative of the imperative that is the fixed price imaginarily calculated in pounds of gold. The symbolic role of money (metal, paper) can by played only when money circulates, for money functions only when it is exchanged for merchandise.

3. The *real* existence of money means that in the monetary system, unlike the barter system, the process $M-A-M1$ can be halted at $M-A$. The real existence of money permits the accumulation of a *reserve* of money, or a *hoard*, the possessor of which can buy without having first sold and then produced something further. Under certain political and ideological conditions, but at the strictly economic level, the monetary system makes possible the appearance of a *class* of nonproductive agents of the social formation, namely the *merchants*.[34] The exchange cycle $M-A-M1$ (producer to consumer) becomes in the case of the merchant (who is neither producer nor consumer) $A-M-A'$. He starts with A (the money reserve) in order to reach A' which represents $A+\triangle A$, where $\triangle A$ is the merchant's *profit* that enables him to consume without producing. Marx calls $\triangle A$ *surplus-value*. The *real* function

of the monetary system is to be seen both in the building up of a reserve and in the payment that follows upon the exchange *(credit)*. The value of money is its *real* weight in gold; it is no longer a simple representative.[35]

Political mode of circulation: a process of exchange whereby agents acquire different functional *places* in the social formation.

Autogestion (or political "barter"):[36] the designation of the one who is to possess the function of *authority* takes place according to various criteria,[37] and can be called in question by the autonomy of the agents (control of authority).

The apparatus of the state: we may take as an example absolute monarchy in the transition from feudalism to capitalism.[38] Its purpose was to place strict limitations on the centers of feudal power (and the masters of the guilds) and to create a state apparatus with a single center of power[39] that covered the whole space of the social formation (such a state of affairs being a political condition for a capitalist mode of production[40]). As in the monetary system, one agent is withdrawn from circulation and loses its bodily value in order to be *established* as a *general equivalent* and consequently as a *law* regulating the circulation of the agents; this one agent is the *king*.

1. An *imaginary* relation is established between the king and each agent, by reason of which the agent becomes a *subject* of the king and acquires an exchange value, his *subjectibility*,[41] which is different from his value as agent (the latter consisting in his *corporality*). His circulation (as subject) is regulated by *law* (the *juridical system,* a collection of normative texts, the reading of which assigns the agents their places); in principle, law deals only with abstract, imaginary subjects. The king, occupying the center of power and seat of the law, takes organizational *measures,* that is, he measures the subjectibility value of the agents who are regarded as all (abstractly) equal before the law (of the king). The king is fatherly: the subjectibility comes about through the production of an imago that overdetermines the parental imago that had introduced the *body* of the child (son or daughter, and subject) into infrapolitical circulation (within the constellation of the family).

2. To make effective the regulation of circulation, the apparatus of the state sets up, throughout the entire space of the social formation, a network of *functionaries* who possess the king's power as his *symbolic* representatives (cf. their bearing and dress). They are the instruments of the circulation of agents and make locally effective the commandments having to do with order (in their double aspect of prohibition and positive enactment).

3. These two functions of the apparatus of state are exercised by the (imaginary, symbolic) means of the text of the political ideology, in the measure that the ideology, by way of identification, finds a consensus among the agents, a consensus which (as an alienation of their autonomy as agents) has constituted them subjects. When the agents *rebel* (a political crisis) and seek to regain their political autonomy or corporality,[42] then the *real* function of the apparatus of state comes into play. Political power is exercised "in person" as repression, with weapons being used to force not "subjects" but

the bodies of the agents to occupy their proper place. When armed repression occurs, the mystification of the imaginary "subject" is dissipated, for it is bodies that are arrested, imprisoned, sometimes tortured, and even killed. The armed sector of the apparatus of state is a *treasury* of political power and is always present in the form of a threat (this is the credit that the dominant class possesses in the line of power), for it is ever-already in reserve against any possible crisis. Thus the cycle of political circulation comes full circle, since armed power, which is at the beginning of class domination, is also at its term.[43]

Ideological mode of circulation: the process whereby texts (oral and/or written) are shifted from the sphere of production (of "writing," in Derrida's use of this term) to that of consumption or reading.

> *Hypothesis 17:* The circulation of the system of sound-producing signifiers that make up oral language takes place in an *empirical mode,* in obedience to the first function of the ideological instance, which is *communication* (circulation) among the agents.

Ideological barter: the empirical mode consists in *naming* real objects (things, actions, qualities, etc.) according to the system of *perception* (the traditional five senses). A *signifier,* S, is attached to each object, creating a mutual and univocal correspondence between each sound-producing S and the perceived image of the type of object named (e.g., "house" is the label for visible, tactile images of the structures in which the agents live). Since there are many concrete objects of the same type, the name has an *ideal* value over and above the material value of the S; this ideal value is the *signified,* s, and it allows language to circulate as communication; it permits the bartering of oral texts.[44]

> *Hypothesis 18:* The setting up of a *logocentric apparatus*[45] has been made possible, on the one hand, by the invention of alphabetic writing, and, on the other, by the production (by scribes, or specialists in writing) of *gnoseological*[46] texts according to a *speculative mode*[47] that is meant to effect a knowledge of the system of the "real." Alphabetic writing entails a "confusion" with spoken language,[48] and oral language plays a dominant political role[49]; consequently, the speculative mode has not succeeded in extricating itself from the empirical mode proper to communication. It is this fact, I suggest, that has made it possible to *establish* one signifier, the *logos,* as a *general equivalent* of the other signifiers, and to make it the key to the circulation of *signs*[50] in these speculative texts.

> *Hypothesis 19:* Depending on the social formation, the logos may be "divine," and we can speak of *theocentrism,* with the dominant specula-

tive text being theological. Or the logos may be "human," and we can speak of *logocentrism* in a strict sense, the dominant speculative text being philosophical and taking priority over so-called scientific texts.[51]

Logocentric apparatus: let us take the signifier "god." Its elevation to special rank sets it over against the totality of things, or the *cosmos,* in accordance with the basic distinction between heaven and earth (to which we shall be returning later).[52] All things are named by signs; consequently the sign that is the name of the god stands in opposition to all the other signs in the system from which this one sign has been set apart.[52a]

1. Being set apart as the transcendent source of the cosmos, this sign, by the very fact of its privileged place, enters into an *imaginary* (or ideal) relation with every other sign. It is the ideal *signified* that makes possible the speculative functioning of the signs, the employment of each signified as a relation to the objects named. This imaginary relation is mediated by the "consciousnesses" of the knowing subjects, and it is this fact that makes it possible, first among the Greeks and later on, in a more radical manner, among the bourgeois ideologists, for its central place to be occupied by the logos, reason, or thought of the human subject. The sound, which is the signifier of the oral sign emitted by the *voice,* is opposed to the *mental* signified, which is interior and inaudible. This the "interior" experience of *thought* (or even religious experience) is the place where the imaginary relation is established and the *dominance* of the signified over the signifier (and of oral language over written) is asserted.[53]

2. The opposition god/cosmos or thought/reality allows the sign which is the general equivalent of all the other signs to play a regulative role in the circulation of the latter in the gnoseological texts. These signs are related to one another by (ideo)logical structures which, at the ideal level of the signified and of thought, determine the textual interplay of the signs (for example, the oppositions soul/body, spirit/matter, subject/object, nature/culture, etc.). In other words, in these texts the signs play a *symbolic* role as representatives of the god-logos and, simultaneously, as representatives of real objects (because of the naming process). Thus, instead of producing knowledge of the system of the real, the signs, because they refer to the perceived images of things, produce a *speculative* effect; they act like a mirror and yield a *reflection* of the cosmos.[54]

3. These gnoseological texts, which are *produced* as complex totalities of various elements, are thus ever-already a prey to the naming process in oral language. "Communication" overdetermines production ("writing," in Derrida's terminology) by deleting, erasing, or repressing it. Here the logocentric apparatus exercises its third function, that of a *real ideological power.* It prevents theoretical knowledge of the relations that structure the real, notably class relations; consequently, the textual lacunae, the blank spaces not written on, are filled by metaphors that adorn the text as symptoms of the

ideology at work. This kind of rhetoric exercises, in the gnoseological text, the function of *repressing* knowledge and the *concept* that would produce knowledge.

An example would be the role played by *dogma* (what theological texts themselves call the *treasure* of the faith) when called upon, as a *reservoir* of real ideological power, to help suppress the heretical texts that subvert dogma. When the *crisis* emerges into the open, the bearers of the heretical texts are tortured or burned *in the name of the god* (the principal equivalent of the signs).[55] Another example is the way *reason* acts in its war against Marxian or Freudian scientificity: it locks up the "madmen" in asylums as a way of getting rid of the communists, of subjecting rebels to psychiatric purification, etc.[56]

THE SUPERSTRUCTURAL ARTICULATION OF THE INSTANCES

Articulation: a key question for historical materialism. The analysis of the logic specific to each autonomous instance and to its various regions[57] must be completed by an analysis of the way in which each instance or region is determined by the other instances and/or regions.

Economic/political: In noncapitalist social formations, the appropriation of the surplus production is effected visibly and in a directly *political* form; the two instances are not autonomous.[58] In capitalist social formations, the appropriation is directly *economic* in character, in the form of surplus value that is subtracted from salaries and hidden in profits; each of the two instances enjoys its own specific autonomy.[59]

Economic/ideological:

> *Hypothesis 20*: The superstructural articulation of these two instances takes place, on the one hand, at the level of the productive forces, around the economic *program* which, insofar as it is a text, also has a place in the ideological instance; and, on the other hand, at the level of the relations of production.

> *Hypothesis 21*: The *theocentric* apparatus is specific to social formations in which empirical agriculture is the dominant element in production. The *logocentric* apparatus is specific to social formations in which industrial production is dominant.

THEORY OF RELIGION

Religious ideology: empirical agricultural production has as its dominant means of production the *earth* or cultivated soil, and as its dominated means the various implements, seeds, etc. The energy used is that of the agents and their draft animals. The agents of production exercise real control over the latter means, but there is another kind of energy they do not control: the energy of sun and of rain (this holds even where there are irrigation systems).

There are also elements that can positively hinder production, for example, snow, wind, frost. What this second group of elements has in common is that all of them come from above, from *heaven* (as opposed to *earth*, where production takes place). In the *text* of these productive forces there is a blank space when it comes to *knowledge* of the biological process whereby seeds are reproduced and vegetation grows. The blank space is filled in by the religious text that articulates itself into the program intrinsic to the productive forces. These forces thus play a *determining* role in the constitution of the dominant parametric code in the ideological instance: the code expressed in the *heaven/ earth* opposition, where heaven is understood as the dwelling place of the *god* who occupies the center of the theocentric apparatus, and earth is understood as the place of the productive agents, the fruit of whose toil is a condition for *life* (abundance), while mishaps in production bring *death* (scarcity). The relations of production assure the *closure* of the ideological circle: the god is represented as "lord" and people as his "servants," in imitation of the relations of political power.[60]

Tribal religions: these are proper to embryonic social formations that lack social classes. They are organized around the cults of the local gods, cults that are connected with the ancestors (and therefore determined by relations of kinship). The recital of the *myths* about the god(s) play a preponderant part in these cults, for they organize the ideological space of the social formation inasmuch as the victory won by one or several gods in combat with the other gods makes possible the separation of *heaven* from *earth* and thus does away with the primeval chaos. A principle of ideological order is thus produced that organizes the parametric codes by which the "real" is classified for the social formation.

State religions: these arise when, thanks to the development of the productive forces and of the commercial and military exchanges, a group of tribes becomes subject to a state apparatus.[61] The god of the clan or tribe to which the head of the state belongs becomes the *god* of a theocentric state religion, and the king is more or less closely associated with this god. The result can be a more or less strained coexistence of tribal cults and state religion, or, in other words, *polytheism*[62]; however, depending on the transformations the social formation undergoes and the way the contradiction between state and village communities develops, the theocentric religion can gain the upper hand and thus lead to *monotheism*.[63]

Sectarian religions (or religions of interiority): these arise along with the development of urban centers. Since cities are the result of a greater specialization in work and of increased exchanges, they are the place where a new class of artisans and merchants comes into existence alongside of, and in dependence on, the dominant and dominated classes. This class is not subject to the relations between the agricultural productive forces to which the theocentric religion is linked; it does not, however, escape the political domination of the class-state (social formation of the Asiatic type) or of the class that controls the apparatus of state (slavery; feudalism in transition toward capitalism), especially as regards taxes. On the other hand, the productive forces of this new class foster individualization of work and create a space for *"interiority,"* while making of this interiority a door that leads nowhere, from the political viewpoint, since it cannot become a social force capable of transforming the relations of political domination to which it is subject. Within the ideological space of the dominant religion, *sects* form that put the emphasis on an interior (or salvational) religion of direct experience of the god as present in the soul of the devotee.[64] Although ideology cannot permit liberation through a transformation of the structures of the social formation, it does promise liberation in the sphere of the imaginary. The statement that "religion is the opium of the people" holds true especially for this third type of religion.

The ideology of reason: industry is characterized by technical methods and the scientific character of its economic *program,* which fills in the blank spaces of the empirical agricultural text. Human *reason* replaces the god at the center of the ideological apparatus, and the result is *bourgeois logocentrism.*[65] This apparatus undergoes revision but does not disappear.[66] The science produced by reason aims at promoting *progress,* that is, like the agricultural god of the past, it proposes to give abundance *(life)* to the agents of the social formation, and to struggle against scarcity, famine, sickness (in short, against *death*).

History, which is the ideologized narrative of the conquest of economic, political, and ideological power by the bourgeoisie, replaces the myths and sacred histories of the religions. This history is the history of humanity's victory over god and nature, the victory won by humanity, which in its turn has become "lord." The lordship continues to reproduce ideologically the relations of production between the new lords and their proletariat. The universalization of the abstract idea "humanity" both hides these relations and renders them effective, since the proletarians, who have now become political "subjects" through the application of juridical categories, make their own the song of the bourgeois ideology and think of themselves as "lords" of nature, when in fact they are simply productive objects submissive to bourgeois domination, objects that are not distinct from "nature," since the means of production they utilize hardly belong to them in any proper sense.

Hypothesis 23: The function these two dominant ideologies have in common is of organizing the social formation, at their own level, so as to exclude what threatens the formation ("violence," in Bataille's sense of the term). But while the sacrality proper to the religious ideology accepted this violence in part as a source of purification, logocentric reason wishes to be its own source of purification through the progress it so richly bestows, and it claims to eliminate all violence.[67]

Hypothesis 24: Logocentrism has effects (1) in the *political* instance: *sex,* one of the major locations of violence, is excluded along with the *body* by the abstract "subject"; the old religious taboo on sex is reproduced, and bourgeois ideology is austerely puritan as a condition for bringing the exploited classes into the industrial production process. Logocentrism also has effects (2) in the *economic* instance: the technocratic ideology, which hides the relations of appropriation of surplus-value behind relations between the technicians-who-know and the workers-who-do-not-know, is reproduced by the educational system as a condition for the reproduction of capitalism itself. Logocentrism, finally, has effects (3) on the *class struggle:* the social formation claims to be highly rationalized and the "best possible" formation; every plan for a noncapitalist industrial social formation is excluded as being utopian and unrealistic, and revolutionary practices are excluded as madness, violence, danger, and sheer delirium.

Political/ideological: the articulation of these two has for its aim the repro-duction of the conditions that make the social formation possible. The political apparatuses that reproduce ideological apparatuses and are decisive for the purpose just mentioned are the family/school pair, which replaces the family/church pair of the feudal mode of production.[68] The family provides for the physical reproduction of the bodies of the agents, and of the symbolic order (within the respective classes); the school provides for the reproduc-tion of productive competence; family and school together provide for the reproduction of the two dominant parametric codes in the social formation.

Hypothesis 25: We must carefully distinguish between political ap-paratus and ideological apparatus. The *political apparatus* is concerned with the circulation or exchange of agents among the places of the social formation, whether in economic production that directly conditions the relations of production (therefore, political apparatuses in the economic region, as, for example, the bureaucracy in a capitalist enter-prise), or in the production of the overall political order (the apparatus of the state), or in ideological production (political apparatuses of the ideological region, such as the school and the churches). I disagree on this point, therefore, with Althusser, who calls these last "ideological apparatuses of the State."[69] Althusser apparently cannot conceive of a political apparatus that does not belong to the state; Poulantzas criticizes him on this point,[70] but I must also disagree with Poulantzas since he does not make the distinction I am proposing in this hypothesis.[71]

THE MODES OF CONSUMPTION
AND THE SYSTEM OF SOCIAL CLASSES[72]

Economic mode of consumption: the region of the economic instance in which production and circulation achieve their purpose.

Economic demand[73]: the field of these demands is the totality of the "economic needs"[74] of the social formation.

Utopia: the analogue, in a social formation, of the Freudian *drive* ("a constant force tending to the suppression of every state of tension"[75]). Since "utopia," according to its etymology, means that which has no *site* (Greek: *topos*), the term strikes me as an appropriate name for this quasi-drive, which is antecedent to any social formation, cannot be apprehended in itself, and can be discerned only in its effects. If the analogy is to be complete, we need another term for the social analogue of *desire*. Since I have been unable to find a satisfactory term, I shall risk being imprecise and shall use "utopia" once again for this quasi-desire that is ever-already historically marked by the economic structure of the social formation.[76]

> *Hypothesis 26*: Carrying the analogy a step further, I shall say that the satisfaction of utopia-desire is accomplished in the consumption of the *bodies* of economic products, to which Marx's *use value* corresponds. But since the (a)social object, the (mother-)earth, is ever-already lacking, the realization of utopian satisfaction can only be partial. Here I intro-duce the idea of *expenditure*, so dear to Bataille: In every social forma-tion part of the surplus is *cursed (maudit)*[76a] and expended unproduc-tively and *consumed* and lost. *Economic consumption* would thus have for its purpose to fill, in a form other than use, the *gap* between economic demand and real consumption.

Political mode of consumption: the region of the political instance where the *political field* takes concrete shape as a systematization of the places of the agents of the social formation, thus assuring the cohesion of the formation.

Utopia-order: analogue of the Freudian *death instinct*[77]; it supports political production as a response to *commands* of the political order. It moves in the opposite direction from utopia-drive, for it wards off the danger of disin-tegration into chaos, which utopia-drive always implies.

> *Hypothesis 27*: Utopia-order is what engenders the tension resulting from the postponement of economic consumption (cf. Hypothesis 3). Utopia-desire tends to dissolve this tension which is the source of political violence, and does so in the *festival,* in which the utopian violence is given an outlet and the political law is violated from time to time; here we have *political consumption*.[78] In the festival there is a partial transgression, in greater or lesser degree, of the taboos relating to sex (orgiastic aspect of the festival) and to murder (war in its primitive form,[79] the knightly tourney, competitive sports, and even suicide[80]). We are made aware here of the strange extremes to which life (essen-tially prodigal) can go, and which enable Bataille to say that "in the end we resolutely desire that which imperils our life."[81]

Ideological mode of consumption: the (nontheoretical) knowledge of the "reality" of the social formation on the part of its agents, a knowledge gained through the *reading* of the ideological texts (which answer ideological questions).

Hypothesis 28: This (empirical and/or speculative) "knowledge" is the effect of signifiers that name objects (nouns) and actions (verbs) that are a prey, semantically, to the parametric codes. Utopia-desire is ever-already marked by this semantic naming process that tells utopia-desire what its object is to be; the object, insofar as it is "real," is *perceived* according to images, and consequently the relation detected between the names and the images as a result of the naming process is the specific contribution of utopia-desire to the ideological instance; its unachieved object is *fusion* with the cosmos.

Hypothesis 29: This utopia-desire, which is not to be confused with the individual desires it determines, is not a simple reality but is as highly diversified as the processes of production in each instance. That is why, in addition to utopias relating to economic products, we also find utopias focused on (political) authority or (political) power and other objects relating to the ideological texts.

Hypothesis 30: The gap between the questions and the readings is variously filled in by processes of writing that are not useful for "knowledge" of the social formation, namely, processes that are religious and/or "artistic" (communion with the consecrated victims; mystical and/or esthetic contemplation; etc.).[81a] Here we have *ideological consumption;* I shall speak of this as *sacrificial* (I shall be using the term in a broad sense that has the advantage of connoting life and death).[82]

Hypothesis 31: The play of the utopias (characterized by such differences as useful/useless, everyday life/festival, profane/sacred) thus proves to be *contradictory.* Here we have the *infrastructural level* of the contradiction that marks every social formation; the issue is life/death (cf. Hypothesis 6).

The sphere of the "proper to": defined by the diversity of the bodies of the agents of the social formation and the diversity of their individual desires. The boundaries of it are marked by the signifiers that differentiate each agent, that is, the products that depend on his or her *ability* (or "creativity"), his or her *personal* competence, his or her *bodily* strength (or power), and lastly, in connection with his or her "face," his or her *personal name.* The sphere of the proper-to is the sphere of the body.

Hypothesis 32: The agents being ever-already grouped, their spheres of the proper-to are the property of their groups before they themselves can appropriate these spheres in an act of rebellion. Indeed, these spheres are first and foremost the property of their kinspeople, since we have a family name before having a personal name. The activity of the desires of each body is determined by the activity of the utopias of the group to which each body belongs.

The system of social classes: after a certain threshold of development of productive forces, of arms, and of ideological specialization of the inscriptive forces has been crossed, some groups, by means of their own utopia, have appropriated to themselves the spheres of property of other groups, while repressing through overdetermination the utopias of these other groups.

Hypothesis 33: A second level of contradiction that overdetermines the infrastructural contradiction has led to a further specification of these social formations, namely, the contradiction between two (or more) classes that acts as a *superstructural contradiction*. Historically, this means the transition to class social formations.

Class social formation: the violence of appropriation has had as its effect the formation of a *class system* that overdetermines the systems based on kinship and lineage that were characteristic of classless societies, or segmentary societies as they are also called.[83] In class social formations, the surplus appropriated by the dominant class is largely consumed by it in the form of *wealth* or *luxury*. It is as an object of display that *gold* will become the principal equivalent in the monetary system and thus be able to *lead astray* the utopian dreams of the productive classes, focusing these dreams on the signifiers of wealth that the dominant class employs, and on gold itself when the forms of commercial circulation have been sufficiently developed. The paths left open for the utopia of the dominated classes are strictly controlled, however, by the political law which in turn is determined by the reproduction of the relations of economic production, that is, by the economic interests of the dominant class.[84] These interests exist in a superstructural contradiction with those of the dominated class, a contradiction that overdetermines the tension (infrastructural contradiction) proper to the political instance. As a result there is an *excessive political tension* (political overtension) in class social formations; that is why the apparatus of the state is necessary in these formations, since the identification of the "subjects" with their general equivalent engenders, by way of the utopia-order, a submission, and even a *fear,* on the part of the dominated class, which is left various festivals, although these have definite limits placed on them.[85] Finally, the ideological apparatus, which excludes the dominated classes from "knowledge" of the social formation, is articulated, by the mediation of its principal equivalent (god or logos), with the apparatus of the state.[86] The sacrificial forms are then established, by means of identification mechanisms, at a level that is purely imaginary; they function in a manner analogous to dreams, so as to keep the social body asleep (developed forms of religious cultus in theocentric social formations; sectarian forms; novels and films for current consumption; etc.).

THE MODES OF CONSUMPTION
AS SITES FOR READING THE SOCIAL FORMATION

Hypothesis 34: The processes by which the instances and their articulations in the class social formations[87] are given an empirical reading are *ever-already deformed* by specific mechanisms in accordance with what Marx (referring to a mercantile economy) has called *fetishization*.[88]

Fetishization: as a result of the division of products into objects for use and objects of value, the process of exchange which makes pieces of merchandise equivalent to one another produces a form of relation of things to each other that is *fanciful*. It does so by bestowing on things an exchange value that "seems" inherent in the product itself, like a quality that springs from the very nature of things. (The consumer buys with the thought that the price he pays is somehow an inherent property of the thing itself.[89])

Idealist site for economic reading: consumers, whose utopia is fascinated by signifiers of wealth and by money, read the text of prices "through the eyes" of the general equivalent, namely, gold, the establishment of which has had for its effect to make available an imaginary or idealist site for reading.

Materialist site for economic reading: but since what consumers consume is in fact the *bodies* of the merchandise, these consumers can always do their reading also from the materialist site, provided they can break away from the idealist site and the fascination which they have experienced. That is, they can become aware of the *inequality* between their own (the producers') consumption and that of their bosses, the nonproducers, and consequently they can strike in order to gain a readjustment in this matter of consumption (to take one example).

Hypothesis 35: A materialist reading of the process of production is a condition for an economic class struggle.

Idealist site for political reading: by separating the *bodies* of the agents from their abstract role as *subjects*, the juridical text and the text of the bourgeois political ideology make available a site for an idealist reading in which the agents, fascinated by the signifiers of power (finery, outward bearing, etc.) and cowed by *arms*, read according to the discourse of power, that is, "through the eyes" of the principal equivalent, and find the existing political order to be quite *natural*.

Materialist site for political reading: the repression of the bodies of the agents, at the level of sex as well as of constricted working conditions and resultant illnesses, of fatigue as well as of imprisonment, etc., makes it possible to *break* through fascination and fear and do a materialist reading of the inequality of position (power/lack of power) and thus of the political conjuncture (for example, abortion).

Idealist site for ideological reading: the ideological text brought into existence by the establishment of the logos (or the god) effects a division between the signifier (ever-already in a textual body) and the signified (which is put in an imaginary relation with the logos and with things). The ideological text thereby makes available the idealist site for an empirical or speculative reading of the social formation according to the codes of the logocentric apparatus, a reading in which the elements of the whole are isolated from what determines them. As readers fascinated by rational evidence (or divine revelation) or even by literary beauty or by the scholarly authority of the specialists in ideology, the agents read only "through the eyes" of reason (or faith) and in accordance with its codes.

> *Hypothesis 36*: In every case a deformed reading of the social formation is proposed that operates on the two levels of contradiction in the social formation and presents the infrastructural as determining the superstructural. In fact, however, only the superstructural is reducible through a revolutionary transformation of the social formation. The mechanism of ideological deformation hides the reducible behind the irreducible, the superstructural behind the infrastructural. Society is organized according to the will of the god or the law of nature and/or reason; in short, to put it in Leibniz's words, society is "the best of all possible worlds."

Materialist site for theoretical reading: it is by way of the *materiality* of the bodies of the agents and their products that the site for a materialist reading can be made available through a break with the idealist fascination. It is by way of the economic and political struggles of the proletariat that the ideological mask has been torn away (through the access to the *problematic* these struggles create) and the *theoretical* production of materialist texts has become possible (initially through the accomplishment of Marx which was, and continues to be, followed up in many areas).[90]

DETERMINATION AND CLOSURE

Economic field: the system comprising all the economic demands of a social formation.

> *Hypothesis 37*: The economic field is in turn composed of three principal fields, relating respectively to the restricted reproduction of the social formation (field I), to its expansive reproduction (field II),[91] and

to expenditure (field III). The economic field has *historical* limits and is *determined* by the processes of production or the productive forces concretely existing in the social formation.

Political field: the system comprising all the commands aimed at the order of the social formation.

Hypothesis 38: The political field is in turn composed of three principal fields, relating respectively to the relations of economic production as to a condition for the reproduction of the political field (field I, occupied by the economico-political apparatuses), to the cohesion of the social formation (field II, occupied by the apparatuses of the family and the State), and to ideological production (field III, occupied by the schools, churches, press, etc.). The political field is *determined* by the processes that produce order or the organizing forces concretely existing.

Problematic: the complex and structured set of *questions* (or problems) relating to the knowledge (or ignorance) of a given region of what is "real" in the social formation.

Ideological field: the system comprising all the problematics of a social formation.

Hypothesis 39: The ideological field is in turn composed of three principal fields, relating respectively to the economic programs (field I), to taboos (morality) and the juridical text (field II), and to the function of distinguishing between life and death (field III). It is *determined* by the various existent processes of writing (this last term being taken in the broad sense).

Hypothesis 40: The *determinations* to which we have been referring are intrinsic to each instance understood as a collection of practices. The determinations produce invisible limits within which certain practices are possible. The relations of economic production, the relations of the appropriations of order, and the ideological relations also have a limiting effect within their respective instances, effects that are distinct from and combine with the determinations. I shall call the effects *closures*.[92]

Hypothesis 41: A *determination* defines the field of *all* the conditions for the reproduction of each instance in the social formation. A *closure* overdetermines and restricts this field solely to the possibilities of reproduction according to class relations. I am not concerned here with possibilities that relate to the transformation of a social formation into a classless social formation.[93]

Overdetermination: the various instances also have effects that overdetermine the fields of the other instances; within each instance, moreover, some regions determine others, all this being the effect of the determination and closure as ever-already combined. Althusser has formulated two theses regarding these effects of overdetermination. The first is that in all historical social formations there is one instance, and only one, whose overdetermining effects are *dominant*; there is always one *instance* that is (or: whose mode of production is) *dominant*. This instance is said to overdetermine the social formation. Second, Marx's thesis that the social formation is in the last analysis determined by the economic mode of production is formulated thus: in the last analysis the economic instance determines the social formation, either by having the dominant role in it or by determining whether it is the political or the ideological instance that is to have the dominant role. This second thesis is what justifies giving the name *historical materialism* to the science of history established by the texts of Marx.

> *Hypothesis 42*: A concrete analysis of a concrete social formation, especially during the phases of transition from one mode of production to another must pinpoint this overdetermination. A good symptom to look for is the interplay of the reciprocal determinations of the general equivalents.

Saturation of the fields: the gap between utopian demand and economic demands that are really satisfied becomes a challenge to the utopia to fill the gap; the gap can be eliminated, according to the measure of the *surplus* of available production, by means of growth or expansive reproduction (field II of the economic field). It is possible, however, to reach a *point of saturation* beyond which no significant growth is any longer possible. This may be due to the effect of determination (a fall-off in labor power because of a great slaughter or an epidemic or a war; or excessive labor power, as when unemployment cannot be countered because of a lack of means of production or a stagnation in the programs of production).[94] The saturation may also be due to a closure of the relations of economic production. In this case a further effect may be an internal political saturation of the social formation (excessive exploitation by the relations, both economic and political, of production), and ultimately a utopian explosion. On the other hand, political saturation may be due to the superior armed force of a neighboring social formation, which results in *war;* a war of occupation will engender a war of liberation, the stakes always being the reproduction of one or other of the two social formations.[95]

SUBASIATIC MODE AND SLAVE SYSTEM

Historical modes of production: Georges Dhoquois distinguishes, from the historical point of view, between the "Asiatic sphere" and the "precapitalist sequence."[96] Within the "Asiatic sphere" he distinguishes an Asiatic mode of production (A.M.P.), a subasiatic mode of production (S.M.P.), a paraasiatic mode of production, and an Asiatic feudalist mode of production (A.F.M.P.). Under "precapitalist sequence," Dhoquois distinguishes slavery (S1.M.P.) and European feudalism (F.M.P.) as the principal types of noncapitalist class social formations.

Hypothesis 43: There are several marks by which to distinguish capitalist from noncapitalist social formations. In the latter, empirical agriculture is dominant (covering especially field I); in the former, technologized industry. In the noncapitalist, expansive reproduction (field II) through the activity of the productive forces is quite limited; in the capitalist, it is very extensive. The monetary apparatus regulates circulation throughout the economic instance in the capitalist social formations, while in the noncapitalist it is for practical purposes excluded from fields I and II and sometimes even from field III; in the noncapitalist social formations the relations of economic production are directly political (dominant production).

Hypothesis 44: In noncapitalist social formations expansive reproduction often becomes important because of relations of production that are brought into existence by war. In these social formations field II is the field of the production of arms and state buildings (palaces, castles, temples, roads, waterworks, etc.). Field III is dominated by the production of luxuries that profit only the dominant class; it is the field of that class's economic interests.

Hypothesis 45: Another classification of class social formations would contrast *group P* (A.M.P., S.M.P., A.F.M.P., and F.M.P.) and *group S* (S1.M.P. and C.M.P. [capitalist mode of production]).

Group P: this group comprises social formations in which there is no differentiation between fields I and II of the political instances, since the apparatus of the state has taken complete control of the economic instance. The producers thus have *possession* (P) of the means of the dominant production; the dominant class is identified with the state; there is a "class-state."

Group S: field I of the political instance is dominated by private political apparatuses, and the apparatus of the state is active chiefly in field II.[97] The producers are *separated* (S) from the means of the dominant production (a slave system; an industrial-wage system). Therefore there is *private ownership* of these means of production by a class, and the law that conditions this ownership produces the distinction between private and public which is specific to group S; on the other hand, "the state here plays a coercive role in behalf of the dominant class,"[98] without the state and the dominant class thereby becoming identified.

Asiatic sphere: the various Asiatic forms are characterized by an opposition between the peasant class, which is organized into village communities (where relations of kinship play an important role in social organization[99]), and the class-state, which directly appropriates the surplus for itself.

Asiatic mode of production: the state acts directly on the productive forces through great river-connected irrigation systems, without which agriculture would be impossible.[100]

Subasiatic mode of production: the state interferes "only at the level of the relations of production, by appropriating in advance a good part of the overproduction and also by controlling part of the exchanges during both peace and war."[101]

> *Hypothesis 46*: Wars between neighboring social formations provide a general explanation of the subasiatic mode. A social formation that is growing (expansive reproduction) because a warrior aristocracy is impelled by a utopian dream of conquest, manages to control the neighboring social formations until it reaches a saturation point (great increase in expenditure on luxuries) and then either falls prey in turn to another conquering social formation or becomes an A.F.M.P.,[102] because of conflicts between king and aristocracy.

Rebellion: in a movement of utopian explosion, the productive class, even while remaining the dominated class, imposes political changes on the dominant class, so that the latter may defend its own economic interests.

Revolution: a process whereby the dominant economic mode of production in a social formation is transformed through the imposition of another mode of production. A dominated class—though not necessarily the productive class in the hitherto dominant production—takes over the power of the state from a class that now ceases to be dominant (cf., e.g., the various industrial revolutions, the French and Russian revolutions, and a number of anticolonial revolutions).

(Radically) communist revolution: the process whereby a class social formation is transformed into a classless social formation, in which the monetary apparatus, the apparatus of the state, and the ideological apparatus are all abolished. Though it has never been completed, the two-stage Chinese revolution (1949 and the proletarian cultural revolution) is the one that seems to come closest to this utopian ideal.

> *Hypothesis 47*: What the villagers of a S.M.P. might achieve through revolution would be a return to primitive "communitarian" forms. Revolution is impossible for them, however, since they have no access to arms; in fact, "military protection" furnished by the state or the feudal classes becomes for the villagers a condition for the permanence of the political order, since otherwise they would simply go on changing masters according to the fortunes of war.[103]

Genesis and dissolution of the slave-based mode of production: all the modes of production in group P have a more or less developed exchange sector connected with economic field III; the sector contains a class of skilled artisans, often working for the state, which controls the exchanges. Except for Phoenicia, the *sea* never played an important role in these social formations. In all probability, it is precisely in the fairly intensive development of *maritime trade* that we are to find the origin of the slave-based mode of production, which began in Greece and was worked out to its ultimate consequences by Rome. This is all the more likely since we find the same kind of development occurring in the transition from the feudalist mode of production to the capitalist mode of production.

Greece had experienced a paraasiatic mode of production[104] in the period of the Mycenaean kings. Since the country did not lend itself to large-scale public works and was in any case broken up into small sections, the kings were unable to retain their position once they had reached the end of the growth phase. The royal bureaucracy collapsed and was succeeded by an Asiatic feudalist mode of production in which the dominant class, helped by "the division of Greece into a multitude of cities,"[105] gradually "developed exchanges" by sea, with "certain cities reaching a high degree of specialization in trade and craftsmanship."[106]

This development of exchanges required extensive individual initiative and an appropriate economic base. The absence of a strong state made possible a movement away from group P; Dhoquois describes the movement as one in which "the state played a qualitatively lesser role, and private property played a qualitatively superior role."[107] This separation of fields I and II of the political instance, along with the development of maritime commerce, led to important changes in the relations of production: the dominant class needed large numbers of productive agents and acquired them in the form of *slaves* (prisoners of war; insolvent owners of small properties; etc.), to such an extent that slavery became the dominant, though by no means exclusive, mode of production.[108]

"Based as it is on private initiative and the relations of exchange, slavery is eminently *precapitalist* in character. It was Roman law that authoritatively established the classic right of private property, which is as absolute as possible, even to the point of allowing abuses."[109] It is this right that the capitalist mode of production has made its own and developed to fit its needs. The Romans with their superior military skill extended their slave-based empire throughout the Mediterranean world, experiencing in the process a phase of growth unparalleled in the world of antiquity. The contradiction caused by slavery became ever more pressing, and the phase of expenditure (great luxury on the part of the ruling classes; formation of urban classes that were idle and fed by the state) led to collapse, although the empire managed to last for several more centuries by an unparalleled strengthening of the state bureaucracy and its apparatus of repression and by a religious ideol-ogization of the emperor in the well-known worship of the Caesar (identification of the political and ideological general equivalents).

NARRATIVE, PRACTICE, IDEOLOGY
(or the Functions of Narrative in the Mode of Production)

Hypothesis 48: I propose a typology of the texts in certain social formations, a typology based on two different analyses by Emile Benveniste
that are valid both for the Greek (Gospel of Mark) and French lan-
guages (translation of Mark, and the present text). I am referring to
Benveniste's person/nonperson[110] and history/discourse systems.[111]

Locutive texts or discourses: corresponding to Benveniste's "discourses."
Narrative texts: corresponding to Benveniste's "history," with the qualification that the verbal forms are those of *verbs of action*.
Gnoselogical texts: are located in the system of the nonperson, the verbal
forms being those of *stative verbs*[112] (discourse can achieve articulation with
these, especially through use of the present tense, as an "author's level").

Hypothesis 49: Gnoseological texts always have narrative texts as their
raw material (see Hypothesis 54) and achieve an "effect of [ideological
or theoretical] knowledge" of the parametric "stative real," a knowledge that does not change to keep pace with duration; duration, on the
contrary, is constitutive of what is "represented" in narrative texts, in
accordance with a *law of successivity*.[113]

Hypothesis 50: A narrative text—"narrative" in a broad sense—is a text
on practice and recounts one or more practices. If we bear in mind
Benveniste's statement that in history (narrative) "no one speaks
. . . ; the events [practices] seem to narrate themselves. The fundamental tense is the aorist, which is the tense of the event outside the
person of a narrator,"[114] we can say that a narrative is a *discourse of a
practice,* a narratorless text in which the practice tells its own story.

Hypothesis 51: Since a social formation is a complex set of structured
practices, its ideological text is largely a narrative text, a set of narratives, a text that has no beginning or end and moves onward indefinitely. Why tell the story of practices? Because people must go on
practicing, and narratives are, speaking generally, grills for reading
other narratives now being composed, narratives that are still open as
far as how they will turn out is concerned. If agents produce and read
narratives, it is because they are looking for keys to their own practices.

Relation of narrative to ideological relation:[115] the relation of a practice
narrated (containing a textual element as a constitutive component) to the
parametric codes of the ideological relation.

Hypothesis 52: Narrative can have two *functions* in a given social formation: (1) to *establish* and/or *reproduce* the parametric codes of the social formation (mythical narratives[116]; in theocentric religions, "sacred histories" that exalt the god[117]; "bourgeois history" that exalts the logos[118]; narratives of consumption[119]); (2) to *subvert* these codes with a view to transforming them. It is with this second function that we will be concerned later on.

Hypothesis 53: The transformations of the modes of production (from feudalism to capitalism; Russian, Chinese, Vietnamese, etc., revolutions) suppose, prior to the revolutionary class struggles, practices that are more or less localized and confined (economic, political, ideological, theoretical practices) and that are the work of individuals or small groups. These practices are *subversive* of the structures of the social formation.

Subversiveness: its general *determining* conditions can be stated as follows: the totality of the productive forces determines the *strict* limits of any subversive economical practice; the totality of the organizing forces determines the strict limits of any subversive political practice; the totality of the inscriptive forces (or the totality of oral and written texts) determines the strict limits of any subversive theoretical practice. On the other hand, the *closures* define the limits that the class in power cannot permit to be overstepped. Subversiveness is possible, then, if the practices in question are *displaced* outside the field of the closures, and break away toward materialist sites for reading.

Competence of an agent: the *effect,* inscribed in the agent's body, of all his or her earlier practices; it takes the forms of economic skill, political power, competence in reading/writing. An agent's competence is determined by the field of possibilities for his or her practices (for example: within the totality of all the texts that determine the ideological field of a social formation, each agent is determined by the concrete readings he or she has made).

Hypothesis 54: Every practice that takes place within the limits of a field that is defined by its determination and overdefined by its closure obeys a law of repetition. It can be said (expressed) in its *singularity* only by a narrative text, and the theoretical knowledge of it is obtained statistically, by the work of theoretical concepts on a set of repeated narratives. For example, in order to bring the concept of "salary" to bear on a concrete economic production, one must collect the narratives of the concrete payments made by capital to the labor force; then one can produce the knowledge, in figures, of the salaries. The absolutely primary "raw material" of theoretical production is a set of repetitive narratives (the "facts").

Theoretical knowledge of subversiveness (or Hypothesis 55): the question raised by this theoretical knowledge can be expounded as follows. In breaking with the closure(s), a subversive practice "frees" itself from the law of repetition, and escapes the grip of the statistical (we touch here on the old question of determinism and "freedom"). The practice is singular and is recounted in the *narrative* of the *new* thing that is produced. As a matter of historical fact, *there have been subversive practices,* for otherwise a single social formation would have reproduced itself indefinitely. The very fact that social formations have been *transformed* (and have not simply been reproduced, even in an expansive way) supposes a series of practices that have subverted not only the various closures but also the various determinations. (A new machine or a new science breaks with the previous determinations, and enlarges or transforms the field in question.)

The question, then, is: How does the break take place? Not suddenly, but by a long, slow process, a *genesis* (a first sally outside the ideological closure permits a reading of that closure; then the writing of a program for *another* closure that is slightly different; then a first, slightly variant practice; etc.). New reading(s), new writing(s), new subversive act(s). What takes place in the always flexible field between closure and determination steadily enlarges the field of the determination. The dialectic of these readings, writings, and subversive acts (economic or political or ideological or theoretical struggle, or even a struggle involving the three instances) can, when a certain threshold has been reached, make possible the production of something *new* that will later impose its own expansive reproduction. A subversive practice is thus the result of a slow development (because of the "strict" limits placed by the existing determination) that can be called *seminal* and eventually produces new fruits.

How is the theoretical knowledge of this subversive practice possible? Being singular, the practice is recounted in a *narrative* or series of narratives, and a *semiotic methodology* must be applied to produce an analysis of this narrative. Historical science (historical materialism) cannot, therefore, do without the analysis of subversive narratives, which I shall distinguish from stories of reproduction by reserving the word "narrative" to the former. *"Narrative" means a narrative of a subversive act, a subversive narrative.*[120] The relation between subversive practice and the narrative of it is such that we know only the fruits and the account of the practice as such. By recounting the practice, the narrative subverts the ideological codes opposed to the subversiveness in question; being itself subversive, the narrative opens up, within the text of the social formation, the space for new practices. As proclaimer of the subversive acts, the narrative makes it possible to read them, repeat them, enlarge upon them, and extend them. The narrative thus has an important and unappreciated role to play in a revolution.

Narrative and ideology: it is a fact, however, that subversive narratives, precisely to the extent that they are effective in transforming the social formation, can be absorbed into a new ideological field. The ideological relation, on the basis of the transformations effected in its codes, will rework the narrative in order to make it serve the reproduction of the ideology; the narrative is now reideologized. The purpose of this book is to analyze a subversive narrative and the ideological work that has already been done within it.

PART II
THE MODE OF PRODUCTION
IN BIBLICAL PALESTINE

The reading of the text of Mark will be introduced by a short chapter on methodology. But, since we aim at a *political reading* of the Gospel, we must first relate what is "represented" in the narrative (in other words, the story told) to the social field in which it is supposed to have taken place, namely, Palestine in the first century of the Christian era. Our object in this second part, then, will be to apply the concepts we have been examining and to produce the concept of that particular social formation.

The very abundant historical materials on the Palestine of the first century are, for the most part, the work of exegetes who tend to emphasize ideological and religious questions and to undervalue the connection between these and structures, both economic and political. I am not a professional historian and must work at second hand, but I have nonetheless been compelled to write the following two chapters as necessary background for the reading of Mark and for the required epistemological break with the prevalent bourgeois exegesis.

The first part of von Rad's text, which I shall be using frequently in this part of the book, gives a good overview of the history of ancient Israel.[1] Three quite different periods may be discerned. The first is the period of distinct tribes that lack social classes; the elements for analysis are very fragmentary, and any historical reconstruction is quite problematic. The second is a period in which a rather fragile subasiatic society is formed; this is due to the establishment by Kings David and Solomon of an organized state, which, however, breaks up into two parts immediately upon the death of Solomon. The third period is that of postexilic Judaism; this period sees a subasiatic society that is dominated by a high-priestly caste and an aristocracy of rich landowners but is always politically subject to surrounding empires, from the Persian Empire of the Achaemenids to the Roman Empire with its slave system in the last century B.C.

To each of these three principal periods corresponds one of the three states through which the sacred texts of the Hebrew religion passed. First, there were the oral myths of the various tribes. Second, these were committed to writing and arranged to form the great narratives concerning the origin of

Israel, and two distinct collections of laws; this took place in the time of the monarchy. Third, these texts, which had taken four main forms (J, the Jahwist; E, the Elohist; P, the Priestly; and D, the Deuteronomist), were rewritten to form a single text, the Torah, which was finished by priestly writers after the exile.

Chapter 1
The Symbolic Order of Ancient Israel

THE QUESTION OF THE LAW

Everyone is aware of the importance of the Law throughout the Bible as a whole, and of the polemic against it in certain parts of the New Testament. The Law certainly played a very large part in the life of first-century Palestine. How are we to analyze this role and to relate it to the other instances of the social formation?

The Law constitutes what we defined in the first part of this book as the *symbolic order* that regulates the relations between the bodies of the agents of the social formation, which is the Law's symbolic field.[1] The symbolic order is the sphere especially of kinship relations[2]; if then we bear in mind the earlier remark about the importance of these relations in the social organization of the social formation in the "asiatic sphere,"[3] we are justified in postulating, for purposes of analysis, the permanence, throughout the period of the subasiatic monarchy, of the *logic* proper to the symbolic order, a logic that originated in the period of the tribes. Proceeding somewhat as ethnologists do, we shall analyze this logic on the basis of the legislative texts that have come down to us. In so doing, we shall not take into account the diachronic order of the various strata or sources that may be found in these texts, but shall assume that every addition was integrated into a synchronic logic that underwent no deformation until the Torah was completed.

We shall have to look for the system that binds together the seemingly empirical prohibitions and ordinances[4] that have been brought together in the legislative texts; among the latter we shall concentrate especially on the two lengthier collections: the one in Leviticus (P document) and the one in Deuteronomy (D document).

We are confronted here by a very complicated exegetical problem. It concerns two notions that are distinct yet related: impurity and sin. E. Beaucamp has written:

The primitive character, in the Old Testament, of the biblical notion of impurity is quite clear. . . . Sin and impurity are in fact two ideas that are basically distinct and have different origins; they always existed side by

37

side, the one never replacing the other. . . . We cannot of course deny that sin and impurity are two categories of thought that are fairly close to one another and that often intermingle. We can even observe a certain confusion of the two at times in biblical language.[5]

I shall be developing two theses which may be stated here as follows:

1. Two distinct systems are to be found in the legislative texts of the Old Testament: a system of *pollution or contagion* and a system of *debt*, the former being dominant in texts belonging to the priestly document (P), the latter in texts belonging to the Elohist (E) and Deuteronomist (D) documents (and most fully elaborated in the second of these two sources). The two systems follow quite parallel logics and are thereby brought into close relationship.

2. Beginning at a certain period in the subasiatic monarchy, the two systems are related by a dialectic which is that of a class struggle.

In Israel the symbolic field was organized around three centers, each of which corresponds to one of the three instances of a social formation.[6] All three were centers or foci of consumption: the *table,* the *"house"* (in the sense of a group of kinspeople; that is what the quotation marks around the word indicate), and the *sanctuary*; this means the consumption of food at meals, consumption of bodies in sexual activity, and ideological consumption in religious sacrifice.

I can illustrate the twofold principle that operates in the logic of the pollution system by an innocuous example: "You must not sow any other seed in your vineyard lest the whole of its produce become consecrated, both the crop you have sown and the produce of your vineyard. You must not plough with ox and donkey together. You must not wear clothing woven part of wool, part of linen" (Deut. 22:9–11).[7]

In the Hebraic classification of plants and animals, in the parametric codes of the social formation,[8] wheat and vine, ox and donkey, wool and linen are *incompatible* pairs. To unite the disparate elements (of a harvest, a team of draft animals, or of clothing) is to create a confused hybrid and to do violence to the classifying mind; the result is that the mixture becomes *consecrated.* By the same principle, bestiality (for example) is excluded.

On the other hand, even compatible elements can be joined only if they are *different.* Incest is forbidden because it is a union of the *same* flesh, homosexuality because it is a union within the *same* sex; here again the result would be confusion.

If we accept Mary Douglas's thesis, we will say that pure and impure are opposed as the formed, the classified, and the compatible are opposed to the shapeless, the confused, and the hybrid.[9]

In Israel, then, as in other human societies, the symbolic system is organized first and foremost as a defense against the *violence* of contagion, the impurity of the confused and formless, and this according to the two principles of *compatibility* and *difference.*[10] According to Bataille, the idea of contagion originates in the horror felt at human corpses which "had fallen prey to the violence of decomposition, the corruption of death."[11] The rational organization of productive work and everyday life therefore requires *taboos* relating to pollution and warding off the threatened danger which pollution represents. The focal points of the symbolic systems are all *centers of purity* from which is excluded the impure, the misshapen, the undifferentiated, anything that breaks down forms.

The consumption practiced at table, in sexual union, and in religious worship is a fusion, an eating that is sought as a goal of human life and a *blessing*; it involves two different but mutually related and mutually compatible elements: humanity and its food, the bodies of man and woman, God and his people. These forms of consumption are *life*.

Pollution means confusion and the dissolution of the elements involved; it is a *curse*. People reject it to the point of avoiding even simple contact or *touching*, since the impure is so violent as to be contagious. It brings *death*.

There is another kind of violence that must be forestalled by prohibiting it in accordance with a second system. The violence takes the form of human *aggression*; the system of prohibitions I shall call the *debt system* (the word "debt" usually being translated as "sin").

Like the first system, this one involves two principles, *gift* and *debt,* which are mutually exclusive, as are pure and polluted. Over against a principle of the *extension* of corporality (and, more broadly, the extension of the "property sphere"[12] which prolongs corporality and includes food, women, tithes) there stands a principle of *restriction*, which operates in everything that attacks the body: theft, murder, aggression, hostility, desolation.

Why the word *debt*? I have chosen not to use the word "sin," because the meaning attached to it is quite different from that given it in the Bible, and I have preferred "debt," because that is the meaning underlying the Aramaic word that New Testament Greek translates as *aphesis* or "remission, cancellation (of sins)."[13] An argument against its use is that among the words for "sin" that von Rad analyzes[14] "debt" does not occur. A further argument is that "debt" carries juridical overtones that do not seem to fit into the description of the disintegrative disorder the Hebrews knew as sin.[15] Von Rad himself, however, emphasizes the fact that the Book of the Covenant, which is the first compilation of prohibitions belonging to the system in question, was based on early legislation concerning debts.[16] In addition, debtors who could not meet their obligations had to become, with their families, the slaves of their creditors until their debts were paid; this shows that debts put a lien on the very bodies of the debtors even to the point of making them slaves, and slavery, as we shall see, is part of the debt system.

TABLE AND POLLUTION

In Israel, the dietetic system was governed by a principle of classification that was based on the distinction between the pure (the eatable) and the mixed, hybrid, or impure (the noneatable).[17]

For land animals, the distinguishing factors used in the classification are these: "You may eat any animal that has a cloven hoof, divided into two parts, and that is a ruminant" (Lev. 11:3).[18] For water creatures: "Anything that has fins and scales, and lives in the water, whether in sea or river, you may eat" (Lev. 11:9b). For flying things: "All winged insects that move on four feet you must hold detestable" (Lev. 11:20); and: "Anything that moves on its belly, anything that moves on four legs or more—in short all the small beasts that crawl on the ground—you must not eat these because they are detestable" (Lev. 11:42). Wings and four feet, for one thing, and crawling on the ground, for another, are instances of the hybrid, the combination of incompatible elements.

The table, or consumption at meals, is thus subject to strict regulation: "Such is the law concerning animals, birds, all living creatures that move in water, and every creature that crawls on the ground. Its purpose is to separate the clean from the unclean; creatures that may be eaten from those that must not be eaten" (Lev. 11:46–47).

Why this separation and taboo? Another prescription in Leviticus may shed some light on it: "If any man of the House of Israel or stranger living among you eats blood of any kind, I will set my face against the man who has eaten the blood and will outlaw him from his people. The life of the flesh is in the blood" (Lev. 17:10).

The *shedding of blood* means the end of life; it means death. Yet death is the very thing nourishment aims at preventing, at putting off from day to day. On the other hand, to live means to feed upon death, since it demands the eating of corpses. Death is thus at the very heart of life, and the table is one of the places where the life-death struggle goes on. This is the reason why the utmost caution must be used in approaching the table, and the principles regulating diet must be applied with extreme rigor.

A confirmation of this explanation may be found in the legislation dealing with excrement (which must be excluded from the confines of the military encampment, according to Deuteronomy 23:13–15).

Excrement is the supreme example of the impure, the formless, the undifferentiated. Moreover, as Bataille points out,[19] it is part of a body that is losing its hold on life, a body whose existence is being curtailed; excrement is related to death. Later on, in Judaism, Gehenna, the place where offal was burned, became the metaphor for hell, that is, for the place of eternal death.

"HOUSE" AND POLLUTION

The "house," that is, kinship, is likewise built on the principle of difference: husband and wife each spring from a different *flesh*. That is why the *taboo on incest* is formulated thus: "None of you may approach a woman who is closely related to him [literally: approach a woman belonging to his own flesh]" (Lev. 18:6); or "You must not uncover the nakedness of . . . They are your own flesh; it would be incest" (Lev. 18:17). These two "definitions" respectively begin and end the exhaustive list of cases of incest. There is only one exception among people closely related, and that is that sexual relations are not prohibited between a man and the wife of his mother's brother. The taboo affects all other areas of close kinship, whether the flesh in question is the individual's own or that of his father or his mother or his sister or his brother. In all these instances, the flesh is always his own, and, as the Jerusalem Bible observes, "flesh must not fertilize itself."[20] (The exchanging of wives also comes under this principle.)

With Bataille,[21] we may go a step further and see behind the prohibition of incest the will to restrain sex conceived as a form of violence, that is, to restrain the desire of the flesh which, if not subjected to a taboo, threatens to make impossible the organization of work and the daily life of the household.[22]

The principle of sexual differentiation leads to the prohibition of homosexuality (Lev. 18:22), which involves a mingling of the same sex, and to the prohibition of bestiality (Lev. 18:23), which is a union of incompatible elements: "This would be a foul thing."

Here is how the list of sexual taboos, excluding or strictly limiting the violence of the flesh, closes: "Do not make yourselves unclean by any of these practices, for it was by such things that the nations that I have expelled to make way for you made themselves unclean. *The land became unclean*; I have exacted the penalty for its fault and the land had to vomit out its inhabitants" (Lev. 18:24–25; italics added). At issue, then, is the purity of the inhabited space; the symbolic field takes the form of a *pure space,* from which everything impure is cut off and cast forth.

This last remark applies especially to *corpses,* which render impure everything that touches them; thus a man becomes unclean for seven days (Num. 19:11). Along with excrement, corpses make clear to us the impulse that structures the field of pollution, for the corpse is the strongest affirmation of death's violence; it is there that this violence must be denied. Corpses must be buried,[23] even those of persons condemned to death for capital offenses and hanged (Deut. 21:23).

In this context, we may mention the leper, that is, the person whose body secretes pus, for here we have another sign of decay and of the death that lies in wait for human beings (Lev. 13). Though illnesses are not expressly listed as forms of impurity, they are nonetheless regarded as punishments (cf. Deut. 28:21–22); Judaism was to see in them an enslavement to Satan.

Being a sign of the violence associated with sexuality and death, menstrual blood and the blood of childbirth render women impure for seven days and forty (or eighty) days respectively (Lev. 15:19–28; 12) (it is tempting to see in these regulations a sign of woman's inferior position in Israel). A seminal discharge (Lev. 15:16) and the discharges of venereal disease (Lev. 15:1–13) render impure a man and everything he touches. In all these cases, as in the case of excrement, the human body suffers losses; the organs and orifices through which these losses occur are regarded as the *shameful* parts of the body,[24] parts closely connected with pollution. Those who undergo these forms of violence become *untouchable* during the period of the impurity; that is to say, they are *separated* from the pure in the space of the house and of everyday life.

SANCTUARY (TEMPLE) AND POLLUTION

Sanctuaries (after the Josian reform, only the temple at Jerusalem) are the place of sacrifice where the individual Israelite (and the whole people) enters into communion (ideological consumption) with his God. But such communion is reserved to the pure, and the sacrifice is the link with the source of purity. Sacrifice is thus the place of purification. The purification is accomplished by means of the *blood* of the expiatory victims (that are substituted for a human being); violence practiced on animals has the power to ward off the violence of pollution.

Not any and every animal can be a victim. The animal chosen for sacrifice must be not only pure but "without blemish" (Lev. 1:3), that is, "no defect must be found in it. You must not offer to Yahweh an animal that is blind, lame, multilated, ulcerous, or suffering from skin disease or sore" (Lev. 22:21–22). In short, only those animals may be sacrificed that are not being subjected to the violence of death.

A priestly caste is set aside for this service. They are the subject of special care as far as the purity of their blood is concerned: they may marry only the daughters of Israelites who are pure[25]; they may not marry women who are profaned by prostitution or who have been dismissed by their husbands (Lev. 21:7). The high priest, moreover, may marry "only a virgin from his own family" (Lev. 21:14). A priest, in addition, may not make himself unclean "by going near the corpse of one of his family, unless it be of his closest relations—father, mother, son, daughter, brother" or "his virgin sister" (Lev. 21:1–3). Even more is required of a high priest: "He must not go near a dead man's corpse, he must not make himself unclean even for his father or mother" (Lev. 21:11).

Only priests and their families may eat the consecrated food that consists of the sacrificial victims (Lev. 22:2); a priest may eat even if he has an infirmity (Lev. 21:22). However, "none of your descendants [i.e., no priest], in any generation, must come forward to offer the food of his God if he has any infirmity—no man must come near if he has an infirmity such as blindness or lameness, if he is disfigured or deformed, if he has an injured foot or arm, if he is a hunchback or dwarf, if he has a disease of the eyes or the skin, if he has a running sore, or if he is a eunuch" (Lev 21:17–20).

Like the victims, the priests are acceptable for the sacrifice only if they are *without blemish.* This rule manifests one of the principles that order the Hebrew symbolic field, namely, that within the realm of the *pure* there is a further distinction between the completely pure and the less pure, the latter being unfit for worship, just as the impure is unfit for consumption. The "less pure" is the nonperfect, that which has defects; in short, that which is not fulfilled. Something is *lacking* to it; it is not completely *blessed.*

MEANING OF THE POLLUTION SYSTEM

At the level of the system based on the pure vs. the polluted, the Israelites made a ceaseless effort to preserve the purity of their tables, their "houses" (kinships), and their sanctuaries. If the effort was ceaseless, the safeguards being multiplied through prohibitions, the reason is that the threat of pollution was a constant thing. Even if, within the space proper to a social formation, it is not always possible to distinguish in a clear-cut, concrete way, a pure space (like the temple) and an impure space (like cemeteries or the place for offal outside the inhabited camp), the purpose of the Law nonetheless is precisely to trace the *line of separation* and clarify the pattern of this symbolic field with its twofold orientation.

In my view, only the conception that Bataille sets forth in his *Eroticism* enables us to grasp the why and wherefore of what we may call the dialectic of the pure and the polluted. This dialectic, says Bataille, reflects and corresponds to a prior dialectic of life and death. In this latter dialectic, moreover, each of the terms is not simply extrinsic to the other; according to Bataille, death is at the very heart of life. If there is a permanent concern about food and the purity of the table, this is because all that humanity has to eat is corpses. If there is a permanent concern about sex, the reason is that sexual desire is a form of violence and deadly on two scores. It is deadly in itself; there we have Bataille's essential thesis: he maintains that the taboos on incest, for example, are only specialized forms of a general, unformulated taboo relating to the danger inherent in sex.[26] Sex is also deadly in the long run, inasmuch as the children who are the result of sexual activity ultimately take their parents' place. Finally, if the *blood* of the victims, that is, something impure, is what serves to purify the altar and the offerers, the reason is that at the very heart of the blessing bestowed by God on the pure and just Israelite (in the form of an abundance of food and children) the curse of death is at work against that same Israelite. Life, according to Bataille, involves an immense, prodigal waste; everything dies so that life may go on in profusion.

Here is what Leviticus says of blood: "The life of the flesh is in the blood. This blood I myself have given you to perform the rite of atonement for your lives at the altar. That is why I have said to the sons of Israel: None of you nor any stranger living among you shall eat blood" (Lev. 17:11–12). In other words, the blood is both life and death; it is the polluted thing that purifies.

The Hebraic conception of Yahweh himself reveals the same contradiction. He is the holy One, the source of all holiness, the one who is separated from everything that is polluted. But is he not also the one at the *sight* of whom men die?[27]

TABLE AND DEBT

We use the word *table* here in a more comprehensive way to include the fruits of the Israelites' work as farmers and stockbreeders. These are the fruits that are heaped upon the Israelites' table and determine the extent of their *property,* their wealth, their abundance.

The principle of *extension* implies the *giving* of a tithe "of all your produce," every third year, "to the Levite, the stranger, the orphan and the widow" (Deut. 26:12), that is, to all who have no fields of their own or, in short, to the *poor.* The latter may eat their fill of their neighbor's grapes, but may not put them into their own basket; they may pick their neighbor's ears of corn, but may not take a sickle to the corn (Deut. 23:25–26). Anything overlooked in harvesting and in picking the olives and the grapes belongs to the poor (Deut. 24:19–21); the petty thefts committed by the poor are thus legalized. The pledges to be accepted for loans may not be seized (Deut. 24:10), and, in the case of loans to the poor, the pledges must be returned by evening (Deut. 24:12–13). There is to be no interest taken on loans (Deut. 23:20), and wages must be paid daily (Deut. 24:14–15). Every seven years the pledges left for loans not repaid are to be returned, and the debts cancelled (Deut. 15:1–11).

A Jewish slave must be set free at the end of seven years of service (people usually became slaves by being unable to pay their debts[28]) and sent away with generous provisions (Deut. 15:12–18). This seventh year, during which the land is to lie fallow (Exod. 23:11: "Those of your people who are poor may take food from it") is called the sabbatical year.

People have the right to buy back lands they have sold because of need ("Land must not be sold in perpetuity, for the land belongs to me, and to me you are only strangers and guests": Lev. 25:23).[29] This right is enforced by the practice of the jubilee year (every fifty years) during which landed property returns to its original owner (Lev. 25:23–55). De Vaux maintains that the prescription was never put into practice (and with reason)[30]; nonetheless the principle of extension is evident in it, as is the purpose, which is justice and social equality: "He may not exact payment from his fellow or his brother" (Deut. 15:2); "Let there be no poor among you" (Deut. 15:4).

Correlative with this principle of extension is the principle of restriction in the form of prohibitions: "You shall not steal" (Deut. 5:19); "You shall not set your heart on his [your neighbor's] house, his field, his servant—man or woman—his ox, his donkey, or anything that is his" (Deut. 5:21).

The second formulation points to the locus of the violence that must be exorcized: the *desire* that is brought to bear on the other's source of subsistence, the desire that is the orgin of aggressive violence. To disobey this prohibition is to fall into *debt* (sin)—another kind of disorder and violence that threatens the social formation. The prophets will denounce it as a cause of the curses that fall upon Israel. This violence (we shall return to this point) is the source of the class system, the enrichment of some at the expense of others, and the formation of large scale ownership.

"HOUSE" AND DEBT

The correlative of the taboo on incest is the rule of exogamy. This is Lévi-Strauss's major thesis. Bataille, for his part, shows how the *gift of a woman*, by father or brother, to another man is to be explained as the effect not of the commercial spirit but of the festive spirit, the sense of effusion; it reflects the operation of the *principle of extension*.[31]

We are familiar today with the idea that humans in modern society have an unlimited range of possibilities open to them when it comes to marriage; in addition, there is a great deal of anxiety abroad about population growth. If we prescind from all this and try to imagine "the tension inherent in life in restricted groups kept apart by hostility," we may be able to "grasp the anxiety that calls for guarantees in the form of rules [concerning exogamy]."[32] The anxiety has to do with the acquisition of wives but *also* with the begetting of children. This latter is a point that Bataille overlooks, but it is extremely important if we are to understand the Hebrew system.

Every Jew was concerned for his "house," and the greatest blessing for him was to have many children who would keep that "house" alive from "generation to generation."[33] Here we find again the struggle between life and death. The forebears continue to exist in their descendants through their *name*. That is the point of the promise made to the elderly Abraham who has no legitimate children: "Look up to heaven and count the stars if you can. Such will be your descendants" (Gen. 15:4), and "Your heir shall be of your own flesh and blood" (Gen. 15:4). Or, according to a different tradition: "I will make you a great nation; I will bless you and make your name so famous that it will be used as a blessing" (Gen. 12:2).

The same notion explains the "levirate law," which prescribes that the brother of a man who has died without leaving children is to marry the man's widow, "and the first son she bears shall assume the dead brother's name; and so his name will not be blotted out in Israel" (Deut. 25:5–6).

This triple extension (exogamy, procreation, perdurance of the *name*) is matched, on the side of the principle of restriction, by three prohibitions. First, there is the prohibition of *adultery*. The woman who is accepted by a man becomes his possession and hence forth belongs to his "house." Adultery is therefore a form of *theft* and the reverse of the exogamic gift.[34] Since the woman is the *giver* of children,[35] adultery also brings the danger that mixed blood will be introduced into her husband's house. ("No bastard is to be admitted to the assembly of Yahweh": Deut. 23:3.) For this reason, an adulterous woman is to be slain on the spot, even if she is only betrothed.[36] In all this, we are clearly involved in a system of debt, as is clear from the prohibition, "You shall not covet your neighbour's wife" (Deut. 5:21), which points to desire and its violence.

Corresponding to the extension of life that procreation represents, the principle of restriction establishes the most important taboo in the debt system: "You shall not kill" (Deut. 5:17). In the pollution system it is the violence of *death* (violence from within, as it were) that is the principal object of the prohibitions. In the debt system, the determining object of the prohibitions is *murder* (death as aggression from outside).

Finally, over against the affirmation of life through the *name* of the "house" there is the debt of defamation: "You shall not bear false witness against your neighbour" (Deut. 5:20). Before a tribunal, two or three witnesses are required to prove a case, and if it turns out that a witness has lied, "you must deal with him as he would have dealt with his brother" (Deut. 19:15–19). The false witness's heart and desire therefore become the norm for dealing with him or her.

Let us look a little more closely at *marriage*. "A man leaves his father and mother [his "house," his flesh] and joins himself to his wife, and they become one body [flesh]" (Gen. 2:24). This "one flesh," the result of fusing two fleshes, can become fruitful. (We are talking always of extending the "house" through exogamy.) At the same time, the father's "house" must live on in that of the son; the principle of extension therefore forbids children to abandon those whom they left when they married. This is the point behind the commandment: "Honour your father and your mother, . . . so that you may have long life and may prosper in the land" (Deut. 5:16).[37]

The purpose of exogamy is to weave a whole fabric of familial relations between various "houses" and to strengthen the relations within the clan, the tribe, and the nation; in short, all the *blood relationships*. The principle of extension through exogamy thus leads to what the texts often call "the house of Israel." The principle of restriction, on the other hand, operates to exclude *pagans* from the house of Israel, marriage with them being expressly prohibited (Deut. 7:1–4). The debt system does not come into play toward pagans as it does toward Jews. Pagans can, or even should, be killed in war (Deut. 20:16–18) or at least be subjected (Deut. 20:11) and be permanently enslaved (Lev. 25:44). Interest can be demanded on loans to them (Deut. 23:21). Pagans are excluded from the assembly of Yahweh (Deut. 23:4–7).

Exclusivity was increasingly emphasized after the exile, when Jews found themselves more and more mixed in with pagans in Palestine and especially in the Diaspora. As the racial and symbolic boundary between Hebrews and pagans became less clear and strong, ideology was called upon to strengthen it.

All that we have been talking about here is located in the political instance that structures a social formation so that it may *survive* in proper order from generation to generation: survival of "names," of "houses," of "tribes," and of the "house of Israel."[38] The system based on debt aims to assure this survival, and to its basic prohibition, that against killing, all the others can be reduced: the prohibitions against theft (the stealing of what people need for the lives of themselves and their families),[39] against adultery, and against false witness (Deut. 5:17–20).[40]

SANCTUARY (TEMPLE) AND DEBT

The worship of Yahweh is opposed to the worship of the gods of Israel's foreign neighbors as gift/debt (sin). The opposition impinges first of all on places of worship:

> You must destroy completely all the places where the nations you dispossess [in the conquest of Palestine] have served their gods, on high mountains, on hills, under any spreading tree; you must tear down their altars, smash their pillars, cut down their sacred poles, set fire to the carved images of their gods and wipe out their name from that place. Not so are you to behave towards Yahweh your God. You must seek Yahweh your God only in the place he himself will choose from among all your tribes, to set his name there and give it a home. There you shall bring your holocausts and your sacrifices, your tithes, the offerings from your hands, your votive offerings and your voluntary offerings, the first-born of your herd and flock; there you will eat in the presence of Yahweh your God and be thankful for all that your hands have presented, you and your households blessed by Yahweh your God (Deut. 12:2–7).

To Yahweh are given victims, holocausts and sacrifices. Tithes too are given: every three years for the Levite or priest,[41] the stranger, the widow, and the orphan (Deut. 14:28–29)[42]; and annually a tithe of crops and of the first-born of flock and herd, to be offered at Jerusalem (Deut. 14:22–23).[43] These tithes are regarded as consecrated (Deut. 26:14). The lengthy text we quoted in the preceding paragraph connects all this with the *temple*, the place for the *gift* to Yahweh of what Bataille calls "the cursed [=consecrated] part"; this is to be expended freely and consumed as excess that is lost (from the viewpoint of daily, profane, utilitarian consumption).[44]

One day a week, the sabbath, is *given* (consecrated) to Yahweh. On that day there is no work (Deut. 5:12–14), just as there is no work during *festive periods*, when joy overflows and the people consume the annual tithe. The most important of these feasts is Passover: ". . . in the place where Yahweh chooses to give his name a home . . . you must eat [the Passover] with unleavened bread, the bread of emergency, for it was in great haste that you came out of the land of Egypt . . . and you must do no work" (Deut. 1:6–8). Other feasts celebrated are the feast of Weeks and the feast of Tabernacles, which were connected with the wheat and grape harvests respectively (Deut. 16:9–15).

Remembrance of the *exodus,* the liberation from slavery, and the passage from curse to blessing; remembrance of the covenant concluded between Yahweh and Israel as God and people, after the fashion of husband and wife; remembrance of the conquest of the promised land: the *narrative* of the establishment of Israel as a people (together with the narrative of the promise to the patriarchs or tribal ancestors) brings the people together in the place where Yahweh's name dwells, namely, the temple in Jerusalem.

Principle of restriction:

> You shall have no gods except me. You shall not make yourself a carved image or any likeness of anything in heaven above or on earth beneath or in the waters under the earth [no images of animals and no human figures]; you shall not bow down to them or serve them [as other peoples do]. . . . You shall not utter the name of Yahweh your God to misuse it (Deut. 5:7–11).

The images of these false gods will be destroyed and their names will disappear. The peoples who now occupy Palestine must be exterminated: "You must lay them under ban, the Hittites, Amorites, Canaanites, Perizzites, Hivites, and Jebusites . . . so that they may not teach you to practice all the detestable practices they have in honour of their gods and cause you to sin against[45] Yahweh your God" (Deut. 20:17–18). There is operative here a principle similar to the one we saw at work in the system based on pollution: the principle that *contagion* must be avoided, but a contagion that now affects the *heart,* not the body. To prevent such contagion, assassins, the incestuous, adulterers, and the debauched must likewise die: "You must banish this evil from Israel" (Deut. 22:22; cf. 21:21).[46]

In my opinion, it is in relation to this idea of the *heart* as place of desire, an idea that governs the system based on debt ("Circumcise your heart and be obstinate no longer": Deut. 10:16), that we must understand the prohibition against carved images. Such images fascinate the hearts of people and stir their desires, for they are visible, palpable *signifiers*; they are "the work of a craftman's hands" (Deut. 27:15), and are adorned with gold and silver. "You must set fire to all the carved images of their gods, not coveting the gold and silver that covers them; take it and you will be caught in a snare" (Deut. 7:25).

Israel has quite different means of knowing its God: his "word," his "voice . . . speaking from the heart of the fire," the "ordeals, signs, wonders, war with mighty hand and outstretched arm," by which Yahweh sought out Israel in Egypt and rescued it. "This he showed you so that you might know that Yahweh is God indeed and that there is no other" (Deut. 4:32–35). In brief, it is the *might and strength* of Yahweh as told in the *narratives* of the exodus that are the means of knowing him. The seductive images of the foreign gods, those "things of nothing" (Lev. 19:4, literal translation) "that human hands have made, of wood and of stone, that cannot see or hear, eat or smell" (Deut. 4:28), stand in sharp contrast to the "might" of Yahweh that is evidently signified in that history of Israel which generation after generation is bidden to remember (Deut. 6:20–25).[47]

BLESSING AND CURSE

The two books, Leviticus and Deuteronomy, which set forth the two systems we have been reviewing, culminate in lists of the blessings and curses that will come upon the people according as they respect or violate the prohibitions of the two systems: "I set before you life or death, blessing or curse" (Deut. 30:19).[48] The two lists are too long to transcribe here, but a reading of them will clarify the meaning of the two systems.

If the people respect the prohibitions and thereby exorcize the two kinds of violence that threaten the social formation, blessing is assured: "You shall eat your fill of bread and live secure in your land. I will give peace to the land. . . . I will make you be fruitful and multiply" (Lev. 26:5-6, 9). "Blessed will be the fruit of your body, the produce of your soil, the issue of your livestock, the increase of your cattle, the young of your flock. . . . Yahweh will summon a blessing for you in your barns and in all your undertakings, and will bless you in the land that Yahweh is giving you" (Deut. 28:4, 8).

The blessing thus takes the form of *fruitfulness*: of field and animal, so that people have an abundance at the table and are filled; of woman's womb, so that children are numerous and the name of the "house" perdures from generation to generation, while the house of Israel too is extended, increasing in peace and becoming great among the nations, thus making Yahweh's *name* known.

If this fruitfulness is to be assured, life must prevail over death in the life/death cycle. For example, the seed cast into the earth must die and then, at the right moment and under the action of the rain,[49] the fruits must spring up in abundance. But only Yahweh, who is in *heaven*, can cause that to happen: "Yahweh will open the heavens to you, his rich treasure house, to give you seasonable rain for your land" (Deut. 28:12); he alone can make *fruitful* the *earth* on which people live, provide water for the cattle, etc. Everything, then, depends on Yahweh as far as Israel is concerned.

The essential difference *heaven/earth* dominates the ideological conception by which the two symbolic orders we have been analyzing are organized. It underlies, for example, the principle that the two fleshes that render one another fruitful must be different, for heaven and earth, while related each to the other, are very clearly separated and differentiated. Like heaven and earth, the pure and the impure must be kept *separate,* the pure being the space of fruitfulness, life, growth, multiplication and blessing, and the impure or polluted being the space of barrenness, death, curse, and violence that must be exorcized. "Be holy, for I, Yahweh your God, am holy" (Lev. 19:2); in other words, "Separate yourselves from pollution."

It is now possible to determine more accurately the meaning of the *debt system*. The earth which humans till and on which they live with their livestock can only *receive* the rain which is *given* to it to make it fruitful; thus a *gift* is the source of fruitfulness and blessing. This basic fact explains the *principle of extension* that rests on the notion of giving; it says that what Yahweh has given to human beings, they must in turn give to their fellow humans who lack it; as they have been filled, so they must fill their brothers and sisters. Similarly, a man must give the daughter that has been given to him to another man who wants a wife so that the other man too may have children.

The victims and tithes given to Yahweh, the sabbath and feasts on which people stop working so that they may give the time to Yahweh—these simply make evident the *gift* that lies behind people's work and their abundance at table. Consequently, to give of their abundance and blessings is an assurance that the blessing will continue, as is their vigilance in the matter of purity. To give what one has is the only means of continuing to have; people must *lose* if they are to receive.

At the same time, the giving of people helps them avoid coveting the abundance of others—their property, their lives, their blessings. Giving thus forestalls violence against the neighbor, the brother, the equal. This equality between people and "houses" is the purpose of the principle of extension: "Let there be no poor among you" (Deut. 15:4); "You must love your neighbor as yourself" (Lev. 19:18). The violence proper to covetous desire militates against this equality and tends to make some people rich and others poor. For this reason, the principle of restriction comes into play to prohibit this covetous desire: "He may not exact payment from his fellow or his brother" (Deut. 15:2).

We must go a step further, for Yahweh is not the God of any and every people in any and every land. He is the God of the Israelites to whom he has *given* "a land where milk and honey flow" (Deut. 6:3), a land which belongs to him and which he makes fruitful. The gift of the *land,* already promised to the forefathers—"the land which he swore to your fathers Abraham, Isaac and Jacob that he would give you" (Deut. 6:10; cf. Gen. 12:1)—is normative for the blessing; in fact, it is the first of the blessings and the pledge of all the others.[50]

It is in this context that we can grasp the absolutely basic importance of the exodus narrative: how Yahweh brought Israel out of slavery in Egypt and thus liberated it from the *curse,* brought it across the wilderness, and *gave* to it the land. The Decalogue, which summarizes the prohibitions of the debt system, began with the assertion: "I am Yahweh your God who brought you out of the land of Egypt, out of the house of slavery" (Deut. 5:6).

The *gift* character of the land emerges clearly from the narrative of the struggles involved in taking possession of it. These struggles, too, fit into the debt system because they are an exorcizing of the aggressive violence brought to bear on Israel's frontiers by other nations. These other nations are "greater and stronger than yourself" (Deut. 9:1); they have "horses and chariots and an army greater than your own" (Deut. 20:1). Yet "you must not be *afraid* of them; Yahweh your God is with you, who brought you out of the land of Egypt. . . . Do not be faint-hearted. . . . Then the scribes are to address the people in words like these [there follow three exhortations to soldiers who have a blessing they have not yet enjoyed: a new house not yet lived in, a vineyard not yet harvested, a wife betrothed but not yet taken; cf. 2:30]. . . . Is there any man here who is fearful and faint of heart? Let him go home lest he make his fellows lose *heart* too" (Deut. 20:1, 3, 5, 8), i.e., lest he *contaminate* them.

Chapters 7 and 8 of Deuteronomy develop at length the theme that Israel is small in comparison with the other peoples but that it will overcome them, as formerly in Egypt (Deut. 7:17–21). The conclusion to be drawn from the unequal strength of the opposing nations is this: "Beware of saying in your heart, 'My own *strength* and the might of my own hand won this power for me.' Remember Yahweh your God: it was he who gave you this strength and won you this power" (Deut. 8:17–18).

Chariots are the mark of a professional army, a standing army (such as that of David would be at a later date[51]). In contrast to such an army Deuteronomy thinks in terms of a "militia composed of the free peasantry" fighting what von Rad calls a "holy war" (we today would call it a "people's war").[52] Von Rad explains that this ancient idea (it is to be found in Joshua and Judges) was revived by the Levites in their antimonarchist effort at reform.[53]

This conception, which Deuteronomy applies in augmenting the courage of the combatants and overcoming their fear, amounts in fact to contrasting the *strength of bodies* with the (bodily) *weakness* that armaments presuppose.[54] We are evidently in the field of the symbolic here, and the *gift* character of the strength in question indicates the presence of the debt system. This conception is manifest in the narrative of the taking of Midian by Gideon: "Yahweh said to Gideon, 'There are too many people with you for me to put Midian into their power; Israel might claim the credit for themselves at my expense: they might say, "My own hand has rescued me" ' " (Judg. 7:3). It is also clear in the narrative of David's fight with Goliath: "You come against me with sword and spear and javelin, but I come against you in the name of Yahweh" (1 Sam. 17:45).

The issue (as seen by Deuteronomy) between Yahweh and the gods of other peoples now becomes clearer. The latter gods rely on the power of wealth, the power of armaments, the political power of kings; their images are signifiers that are wedded to silver and gold (Deut. 7:25) and to war horses and war chariots (Deut. 20:1).[55] In contrast to such *signifiers,* the absence of *images* of Yahweh and the remembrance of the story of his strength show the preponderance in Israel of the principle of *gift.*

In Deuteronomy, the fear of abuses by kings shows in the reservations concerning the idea of royalty in Israel:

Ensure that he [the king] does not increase the number of his horses, or make the people go back to Egypt to increase his cavalry. . . . Nor must he increase the number of his wives, for that could lead his heart astray. Nor must he increase his gold and silver excessively. . . . So [by observing the Law] his heart will not look down on his brothers" (Deut. 17:14–20).

The narrative in 1 Samuel, chapter 8, of the people's request for a king ("Give us a king to rule over us, *like the other nations*": 1 Sam. 8:5, italics added) sets forth in detail how the king will exploit his brothers; that is why Samuel refuses to yield to the demand, though he is forced to do so in the end. Von Rad says: "The place occupied in the pagan religions by the cultic image was in Israel taken by the word and name of Yahweh,"[56] that is, by the narrative of his manifestations of power, the commemoration of which, especially at Passover, will reveal to successive generations of Israelites the true source of the blessing they enjoy: "You shall tell your son, 'Once we were Pharaoh's slaves in Egypt, and Yahweh brought us out of Egypt by his mighty hand' " (Deut. 6:21).

If, however, people are not on guard to keep the pure and the polluted separate, the latter will gain the upper hand; violence and the *curse* will then fall upon Israel. If they do not avoid covetous desire and the violence inherent in it (theft, adultery, murder, defamation, worship of the images of foreign gods), then desire and violence will gain the upper hand. The result will be, not abundance and multiplication, but *devastation,* plague, famine, barrenness, and enslavement by other nations. We are astounded when we read the lists of curses; I shall quote but a short example: "A nation you do not know will eat the fruit of your soil and of your labour. You will never be anything but exploited and crushed continually" (Deut. 28:33–34). The sight of a people and its children subjected to unimaginable rage and violence (the condition of Israel in Egypt, according to the exodus narrative) will be unbearable to anyone who sees it.

The *debt* system can be summed up in the concept of the *covenant* between Yahweh and Israel; it is a covenant that involves love on both sides, but the initiative belongs to Yahweh.

> If Yahweh set his heart on you and chose you, it was not because you outnumbered other peoples: you were the least of all peoples. It was for *love* of you and to keep the oath he swore to your fathers that Yahweh brought you out with his mighty hand and redeemed you from the house of slavery, from the power of Pharaoh, king of Egypt. Know then that Yahweh your God is God indeed, the faithful God who is true to his *covenant* and his graciousness for a thousand generations towards those who *love* him and keep his commandments (Deut. 7:7–9, italics added).

"Listen, Israel: Yahweh our God is the one Yahweh. You shall *love* Yahweh your God with all your heart, with all your soul, with all your strength" (Deut. 6:4–5). To *love* is to *give*; in the terminology used by Bataille, to love is to consume and to lose. To steal and kill, on the other hand, is to be in *debt,* or, in Bataille's terminology, to be cursed and destroyed.

The Decalogue, which is a summary of the prohibitions that involve *debt,* is at the heart of the covenant, as is the commandment to love one's neighbor (Lev. 19:18), which is a summary of the idea of *gift.* "You will be his very own people as he promised you, but only if you keep all his commandments; then for praise and renown and honour he will set you high above all the nations he has made, and you will be a people consecrated to Yahweh" (Deut. 26:18–19). That is, the blessing of Yahweh will make Israel a great nation in the eyes of other peoples: "When they come to know of all these laws they will exclaim, 'No other people is as wise and prudent as this great nation' " (Deut. 4:6).

Chapter 13, verse 3 of Genesis had already opened up the same vista to Abraham: "All the tribes of the earth shall bless themselves by you." Yahweh's blessing, brought about by his power and *gift,* causes Israel to increase, and therein lies Yahweh's *glory,* which has come to "dwell" in Israel (according to the conception dominant in Leviticus). "The glory of God will fill the whole earth" (Num. 14:21),[57] but not by means of a going forth of Israel to the nations; on the contrary, it is the nations who will *come* to Israel, the blessed land. The eschatology to be developed by the prophets is already inplicit in the Pentateuchal conception of Yahweh's blessing.

POLLUTION AND DEBT

The time has come to emphasize the approximative character of the foregoing reflections. It would take intensive work by specialists, especially in Hebrew semantics and in the various textual strata with their historical origins, to confirm or undermine them. I make no claim here to be a historian. I have only read the modern French translations of these texts and tried to find therein a logic that guides the organization of the two systems and that may later serve in the reading of Mark's gospel narrative.

It is with the same intent and in the same perspective that I now carry the argument forward. The next step is to compare the two systems in order to determine their points of likeness and difference.

Purity, as we have seen, brings fruitfulness and multiplication; that is, it brings Yahweh's blessing and gift. In the system based on debt, what I have called the principle of expansion or of gift is at work. Pollution, on the contrary, brings corruption, death, destruction, diminution; in other words, a principle of restriction is at work.

The punishment of "debtors" (or sinners), namely, their death or at least their separation from the just, flows from the concern to avoid a *contagion* that affects hearts, just as the separation of the pure and the polluted keeps bodies free from the contagion of impurity. This element of contagion, according to von Rad, is intrinsic to the very concept of *debt* (sin): "The evil deed was only one side of the matter, for through it an evil had been set in motion which sooner or later would inevitably turn against the sinner or the community to which he belonged."[58] Smend (whom von Rad cites) had already said the same: "For the Jews sin was rather a power which brought the sinner to destruction, because it was basically identical with the penalty."[59] This is to say that the debt, like the pollution, is itself the violence that by contagion breaks down and destroys the social formation; the debt or pollution *is* the curse.

I might note further that, while the areas covered by the two systems are mutually exclusive (except perhaps [60] for the case of incest), nonetheless the term *abomination*,[61] which seems to me to convey the maximum degree of pollution, often appears in Deuteronomy to characterize transgressions that clearly belong in the debt system (see, for example, Deut. 25:13–16).[62]

A further similarity is that the debt system has within it a contradiction much like the one we found in the pollution system. It consists in this, that blessing and abundance engender the covetous desire to have more; this means that the blessing may well develop under its aegis the violence that is the curse.

> Take care you do not forget Yahweh your God, neglecting his com-
> mandments and customs and laws which I lay on you today. When you
> have eaten and had all you want, when you have built fine houses to live
> in, when you have seen your flocks and herds increase, your silver and
> gold abound and all your possessions grow great, do not become proud
> of heart. Do not then forget Yahweh your God (Deut. 8:11–14).

"For failing to serve Yahweh your God in the joy and happiness that come from an abundance of all things, you will submit . . ." (Deut. 28:47; cf. Deut. 6:10–13).

Wherever there is abundance, even if part of it be dispensed in the form of a gift out of pocket, there is also *increased* wealth—and increased danger of covetousness and of taking from the weak so that one may have still greater wealth; this means there is increased danger of debt and its curse. As in the pollution system, so in the debt system death (curse) is at the heart of life (blessing). This contradiction leads to the formation of class societies, and Israel was no exception.

The two systems thus follow the same logic, the same dialectic of blessing (=purity=gift) and curse (=pollution=debt). We might even be tempted to say that there must initially have been but a single system, so much do the two resemble each other. Nonetheless, even specialists who, as they read, want to object to what they regard as a simplification, will grant me:

1. that as I have described the two systems, the domains in question are mutually exclusive, being two forms of violence; and

2. that I have not forced the texts in describing the pollution system on the basis of Leviticus and the debt system on the basis of Deuteronomy. Deuteronomy, for practical purposes, says nothing of what Leviticus speaks of as pollution. Leviticus, on the other hand, does not ignore the idea of debt, but it does evidently give it less importance; Leviticus, throughout the Priestly document, even seems to pay no attention[63] to the Decalogue, which

is the summary of the taboos in the debt system, just as the Decalogue says nothing of incest. I do not regard all this as mere accident, and I must now account for the relative opposition between the two systems: an opposition that is certainly of late provenance, although it would be inexplicable if the distinction as such between the two were not archaic.

POLLUTION, DEBT, AND CLASS SOCIETY

Among the four source documents for the first five books of the Bible, J and P are usually regarded as having originated in the groups (including the clergy) that comprised the royal court at Jerusalem; E and D, on the other hand, issued from circles in northern Palestine that had achieved a separate political organization after the death of Solomon but were decimated in the eighth century by the Assyrian invasions, at which time part of the population took refuge in the south and brought their traditions with them.

Two different theological traditions are to be found in the prophetic literature. One is the northern tradition, represented especially by Hosea, Jeremiah, Ezekiel, and Second Isaiah; it focuses on the exodus from Egypt, the covenant at Sinai, and the conquest of Palestine. The other is the southern tradition, represented especially by Isaiah; it is monarchic and develops a theology of the covenant with David, the anointed king, and of the choice of Zion (the hill on which the temple at Jerusalem was built), as Yahweh's dwelling place. The two traditions are independent, even if the last three prophets of the first list are acquainted with the tradition concerning David and Zion.[64]

It is an interesting fact, however, that all the prophets, even Isaiah, are at one with Deuteronomy in following a dialectic that sets them in opposition to the circles at the subasiatic court and to the Jerusalem clergy.[65] The dialectic involves the two systems of pollution and debt, and, in my opinion, reflects a class struggle, as I shall now attempt to show.

The exploitation of the rural communities by the subasiatic state is thus described by von Rad:

> In spite of the inadequacy of our information, we can well imagine that the rural population, which was tied to the patriarchal way of life, did not by any means accept without protest the great innovation of the imposition of the kingdom. Quite apart from religious considerations, the monarchy, as we know, also brought in its train a considerable curtailment of the rights of the free landed peasantry, as well as considerable economic burdens. The "right of the king" which Samuel is said to have recited to the people (I Sam. VIII. 11–17) is of course thoroughly tendentious in its formulation—this whole account of the choice of Saul as king also derives from a considerably later time. Nevertheless, the details of this right of the king are far from being without foundation in fact. The king actually did conscript the young

men of the country population in order to put them in his garrisons as regular soldiers. He laid hands on landed property to set up estates of his own throughout the country; and from the country population, too, he drew the labour forces for these estates. Other landed property he confiscated as rewards for his henchmen (I Sam. XXII. 7). He taxed the whole population to defray the expenses of his court (I Kings IV. 7, XX. 15); indeed, even womenfolk were not safe from his requisition, for he needed them as perfumers, cooks, and bakers. It is easy to imagine how the free peasantry in Israel, who still lived by a feeling of freedom acquired in nomadic life, must have regarded such interferences with their life. An utter repudiation of the monarchy finds its strongest expression in the fable of Jotham (Jg. IX. 8ff.), which has been designated the most forthright anti-monarchical poem in world literature.[66]

The logic of the debt system, which we have already analyzed, is certainly that of the early pre-subasiatic tribes. It corresponds to "the old ethic of brotherhood obtaining among the neighbourly nomadic tribes," in which "the human element . . . conspicuous in ancient Israelite law . . . has its roots in the time long before the Settlement."[67] The archaic character of the idea of blessing[68] and of the idea of "sin" as curse and maleficent power[69] seems to me to be likewise beyond question.

Now, the aim of the debt system, as we have seen, was social equality[70]: "Let there be no poor among you" (Deut. 15:4), and the avoidance of any class system or subasiatic monarchy. The fact that Deuteronomy was not written until four centuries after the irreversible event in which such a monarchy was established shows only that "faith in Yahweh," in accepting the monarchy,[71] did not determine the social order; the fact does not exclude our presupposition that the logic of Deuteronomy continues to be the logic of the earlier Elohist.

An exegesis of the prophetic texts would, I am sure, easily confirm the brutal conclusion that is already clear and that bourgeois exegetes systematically avoid[72]; the class system established by David and the exploitation of brother by brother are the curse that fell on Israel and brought it to devastation and exile. We shall see that the gospel of Mark is located in the same field as far as the reading of the history of Israel is concerned.

Evidently, the priestly class did not read this history in the same way, for the priestly class was connected with the royal court and, after the exile, replaced it. It is a fact, however, that in Deuteronomy the Levites, "the whole of the tribe of Levi" (Deut. 18:1), are considered to be priests of Yahweh, while the P document (Leviticus) insists on distinguishing between the priestly caste consisting of Aaron and his descendants, on the one side, and the rest of the Levites, on the other (the difference between priest and Levite being always strongly marked in P[73]). This fact is already a symptom of the conflict between the circles from which the D and P documents respectively emerged, and of the opposition between countryside and court[74] on which this conflict is based. The fact is thus a symptom of different sites for reading.[75]

The class reading that the priests make of Israel's history depends on their cultic function and is even reflected in what I have called the pollution system, which is at the very heart of the cultus and is by definition the business of the priests, just as it is their business to determine in doubtful cases what is pure and what is polluted (cf. Lev. 14 on leprosy, for example). The cultus is the place for purifying people and things from purifiable pollution and for exorcizing the violence that pollution represents.[76] According-ing to P, moreover, it is the very violence of birth that separates the tribe of Levi from the others,[77] that is, that sets apart the tribe in which the priestly caste has a privileged place.

As I have shown, the violence that is exorcized by taboos bearing on pollution is the violence of death; the violence, in other words, that relates to what I have called the *infrastructural, irreducible* contradiction with which every social formation is confronted.[78] The violence, however, with which the debt system is concerned—the violence of murder as aggression—relates to the *superstructural* contradiction, which is *reducible.*[79]

Our reading of Leviticus has shown us that in that book the debt system, if not entirely absent (as is the Decalogue), is to some extent confused with the clearly dominant pollution system. Deuteronomy, on the contrary, distin-guishes them to such a degree that the pollution system is completely shunted aside by the debt system; the latter is entirely to the fore, a symptom of this being the primordial importance assigned to the Decalogue, in imitation of the Covenant Code (E).

Why this divergence? For an answer we need only look to those who were responsible for the two texts. Von Rad has shown that Deuteronomy repre-sents in writing the extensive preaching activity of the Levites of the northern kingdom, who undertook a reform movement that preceded the radical cultic changes of the Josian period.[80] In other words, Deuteronomy results from a clearly *reformist* practice. It is because these Levites are seeking a reform of the social formation that they assert the primacy of the debt system, for the domain of the latter is precisely that of the reducible.

The *conservative* practice of a dominant class, however, such as was the practice of the priestly caste at Jerusalem, gains by keeping the two systems confused and by maintaining the preponderance of the system that focuses on the irreducible. Since the priests were functionaries of the king, the centrali-zation of the cultus in the Jerusalem temple, along with the suppression of all other sanctuaries (this, paradoxically, was the doing of the Deuteronomist reformers), meant the consolidation of their power over the whole social formation, to the point where they became the possessors of the political power once the Babylonians had swept the monarchy away.

It is precisely from this postexilic period that final redaction of the P document dates, as does the canonization (fixing in a "canon" or normative collection) of the entire Torah with P being, as it were, the glue holding opposing texts together. By thus establishing the canon of the Torah, the priestly caste in power closed the book and made themselves its masters, for, by this double closure, textual and political, the priority of the pollution system was asserted so strongly that at the ideological level it would dominate Judaism down to the destruction of the (second) temple, with which the destinies of this system had been bound up ever since the establishment of the subasiatic monarchy. It was by this act[81] of asserting the priority of the pollution system (of which the schematization and coordination of ritual[82] and the multiplication of expiatory sacrifices[83] are but corollaries) that the priestly caste gave their class power a solid foundation in the sacred text.

Meanwhile, once the debt system was reduced to juridical casuistry for use in the courts, it was *forgotten* that the violence of murder was the violence, in the service of appropriation, that had led to the formation of the social classes.[84] Now the political powers used the Law to repress the "violences," and even rebellions, of the humble folk.[85] This, despite the fact that the preaching of the Deuteronomistic Levites and the prophets had aimed at stimulating movements against class injustice!

The primacy of the pollution system has another effect which it is worthwhile to point out, since we are preparing to read the Markan narrative. The primacy of the pollution system tends to reduce the importance of the narrative of Yahweh's power and to lay it away in a past that is over and done with (in the priestly closure, *the Law closes the narrative*), thus preventing it from coming alive again to confront priestly legalism and the vast cultic edifice that is structured according to the rhythm of the seasons and the years.

The primacy of the pollution system thus tends to repress prophetism with its critique of subasiatic institutions and its proclamation of a future action of Yahweh.[86] As against such as outlook, Deuteronomy sets down a criterion for distinguishing the true prophet from the false. "When a prophet speaks in the name of Yahweh and the thing does not happen and the word is not fulfilled, then it has not been spoken by Yahweh" (Deut. 18:22). Here the criterion is simply the power or powerlessness of the prophetic practice. However, "if a prophet . . . offers to do a sign or a wonder for you, and the sign or wonder comes about; and if he then says to you, 'Come, then, let us follow other gods (whom you have not known) and serve them,' you are not to listen to the words of that prophet" (Deut. 13:3–4). Here the criterion of power is applied, but it is subordinated to the criterion of fidelity to the covenant. The aim always is to discern those new narratives that can claim to be in the line of the foundational narrative. For, according to Deuteronomy, *the Law remains open to new prophetic narratives.*[87]

Having thus boldly presented my thesis, I now sink back into the modesty that befits the amateur, the nonspecialist. I do not *know for sure* that what I have proposed is true; I simply *believe* it to be true. I have been pointing out the direction in which, as I see it, a materialist exegesis of the Old Testament must proceed. It must take account of the factors already at work in the texts as we have them (texts which all date from a time when the monarchy had already been established) and bring to light the ideological process concerning the two systems in the symbolic order of ancient Israel. It seems probable to me that such an elucidation of ideology must lead to revisions of accepted Hebraic semantics, for it is quite possible that the dominant idealist exegesis has slanted the semantics in accordance with its own class interests. The reading of Deuteronomy and the prophets would be the privileged place for this elucidation.

There is, moreover, some real justification for my boldness. Read, for example, the note in von Rad in which he cites Martin Noth's "penetrating criticism" of blessing as recompense: the latter exegete, with his great erudition, cannot accept the blessings promised to Israel if it obeys the Law, because they imply the "Catholic" concept of merit![88] In another passage, von Rad tries to show that the Israelite sacrifices did not have their effect "ex opere operato"![89] Moreover, the "material view of salvation" in Deuteronomy is the result of "a lengthy process," for "in its earliest days Jahwism was not yet able to make the proper theological connection between God and the gifts of the arable land."[90]

And yet, far more than the Catholic exegetes, von Rad does take into account the relation between the texts and economic and political questions; at least he pays some attention to it, as is clear from the long passage we cited from him a few pages back (in this final section of the chapter). In the face of this kind of exegetical world, which has made such an enormous scientific investment for the sake of serious work on the original texts and which nonetheless works within the kind of ideology we have indicated, surely my inquisitive approach to these venerable texts will be understood and forgiven.

Chapter 2
Palestine in the First Century A.D.

THE ARTICULATION OF THE
SUBASIATIC MODE AND SLAVE SYSTEM

In the preceding chapter we assumed that the social formation of ancient Israel was a subasiatic mode of production. Our task now is to analyze this social formation in its final state. There is no doubt that the history of Palestine unfolded entirely within the "Asiatic sphere"[1] down to the wars of Alexander (died 323 B.C.); there was plenty of time for the social formation to achieve its structure and even for it to undergo a restructuring. The problem, then, is not so much the subasiatic mode of production ("subasiatic," because the important irrigation systems characteristic of the Asiatic mode of production were lacking) as the articulation of this with a slave system. In other words, the problem is, first, the "hellenization" of the mode of production (against this hellenization the Maccabees rebelled in the second century), and then its "romanization," once Pompey in 63 B.C. had made Palestine a part of the Roman Empire.

The result of these two successive changes was the development within the subasiatic mode of production of a large private sector of mercantile trade— the kind of development that occurred in the later stages of many Asiatic social formations.[2] The question we must answer is whether the subasiatic mode of production remained dominant or became secondary, and what kind of transformations it underwent.

The answer seems easy for Judea, which was geographically isolated and entirely centered on Jerusalem and its temple. Here the subasiatic mode seems to have remained dominant, as we shall see. The answer is more difficult for Galilee, since this section of the country was crossed by two great trade routes, the one connecting the sea (at Ptolemais in Syro-Phoenicia) with Damascus, and the other connecting Damascus with Jerusalem. The latter route followed the Jordan valley and was subject throughout the first century A.D. to the political power of the Herodian family; it was thus isolated from Judea.

Agriculturally, there is a sharp contrast between arid Judea and fertile Galilee where rain is not infrequent. In Galilee, therefore, large estates were more readily to be found, as well as non-Jewish groups devoting themselves to trade, while the Jews were peasants for the most part.[3] The juxtaposition of races laid the Galileans open to the suspicion of legal impurity in the eyes of the Judeans, but it did not prevent the Galileans from being rather nationalistic; it was in Galilee that the various zealot movements had their origin.

The trouble is that we have far more information on Judea and Jerusalem[4] than we do on Galilee, and the following pages will inevitably reflect this fact. Moreover, as is usually the case for most of ancient history, we have no economic statistics. Consequently, our analysis, which is mainly qualitative, must depend on data relating to the political and ideological spheres and to the first-century conflicts that reveal the class interests at stake.

THE ECONOMIC INSTANCE: PRODUCTION AND CIRCULATION

Agriculture and stock-farming. As far as the productive forces were con-concerned, the methods of cultivation were empirical (wheel-less plows; scythes). Wheat was grown in Transjordan, Galilee, and Samaria. Judea was less favorable to large-scale cultivation, and farmers went in for wine, olives, fruits, vegetables, and cereals. There were some wooded areas, so that the woodcutter's trade was possible to some extent. Sheep and goats were raised in Judea, and larger cattle in the coastal plains and in Transjordan. Pigs, being impure animals, were not raised in Palestine. (Mark 5:1–20 takes place in a foreign country.)

As for the *relations of production*, the peasants in the *village* communities were small-scale proprietors (the division of labor was not very advanced) and had to pay a tribute to the state. They formed one sector of the subasiatic social formation, in which property was, in the abstract, collectively owned but was in fact worked by individuals and could be inherited; the land outside the villages was "common land." In addition to the peasant holdings, there was an extensive area of production in the form of large estates. These were worked either by salaried day laborers (cf. Matt. 20:1–16) who were frequently the peasants just mentioned, or by slaves (these were fairly few in number, according to Jeremias). Stewards or managers quite often organized the work in behalf of an owner who lived in the city (cf. Luke 16:1–9) or even of a tenant-farmer (cf. Mark 12:1–9).[5]

In parallel fashion, the peasants in the villages raised a few animals around their houses, while the big landowners hired shepherds to take care of their vast flocks.[6]

The Sea of Galilee was fished by various methods; even great nets up to five hundred meters long were used, involving several boats and teams of six to eight fishermen. The description in Luke 5:7 and 10 seems to indicate a simple collaboration of several fishermen, with the catch being equally shared.

Artisans were to be found chiefly in the cities, and especially at Jerusalem; they dealt in clothing (wool, flax, woven cloth; fullers, tailors, curriers), food (oil, meat, cheese, eggs, baked goods), and construction (carpenters, smiths). There were also potters, water carriers, makers of ointments, spices, and perfumes, makers of luxury items, goldsmiths, seal makers, copyists, etc. As a general rule, artisans were self-employed.

The state itself hired thousands of workers (rebuilding of the temple, building of Herod's palace, monuments, aqueducts, city walls): workers in stone and wood, sculptors, goldsmiths, mosaicists, etc. It is estimated that around A.D. 60 the state was employing about eighteen thousand men.

Consideration of the *mode of circulation* will enable us better to distinguish the two economic sectors of Palestine: one connected with the *villages,* the other with the *city*. In the *villages*, circulation involved only some items produced by artisans (Jesus was a carpenter in a village) and usually took the form of barter. For essential products the villages were self-sustaining. Any surplus of such production went either to the temple in the form of an annual tax (the double drachma) or to the lower clergy in the form of a tithe, or was set aside for the great feasts, as a second tithe that had to be spent in Jerusalem. Evidently, what we have in the villages is the "base" of a subasiatic social formation.

The *cities* must be taken in connection with the great landed estates and with the vast herds of cattle that provided food. Unlike the villages, the cities were centers for a rather intensive trading activity that was connected either with the Herodian court (at Tiberias, founded by Antipas in A.D. 17) and the international trade route that passed through Galilee, or with Jerusalem in Judea.

The source of production for such trade, as far as agricultural produce and cattle went, was the great estates whose economic interests were bound up with the cities and especially with Jerusalem and its very large influxes of pilgrims. (Jeremias estimates about sixty thousand for the feast of Passover.) A class of wholesalers assured the circulation of goods; these people were also involved in the slave trade and in trade in raw materials. (Metals—gold, silver, bronze, iron—were imported from abroad.)

The pilgrimages also supported the artisans of Jerusalem who engaged in retail selling without an intermediary. Their trade was connected with the temple (animals for the sacrifices; souvenirs) or the hotel business, or they dealt in luxury items. It is to be noted that all this trade was concerned with *expenditure*; it was field III of the economic field that supported Jerusalem.

Trade was regulated by a monetary apparatus in which Jewish coins circulated side by side with foreign coins: Roman (the denarius), Greek (the silver drachma), and Phoenician. The mixed coinage shows the international character of trade in Palestine, and also reflects the fact that Jewish pilgrims came from all over the known world.

The importance of this trade and its connection with the great estates explains why the day laborers working for these estates were paid in silver (a denarius a day according to Matt. 20:1–16), as were the officials and work-men of the temple (who seem to have been fairly well paid[7]).

What emerges clearly from Jeremias's account is the economic and finan-cial importance of the Jerusalem temple with its vast income comprising gifts received from all over the world, taxes assigned by the Law in the form of the double-drachma levy, the trade in sacrificial victims, the fulfillment of vows, deliveries of wood, etc., etc., and, in addition, the revenues from its real estate. On the other hand, there were also enormous expenditures, especially for the rebuilding of the temple that began in 20 B.C. and ended A.D. 62–64.

This *treasury* was administered by the chief priests, three of them being treasurers in chief with a staff of officials under them. They dealt in "public finances," since the treasury was a state treasury that did not legally belong to the priestly aristocracy that administered it and drew a regular income from it.

The families of the chief priests (four families provided most of the chief priests during the Roman period) were very rich and were probably land-owners as well. Moreover, the concession for selling sacrificial animals within the temple precincts (Mark 11:15) belonged to one of these families, proba-bly that of Annas.

While taxes from Jews scattered throughout the Roman Empire flowed into Jerusalem, the taxes collected by the Roman occupiers were draining off a good deal of the Palestinian surplus to the profit of Rome. Judea had to pay six hundred talents a year to Rome; this was the equivalent of six million denarii, with a denarius representing a day's wages for a farm worker.

This total tax comprised: the tribute (*tributum*), which was a personal tax and a land tax; the "yearly produce" (*annona*), an annual contribution to meet the needs of the garrisons, taking the form of food and of forced labor; the "public" tax (*publicum*), consisting of indirect taxes and duties, the collection of which was usually farmed out to "publicans" or tax collectors.

What we have said thus far will enable us to give a description, from the economic angle, of the social formation of first-century Palestine.

1. The villages, as we have seen, were the base of the countryside com-munities that are characteristic of a subasiatic mode of production; the state-temple was the superstructure that appropriated the surplus of the villages.

2. The commercial sector, together with the large estates in the back-ground, is to be located rather among the mercantile forms current in the Roman slave-based mode of production, but with one difference: slavery seems to have been quite limited in Palestine. However, the temple, insofar as it was a treasury, was the economic pole of the mode of circulation, especially in Judea; this fact shows that the commercial sector is also to be regarded as belonging, at least partially,[8] to the subasiatic mode of produc-tion. We know from various sources that a developed Asiatic social formation contained a sector of private property and private trade.[9]

3. The double-drachma tax, which was collected from the Jews of the

Diaspora, gave a rather special character to this subasiatic formation. The tax was a symptom of the social function that was proper to the temple and that also provided justification for the state.[10] We shall return to this point in speaking of the ideological instance.

In summary, there seems to have been in Palestine a composite form in which the subasiatic mode of production was dominant in Judea, and the commercial sector, linked to the international trade of the Roman slave-based mode of production, was dominant in Galilee. The whole, however, was overdetermined by the slave-based mode of production because it was integrated into the Roman Empire, with the taxes collected being the visible economic bond between the subasiatic mode of production and the slave-based mode of production. We shall return to this point in speaking of the political instance.

THE POLITICAL INSTANCE

There are two difficulties involved in dealing with the symbolic in first-century Palestine. The first is the difficulty of knowing the *symbolic order* (a text, and therefore something ideological) that held effective sway. The difficulty exists because the order we analyzed at length in the preceding chapter underwent transformations in the course of time that were due to the social transformations going on. We will speak of these transformations in the next section. The second is the difficulty of knowing the concrete *symbolic field,* and especially the differences between the villages and the city, between Galilee and Judea.

Here we shall simply make a few remarks. The first is that there was a notable dislocation between the symbolic order and the real field. The clearest symptom of this dislocation is that from the second century B.C. on, a whole social force came into existence: the Pharisees. These defined themselves by their strict observance of the ancient symbolic order, and thereby implied that the rest of the people were much less strict in their observance. In particular, the Pharisees regarded certain occupations as inherently impure and their practicioners as polluted.[11] Among these occupations we may note that of the publicans or tax collectors, the men who collected the *publicum* tax in behalf of the Romans and who, in Palestine as everywhere else in the empire, were a parasite class, hated by the masses and condemned by the intellectual leaders. In addition to those in such inherently impure occupations, a number of people publicly violated one or other commandment of the law and were singled out as *sinners.* Finally, the "mentally ill" were regarded as possessed by a demon or impure spirit and were therefore impure and outcasts.

A second remark is that the frequent mingling of Jews with pagans (especially in Galilee but also in Judea) led to an intense concern for purity of Jewish *blood* and origin and thus for the absence of any pagan blood in the ancestral line. If a person was to exercise some very important civic rights,[12] he had to prove his Jewish origins; thus even the ordinary Israelite knew his recent ancestry and could tell to which of the twelve tribes he belonged. After the return from the exile, proof of legitimate origin became the real basis for the community of the restored people. It was especially decisive for the families of levites, priests, and chief priests. Jeremias provides a lengthy analysis of the division of Jewish society into three major groups: families of legitimate origin; families of illegitimate origin that were slightly tainted; and families of illegitimate origin that were seriously tainted.

A third remark concerns the villages: here the whole realm of the symbolic was probably much more respected, since kinship relations still played the economic, political, and ideological roles proper to them in a classless social formation.[13]

At the suprapolitical level, that of the relations of authority or political power,[14] it is likewise necessary to take into account the distinction between the village sector and the city sector.

In the *villages*, the *permanent* relations of authority were the relations within the kinship or "house." As for relations of authority that were not permanent, there was a *council of elders* that met either to regulate community affairs or as a tribunal in case of a lawsuit or a violation of the law.[15] This council was made up of the "elders" (that is, the heads of the Jewish "houses") who were chosen for the purity of their ancestral blood, and a priest who handled questions of pollution and purity.

In the *cities* the same councils existed, but the seats on them were preempted by the heads of the richest families, the "lay aristocracy." The councils in this case already reflected relations of power and class relations, for the members controlled the great agricultural estates that were the centers of the apparatus of political power and of economic activity. Some seats on the city tribunals were held by *scribes*. These were men who had pursued a regular course of study for a number of years and could make decisions on their own in questions of religious legislation and penal law. They were ordained at the age of forty and authorized to be judges in criminal and civil trials. Priests were frequently trained as scribes.

The reason why the scribes could act in this way was that their course of study not only dealt with the religious area, of which we shall speak further on, but also trained them in the complicated casuistry required for interpreting the ancient legislative texts that applied to the systems of pollution and debt. The existence of such a casuistry is further proof of the dislocation between the ancient texts and the new situation in the symbolic field as a result of social changes.

Among the councils of elders the most important was the Jerusalem council, the *Sanhedrin*. The political power of this council extended to all of Judea, and its ideological power to all of Palestine and even to the Jews of the worldwide Diaspora. The Sanhedrin was both the supreme tribunal (criminal, political, and religious) and the seat of government or state power in Judea. It was therefore the focal point of the state superstructure in the subasiatic mode of production after the year 6 B.C., when Judea became a Roman province ruled by a procurator.

The Sanhedrin had seventy-one members: "the chief priests and the elders and the scribes." The "chief priests" were the important priests who formed a permanent temple staff and therefore had a voice in the Sanhedrin where they formed a well-defined group. The "elders" were the *heads of the patrician families of Jerusalem*. The "scribes," most of them Pharisees, were the people's party and represented the crowd over against the aristocracy, in the religious as well as the social sphere. But, from 6 B.C. to A.D. 66, it was the priestly and lay aristocracy, of the Sadducean observance, that played the decisive role in the Sanhedrin.

Meeting as it did in the temple, with the current high priest in the chair, the religious character of the Sanhedrin provided an ideological mask for its political function. However, like all the other councils of elders, the Sanhedrin did not sit constantly but functioned only when convoked for serious business. The apparatus of state, which had permanently appropriated political power to itself in both Jerusalem and Judea, consisted exclusively of the chief priests of the Sanhedrin. The center of this apparatus was the *high priest* whose religious function had been the ideological basis for his political role ever since the fall of the monarchy and the return from Babylon. Originally, the office of the high priest was for life and was hereditary; however, in the first century A.D., the Roman procurator, like the Herods, appointed and deposed high priests as he chose, selecting them from any of the priestly families.

Under the high priest was another chief priest, the *commander of the temple*, who, in addition to being supreme supervisor of the cult, also had supreme police power. He was thus in charge of the repressive sector of the state apparatus in the temple, and it was his police, made up of levites, who must have arrested Jesus. In addition, there were seven *supervisors* of the temple, who guarded the keys to it, controlled access to the square in front of the temple, and saw that external order was maintained. The third function assigned to the chief priests was that of *treasurer*; there were three treasurers, charged with administering the revenues of the temple, its stores, and its wealth: in short, all the finances of the temple.

A large staff of officials—priests, levites, and laypeople—carried on the day-to-day work of this political apparatus of the temple, which also served as apparatus of the state for the whole of Judea.

This strictly Jewish apparatus of the subasiatic state was, however, controlled by the state apparatus of the Roman slave-based mode of production. In A.D. 6 the Romans had appointed a procurator who had charge of Judea (and Samaria), while the Galilee of Herod Antipas remained dependent on the legate of Syria.

In order to underline the internal autonomy left to the Jewish state apparatus, the procurator resided at Caesarea (Samaria) on the shores of the Mediterranean; here the troops of the occupation were stationed: about three thousand men recruited in Syria and Palestine, but from the non-Jewish population. The procurator went to Jerusalem only for the great feasts; the rest of the time a cohort of soldiers under the command of a tribune constituted the garrison at the capital. During his visits to the city the procurator handled cases involving capital punishment, since for political reasons the right to impose the death penalty was reserved to him.

The internal autonomy left to the Jewish state apparatus was, however, subject to controls. One control was that the right to appoint and depose the high priests remained in the hands of the Romans, as it had been in the hands of the Herods before them. In this system only the four most powerful priestly families provided the high priests; the Romans thus assured the complete dependence of the high priests on themselves.

The Romans also secured the dependence of the "elders," that is, of the "lay aristocracy."

> The landowning gentry . . . did not feel altogether secure in their holdings, since theoretically all land belonged to the state.[16] They were also much too frequently decimated or displaced by the arbitrary acts of Herod and the other rulers . . . ever since the Ptolemies had established the "large estate," handed it over to an individual master for direct or indirect exploitation, but also subjected it to arbitrary withdrawal.

Thus exposed to the constant threat of expropriation by the Romans,

> the landowning classes, too, developed those characteristics of servility toward political superiors and of utmost ruthlessness toward underlings which often forced the latter to flee and join the roving bands of brigands. This was the usual extreme way out for oppressed farmers, as well as slaves, in the ancient world.[17]

In addition, "the procurator was careful to choose his officials from among the 'elders' of the Sanhedrin and other heads of families—his tax officials, the *dekaprotoi* (*Ant.*, 20. 194). These were charged with assessing the citizens liable to taxation, the tribute which Rome imposed on Judaea, and guaranteed the correct payment from their own resources."[18]   In these ways, the Roman state apparatus could leave an area of internal autonomy to the Jewish apparatus and reserve to itself only a few decisive functions, and still exercise an indirect control over the classes that exercised power in the Jewish apparatus. We shall return to this point when we come to analyze the class struggle in first-century Palestine.

THE IDEOLOGICAL INSTANCE

According to the definition we gave at the beginning of this book, the ideological instance is the instance of the production (writing), circulation (among the agents), and consumption (reading) of the texts of the social formation. We can shift here to the singular number, for in the last analysis there is but a single text that is constantly being taken in hand, continued, enlarged, read, and rewritten, a single text that is ever-already *ideologically appropriated*, in its complex semantic, by means of various codes.

In first-century Palestine, the oral text was in the language that had been in common use throughout the whole Near East for several centuries: Aramaic. The work of ideological appropriation, on the other hand, was done on the basis of texts written over ten or more centuries, the older ones being in *Hebrew*, the old language of Israel that had now become a "sacred language." Most of the people were illiterate, and access to the written texts was restricted to a caste of "specialists" in writing, the people we call the "scribes" (*grammateis* is the Greek word in the New Testament), and whose political role we discussed a few pages back. The place where they exercised their specifically ideological function was the *synagogue*, where the people of the city or village gathered each sabbath, and the ancient writings were read and commented on.

Another caste, the *priests*, had a different ideological role, that of performing purificatory rites; the place of their ideological production was the *temple*.

Before turning to the effects of these two dominant ideological productions on the text of the social formation, we shall dwell briefly on the processes of reading/writing in the synagogue.

Let us consider first the text that was read and commented on in the synagogue; it consisted of the Torah and the prophets. I am looking at these texts here not in their historical development but as already forming a closed collection ever since the return from Babylon and the beginning of Palestinian Judaism.

The *Torah* comprises six books (Genesis, Exodus, Leviticus, Numbers, Deuteronomy, Joshua). The content of these books forms, in part, four sets of narratives.

1. To begin with, there are (in Genesis 1–11) narratives relating to the origin of the world and humanity. Humanity, ever since the first human couple, has existed in a situation of contradiction that we described earlier as infrastructural,[19] inasmuch as the mythical "fall" of the first couple brought in its train sexual violence, toil, and death.

2. The rest of the Book of Genesis (chapters 12–50) tells of the origins of the Israelite people by means of narratives concerning the three great ancestors, Abraham, Isaac, and Jacob, and concerning the *promise* which Yahweh made to them of a land, a numerous posterity, and the blessing that would come to them in the form of abundance, happiness, and preeminence over other peoples and that would counteract the effects of the infrastructural contradiction.

3. The next four books—Exodus through Deuteronomy—contain narratives about the formation of the people of Israel as Yahweh's people. The formation began with the liberation from Egypt under the leadership of Moses, and the offer by Yahweh, during the forty years' sojourn in the

wilderness, of a convenant:[20] "Now, if you obey my voice and hold fast to my covenant, you of all the nations shall be my very own" (Exod. 19:5). The prophets will repeat the same idea in a lapidary formula: "They will be my people, and I will be their God."

4. Finally, the Book of Joshua contains the narrative of the conquest of Canaan by the Israelite tribes. The book ends with the account (Josh. 24) of the gathering of the twelve tribes at Shechem, where the Mosaic covenant was ratified,[21] and the land was regarded as given to Israel by Yahweh in *fulfillment* of the promise to the patriarchs.

Thus the narrative of the origins of Israel is set within a great structure of promise and fulfillment. But the fulfillment itself is, from the viewpoint of the redactors of the text, only an overture to a further narrative that recounts the prolongation of the blessing into the later generations. This is evident from the place legislative texts have in the Torah, where they fill the books especially of Leviticus and Deuteronomy; we analyzed these texts in the previous chapter. The point is that the blessing will be in fact given only if the people obey the Law that Yahweh gave to Moses. It is to be noted, however, that the narrative dominates, not the Law.

The *prophetic books* (Judges, Samuel, Kings, Chronicles, and the prophets in the usual sense) begin with a narrative recounting the transition from the tribal confederation to the monarchy (Judges, 1 and 2 Samuel, 1 Kings 1–11). David and Solomon are shown as having taken the great step in the fulfillment of the promise. (Note especially the description of Solomon's glory, 1 Kings 3–10; this is really a narrative of Israel's glory in the sight of the other peoples.)

The glory is short-lived, however, and the remainder of the Books of Kings (repeated later in Chronicles) is the story of the curse that the monarchy brought on Israel; it ends with the deportation of the leading classes to Babylon.

The prophetic books (in the narrower sense), whether pre- or postexilic, mix narratives with the threatening or consoling oracles of some great religious personalities, people who, through the centuries when the curse prevailed, read the narratives contemporary with them in the light of the Torah.

They begin to announce a future intervention of Yahweh, which is initially thought to be proximate, but later as quite distant.[22] It will be an intervention by Yahweh as a warrior who will restore the blessing to Israel and subject the hostile nations to it. According to the prophets of the eighth century, the awaited time is the "Day of Yahweh."

Eschatological concepts changed from prophet to prophet and age to age. Central to the hopes that Isaiah fostered was the return of a *king* who would be a descendant of David and the anointed (Messiah) of Yahweh and who would restore righteousness (the debt system) in Israel. This *messianic* hope remained alive until the time of Jesus and permeates the text of Mark, as we shall see. Other prophets, especially Jeremiah and Ezekiel, took as their metaphor the Sinai covenant that had been broken by the infidelity of Israel and her kings, and foretold a *new* covenant that Yahweh would make with his people; these prophets retained the element of Davidic messianism. Second and Third Isaiah offered the vision of a *new Jerusalem*, a Zion reestablished, to which foreign peoples would flock in quest of the Law of Yahweh and the happiness associated with its blessing. Images of abundant meals given without payment, of marriage feasts, of Jerusalem as a city of justice, and of joyous festivals bear witness throughout the prophetic literature that the aim is always the recovery of Yahweh's blessing, which will depend on the *conversion* of Israel to the Law of Yahweh and on the reestablishment of the debt system.

This textual structure will reoccur later on, notably in Mark; it is characteristic of the Jewish redaction of the narratives. People write and read narratives in order to shed light thereby on contemporary practices and on the narratives presently being composed. There is, however, a point I must make right here. It is this: that this metaphorization of the first narrative of Israel, a metaphorization made evident by the adjective *new* (new exodus, new covenant, new Law), is a snare for bourgeois exegesis, as it was for the exegesis that preceded it, for this exegesis claims that, since the newness is in the *heart* (Jeremiah, Ezekiel), the whole affair is a matter of *interiorization*. We shall see why the exegetes think so, but for the moment we must insist that the viewpoint of the prophets is always an *earthly* one, that is, that they are always speaking of material blessings *on earth*. What they always have in mind is the *collective destiny* of Israel *in the land* that Yahweh had given to his people.

Here, then, is a first collection of texts, the sacred texts; the ideological work of the scribes consists of reading them and commenting on them. In the synagogal office for the sabbath, the service began with an opening prayer and the recitation of the eighteen blessings; then

> there was the reading of the sacred text: the Torah (Pentateuch) first, then the Prophets (collection proper to the Jewish canon). This reading was done in Hebrew, the liturgical language, before a Palestinian audience, and in Greek, the language of the Septuagint, in the Diaspora. But in Palestine, the sections of the sacred text chosen for reading were soon translated into Aramaic: this is how the targums originated.[23]

Before continuing with the oral and written texts that circulated in first-century Palestine, we must stop to consider the scribal class that produced these texts. The priestly class, which had achieved the dominant position in postexilic Judaism, shunted aside the eschatological problem that had absorbed the prophets.[24] The priestly class closed the Torah, and their reading of the sacred text became more and more conservative. In the process they laid open a space for textual production that would be occupied by the scribes. The latter, in turn, became increasingly strong as a class until they finally acquired the preponderant ideological place they have in the period that concerns us.

How did the scribes fit into the economic framework? We must realize that they came from various backgrounds. Some were priests, and belonged to the higher or the lower clergy. The great mass of scribes, however, came from other sectors of the people: the merchants and the artisans; with most of them belonging to sectors not blessed with material goods. Since, moreover, the scribes were prohibited from seeking payment for their activity and since many of them had no trade, they lived chiefly with the help of public assistance. At the same time, however, we must conclude that since there were no peasants among the scribes, the vast majority of them belonged to what might be called the petit bourgeoisie (or lower middle class) of shop-keepers and artisans. This means that their ideological concerns corresponded to the economic and political interests of their class.

"It was knowledge alone that gave their power to the scribes," says Jeremias. In other words, their ideological practice was a decisive ideological function. Jeremias also speaks of the scribes' "dominant influence over the people," and goes so far as to speak of the scribes as "a new upper class" alongside "the old ruling class composed of the hereditary nobility of priests and laity," a class with entry into the Sanhedrin itself.[24a]

Three kinds of texts are characteristic of the ideological practice of the scribes:

1. *Wisdom texts*, of which the Book of Job is one of the most important. Something has changed: among these marginalized members of society, the problem of the individual has taken priority, and the scribes interrogate the texts with regard to their personal destiny; they ask why their condition is an unhappy one, even though they are the very ones who have remained faithful to the law of Yahweh. Have not the promises failed, since a curse has proved to be the fruit of the practice of purity and giving in conformity with the law? In the Book of Job, if we prescind from its opening (Job 1–2) and its happy ending (42:7–17), which are later additions, there is no answer to this question, any more than there is in Qoheleth (Ecclesiastes), in many of the psalms, or in the rest of the wisdom literature. The writers continue to hope amid their wretchedness, but only death awaits them. Some of the wisdom writers are interested in the knowledge of nature and society, and offer rules for individual behavior (e.g., the Proverbs and Sirach or Ecclesiasticus).

2. The *targumic texts*, which originated "in the framework of the synagogal service," constitute "a tradition in the interpretation of the Old Testament texts." They represent a process of reading and writing that is constantly renewed and expanded in the form of what A. Paul calls the "Intertestament," which "will reach its full flowering only later on, in rabbinical Judaism" after the first century A.D.[25]

3. The texts that are perhaps most representative for the period we are interested in are the ones called *apocalyptic*. These made their appearance from 200 B.C. to A.D. 100. The problematic they develop is imported from abroad and related to the knowledge of nature and history; the answer is based on "the presupposition that there is a general analogy between God's saving action and the order of nature."[26]

The influence of foreign literature on Israel may be seen first and foremost in the break with the prophetic tradition. The message of the prophets had been rooted in the history of salvation, that is, in well-defined traditions of divine election; the authors of the apocalypses, on the other hand, present a view of history according to which the course of history has been determined from the beginning and events occur in a predetermined succession. The prophets have now fallen silent for good; the apocalyptic writer, like the Persian writers, has received a secret revelation (chiefly through dreams) which will be passed on only to the initiated.

Apocalyptic literature had a very important place in the course of study a person had to pursue in order to become a scribe. In addition, the constitutive elements in the semantic peculiar to these texts entered the ideological text of Israel and are also present in the New Testament texts, especially that of Mark, which we shall be reading later in this book. (I shall be referring to these elements as the "mythological code.") We must therefore examine this semantics more closely; since it was the intertextual effect of Persian religious texts, we must speak briefly of them.

The Persia (or Iran) of the Achaemenids was a subasiatic mode of production (it lacked major irrigation systems); it was also the first great empire of the ancient Near East (sixth to fourth centuries B.C.) and included within it Asiatic social formations such as Mesopotamia and Egypt.

In Persia we find in succession the three types of religion that we described above in Chapter 1.[27] E. Benveniste describes the passage from tribal religion to state polytheism: "Ancient Iran, being an aggregate of peoples and tribes, some sedentary, others nomadic, must have practiced widely varying cults. Gradually, however, a great part of ancient Iran was won over to the religion of Mazdeism."[28]

In Mazdeism, there is a principal god, Ahura Mazda, who creates the world and then governs it with the help of other, secondary gods; he is heavenly light and wisdom. The difference *heaven/earth* is thus primordial. There is also a world of evil and darkness, comparable to pollution among the Jews; this world is ruled by maleficent gods or *demons* (the *daevas*). The ideological universe of Mazdeism is thus one of conflict between the forces of good and the forces of evil; it thus reflects the earthly life of the warring tribes that were driven by envy of their neighbors and the desire to dominate them.

The king too is an earthly image of the god and thus in his way lord of the universe and master of the cosmos; wisdom is his essential attribute as ruler. Iran expected its king to make the needed rain fall and fertilize the soil. We are evidently faced here with an "Asiatic" religion as described by I. Banu.[28a]

The third type of religion, which was more or less contemporaneous with the Greek mystery religions, was the work of Zarathustra, who lived in an age of sedentary living and urbanization. Inspired by personal "revelations," he preached a religion of interiorized salvation and of personal religious experience. Each believer who enters the fray and fights on the side of the good is the locus of an interior struggle against the forces of evil. Here the many episodic battles of the old mythology are replaced by a single ongoing war between good and evil. The victorious believers receive their true reward from the hands of Ahura Mazda after death. What had been a royal privilege is here made accessible to the faithful; the consequence is the introduction of the idea of immortality and a clear distinction between the god and the king.[29]

Zarathustra thus preached a salvation that is acquired in an inner place where a person follows a revealed wisdom; the salvation will be fully manifested on a great day of final judgment by fire, when a redeemer, the "Living One," makes his appearance, and the good and the wicked receive the rewards or punishments they have merited. Along with such a belief in judgment, a belief in a resurrection of the flesh also grew up.

These various themes—the struggle between good and evil, the role of demons in the struggle, an eschatological judgment, a redeemer, and a resurrection—were foreign to the ideology of the Old Testament, but they appear in the apocalypses. It is generally accepted that they represent the influence of Zoroastrianism. Why should we be surprised at this kind of intertextuality? It was Cyrus, after all, who allowed the Jewish exiles to return from Babylon to Palestine; it was Darius who gave permission for the rebuilding of the temple; it was Artaxerxes who permitted Nehemiah to come to Jerusalem as governor and rebuild its walls. In short, the restoration of Israel in the form of Judaism was the work of the Persian kings.

We must now try to determine the political conditions under which this interideological work took place. Apocalyptic literature appeared suddenly and at a precise period. To some extent, this literature carries on the traditions of the wisdom literature, expecially the science of interpreting dreams, oracles, and signs. But this literature is innovative in what is probably the surest sign of the apocalyptic: its glimpse of the end of history, universal judgment, and redemption; in other words, the perspective it opens upon the consummation of history.[30] Despite von Rad's skepticism about the possibility of determining the circles that fostered these ideas,[31] it is easy enough to see what events in Palestine completely upset the political problematic and led to a new textual production on such a massive scale. The events were the Maccabean revolt and its consequences.

Thus it is that even outside the apocalyptic literature we find in the Second Book of Maccabees a defense of the resurrection of the dead: "If he [Judas Maccabeus] had not expected the fallen to rise again it would have been superfluous and foolish to pray for the dead" (12:44; cf. vv. 38–46). We are thus led to think that this "holy war" was the place where the Jews appropriated the belief in a final, eschatological resurrection, on the grounds that the death of those who went to war for Yahweh would otherwise be meaningless and a pure curse.

The Maccabean uprising was also the time when the party of the Pharisees came into existence. They may have been connected with the Hasidim whom the First Book of Maccabees describes as "a community of Hasidaeans [i.e., the "Devout"], stout fighting men of Israel, each one a volunteer on the side of the Law" (2:42). The scribes, in turn, were from the beginning leaders and influential members of the Pharisee party. Guignebert writes: "The greater part of these Apocalypses appear to emanate from Pharisaic centres"[32]; and Jeremias: "The apocalyptic writings of late Judaism . . . contained the esoteric teaching of the scribes."[33]

It was chiefly the tradespeople, artisans, and peasants that provided the membership of the Pharisee party, but it is clear, too, that the members from among the peasantry were few. As with Zoroastrian circles and Greek circles in the sixth century B.C., we are dealing with the lower middle classes of the cities. Apocalyptic hopes of an eschatological consummation are, moreover, typical of a class that is politically distressed[34]; no less typical is the pessimistic vision of humanity and of a history that is marching to its doom—the kind of vision found in most of these texts.[35] A further proof of the political place of this ideological literature is the fact that it reverses the tendency of the wisdom literature to be more interested in the individual's destiny; here, the collectivity is to the fore again, although the individual is not forgotten.

The apocalypses contain a complete picture of the last things. Guignebert describes the principal components of the picture as seen according to two different types of eschatology, the one millenniarist in character (millenniarist = lasting a thousand years; the number was taken over from Persia), the other simpler and closer to the old idea of God's kingdom. We may note the following elements in the picture as presented by Guignebert:

(1) The Messiah would doubtless not come unheralded. Warning of his approach would be given by wars, famines, and calamities of every kind. . . .

(2) But the Messiah . . . would be preceded by Elijah. . . . [cf. Ecclus. 48:10]. That prophet who had been caught up to heaven without dying would now return. . . .

(4) The coming of the Messiah would provoke a coalition of the wicked under the command of a leader, as to whose identity opinion seems to have remained vague. It was left for Christian apocalyptic to fill in the uncertain outline and give this figure the name of *Antechrist,* or rather *Antichrist.*

(5) The hosts of evil would be defeated; but opinions varied as to the identity of the victor. Some said that God himself would thus irresistibly demonstrate his power, but the greater number believed that the Messiah, invested by Yahweh with supernatural power, would be the actual conqueror. This second theory was more in line with the general development of Jewish eschatology.

(6) The overthrow of the wicked would be followed by the establishment of the blessed Messianic Kingdom. The Messiah, prince of peace, would be enthroned at Jerusalem; but the holy city would be renewed and purged of idolatry, or even replaced by a celestial city sent down fully fashioned from on high. In and around this city the chosen people, now no longer scattered, would dwell in all their ancient glory.

This point of time was sometimes chosen for the resurrection of the righteous of Israel. The *Kingdom of God* would bring about a peace untroubled by fear, a prosperity which no chance could destroy, an inalienable bliss. . . .

(8) It was then that the dead would arise. For a long time, as we have seen, this was held to apply only to the righteous, the sinners remaining in perpetual oblivion in the dust of *Sheol*[36]; but at last it was felt that the logic of retribution[37] demanded the punishment of the wicked as well as the reward of the righteous and hence a universal resurrection. . . . This resurrection is usually interpreted as meaning a restoration of the body which had been laid in the grave. . . .

(9) Opinions differed widely with regard to the last judgment. Some supposed that there would be two such judgments, one when the Messiah had overthrown his enemies, and one after the general resurrection at the end of the millennium. Theoretically Jahweh himself was to be the judge and to pronounce sentence. . . .

(10) At the judgment mankind would be divided. The righteous would be privileged to enter God's kingdom, where they would dwell in his divine presence, among the angelic host, gazing upon his countenance, and sharing in his *glory* . . . and they would live forever. . . . As for the wicked, they would share the fate of the demons, being cast into *Gehenna* for eternity. It is only much later . . . that Jewish thought showed any sign of being influenced by the idea which was the climax of Persian eschatology, that of a renewed universe, in which all creation, even the evil spirits themselves, would enjoy happiness and peace.[38]

The effect of the Persian texts on the ideology of Palestine was also felt in the *dominant code* of the Palestinian ideological instance, a code characterized by the heaven/earth opposition. As in the Zoroastrian texts, so here there is a heavy emphasis on the distance between heaven and earth. The end of the ancient prophetic line led to the *closing up* and silence of heaven. ("Deprived of signs, with no prophets left, who can say how long this will last?" the psalmist complains in Psalm 74:9.) Henceforth there is room only for secret revelations through dreams and visions, such as the *mystery* revealed to the "prophet Daniel"; in other words, there is room only for the *religious experience* of the initiated, to whom alone heaven is opened for the space of a vision.

The vision, however, or at least its interpretation, does not come directly from God but through intermediaries, the *angels*. This is a further effect of the great distance between God and man.

To fill the gap, the Jews produced a system of intermediaries, the *hypostases* of God, who were his deputies and assistants in the creation and direction of the world. Such were the *Spirit of God (ruach Elohim)*, his *Word (Memra)*, his *Presence (Shechinah, i.e. Habitation)*, his *Glory (Jekarah, Doxa)*, and his *Wisdom (Hokmah)*. As a matter of fact, these hypostases are almost as difficult to define as God Himself, but since, as Lagrange puts it, *"Their whole object is to evade definition,"* it is fitting that they should remain vague and obscure.[39]

There is likewise a whole hierarchy of angels and archangels who constitute a divine court (similar to the courts of the Asiatic kings). The lowest in the hierarchy "are the communicating links between God and the world, and above all between God and man. It is their business both to convey divine revelations to human ears, and to bear the prayers of earth to the throne of Jahweh."[39a]

A *demonology* was also developed. Here the effect of the Persian texts was even more pronounced, for now the curse ceases to come from God and comes from the evil spirits instead. The demons have a leader, Satan (like Ahriman, the Persian evil spirit), and are thought of as constituting an army that is in conflict with the army of God. "Everywhere people saw new indications of the work of evil spirits; every misfortune, every illness, and particularly, under the name of *possession,* all disorders of the nervous system were ascribed to them."[40] This amounts to saying that in this ideological picture demons held the place that pollution occupied in the Jewish symbolic order.

The working out of human destinies, whether collective or individual, was thus matched, in a way, by a conflict between the heavenly hosts and the army of Satan, God's adversary. (Compare the conflict of good and evil in the Iranian ideology.)

Here, once again, heaven is separated from earth, and a third entity is introduced: the *abyss,* in which the demons dwell. As we have seen, the last judgment takes the form of aligning the just with the angels and the wicked with the demons; in the end there will be only heaven[41] and *hell* (or Gehenna).[42]

The schema of the dominant code (i.e., the *mythological* code) is thus characterized by the opposition of above/below, or heaven/earth, with the abyss (corresponding to the depths of the sea) being that which is "lower than the earth." Moreover, at the level of earth, the mountain is a place that is "higher," closer to heaven. This is true ever since the revelation given to Moses on Mount Sinai and later to Elijah on Mount Horeb. The mountain is therefore the privileged place for theophanies. As a result, the schema above/below works out thus:

heaven	God (stars, angels)
(mountain)	(human intermediaries: Moses, Elijah)
earth	human beings
abyss (sea)	(demons)

From this above/below schema also derive the descending/ascending movements: the descending movement of the rain (the waters above the firmament, in Genesis 1:7, descend upon the earth according to Psalm 104:1–30), and the ascending movement of sacrifice (the Hebrew word for holocaust, *ôlah*, means "to ascend") and of prayer, which mounts to God in heaven. Enoch (Gen. 5:24) and Elijah (2 Kings 2:11) *went up* to heaven, in an ascensional movement that we shall find once again in Mark.

The *desert* is an ambiguous space; it is land that is not inhabited, not written on. It is the place of testing (as at the exodus) and temptation, because the demons have access to it; in short, it is par excellence the place of spiritual combat.

Such, then, are the written texts, produced by the scribal class and circulating in the discourse of the agents of Palestine in the first century. To them must be added another entire and very basic sector of the ideological instance, namely, the sector dealing with the ritual language of the cultus whose center was the temple at Jerusalem, a place of economic consumption. The class responsible for this language was the *priests*. Within the Jewish people, the clergy constituted a strongly organized tribal class which traced its ancestry back to Aaron and within which the priesthood was inherited. The priestly community was divided into twenty-four priestly classes that included all the priests scattered throughout Judea and Galilee; these priests were obliged to come to Jerusalem for their turn in performing the daily sacrificial services in the temple.

Beneath the priests the levites formed a "lesser clergy" who were likewise divided into twenty-four groups and who belonged to the tribe of Levi. They were in charge of the music in the temple and of the secondary services connected with the cultus; for example, they formed the police and kept watch over the gates of the temple. In the time of Jesus, the Jewish clergy counted about eighteen thousand priests and levites.

The bulk of their income came from the payment by the people of a tithe on the products of the earth. Large sectors of the people did not pay the taxes, however, or paid in insufficient amounts, with the result that the clergy lived poorly. They were therefore obliged to exercise a profession or trade in their place of residence; it took the form of manual work for the most part.

If we recall what was said about the economic situation of the priestly aristocracy, we will readily see that there was a profound contrast between the great mass of priests and the chief priests who belonged for the most part to the priestly aristocracy. The higher and lower clergy had interests that were opposed.

In addition to filling the role of an ideological apparatus in the temple worship at Jerusalem, the priest's office also required him to exercise, in his home town, the function of distinguishing between the pure and the polluted. Leviticus had assigned this function to priests; as a result in many places they also had a role to play in the courts of justice.

Thus, while the scribes, with the help of a very detailed system of casuistry,[43] defined the symbolic order, that is, the prescriptions and observances for daily life, the priests made judgments that defined the concrete symbolic field. Not everyone heeded the very strict precepts, however, and so there arose the closed communities of *Pharisees*, who lived a strictly orthodox life, especially in regard to the prescriptions concerning tithes, food, ablutions, the sabbath, and the hours of prayer.[44]

The priests, like the majority of the scribes, belonged to the Pharisaic movement, whereas the Sadducee party drew the chief priests and the elders, the priestly and lay aristocracy, and certain scribes, or, in short, the leading classes. The conservative theology of the Sadducean scribes was based strictly on the text of the Torah and sharply rejected the oral tradition of the Pharisaic scribes; in particular, the Sadducean scribes would have nothing to do with apocalyptic speculations in eschatology, and they denied the resurrection of the dead. We will return to this point when we discuss the ideological class struggle.

In summary, the various ideological texts inscribed these codes in the discourses of the agents of the social formation, just as casuistry (in synagogal preaching, in the courts, and in the priestly discernment of the pure and the polluted) and the rituals inscribed these same codes in the daily behavioral practices of these same agents, and even in their bodies (pure or more or less polluted) and the bodies of their products (food, dwellings, places of work, other objects). In a similar manner, economic structures inscribed the signifiers of wealth and poverty (the rich/poor opposition), and political structures inscribed the signifiers of power on the one hand and these being dominated on the other (the opposition "great men"/masses).

Finally, let us consider the *effects* of the writing of the ideological instance in the *space* occupied by the social formation in first-century Palestine. This space was written on either geographically or topographically (in the modern sense of this term). Ideological discourse concerning this space had the effect of orienting the space symbolically, for as Mircea Eliade says, "Palestine, Jerusalem, and the Temple generally and concurrently represent the image of the universe and the *Center of the world.*"[45] This means that the entire space inside and outside of these boundaries was evaluated positively or negatively according to purity (or greater purity) or pollution (or lesser pollution). Thus, as we noted earlier, Galilee was regarded as less pure than Judea, either because of the greater number of pagans that lived in Galilee, or because it was further removed geographically from Jerusalem and the temple.

The mythological discourse was also inscribed in the temple inasmuch as the latter was seen as the *axis of the world.* "Treating of the symbolism of the Temple, Flavius Josephus wrote that the court represented the sea (i.e., the lower regions), the Holy Place represented earth, and the Holy of Holies heaven (*Ant. Jud.,* III, 7, 7)."[46] In the conceptual scheme I have been applying, the temple, as center of the world, became the *center of Israel's symbolic field.* The temple occupied such a position because it was the axis connecting earth with heaven; the Holy of Holies, but lately the place of Yahweh's presence, was the mythological point where heaven touched earth, and earth heaven. That was why the high priest alone could enter it, and then only once a year, on the day of atonement. That was why all Jews were bound by law to come on pilgrimage to Jerusalem thrice yearly for the great feasts. That was why all Jews, wherever they might be, turned toward the temple when they prayed (just as Muslims bow toward Mecca when they pray). That, finally, was why all the messianic movements, so numerous in the period of which we are speaking, focused their attention on Jerusalem. Many individuals took up residence in Jerusalem so that they might die in that holy place and be buried where the resurrection and last judgment would some day occur.

Palestine and the temple were further subdivided in terms of their holiness.

M. Kel. i. 6–9 describes the ten degrees of holiness which surround the Holy of Holies in concentric circles:

1. The land of Israel.
2. The City of Jerusalem.
3. The Temple Mount.
4. The *hēl,* a terrace with a balustrade beyond which no Gentiles could pass.
5. The Court of Women.[47]
6. The Court of the Israelites.
7. The Court of the Priests.
8. The area between the Porch and the Altar.
9. The Sanctuary.
10. The Holy of Holies.[48]

The segregated areas of the symbolic field, with boundaries based on race and on purity, were thus inscribed in the very architecture of the temple, this "image of the universe," as Eliade calls it.

THE ARTICULATION OF THE INSTANCES AND THEIR RESPECTIVE FIELDS

If we are accurately to define the conjuncture of the class struggle in Palestine, we must now go back over the three instances that we have analyzed separately and consider their articulation and then the determinations and closures of the three fields defined by the instances. Let us first look at the subasiatic mode of production in itself.

After what we have said about the instances, it is easy to conclude that the articulation of the *economic and political* instances is that of a subasiatic social formation. The dominant relations of production involve the countryside communities and the political apparatus of the state, which deducts its taxes in advance. Taxes are also assessed on the production and circulation of the sector defined by the cities.

In the period we are studying, the articulation of the *political and ideological* instances is characterized, on the one hand, by the nondistinction between the political apparatus of the state and the priestly politico-ideological apparatus, since the chief priests, under the authority of the high priest, hold the political power (the situation was different in Galilee, and even in Judea under the Herodians). The articulation is characterized, on the other hand—and always has been—by the sacred nature of the Law that regulates, at the level of the symbolic order, the circulation of bodies.

The articulation, finally, of the *economic and ideological* instances is manifest in the fact that the seat of the state is the temple. In an agricultural economy that is determined by the lack of development of the productive forces[49] and that is saturated, from the growth viewpoint, by foreign occupation, it is the economic field of *expenditure* (field III) that determines the temple to be the center of the state; this has been true since Judaism came into existence in the sixth century B.C. Thus, when we look at the social formation from within, the subasiatic mode of production is determined, in the last analysis, by the economic instance, for it is the economic instance that determines the internal domination of the social formation by the ideological instance.

If we look at the social formation from without, we must consider the articulation of the subasiatic mode of production and the Roman slave-based mode of production. The latter, by the military power of its occupying forces and by the consequent political power of the Roman procurator, exercises political domination over Palestine. The ultimate key to the determination of this political domination is to be found, of course, in the slave-based economy of the Roman Empire. It was this economy that assured Rome of its political power over the whole "civilized" world of the time, because Rome's mighty army was financed by taxes levied on the social formations that were subject to military occupation.[50]

If we look at the situation from the side of the fields of the three instances of the social information, and of their determinations and closures, we can explain the privileged place of the temple in this subasiatic social formation.

In a production quite strictly determined by the degree of the productive forces, whether in agriculture or in the state's crafts and industry, the closure of the economic field is assured by the monetary apparatus and its principal equivalent, *cash*; in addition, the circulation which this cash money regulates is subject to the temple inasmuch as the latter is a *treasury* or store of public resources. There is a sign to designate the dominant place of the temple in the economy, namely, the *gold* that plates the temple: the doors covered with gold and silver, the lampstands and sacred utensils of gold and silver, the facade covered with gold slabs (for example, the wall and door between the vestibule and the holy place, etc., etc., right into the Holy of Holies, the walls of which were covered with gold). "So great is the abundance of gold in Jerusalem, and especially in the Temple, said to have been, that after the sack of the city, the market in gold for the whole province of Syria was glutted, with the result, Josephus says that 'the standard of gold was depreciated to half its former value' (*BJ* 6.317)."[51]

The closure determined by the tax levied by the Romans overdetermines this internal closure of the subasiatic mode of production.

The political field, determined on the one hand by the symbolic field and on the other by the apparatus of the state (Sanhedrin and priestly executive apparatus), is once again the temple. The temple is the seat of the apparatus which, in the person of the high priest with his vestments of office, assumes the central role of principal equivalent in the political instance of the subasiatic mode of production.

The procurator, for his part, is the official who "represents" the Roman emperor. Thus a second principal equivalent, namely, the Caesar, closures and overdetermines the political field.

We have described the ideological field as dominated by the mythological code, the axis of which is again the temple at Jerusalem, since this defines the center of the symbolic field. Inasmuch as the Romans respected the ideological autonomy of the countries they occupied, the temple plays its role alone at this level. The principal equivalent here is the *God of Israel,* who is present in the temple.

We can sum up this analysis by saying that the temple, the specific function of which is ideological, proves to be in fact, in this particular subasiatic social formation, an *element* that is *overdetermined* by the economic, political, and ideological instances, and consequently the place where the *internal* contradictions of each instance (internal, that is, to the subasiatic mode of production) come together. So true is this that the destruction of the temple in A.D. 70 by the army of the emperor Titus brought with it the collapse of the social formation. Except for the brief interlude of the Jewish War in A.D. 130, the unity of Judaism would henceforth be purely ideological; there would be no Jewish state again until the second half of our own century.

The triple internal contradiction was overdetermined by the contradiction of the whole formation's forcible integration into the slave-based mode of production. This integration was economic (assessment of taxes), political (military occupation), and ideological (the presence, in the land Yahweh had given to the Jews, of pagans whose blood was polluted).

The interplay of these two contradictions will provide us with the key to the conjuncture of the class struggle in Palestine. Only the knowledge of this will make possible a political reading of Mark's narrative.

THE CLASS STRUGGLE IN PALESTINE

We shall try to sketch a picture of the class struggle in Palestine.[52] It may be said that economic conditions in Palestine were quite similar, in many respects, to those in neighboring Egypt and Syria. By and large, this southeastern corner of the Mediterranean was the most backward area of the Roman Empire. Despite the fact that Palestine possessed considerable natural wealth and was economically self-sufficient, the working classes both in rural areas and in the cities suffered many privations because of the effort being made to link the economy of Palestine with that of the empire and because of the increasingly heavy burden of taxation.

Unfortunately, we have little information about the movement of prices in Palestine, but it is likely that the same factors which kept pushing up the cost of living in nearby Egypt were also an inflationary pressure in overpopulated Palestine. In addition, the methods of collecting taxes became more ruthless and the extortion more unbridled and universal, since the Roman colonial officials held their posts for a relatively short period and attempted to amass the greatest possible wealth in a very brief time. As a result, the masses lived in utter penury. On the one hand, the religious tithes and the tithe for the sabbatical year "were almost unbearable charges even in the most fertile regions of the country."[53] On the other, the tribute to the Romans, which amounted to a quarter of the harvest every year or two years, must have made the Palestinian farmer's life extremely difficult. It was for these various reasons that the priests rarely received the tithe that was their due, as we noted earlier.

The situation in the cities was hardly better. The low wages paid to skilled workers and the even lower ones paid to the ordinary laborer, the numerous unemployed, the existence of a *lumpenproletariat*, and the possibility that employers might use slaves: all these factors contributed to putting the wage earner into an almost desperate economic situation. This is why strikes were so rare throughout the Greco-Roman world and almost nonexistent in Palestine. The workers and slaves of the great landowners frequently had to flee and join the gangs of bandits who roamed the countryside. Such brigandage (involving not only escaped slaves but also free workers who were reduced to penury) became a permanent part of Palestine life.

In the prevailing situation, there could be a class struggle in any meaningful sense only if the ultimate objective was the takeover of power. Some of the bandits did have such an aim; that is, they took up arms not only for personal gain but to help the people as a whole. They saw their oppression by the Romans as the embodiment of all evil. This is how the faction we call "the Zealots" came into existence,[54] the faction that for decades carried on a life-and-death guerilla war against the Romans in the attempt to establish a Jewish state in the face of Roman power.

Galilee, the richest and most populous area of Palestine, provided numerous hiding places in its hills; it thus became the birthplace and permanent center of the various groups who made up the guerilla sector. The first rebellion, led by Judas of Galilee, is summed up as follows by the editors of the Jerusalem Bible, who date it in 4 B.C., after the death of Herod:

Sabinus [procurator for Augustus in Syria] comes to Jerusalem to make an inventory of the resources of the kingdom of Herod [with a view of collecting the taxes]: sharp opposition and trouble throughout the country. At this time, possibly, the rebellion of Judas the Galilean, cf.

Ac 5:37, and of the Pharisee Saddok who urged disobedience to Rome and refusal to pay taxes. (Origin of the Zealots, cf. Mt 22:17) Sabinus appeals to Varus [legate of Syria] who pursues the rebels; 2000 are crucified.[55]

The great landowners, on the other hand, benefited from the heightened prices for farm produce; their large estates, whether royal[56] or private, were numerous enough to control the rhythm of production and thus of prices. This dominant Jewish class (chief priests, great landowners, large-scale merchants, and Herod and his leading officials) profited to the maximum from the conjuncture, since they were politically hand-in-glove with the occupying Romans, who depended on them. The corruption of all these men and the discredit that had fallen on the chief priests because they were illegally installed were sufficient reasons for the popular classes to be thoroughly dissatisfied with them. This was especially true of the lower middle classes in Jerusalem (the crowds whom we meet in Mark 11 and 12, with their hostility to the Sanhedrin dignitaries), who nonetheless were very dependent, economically, on the temple.

How was this class struggle translated into ideological terms? The focal point was the eschatological perspectives developed in the apocalyptic texts; these texts were the property of the Pharisees and were rejected by the Sadducees who had adopted the logic followed by the postexilic priestly class.[57] Since the Sadducees did not share the utopia of the popular classes, eschatology (including the idea of a resurrection from the dead) was alien to them, bound as they were to a strict reading of the ancient texts.

The *utopian horizon* that marks this eschatological outlook and, at bottom, the eschatology of ancient Israel as well, may be characterized in the terminology of the evangelical "beatitudes." Its dominant component is the kingdom of God,[58] which will be established on earth and in which the poor, that is, the dominated classes, will have the place of privilege: "How happy are you who are poor: yours is the kingdom of God" (Luke 6:20). The kingdom has three dimensions that correspond to the three instances: *satisfaction* ("you [the hungry] will be satisfied": Luke 6:21); *possession of the land and the earth* ("they shall have the earth for their heritage": Matt. 5:4), which implies Jewish domination of the foreign nations; and finally, at the ideological level, the vision of God ("they shall see God": Matt. 5:8; "they shall be called sons of God": Matt. 5:9), which represents ideological *consumption*, according to the ancient idea that to see God is to die.

Among those who adopted these eschatological perspectives, three groups are to be distinguished. First, the *Essenes,* who believed the temple to have been profaned by the illegally installed high priests, and therefore organized their own community outside the Jewish symbolic field that was centered on the temple; by this very separation, their influence on the class struggle was lessened.[59] A second group was the *Pharisees*; because their social base—the artisans and small tradespeople—lacked political power, they concerned themselves rather with "the other world"[60] and prepared themselves for it chiefly by pietism and a legalistic observance of the law.

The third group was the *Zealots* who were Pharisees in their religious ideology but looked to an armed struggle against the Romans, those pagans who were polluting the land of Israel, as the way to restore the kingdom of David. The Zealots were waiting for a warrior Messiah who would lead them in the decisive conflict; they drew their recruits meanwhile from the exploited peasantry. Guignebert observes that "this Messianic hope, under the guise of a Davidic king, who would restore the glories of Israel, was almost entirely a popular one. . . . It undoubtedly was the impulse behind the constant state of unrest in Palestine, the inspiration of the great rebellions against the power of Rome."[61] The Son of man coming on the clouds of heaven (Dan. 7:13), the just and victorious king who comes humbly, riding on a donkey (Zech. 9:9), the Son of David (a current description of the messianic age was "the reign of the house of David")—these various ideas of the coming Messiah[62] were debated in the Pharisaic schools without any agreement being reached. But disagreement of this kind did not prevent the eschatologico-messianic hope from playing a decisive role in the various rebellions against the Romans that arose in the first century A.D. down to the war of 66.

Josephus wrote a detailed account of the war of 66 in his narrative *The Jewish War*, while Pierre Prigent in his *La fin de Jérusalem* has given a lively account of it. We shall limit ourselves here to a few remarks on the various interests at stake in the class struggle.

The peasant class, made up of country people and wage earners on the large estates, was the most oppressed class, as we have seen; its enemies were the Romans, but also the priestly and lay aristocracy, those whom the Gospel narratives call "the chief priests and the elders." This class must have furnished the largest contingent of Zealot fighters. "These revolutionaries included ardent patriots and men full of religious feeling, but others were simply men whom Josephus rightly describes as a rabble of slaves and the dregs of the population."[63] The reference here is no doubt to the *am ha-arets* ("people of the soil"), the sector of the people whose knowledge of Judaism was much distrusted by the strictest Pharisees.

Once the war had begun at Jerusalem in response to the claim of Florus, the Roman procurator, to requisition seventeen talents from the temple treasury,[64] the lower middle class of artisans and tradespeople felt involved from the start, and with them many priests of the lower clergy and many of the Pharisaic scribes. The dominant class, on the other hand, was regarded as allied with the Romans; consequently, when the Zealots captured the city and the temple in 68, Annas was one of the first to be slain; he was followed by most of the dignitaries.

What was the goal of the Zealots? What kind of regime did they intend to set up in Jerusalem once they had driven out the Romans? We must judge by what they did. On the one hand, in 66 they set fire to the files of juridical actions regarding debts; this shows, as Jeremias says, that "the social factor played a large part in the Zealot movement."[65] Prigent echoes this view when he asks, "Did the Zealots dream of a redistribution of property that would be more in accord with God's will?"[66]

On the other hand, the Zealots chose a new high priest by lot from among the old legitimate high-priestly families that had effectively been excluded from the supreme office since 172 B.C.; the choice fell on a simple man who was practicing a manual trade. Finally, the Zealots put up a desperate defense of the temple throughout the war, and especially in its final phase.

All this shows that the Zealots were not seeking a "revolution" that would do away with the subasiatic mode of production, but a "rebellion" that would restore it to its pure form. In a number of ways the Zealot movement reminds us of the Deuteronomist movement (the notable exception, of course, being that the monarchy was no longer an issue). Like the Deuteronomist movement, the Zealot movement was *reformist*; the religious ideology that had the Jerusalem temple for its focus played a determining role, as did the economic interests, also connected with the temple, of the lower middle classes of Jerusalem; once the corrupt high-priestly families had been banished, the new high priest continued to be the center of power in the subasiatic state. Given the determinations that came into play, no other course of action was conceivable for the Zealots; no communist revolution was possible for them, any more than it had been for the Deuteronomist levites or the Maccabees.[67] It is important, I think, before we approach the problematic of a political definition of Jesus' practice according to Mark, to realize that we may not expect of him a "communist revolution" such as might be projected in our own day. Once we do realize this, we will be free to compare Jesus' strategy with that of the Zealots, but within the framework of a subasiatic mode of production. This is why we have taken so much time and trouble to define this mode.

Back to the political project of the Zealots. Not only was it the only one they could conceive, but it was in itself a project that, "humanly" speaking, was doomed to failure. That is perhaps why messianism played such a large part in their thinking: they hoped for a divine intervention in case things did not turn out well for them. The utopian drive was strong, as we can see from Dion Cassius's account of the final struggle inside a temple already in flames:

> The Jews resisted more zealously than ever, as though they thought themselves happy if they fell beside the temple and in its defense. The ordinary people were lined up in the forecourt, the councillors on the steps, and the priests in the very sanctuary. Though they were few in number and faced a great army, they succumbed only after part of the temple had caught fire. Then some deliberately threw themselves on the swords of the Romans, while others cut one another's throats or killed themselves or threw themselves into the flames. All were con-

vinced, especially the groups last mentioned, that it was not a disaster but on the contrary a victory, salvation, and happiness[68] to perish with the temple.[69]

"We have long since resolved to serve neither the Romans nor any other man, but God alone," are the words Josephus puts on the lips of the Zealot leader at Masada,[70] at the beginning of the scene which ends in the collective suicide of the nine hundred and sixty inhabitants of the town, women and children included.[71] That is the kind of people the Zealots were!

Let us bring the story to an end. Josephus tells us that Titus wanted to spare the temple but that his soldiers disobeyed him. Historians have often challenged this version by a man who was a traitor to Jewry and a friend of a future emperor,[72] and yet Josephus is likely to have been right, for what a valuable source of tribute the Romans lost by burning the temple! Why so? Because the destruction of the temple meant the collapse of the subasiatic social formation. The agrarian sector and the commercial sector that continued to exist in northern Palestine functioned henceforth within the framework of the slave-based mode of production. Judaism became definitively rabbinical in character, with the Pharisaic scribes determining its ideological direction. Judaism also became definitively a Diaspora phenomenon.

PART III
A READING OF MARK

Chapter 1
Reading Mark: Structural Analysis
or Textual Analysis of the Narrative?

How should a narrative be read? Let us put this question to Roland Barthes.

What I earlier spoke of as the effect of naming in a language[1] corresponds to what Barthes, following Hjemslev, calls *denotation*;[2] the meaning of this term is to be found in the well-known definition by de Saussure of a sign as a correspondence between a signifier and a signified (S/s). *Discourses* or locutive text[3] can be defined as texts showing the domination of this *denotative* effect or of denomination. We shall reserve the name of *text* for other linguistic complexes in which another effect is dominant, the one Hjemslev calls *connotation*. Barthes defines this last as "a determination, a relation, an anaphora, a feature which has the power to relate itself to anterior, ulterior, or exterior mentions, to other sites of the text (or of another text)."[4] Their grouping "constitute a braid (*text, fabric, braid*: the same thing)."[5]

The dominance of connotation is the basis for a typology of texts[6] and the way into the polysemy or limited plural of a text. But this is true only of certain texts, since "it is not certain that there are connotations in the modern text," which Barthes contrasts with the classic text.[7] In Julia Kristeva, these contrasting texts are said to belong respectively to the ideologem of the *sign* (the bourgeois classic text) and the ideologem of *signification* (the modern text), the latter being the privileged object of her semanalysis.

We shall ignore the ideologem of signification, which is of no concern to us here, and consider the third ideologem that has existed in the history of the western textual tradition. This Kristeva calls the *ideologem of the symbol*; it is anterior to that of the sign, which is proper to economies based on exchange.

According to Kristeva, the ideologem of the symbol (which is proper to "European society until about the thirteenth century,"[8] as it was to the Greek republic[9]) is "a cosmogonic semiotic practice,"[10] the site of "mythic thinking . . . that is manifested in epic, in popular stories, in the *chansons de geste,* etc."[11] This is why I prefer to give the name *"mythic* texts" to texts belonging to the symbolic order,[12] as opposed to the classic texts that depend on the semiotic of the *sign*. For, as Kristeva says, "in the logic [of the symbol] two opposed units are exclusive of one another,"[13] just as in what I earlier called the mythological code. I shall take it as characteristic of *mythic texts* that they show the domination (or closure, according to Kristeva) of a mythological code. This will be the case with the narrative of Mark.

We thus get three types of text. At one extreme, there is the *discourse*, which may be called the zero degree of text. In the discourse the denotative reigns, and the system of the personal (I/you; verbal system of the present here/now; demonstratives; etc.) defines the field of the locutors as the point of reference for the locution. The discourse is the domain of communication. At the other extreme, there is the *poetic* text in the modern sense of the term "poetic." Here the play of meaning is everything; there is nothing but textual productivity (in Kristeva's sense), and all representation is excluded. Between these two extremes come the texts in which the connotative is at work, with its leaning to the side of productivity, although the denotative, the referential, the "representational," is always present. These texts include mythical and classical *narratives,* as well as gnoseological texts.[14]

There are two Roland Barthes. One is the Barthes of the *"Introduction à l'analyse structurale des récits."*[15] The other is the Barthes of *S/Z,* in which he reads Balzac's short story *Sarrasine* and gives what he calls a *textual analysis* of it, as distinct from a *structural analysis.* We must appreciate what is at issue in this shift from the one type of analysis to the other.

R.B. I sets out "to describe and classify the infinite number of narratives." For this purpose he needs "a theory" (in the sense of a "hypothetical descriptive model"), "and it is this that we must first look for and sketch out. The constructing of such a theory will be rendered much easier if we accept from the beginning a model that will supply basic terms and principles. In the present state of research it seems reasonable to accept the linguistic phenomenon itself as the foundational model for the structural analysis of narratives."[16]

This model will depend, to begin with, on the linguistic concept of "levels of description" (borrowed from Benveniste[17]), then on the concept of "functions" (derived from Propp) and of "actions" (taken from Greimas; but this writer also used Propp as his starting point), and finally on a linguistic theory of communication.[18] In short, linguistic theory and Propp are the two influences from which Barthes will be breaking away. The tales Propp studies are mythical texts, and the model they provide is too likely to become a machine for reducing narratives to the already known.[19] That, however, is a risk Barthes finds intolerable when he sets out to read a "classic" text. He therefore dismisses Propp as well as Greimas and his school.

Textual analysis involves studying a "single text . . . down to the last detail." To study a text in this way is "to take up the structural analysis of narrative where it has been left till now: at the major structures"; it is "to substitute for the simple representative model another model, whose very gradualness would guarantee what may be productive in the classic text." "It avoids structuring the text excessively, avoids giving it that additional structure which would come from a dissertation and would close it: it stars the text, instead of assembling it."[20]

Similarly, in the classic narrative the narrator plays far too large a role for the linguistic model of the three levels to be still suitable. What is economical in analyzing the denotations of a phrase becomes too cumbersome in analyzing the connotations of a text.

Between 1965 and 1967, Barthes changed the field of his analytic interests: it is no longer the "structures" of narrative in general that he looks for in reading, but the "structuration" of *a single* text taken with its differences from others, with the plurality of its meanings, and with the "remainder" that the structural model neglects, that is, with the work of textual *production* that is going on in it, or, if you prefer, the work of writing (in Derrida's sense of this last term), the effect of this work being the text, this fabric of connotations.

Of the older model that was structured by several concepts there remains only what can hardly be called a model now, namely two very flexible concepts: the concept of *connotation* or correlations of meaning, and the concept of the assemblage of connotations or the *code*. These two concepts are enough to define two essential points.

The first of these concerns the text as *work*:

> The text, while it is being produced, is like a piece of Valenciennes lace created before us under the lacemaker's fingers: each sequence undertaken hangs like the temporarily inactive bobbin waiting while its neighbor works; then, when its turn comes, the hand takes up the thread again, brings it back to the frame; and as the pattern is filled out, the progress of each thread is marked with a pin which holds it and is gradually moved forward; thus the terms of the sequence: they are positions held and then left behind in the course of a gradual invasion of meaning. This process is valid for the entire text. The grouping of codes, as they enter into the work, into the movement of the reading, constitute a braid (*text, fabric, braid:* the same thing).[21]

The second point concerns the operation of *reading*: "To read, in fact, is a labor of language. To read is to find meanings, and to find meanings is to name them; but these named meanings are swept toward other names; names call to each other, reassemble, and their grouping calls for further naming."[22] Reading is therefore a matter of locating codes and naming them, as the reader moves back and forth through the text. To read is, consequently, to *reread*.

> Rereading, an operation contrary to the commercial and ideological habits of our society, which would have us "throw away" the story once it has been consumed ("devoured"), so that we can then move on to another story, buy another book, and which is tolerated only in certain marginal categories of readers (children, old people, and professors),

rereading is here suggested at the outset, for it alone saves the text from repetition (those who fail to reread are obliged to read the same story everywhere), multiplies it in its variety and its plurality.[23]

Must I choose between the two Barthes, between structural analysis and textual analysis? My reading project deals with a text of the mythic type, and consequently structural analysis can be helpful to me, especially because my reading of it is for the sake of an essay in theory[24] and not solely an exercise in semiotics.[25] On the other hand, it is quite clear, especially after *S/Z,* that I cannot use the schemata of Propp and Greimas but must read Mark's narrative as a *single* text and therefore, as far as possible, conduct a textual analysis of it. I must, however, conduct the textual analysis while taking the structural analysis into account; I must follow the later Barthes while not forgetting the earlier Barthes.

To adopt such an approach is not necessarily to betray Barthes, since despite the break between the earlier and the later Barthes there is also continuity. Thus, when he defines connotation as a relation of meanings or sites of a text, he adds that "this relating . . . can be given various names (*function* or *index*, for example)."[26] A few lines further on, he notes that "analytically, connotation is determined by two spaces: a sequential space, a series of orders, a space subject to the successivity of sentences, in which meaning proliferates by layering; and an agglomerative space"[26a]; but these are concepts from structural analysis. In the latter, *function* was the word for "the smallest narrative units," the criterion for such units being meaning.[27] A small group of functions was called a *sequence,* and *parametric* was the word used for the later "agglomerative."

Henceforth, *function* will be equivalent to *connotation,* and a *group of functions structured among themselves* will be equivalent to *code.*

Following the lead of R.B.I, we shall now single out several kinds of codes.

There are "two main classes of functions, the one being distributive, the other integrative." Functions fall into the one or the other class depending on whether they operate at the same level of meaning or, on the contrary, are related as "lower to higher."[28] We shall speak of them as *function in the proper sense* and *index.*[29]

A first distinction is between cardinal functions or *nuclei* ("You cannot eliminate a nucleus without changing the story" being told) and *catalysts* (which fill the narrative space between the nuclei).[30] It is possible, consequently, to distinguish the *sequential structure* of the codes from the functions in the proper sense.

A sequence (according to Claude Bernard) is a logical succession of nuclei which are united among themselves by a relation of solidarity (in the Hjemslevian sense of mutual implication; each of the two terms supposes the other): the sequence begins when one of its terms has no antecedent that is solidary with it, and it closes when one of its terms has no solidary consequent.[31]

A sequence is therefore characterized by a succession of terms that imply each other according to a *logic of successivity,* the order of the sequential terms according to a chronological before/after being constitutive of the narrative as a type of text, but in such a way that it always contains the *opening* and *closing* of a sequence. "The combination of several sequences readily lends itself to classification according to a formal typology. The following cases are possible: *chaining,* when the sequences are arranged in a 1–2–3 order; *enshrining,* when the order is 1–2–1; and *interweaving,* when the order is 1–2–1–2."[32] Chaining is the rule in Mark; this means that the few instances illustrating the other two types will be all the more interesting because they are rare.

The *sequential code,* in Mark, consists of all the terms designating actions and their actants,[33] and is articulated according to the system of the nonperson and of history.[34] This code will be designated as ACT.[35]

However, in Mark, this ACT code contains two other codes (or subcodes) that are especially important. The first is analogous to the hermeneutic code of *S/Z,* which comprises "the various (formal) terms by which an enigma can be distinguished, suggested, formulated, held in suspense, and finally disclosed," but the terms "will not appear in any fixed order."[36] It is the code of *readings* or analyses that the actants make of the ACT narrative, and for this reason I prefer to call it an *analytic code* and designate it as ANAL. Inasmuch as its verbs are terms of ACT, they will be locutive verbs, introducing *discourses* or statements of the actants. It is in these discourses or statements that the logic of this reading or analysis can be determined. ANAL thus goes beyond ACT, which is limited to narrative statement, and may therefore legitimately be regarded as an independent code.

What we are calling ACT (actantial) is, in *S/Z,* also called *proairetic,* because praxis or action is linked to deliberation; it must be understood, however, that "in narrative . . . the discourse, rather than the characters, determines the action."[37] In other words, every verbal term in ACT represents deliberate choice. Now in Mark certain actants will often have especially important moments of *strategic choice,* the strategies of each actant being defined by relation to those of the others. We are thus led to give special place to a *strategic code* as a subcode of ACT. The terms of the strategic code will define the configuration of the actants who may therefore be classified in function of their strategies in relation to the principal actant. This code will be designated as STR. Here again, it will be the statements of the actants that, by going beyond ACT, make possible the structuration of the actants themselves. It is clear, moreover, that ANAL and STR will be closely related, since strategies result from readings made of ACT or the narrative.

These remarks will suffice for the *sequential codes* in Mark.

Let us turn now to the *indices*, the second major class of functions. The characteristic difference between indicial codes and sequential codes is that the terms of the former belong to *parametric* relations[38] which remain *constant* throughout the text, whatever be their location in the succession of nuclei. In the text-narrative, these codes are really parametric codes of the ideological text of the social formation[39] in which the text-narrative is produced as the result of a process close to what Kristeva calls intertextuality.[40]

In the quite representative[41] text to Mark, the intertextual effect was sought in accordance with a logic of probability. However, historical analysis detects here and there dislocation and distortions between the parametric codes being deployed in the text and those that the analysis determines to have been the parametric codes of the social formation. We shall return to this point later, since the readings of Mark by bourgeois exegetes turn out to be seriously compromised once this kind of analysis is made.

We find in Mark a *topographical code* (TOP) relating to terms that designate places; the *geographical code* (GEO) is a subcode of TOP. We also find a *chronological code* (CHR) relating to terms that are indicative of time and make the succession of events explicit; this code is of lesser importance. The *mythological code* (MYTH) relates to terms belonging to what we have already called the mythological code of first-century Palestine. The *symbolic code* (SYMB) relates either to the symbolic (ideological) order or to the symbolic field as defined earlier in dependence on Barthes.[42] The *social code* (SOC) contains terms dealing with economic, political, or ideological functions, that is, speaking generally, with social functions; the terms of the social code, then, are, like the others, part of the text of the social formation.

A word must be said about a final code that is neither sequential nor parametric but shares in the nature of both. There will be actantial, analytic, and strategic codes for various, often opposed actants and for what I shall call their "practices." (I use this word in the general sense of "what the actant *does,*" and without presupposing, at the level of analysis of the narrative, the theoretical content which the concept of "practice" will receive in the fourth and final part of this book.) Mark's narrative deals chiefly with the practice of an actant, Jesus (J), in relation to whom all the other actants are defined. As the narrative unfolds, it will trace out a *field* for the practice of Jesus, and the field will imply terms of the various sequential and parametric codes. This field I call the "basileic" field (from *basileia*, the Greek word for "kingdom"); I shall be able to justify the name only in the course of the reading itself.[43] Thus, there is a final code, BAS.

As is the case with the other biblical texts, the text of Mark has come down to us in manuscripts from diverse traditions. For this reason, it contains a number of variants, most of which are of secondary importance. An exception is the "canonical ending," that is, Mark 16:9–20, which is clearly late and will be excluded from our reading, although we shall attempt to give a textual explanation of its later insertion. The text we shall be reading is a French text translated from the Greek text established by Kurt Aland.[44]

In making my translation I have used the translations in the *Bible de Jérusalem* and the New Testament by Canon Osty. I have also made use of Zerwick's *Grammatical Analysis*[44a] so that I might keep the translation as literal as possible and not lose a number of connotations of the Greek text that both Osty and the *Bible de Jérusalem* sacrifice for the sake of a more literary French version.[45] When it seems necessary to justify a point of translation, I shall refer to the Greek text (Gr).

Since I am straddling the two Barthes, the reading operations I shall now briefly describe will reflect both the structural and the textual orientations.

The essential operation, which is the patient determination of the codes, was described earlier in this chapter. For a long time I read with a structuralist outlook, but now I believe I am justified in describing the operation as *textual*. Despite this, the divisions I shall introduce into the text of Mark will not follow the "lexias" of the biblical verses, but will be grounded structurally *in the narrative statement*. I first divided the narrative according to nominal and verbal syntagmas, and then collected all these little nuclei into *scenes*, according as they followed one upon the other without the intervention of any actants beside those involved in the first nucleus. The scenes in turn were grouped into *sequences*. For this grouping two criteria were applied. The first is that the opening and closing should be such that, at least implicitly, the sequence forms an independent short narrative with a describable narrative meaning.[46] The second criterion is that, as a general rule, the term in the topographical code remains the same throughout the sequence (but sometimes there is a shift of place).

Finally, in accordance with criteria to be determined on each occasion, the sequences will be combined into a number of *major sequences*. It can be said now that in the construction of these GEO will always play an important role.

The sequences will be numbered S 1 to S 73, and within each the scenes will be designated a, b, etc. Thus, S 23d is the fourth scene in the twenty-third sequence.

The third operation will consist in an analysis at the level of narrator/ readers. In this analysis it will be possible to take up the question of the structuring of the narrative. At this level, given some "contradictions" in the structure of the narrative (and manifested by the narrative itself), we will be led to make a *symptomatic reading* which will bring out the ideological (or theological) function of Mark's writing. We will offer a lengthier justification of such a reading at the proper time.

I shall frequently be picking a fight with bourgeois exegesis and its idealism. Let us note here the semiotic significance of the term *narrative*. *A narrative is a text,* and the whole reading method I shall employ is brought to bear simply on the text-narrative, and this means on the (textual) codes of the social formation that are cited in it. As a general rule, classical exegesis, because its attention is so much focused on the real, historical "referent" of the text being analyzed, goes astray in its reading and quite often ends up by causing the materiality of the text to disappear from view. For that kind of exegesis, the *history* (not the narrative) is the important thing; it is exegesis under the aegis of idealist historicism.

We may apply the name "materialist" to two phases in the history of the exegesis of the three "synoptic" Gospels (Mark, Matthew, and Luke). The first began in 1838 with the *two-source theory* (Wiltke, Weisse, Holtzmann), which postulated that Matthew and Luke depend on Mark for material common to the three synoptics and on a source containing discourses of Jesus (Q) for material common to Matthew and Luke but missing from Mark.[47] This theory, which the majority of German and British exegetes have accepted and the majority of French exegetes have rejected, is described in W. G. Kümmel's *Introduction*.[48]

The second phase began around 1920 when Schmidt, Dibelius, and Bultmann began studying the history of forms (*Formgeschichte*), that is, the changes each pericope underwent, independently of the others, in the time before the various pericopes were brought together in the three synoptic Gospels. The changes were explained by the catechetical or liturgical use made of a given pericope in the early Christian communities; catechesis and liturgy thus provided the "vital context" (*Sitz im Leben*) for each pericope.[49] During the 1950s, the *Formgeschichte* method was supplemented by *Redaktionsgeschichte*, that is, the history of the redaction of each gospel.[50] These two methods meant a partial break with historicism, but the excessive influence attributed to the Christian communities for which the text was intended has meant that with the rejection of the "historical Jesus" problem the text-narrative itself has been emptied of its content.[51]

It must be said, however, that all the exegetes, even the few unbelievers among them, depend on a religious ideology that is a major obstacle to a materialist exegesis.

The narrator/readers level. Instead of postponing a reading of what belongs to this level until after the reading of the sequences, I have thought it better to provide it in the commentary itself. For this reason I must now give a brief description of what this reading is meant to be. (I shall return to this point in greater detail as occasion requires.)

Since the beginning of the second century A.D. the redaction of this text has been attributed to a Christian named Mark. As a matter of fact, we know nothing about him, and therefore we take the name *Mark* here simply as a designation for the text itself. If for some reason we want to refer to the author as such, we shall put the name "Mark" in quotation marks.

It is more important that we should know where and when the text was written. Only internal criticism of the text can provide information that suggests an answer to these questions. Georges Minette de Tillesse urges that

> the second Gospel must have been composed in the years immediately following upon the sack of Jerusalem, that is, in 71 or 72. . . . The language of the Gospel shows that the author is a Jew with a knowledge of Hebrew: he is quite well acquainted with the Scriptures and usually

quotes them according to the Hebrew text or the Aramaic targum (cf. 4:12). He writes for non-Jews (cf. 7:3–4), as the very language of his Gospel and his translation of Aramaic technical terms (cf. 5:41; 7:11; 15:34) show.[52]

Who were the readers for which the Gospel was intended? "The Christian community in the year 71 to which this set of traits [a certain distance with regard to the fall of Jerusalem; recent persecutions which have shaken the community to its foundations; existence of renegades as a result of the persecutions] best applies is very likely the community at Rome, which has traditionally been regarded as the intended recipient." "The Latin words used by Mark"[53] offer corroboration for this view.

The persecution of the Roman community by Nero (64–67) occurred shortly before the destruction of Jerusalem (in 70). . . . By now the persecution was probably over, but it had certainly claimed many victims in almost every Christian family of Rome. According to tradition, it had also taken the two leaders, Peter and Paul, of the ravaged community. . . . All these events [of the Roman war against the Jews] must have inflamed Roman anti-Semitism and created a threat of terrible persecution for the little remnant of the Roman church.

Our reading will provide what I regard as decisive confirmation of these views of Minette de Tillesse, which are far from winning unanimous agreement among the exegetes in regard to the dating of the Gospel, and are rather rare among Catholics.[54]

While we shall find that the narrative of Jesus (ACT) is most often related to the final, eschatological narrative, the level of narrator/readers will also relate the narrative of Jesus to the *ecclesial narratives* of the Roman community, locating these between the narrative of Jesus and the eschatological narrative.[55]

Chapter 2
"Have You Never Read" Mark?

Beginning of the good news of Jesus the Messiah (1:1)

Gr. *Christos* → Messiah.[1]

This is the *title* of the text. "Beginning" already tells us that the text will be a *narrative* with sequential codes that open with a beginning and close with a conclusion. There is nothing prior to this beginning; the events to be narrated will begin with the first sequence after the title. A question arises: what ending can there be for such a beginning? As we will see, the question proves meaningless, because the text will not have an ending; it will be suddenly interrupted before the open-ended sequences are brought to a conclusion.[2]

"Of the good news": This, as we shall see, is the title of the narrative. In the midst of all the texts read (heard) by the readers, this one stands out as *news*: something *new* is told, and it is described as *good*. New/old, good/evil: only the rest of the text can make it clear what codes are in question.

"Of Jesus:" the principal actant of the narrative.

"The Messiah": in ideological texts, this term connotes the one sent by God to free the people. The narrator sees Jesus as being this personage; the narrative will be in effect the narrative of his practice and of the recognition (ANAL) of this practice as messianic. "Good news" (Gr. *evangelion*) has become the *title* of the narrative of Jesus in the text of the West.

S 1 (1:2-8, 14a)

As it was written in the prophet Isaiah: "See, I am sending my messenger before you to prepare your way. A voice is crying in the desert: prepare the way of the Lord, make his paths level."

a1 John the Baptist appeared in the desert

b proclaiming an immersion of conversion for the cancellation of debts. And to him the whole land of Judea and all the inhabitants of Jerusalem went out, and they had themselves immersed in the river Jordan while they admitted their debts. And the John was clad in a camel's skin; he fed on grasshoppers and wild honey. And he proclaimed saying: "There comes after me one who is more powerful

98

than I, and I am not worthy to stoop and untie the thong of his sandals. I have immersed you in water, he will immerse you in the Holy Spirit."

a2 (After the John had been handed over into custody)

Gr. *aphesis* — cancellation. "The biblical meaning of the word is that of the act of God whereby sin, as a debt, is cancelled."[3]

"As it was written" (level of narrator): the writing (of the prophet) makes it possible to decode the voice (of John). The opposition I/you (my messenger/you, your way), here found in the writing, will be repeated in S 2 by the "heavenly voice" ("You are my son"); at the level of the narrator, the writing is interchangeable with the MYTH and vice versa. John, the actant in S 1, who makes his appearance in S 1a1, is arrested in S 1a2 (which comes between S 2 and S 3), and returns to the narrative only in a retrospect, is reduced by the narrative to the sole function of being a *voice* that prepares for the narrative (the way) of the actant Jesus. Even his practice, namely immersion (baptism), is a proclamation and thus a voice. The way of Jesus is the way of the (expected) Lord; his leveled paths are eschatological.

a1, b. "In the desert," "clad in a camel's skin," etc.: John is connoted as strange, outside the system of practices current in the social formation. The immersion (SYMB: purification) and the cancellation of debts (SYMB: debt system) put him on the side of *heaven*, whose voice or prophet he is (cf. S 55b).

"There comes after me one who is more powerful than I": John's prophetic discourse repeats the opposition John/Jesus, presenting John as inferior to and the precursor of Jesus (cf. S 43). To the water of the SYMB code (washing of the body) is contrasted an immersion in the Holy Spirit (MYTH), the eschatological purifier, that will take place at the judgment when there will be a washing of hearts (cf. S 35 for this opposition).

"Judea, Jerusalem, Jordan": TOP.

"All the inhabitants": actant *Crowd* (C).

S 2 (1:9-13)

a   And it happened in those days that Jesus came from Nazareth in Galilee

b   and he was immersed by John in the Jordan. And immediately, as he was coming up from the water,

c   he saw the heavens divide and the Spirit like a dove descend on him; and from the heavens a voice: "You are my beloved son, on you my favor has rested."

d   And immediately afterwards, the Spirit drives him into the desert. And he was in the desert for forty days, tempted by the Satan, and he was with the wild beasts, and the messengers were serving him.

(S 1 a2) After John had been handed over into custody,

a. "And it happened in those days that Jesus came": the principal actant is introduced. "From Nazareth in Galilee" (TOP-GEO): he is not a native of Judea, the central region in the Jewish SYMB field. We will see him later in his own country; his trade, his mother, his brothers and sisters, etc., will be mentioned, showing that, unlike John, he fits into the normal framework of the SOC. Jesus is also immersed like the other people in the C. "Immersed/coming up": descent into the *abyss,* return to the *earth*, according to the spatial schema of the MYTH.[4]

c. "He saw": a new scene in which John is no longer an actant; it is rather J who will have a "vision," as the prophets of old did, for the heavens, long closed,[5] open again. The immersion of Jesus simply provides a scenario, as the water makes way for the Spirit, in accordance with John's proclamation. "Descend on him": again the spatial schema of the MYTH, but here used to relate *heaven* and *earth*. This *descent* of the Spirit opens something, namely the narrative of J, and establishes that its term or completion will be an *ascent* to heaven as "Son of man" (as we shall see).[6]

"From the heavens a voice": The voice is that of God who is located in heaven (MYTH). "You are my beloved son": J is declared to be in a relation of sonship with the God of the MYTH. This intervention of the Spirit thus *separates* J from the other members of the C who, like him, had been immersed (baptized). "On you my favor has rested": this narrative is presented, therefore, as a narrative of election by *heaven,* whose *voice* addresses J according to the I/you system.

"And immediately afterwards, the Spirit drives him": J remains passive over against the actants who belong to the MYTH; his separation from other men will be completed by the forty days in the desert, as it had for Moses and Elijah before him. "Satan" (the adversary: MYTH): the evil counterpart of the Holy Spirit. The latter draws J to the coming struggle (the word "temptation" will be used in the narrative for the opposition of J's adversaries). The wild beasts and the messengers (angels) complete the mythic scenario for the scene.

"After John . . . ": John disappears from the text. J has resumed his traveling, but in the opposite direction, and the text creates a small loop in the TOP: desert → Jordan/Jordan → Desert. J too is now on the side of heaven, and separated from the SOC.

S 3 (1:14b-15)

a The Jesus came into Galilee
b proclaiming the good news of the God, and saying: "The time is fulfilled and the kingdom of God has drawn near; be converted and believe in the good news."

a. "The Jesus came into Galilee": a new loop in the TOP: Galilee→Jordan (Judea) → desert (temptation) → Galilee.

b. "Proclaiming": J in turn becomes a *voice*. "Good news": refers back to the title, which had spoken of the beginning of the good news. "The time is fulfilled": the fulfillment of the time is also the fulfillment of the narratives which unfold as a succession in time; what draws near with the kingdom of God is the completion, the final closure of the indefinitely long text of the narratives. This drawing near will therefore be the final, eschatological narrative. S 58 will oppose it to the beginning (that is, the creation of heaven and earth) and speak of it as the "passing away" of heaven and earth, the removal of the mythological difference or *divergence* that has caused time to exist. Between the prediction and its accomplishment there is the time of conversion and faith, amid a nearness that is proclaimed to be good and a source of happiness.

S 1–S 3: The Program of the Markan Text

The narrative has not yet begun; it will begin only in S 6. Thus far there has been only a circuit of voices: the voices of John, of heaven, of Jesus, the voice from heaven that bestows a voice on Jesus and silences the voice of John the forerunner. Yet the text has already begun its work: specifically, the work of programming, that is, the introduction of the *codes* whose *divergence* will make the narrative possible. On the one side, there is the TOP code, the second loop of which (Galilee → Judea → [temptation] → Galilee) anticipates the overall itinerary of Jesus (Galilee → Jerusalem (Judea) → temptation [and death] → Galilee). On the other side, there is the MYTH code; the *descent* provides the first term in this code, with the last being an ascent that will eschatologically remove the difference that makes possible the time proper to the narratives. The time remaining will be the time of the narrative of Jesus, who until this point has been a mere *voice* that does not even have any hearers. The Crowd will be convened only in S 6 for the opening of the narrative of Jesus; the latter at that point will cease to be a voice and will become a practice, the narrative of which will become in its turn the announcement of the final narrative, the good news of the closing "of the days of tribulation" that precede the end (S 58).

In short, according to J. Kristeva's conception (in her essay *"Le texte clos"*), the text (mythical or in the ideologem of the symbol) begins with a programmatic loop that has its own opening/closure, that is, the limits it will not be able to transgress, or, in a word, its determination.

S 4 (1:16-20)

a And as he was passing along the sea of Galilee
b he saw Simon and Andrew, the brother of Simon, who were casting their nets into the sea, for they were fishermen. And the Jesus said to them: "Come after me and I will make you fishers of men." And immediately, leaving their nets there, they followed him.

c And going on a bit further
d he saw James, son of Zebedee, and John, his brother, likewise in their boat putting the nets in order, and immediately he called them. And leaving their father Zebedee in the boat with the hired men, they went off after him.

a. "He was passing along the sea of Galilee": A line which separates sea/land and plays a role in the strategic metaphor "I will make you fishers of men." In a movement opposite to the one recounted here (the movement of casting nets into the sea), the disciples will pull men like fish from the sea (which is the mythological location of Satan, death, and the abyss) toward the land.

b-d. "I will make": indicates a project of J and consequently a *strategy* relating to "men." "After me," "they followed him," "they went off after him": This *following* (STR) places the four fishermen named (Simon, Andrew, James, and John) at the *beginning* of J's road; this will qualify them to be questioners about the *end* of the road (cf. S 58). "Fishermen" (SOC): in a dominated class. "The boat": will reappear later on (S 18).

The practice of J has not yet begun, but, though separated from men by the Spirit (in S 2), he will not be alone in his narrative, but will be part of a group: the narrative will be concerned not with individuals but with a collectivity.

S 5 (1:21a, 39a)

a1 And they entered Capernaum
a2 (and he went throughout Galilee)

a1. A shift of scene, according to the TOP code, from the shore of the sea to the city. The opposition city/outside the city will quickly become strategic: in S 18 J will be forced to withdraw to the shore of the sea. The present sequence will be completed after S 8.

S 6 (1:21b-29a)

a1 And immediately, on the sabbath, having entered the synagogue,
b he was teaching. And they were amazed at his teaching, for he was teaching them as one having authority, and not as the scribes.
c And just then there was in their synagogue a man with an unclean spirit, and he began to cry out: "What have we to do with you, Jesus the Nazarene? Have you come to destroy us? I know who you are, the holy one of God." And the Jesus rebuked him very severely, saying: "Be silent and go out of him." And convulsing him, the impure spirit went out of him with a loud cry.
d And all were startled, so that they asked one another: "What is this?

Here is a new teaching with authority. He commands even the impure spirits, and they obey him!"
e   And his reputation immediately spread in all directions through the whole region of Galilee.
a2   And immediately, having left the synagogue,

a. The opening and closing of the sequence (ACT) is made quite clear: "having entered the synagogue"/"having left the synagogue." These explicit openings and closings occur frequently throughout the narrative, and we shall not advert to them on every occasion.

"Sabbath, synagogue, scribes": SOC.

b. "He was teaching": this is the first term indicating a specific practice of J, who here acts as a "master" (rabbi), a title he will be frequently given in the narrative. We must observe however (a point on which we shall dwell at length in S 22) that the teaching is not specified. What attracts attention is the authority (*exousia*) with which he speaks, for it contrasts with the habitual teaching practice of the scribes (SOC). Further on, the contrast is brought out again by the word "new." A *new* practice stands over against a habitual, repetitive ideological practice: there is a *difference* between the practice of the SOC and the practice of J.

c. "Unclean spirit": MYTH. The discourse of the spirit raises the question (ANAL) of the newness of this practice as an opposition of you/us, with the opposition taking the form of a *combat* in which the unclean spirits admit themselves to be already the losers (S 18, S 24). The outcome of the combat is already determined; in the MYTH heaven is already victor over the abyss. The spirit goes on the offensive (STR): "I know who you are: the holy one of God." Our attention is here drawn back to S 2 ("you are my son") (cf. S 18, S 24); the spirits too have heard the "voice from the heavens."

Be silent": J counterattacks, thus rendering more urgent the question, "Who is Jesus?" (Q 1), which will be one of the riddles of the ANAL. J is seeking to repress the response to the question. As a matter of fact, however, the narrative itself is leading to the response through the interplay of the three sequential codes. The MYTH (S 2, S 6a) has already given a response; it thus contradicts the narrative (MYTH/ACT contradiction) and in a sense cancels out the narrative by a response that already stands within the semantic field of the ideological system.[7] The command, "Be silent," is a strategy (STR) of J which denies that response by silencing it, and leaves it to the narrative to bring out, later on, the response that is in accord with his practice.

"Go out of him": the command and the spirit's obedience represent a victory of J over the unclean spirit (ACT). J is called the "Nazarene" after his place of birth (S 2). Nazareth is also inscribed in the SOC code; it was a small town in Galilee (cf. S 27).

d. The ANAL code is highlighted by the startled Crowd: "What is *this*?" This is question Q 2 and will determine the answer to Q 1. "This" refers to the twofold practice of J: his new teaching and his victory over the unclean spirit, which is the object of the ACT in this sequence. We are at the beginning of the narrative (ACT), and the term "new" brings out the difference between J's practice and the practices common in the SOC.

   e. "His reputation immediately spread": the narrative begins to circulate "in all directions through the whole region of Galilee" (GEO). The program enunciated in S 3 is beginning to be implemented, but it is now no longer the voice of J that circulates but the narrative concerning him. We will see later the textual importance of this substitution.

S 7 (1:29b-35a)

al He entered the house of Simon and Andrew along with James and John.
b   Simon's mother-in-law was in bed with a fever, and they immediately told him of her.
c   Drawing near, he took her by the hand and helped her up; and the fever left her,
d   and she served them.
el In the evening when the sun had set, they brought all the sick and possessed persons to him,
f   and the whole village was gathered at the door.
e2 And he healed many sick people who were afflicted with various ills, and he expelled many demons, and he prevented the demons from speaking because they knew him.
g   Early in the morning, while it was still dark, he rose,
a2 left the house,

   a. Synagogue/house: within Capernaum, the TOP contrasts two spaces, one dominated by the scribes (S 6, S 16), the other being the house of Simon, one of J's followers; this second space will soon be characterized as a space of the DD (disciples).

   b, c, d. If we characterize the actant "Simon's mother-in-law" as an Ic (individual under a curse), then the effect of the ACT is the passage from Ic to Ib (b = blessed). "The fever left her": c → b, a passage from emptiness to fulness, from curse to blessing, the blessing being suggested by the woman's service at table. In addition, at the level of the body (SYMB), there is a contast lying/standing, as well as a contract between two bodies ("he took her by the hand"). The standing body is restored to daily life ("she served them").

   e1. The narrative that has spread abroad (S 6e) brings the Crowd from the town to the door of the house; the sunset puts an end to the sabbath, during which all work was forbidden, such as "bringing the sick."

   e2. A brief summation of numerous narratives like S 6c and S 7c. Attention is called to the effect of J's power (c → b, demons expelled), and to the STR regarding the "secret" of J's identity.

S 8 (1:35b-38)

a   and went off to a deserted place
b   and prayed there.
c   Simon and his companions went right after him and found him
d   and say to him: "Everyone is looking for you." He says to them: "Let us go elsewhere into the neighboring towns, so that I may make proclamation there too, for it is to that end that I have come out."

a. "A deserted place": in opposition to an inhabited place, a town (TOP).

d. "Everyone is looking for you": the STR of the C is made explicit here (already implicit in S 7f) and will be mentioned frequently from here on. Note however that Simon is the spokesman for this strategy, a fact that will allow us later on to connect the STR of the DD with that of the C. To this strategy Jesus opposes his own: the geographical expansion of his practice (of proclamation) throughout all of Galilee; this STR is indicated in the words "for it is to that end that I have come out" of the town (S 7a2).

S 9 (1:39)

a   And he went throughout all of Galilee,
b   preaching in their synagogues
c   and expelling demons.

This summarizing, multiplicative narrative of J's practice reminds us of S 6, since "preaching in their synagogues" is to be connected with the "new teaching" of which the C speaks there, and the "expelling of demons" with the narrative of expulsions given there. Galilee (S 3, S 6e) is the region (GEO) for the circulation of this practice.

The narrative statement thus fulfills the strategic statement of J in S 8d. S 8–S 9 illustrate the code to which we have given the name strategic (STR), so that S 8 might be described as a sequence dominated by a STR.

We can now read a term in the ACT which we passed over without comment in S 8b: he "prayed there."[8] What is registered here (cf. S 22, S 32, S 54, S 64) is the relation between *prayer* and *strategy*: prayer depends on narrativity and can be understood only in terms of its function in the narrative. The TOP (deserted place) shows prayer as J's distancing of himself from the narrative (in S 6–S 7), that is, as a reading by J of the ACT narrative, and therefore as a site of the ANAL.

S 10 (1:40-45a)

a1   And a leper comes to him,
b   calls upon him for help, and, falling to his knees, says: "If you wish, you can cleanse me." Taking pity, he extended his hand, touched

him, and says to him: "I do wish it: be cleansed." And immediately
the leprosy left him and he was cleansed. And sternly warning him,
he sent him away, and he says to him: "See to it that you say nothing
to anyone, but go, show yourself to the priest and offer for your
cleansing what Moses prescribed, as a testimony against them."

a2   But, once the man had gone away,

c   he began to proclaim very loudly and to spread the word,

Gr.: "as a witness against them" (cf. Mark 6:11; 13:9–10).[9] Gr. *polla* =
"very loudly"; cf. 3:12; 5:43; 9:26.

b. The ACT is equivalent to that of S 7b, c. There are some differences,
however. The petition here comes from the Ic (in a discourse that links the
will and the power of J, a linking which the latter accepts, for he repeats it in
his efficacious words of cleansing), whereas in S 7 the petition comes not
from the sick person but from others.

The word "cleanse" occurs four times in various forms: the SYMB is not
allowed to go unnoticed. When J touched the leper, he should have himself
been made unclean, but in fact the opposite happens; we are told here of the
subversion of this symbolic order, for Jesus *touches* the leper, and the leper
becomes clean. It is the *power* of J's body that is thus made known in the
SYMB code, and we see how this power ("you can") is related to J's wish or
will ("you wish"): it is the heart of J ("taking pity") that is the source, in his
body, of this power to cleanse.

To this ACT a strategy is connected: the ACT narrative is to remain a secret
(except from the priest who must verify the cleansing), not in its effect, which
is the integration of the Ib into the field of Jewish purity, but in the manner of
its occurrence (including the principal actant of the narrative).

c. This instruction is not followed; on the contrary, the former leper begins
to *proclaim* very loudly "the word." This term ("the word": *ton logon*) occurs in
the text for the first time and evidently means a *narrative* and, more specifically, a narrative about J (ACT). Note that "proclaim" is an index of a
narrative; it has already occurred in S 1 and S 3 to indicate the announcement
of a narrative to come (the narrative of J, in S 1, and the final, eschatological
narrative, in S 3), but here it points to a past narrative.

S 11 (1:45b)

a   so that he could no longer go openly into a town, but remained
     outside, in the deserted places.

b   And they came to him from all directions.

a. The disobedience of the Ib affects the STR of J, which is summarily
stated in this sequence: the space of the towns is closed to him, and he stays in
the deserted places outside the towns (TOP).

This STR will be intensified in S 18, apparently in contradiction to the present sequence, since we will find J in towns in S 12, S 13, and S 16 (although S 12b shows that J had entered Capernaum secretly, and that the crowd gathers only because it has heard that J is there). S 10–S 11 would seemingly be better placed after S 17, and we must therefore ask why they have been placed here. The usual answer is: the author takes advantage of the fact that J is outside the towns and far from the CV, in order to make plausible his being approached by a leper, who was forbidden to go near inhabited places. But this answer does not really tell us anything, since S10–S 11 could have been placed at a later point. In my view, the placing of S10–S11 at this point sheds light on the STR of J, which has been begun in S 8–S 9. There are two reasons for this STR. One will be given in S 17–S 18, which tells us of the birth of a STR opposed to that of J and thus tending to define it. The other reason is given to us here: The town is the place of the C, and J, who in S 8 has already rejected the STR of the C that seeks him out, confirms his rejection in S 11. Let us say, for the moment, that J wants to avoid too conspicuous a success in relation to the C; he does not want his body to become enclosed in the large circle of the C. This is why he had ordered the cleansed leper to be silent.

  b. "And they came to him from all directions": J's STR is only half success-ful. He cannot prevent the crowds from surrounding him; he can only keep it from happening in the towns. This movement that draws the C away from the inhabited places (TOP) will be intensified in proportion as the spread of his narrative will increase the number of those who seek him out.

S 12 (2:1-12)

a A few days later, after he had entered Capernaum again,
b it was heard that he was at home. And many gathered so that there was no more room, even in front of the door. And he preached the word to them.
c1 And they come bringing him a paralytic carried by four men; since they could not bring him to him because of the crowd, they removed the roof at the spot where he was, and, having made a hole, they lower the bed on which the paralytic was lying. And the Jesus, seeing their faith, says to the paralytic: "Child, your debts are cancelled."
d Now some of the scribes were sitting there and saying in their hearts: "How can this man speak like this? He is blaspheming! Who can cancel debts but the God alone?" And immediately, knowing in his spirit that they are saying these things within themselves, the Jesus says to them: "Why do you speak thus in your hearts? Which is easier to say to the paralytic: 'Your debts are cancelled,' or 'Arise, take your bed, and walk'? Well, in order that you may know that the Son of man has authority to cancel debts on earth,"
c2 he says to the paralytic: "I say to you: arise, take your bed, and go

home." And he arose and immediately, taking his bed, went out in the sight of everyone,

e   so that all were beside themselves and praised God, saying: "never have we seen anything like this."

Gr. *lalein* ("speak") will be translated "preach" when followed by "the word" or "in parables."

a. "A few days later": concordance (CHR) with S 11, according to the narrative logic of successivity. J returns secretly (STR) to Capernaum, that is, not openly (cf. S 11a). "It was heard that he was at home": This presupposes he had done something that had attracted attention; it is the narrative that brings the C, as in S 6e and S 7f. "And he preached the word to them": this is comparable to the teaching of S 6b (cf. S 22); the scribes then come on the scene, and the narrative will show the opposition of two teachings.

c1. The *request* of the Ic is told in the form of a little strategy for approaching the body of J (remove, make a hole, lower), with the C playing the role of obstacle; the narrative speaks of this little strategy as *faith* ("seeing their faith": cf. S 26, S 51). "Child, your debts (sins) are discharged": according to the logic of the debt system, the curse of paralysis (a sickness or defect) is attributed to the man's debts (therefore Ic) which keep him on the side of the sinner and separated from the upright (SYMB).

d. This logic of the debt system is accepted by the scribes (SOC); they read (ANAL) the narrative by denying J the authority to discharge or cancel debts. Only God has such authority, and he bestows his benefits chiefly through expiatory sacrifices (SYMB). J's words are therefore read as blasphemous, and the blasphemer is read as being opposed to God on whose side the scribes are; therefore, the schema would be: God (scribes)/J.

J begins the discussion by giving a *lesson in reading* (ANAL): to the first narrative (c1) he opposes a second, and invites the scribes to read it ("in order that you may know"). The issue is the authority of his words of forgiveness that end the first narrative (c1); he compares these with words of healing ("arise, take your bed, and walk") according to the norm of effectiveness or power, as indicated by the term "easy" ("which is easier . . . ?").

c2. Once the scheme for reading has been established, the second narrative can proceed according to the pattern already suggested: Ic/Ib, with the SYMB opposition taking the form of "lying"/"he arose." The effectiveness of the practice of J consists in the free *walking* of the former paralytic.

e. The C reads (ANAL) this second narrative (c2) and reverses the scheme set up by the scribes in their thoughts. For the practice of J makes the crowd give glory to God. J is now located on God's side: God, J/scribes.

The second narrative shows the authority (power) of J over the pollution system (c/b), whereas the first (c1) had shown his authority over the debt system. The reading by the C fuses the two narratives: "Never have we seen anything like this," the "this" including both J speaking "like this" and his healing of the paralytic, in a double subversion of the Jewish SYMB field.

Still to be explained are the term "Son of man" (linked to the term *heaven* of the MYTH; cf. S 42, S 58, S 66) and the authority "on *earth*," the other term of the MYTH, which links the ACT narrative with the final eschatological narrative. We shall leave these two points for the moment, and return to them later (S 22, S 42).

S 13 (2:13-17)

a   And he went out again along the sea.

b   And all the crowd came to him, and he was teaching them.

c   And as he passed he saw Levi, son of Alphaeus, sitting at the tax office, and he says to him: "Follow me." And standing up he followed him.

d   And he was at table in his house, and many tax collectors and debtors were at table with the Jesus and his disciples, for they were many and they followed him.

e   And the scribes who belonged to the Pharisees, seeing him eat with the debtors and tax collectors, said to his disciples: "Why does he eat with tax collectors and debtors?" The Jesus, having heard them, says to them: "It is not the strong who need the physician, but the sick. I have not come to call the upright, but the debtors."

a. "Along the sea" has two functions: on the one hand, it recalls S 4 (calling of the four fishermen), which will be repeated in S 13c and will set the stage for d and e; on the other hand, it also prepares for S 18, S 22, and the whole series of meetings of J/C beside the sea. The differentiation and contrast between the DD and the C will thus be effected strategically, down to S 42.

b. We shall simply observe that this scene is differently structured than S 7f, S 11b, and S 12b, where the C is brought together by hearing the narrative of J's practice. Here, J moves to a different place, the C follows him, and he teaches them: the rabbi (teacher) thus calls them together.

c. The same structure is found here as in S 4 (it will be analyzed in S 49). Note that Levi as a tax collector or publican is a social outcast (SOC).

d. Tax collectors and debtors are lumped together with the disciples of J, so that it is difficult to decide whether the words "for they were many and they followed him" ("following" being a mark of the DD) refers to the tax collectors and debtors or to the disciples; there is a textual ambiguity.

From another viewpoint the narrative shows the shape of a *circle* around the table, in the house, and this shape or figure will become a decisive one in the BAS code. *Table* and *house* (TOP) will indicate, by synecdoche, this *circle* of which J will reveal himself to be the *center* (*eating* will be another term in this series).

e. The scribes, who are defined as "belonging to the Pharisees" (SOC), read (ANAL) this practice of J (eating with tax collectors and debtors) as subversive of the Jewish SYMB field at the point where the two systems intersect:

those who in fact are excluded from the debt system are the unclean; their table is a source of pollution, and every Jew who would be clean must steer clear of it if he is not to be polluted.

J gives a lesson in reading (ANAL), which is based on the opposition "the strong" (or: healthy)/"sick," or clean/unclean (pollution system) and upright/debtors (debt system). "I have not come" (words indicating J's STR) in order to maintain the SYMB but to subvert it; this is expressed in the image of the physician and his practice of "salvation" in the sense of a passage from a state of being cursed to a state of being blessed. J's STR will lead to a new circle, inscribed in accordance with the BAS code, as contrasted with the circles of cleanness proper to the Jewish SYMB code; this antithesis is what I am calling *subversion* (i.e., of the dominant codes).[10] J's reading (ANAL) is meant to bring out this *antithesis*.

S 14 (2:18-22)

a   And the disciples of John and the Pharisees were observing a fast.
b   And people come to him and say: "Why is it that the disciples of John and the disciples of the Pharisees fast but your disciples do not fast?" And the Jesus said to them: "The guests of the bridegroom cannot fast, can they, while the bridegroom is still with them? As long as they have the bridegroom with them, they cannot fast. Days will come when the bridegroom is taken from them, and then, on that day, they will fast. No one sews a patch of unshrunk cloth on to an old garment. If he does, the added piece pulls away from it, the new from the old, and the tear becomes worse. And no one puts new wine into old skins; if he does, the wine will burst the skins, and both wine and skins will be lost; instead, new wine into new skins.

a. The disciples of John, who has been arrested (S 1a2), have joined the Pharisees in a fast, probably to petition God that he would rescue John from this situation of curse.

b. Those who fast show that their bodies are clean (SYMB) and upright. The question put to J opposes his DD, that is, the circle around J, to this circle of upright men. The reading (ANAL) J makes of this difference in practices follows the logic of the SYMB code: the bridegroom is with them, and a wedding is a time of blessing, not a reason for fasting. In contrast, the disciples of John have a reason for fasting (John's arrest). The circle of the BAS code is thus signified by the metaphor of the wedding feast (satisfaction of hunger around the table), and J, as the bridegroom, is made the center of the circle. The metaphor is based on the antithesis eat/fast, which will be found later on as: be hungry/be filled (S 31).

The two metaphorical antitheses that follow indicate that the difference between the practice of J, which establishes the circle, and the practice of fasting, which belongs to the Jewish SYMB field, is the difference of new/old.

On the one hand, the Jewish symbolic field is described as an old fabric (or text), which cannot be attached to a new fabric (or text); on the other hand, it is described as an old framework or order (a wineskin) that cannot resist the force exerted by a new wine. The aspect of subversion emerges clearly: *tearing* of the old symbolic text, *bursting* of the old order. Note too that the Greek word here translated as "added piece" is *pièrôma,* which in S3 (in a verbal form: *peplèrôtai*) connotes the final narrative: "The time is fulfilled."

"Days will come": the restriction on the time of celebration is to be located at the level of the narrator who is writing to communities of DD which are being subjected to persecution; the bridegroom has been "taken" from them and "on that day, they will fast," that is, when they in turn find themselves in prison (cf. S 62).

S 15 (2:23-28)

a   And on the sabbath he was passing through a field being harvested, and his disciples began to make a path for themselves by pulling the wheat.

b   And the Pharisees said to him: "Look! Why are they doing that which is not permitted on the sabbath?" And he says to them: "Have you never read what David did when he was in need and when he and his companions were hungry? How he entered the house of God in the time of Abiathar the high priest and ate the loaves of offering, which only priests may eat, and gave them also to his companions?" And he said to them: "The sabbath was made for man's sake, not man for the sabbath, so that the Son of man is lord even of the sabbath."

Gr.: there is a problem of translation here. The New American Bible (for example) translates: "His disciples began to pull off heads of grain as they went along," and implies that the disciples pulled the grain in order to eat it. In fact, that is also how J reads the text. Yet the correct translation, as explained by P. Benoit,[11] is that they pulled the wheat so as to open a path for themselves. Matthew and Luke have corrected Mark's text at this point so as to make it conform to J's reading. The difficulty seems insoluble to me. Since this sequence exemplifies the structure of the ANAL code, I shall read J's reading as though the textual incongruity did not exist.

a. The ACT narrative is presented.

b. The reading by the Pharisees and the reading by J are opposed to each other. The Pharisees contrast the narrative ("They are doing") with the law ("that which is not permitted") (SOC), according to the grill: sabbath (rest)=not to work/other days=to work. J sets up a different schema for reading ("Have you never read?), by comparing the ACT with a narrative about David from the Old Testament; the logic he is invoking says that what David did was not against the law. Here are the two narratives side by side:

What David Did	They Are Doing
when he was in need and when	
he and his companions were hungry,	J and his disciples[12]
he entered . . . ate . . . gave	they plucked the wheat (to eat it)
in the house of God, loaves of offering	on the sabbath
which was not permitted	which is not permitted,

The logic of the comparison is evident: what the ACT narrative omits is to be read in the narrative of David. If the disciples pluck the wheat, it is because they are in need and are hungry. Therefore, the conclusion: the sabbath was made for the sake of humanity and its needs, and not vice versa; humanity's needs take precedence over the law of the sabbath in the field of the BAS, in the new dispensation that the practice of J is in process of writing, so as to subvert the dispensation proper to the Jewish SYMB field.[13] The BAS field has its justification as a function of the final, eschatological narrative, to which reference is made in the words: "The Son of man is lord even of the sabbath."

S 16 (3:1-5)

a   And he entered again into the synagogue.

b1 And a man was there who had a withered hand,

c1 and they were watching him closely to see whether he would heal the man on the sabbath, so that they might accuse him.

b2 And he says to the man with the withered hand: "Stand up in the midst."

c2 And he says to them: "Is it allowed on the sabbath to do good rather than evil, to save a life rather than kill?" But they remained silent. And looking around at them with anger, and deeply grieved at the hardening of their hearts,

b3 he says to the man: "Stretch out your hand!" And he stretched it out and his hand was restored.

The issue is still the sabbath law (SOC): to heal someone was regarded as doing a form of work and was therefore prohibited on the sabbath. Violation of this law was an offense punishable by death[14]; that is why J's enemies keep a close eye so as to be able to accuse him.

The proper approach to a reading (ANAL) is established here, even before the ACT narrative, just as in S 12. "Stand up in the midst": J puts the man with the withered hand (Ic) in the center of the circle, so that his deficiency (need) may be the object of a reading. "And he says to them: 'Is it allowed . . . ? ' ": J approaches them as interpreters or readers of the law. The point at issue is not what people can or cannot do on the sabbath (this was the object of casuistic debates among the scribes), but whether they are to *do good or evil.*

The object of the law is those practices that lead to blessing (to the good), that is, to the saving of lives (passage from curse to blessing). The law can therefore only forbid the doing of evil, the taking of lives. The enemies of J are unable to answer him; the very logic of the SYMB forces them to remain silent. The ACT narrative can now unfold (Ic/Ib), for the reading: "He has worked on the sabbath," has already been replaced by the reading proper to the BAS code: "He saved a life on the sabbath." But the accusers do not accept this reading because (says the narrative) of "the hardening of their hearts." The *heart* has already been mentioned in S 12; here, in S 16, the heart is shown to be the place where decisions are made, the place that determines the division among actants and readers, in relation to the practice of the actant J. The *hardened heart* cannot read the practice of J, that is, his narrative.

S 17 (3:6)

a When they had gone out,
b the Pharisees immediately formed a plan against him with the Herodians on the way to destroy him.

b. "The Pharisees": these were the "they" of S 16; in S 13 they are linked to the scribes (SOC). "Immediately formed a plan against him": the STR of the scribes and Pharisees (along with the Herodians[15]) is specified, as is their place in the constellation of actants. These men are the *adversaries* (AA) of the actant J. Their strategy is to "destroy him" and defeat his STR, that is, the circle which is subversive of the field, both SYMB and SOC, in which they exercise a certain ideological power.

In addition, S 17 ends the set of sequences that began in S 12. Sequence 18 begins with the withdrawal of J to the sea, which picks up the words "he could no longer go openly into a town" of S 11a. We may therefore pause here to reread the series of sequences we have already examined, namely S 5–S 9 + S 10–S 11, and S 12–S 17, and to characterize them briefly.

Rereading of S 5-S 11

After the three programmatic sequences S 1–S 3 (and S 4, which situates J in a group, before beginning the narration of the "new"), this first major sequence, which unfolds initially at Capernaum and then in Galilee at large (GEO), is characterized by the narrative of three types of practice on J's part (new teaching, expulsion of an unclean spirit, healing) and its multiplication in the form of a summary. This practice gives rise to a strategy of the C (C seeks out J), to which J opposes a STR of avoiding the C, a strategy which is underlined in S 10–S 11 by the further choice (STR) of not going openly into the towns. This *major sequence* comprises, then, the confrontation of two STR, that of J and that of the C.

Rereading of S 12-S 17

When we read these sequences as a unit (their TOP is rather uncertain), we see that J's practice is being systematically presented as subversive of the Jewish SYMB field, and even of the entire Jewish SYMB order. This practice elicits a strategy from the scribes, Pharisees, and Herodians; this may be described as a *strategy of temptation*, and a consequence of this in turn is a STR for doing away with J (S 17).

This major sequence is also the site for the deployment of the ANAL code as the code for the procedures for reading the ACT narrative, with the readings differing according to the site (SOC) of the reader. Especially to be noted is the fact that S 16 provides a very important key to J's reading (BAS), with its antithesis "save a life/take a life." This antithesis will define the goals of the two opposed strategies.

We may note a further point: the two mentions of the "Son of man" (the first links S 12 and S 13, which deal with "sinners"; the second links S 15 and S 16, which deals with the sabbath), as well as the metaphor of the bridegroom (with its allusion to the "eschatological wedding feast"), relate the ACT narrative to the eschatological narrative, which has been announced in S 3 in the term "kingdom of God." We will come back to this point in S 22 and S 42.

S 18 (3:7-12)

a   And the Jesus took refuge by the sea with his disciples

b   and a great crowd followed them from Galilee;

c   and from Judea and Jerusalem and Idumea and from beyond the Jordan, and from around Tyre and Sidon, a great crowd, hearing of all that he was doing, came to him.

d   And he told his disciples to have a boat ready for him because of the crowd, so that they might not press upon him.

e   For he healed many, so that all those with sicknesses crowded in upon him to touch him. And the unclean spirits, when they saw him, fell down before him and cried out, saying: "You are the son of God!" And he sharply rebuked them lest they make him known.

Gr.: *anechōrēsen*, "took refuge" implies here a real "emigration," as the STR code makes quite clear.[16]

a, b. "By the sea," "disciples," "followed": these three elements recall S 4 and S 13. "A great crowd" brings the C back into the narrative, after it had been almost wholly absent from S 12–S 17. Its reintroduction points to the main issue of the next major sequence (S 18–S 42) that is beginning here, namely, the division between the DD and the C; the circles which these two groups form around the body of J have until now been rather undifferentiated, as we remarked in S 13.

c. The field for hearing the narrative of J's practice ("hearing of all that he was doing") extends beyond Galilee into Judea and Jerusalem and even beyond Palestine: southeastward into Idumea, eastward beyond the Jordan, and northward (to Tyre and Sidon). For the first time, the narrative breaks through the Jewish frontier and reaches out to the horizon proper to J's practice. We are thus given a first indication of what his strategy will be with regard to the Israelite SYMB-GEO field.

d. In this major sequence (S 18–S 42) "boat" will be the element that defines the circle of J + DD, and will enable it to put distance, both topographical and strategic, between this circle and that of the C.

e, f. A repetition of the summary in S 7e, defining the STR of the C and emphasizing once again the value of the *touch* of J's body (SYMB).

In short, this sequence is simply a *program* for S 18–S 42; we are still in the "closed text" as defined by J. Kristeva.

S 19 (3:13-19)

a   And he ascends the mountain
b   and calls to him those whom he himself wished, and they came to him. And he made twelve, so that they might be with him and he might send them to proclaim and have authority to cast out demons. And he made them twelve: he gave the Simon the name Peter, and James, the son of Zebedee, and John, the brother of James, and he gave them the name Boanerges, that is, sons of thunder, and Andrew and Philip and Bartholomew and Matthew and Thomas and James, the son of Alphaeus, and Thaddaeus and Simon the Zealot and Judas the Sicarius, the one who betrayed him.

Gr.: Simon *Kananaios* = Cananaean = Zealot. Iscariot = a Sicarius (daggerman, assassin).[17]

a. "He ascends the mountain": in the MYTH the mountain is a place closer to heaven; it is also the place where the revelation was given to Moses, "author" of the Law and the Jewish symbolic order over which J claims to be "lord" (S 15).

b "And calls to him those whom he himself wished" (STR), "so that they might be with him" (defining a *circle* even narrower than the circle of the DD who were following him), "and he might send them," prolonging (STR) his practice in Galilee (S 9; cf. S 28). The mention of the crowds of pagans in S 18 now takes on further significance: the goal of the STR will be to send the twelve to the gentiles outside of Israel.

"And he made twelve": the text emphasizes this by saying it twice. The number "twelve" recalls that Israel was made up of "twelve tribes." The indices are interrelated, even if this will be developed textually only later on: this circle (SYMB) of twelve bodies around the body of J (cf., e.g., S 26) is intended as a substitute for the entire symbolic field of Israel and is also meant to spread outward among the pagan nations.

"He gave the Simon the name Peter": This confirms the fact that the call in S 4 is strategic ("fishers of men"), for the change of name implies a change of profession or calling. The same for James and John who, with Peter, will on three occasions be privileged witnesses of the ACT narrative. Andrew, on the other hand, is excluded from this special group. Why?

The interpretative phrase, "that is, sons of thunder," is the work of the narrator who translates into another linguistic field (the Greek linguistic field of the pagans) a narrative based on Jewish codes. "The one who betrayed him": the phrase again points to the narrator as knower of the narrative and its ending, and thus as weaver of the fabric of codes that is the text.

S 20 (3:20)

a   And he returns to the house,
b   and again the crowd gathers, so that they were not able even to eat bread.

S 21 (3:21)

a1 Having heard this, his relatives came to lay hold of him, for, they said: "He is out of his senses."

S 20 (3:22-30)

c   And the scribes who came down from Jerusalem were saying: "He is possessed by Beelzebul," and again: "It is through the prince of demons that he casts out demons."
d   And having called them to himself, he spoke to them in parables: "How can Satan cast out Satan? If a kingdom is divided against itself, such a kingdom cannot stand. And if a house is divided against itself, such a house cannot stand. And if Satan rises up against himself and is divided, he cannot stand but is finished. But no one can enter the strong man's house and plunder his property unless he first binds the strong man; then he can plunder his house. In truth (amen) I tell you: all things will be forgiven the sons of men: the sins and the blasphemies they shall blaspheme; but who-ever shall blaspheme against the Holy Spirit will not receive cancel-lation of his debt forever, but be guilty of an unending debt." For they were saying: "He has an unclean spirit."

S 21 (3:31-35)

a2 And his mother and his brothers come
b   and, standing outside, they send in to him and call him.

c   And the crowd was sitting around him, and they say to him: "Look! Your mother and your brothers are outside looking for you." He answers them: "Who are my mother and my brothers?" And looking around at those sitting about him he says: "Behold, my mother and my brothers! Whoever does the will of God, he is my brother and sister and mother."

S 20

a, b. "House," and "again the crowd gathers" echo S 12; secrecy is being maintained. Just as the size of the crowd was indicated in S 12 by the fact that the house could not contain it, so here its size is indicated by the fact that J lacked time even to eat (cf. S 31), the term *bread* being the index that will be very much to the fore in S 29–S 42.

c. "The scribes who came down from Jerusalem": the center of ideological power (SOC) sends scribes to conduct an inquiry; the narrative of J's practice and the enthusiasm of the CC had therefore reached Jerusalem. "They were saying: 'He is possessed'": this is the result of their reading (ANAL) of the question (Q2) raised in S 6: By what authority? By what power? The scribes thus recognize that J is delineating an antifield (SYMB), and they attempt to discern the power in it; they situate it on the side of pollution, of which Beelzebul (or Satan) is the center.[18] This accusation is a result of S 17, for it aims at establishing, in the minds of the C, the conditions needed for getting rid of J (STR AA). The second accusation selects, from the entirety of J's practice, the practice of expelling demons; this enables J to develop his answer.

d. "Having called them to himself": almost everywhere in the narrative this phrase has the DD for its object.[19] Here, however, the context shows that it is the scribes who are called so that J may reply to them. At the same time, the secrecy enables us to read that this call goes out to the DD who are among the C. This textual unclarity shows that the interweaving of S 20–S 21, which anticipates and prepares for S 22, is the site of a clearly defined separation of the DD from the AA, and is thus a STR site. STR and ANAL are thus articulated with one another, as is already the case in S 12–S 17.

"In parables": a new scheme for reading is set up, with the theory of it to be given in S 22: a narrative-fiction is recounted as a grill for reading the ACT narrative (this narrative fiction functions like the narrative of David in S 15). First, a parallel series of two parables challenges the reading by the scribes (namely, that the demons expel the demons): a kingdom whose leaders are at odds with one another and a house whose components are at odds with one another are both destined for destruction. If, then, the demons and their prince are on opposite sides, they are betraying their own interests and destroying themselves. Thus it is not Beelzebul but an X that is the key to deciphering the narrative of J. The third parable shows where this X is to be found, although he is not named; the naming is left up to the hearers, who are once again established as readers. The demons who "possess" sick bodies are the house of a strong man; if this house is plundered, then the X who succeeds in plundering it is stronger than the demons. In the logic of the Jewish ideology only God is stronger than Beelzebul; the hearers and readers may draw their own conclusion (ANAL).

"In truth I tell you": a frequently recurring expression, the function of which we shall examine later on (cf. below, p. 236). Note the future tense in "they shall blaspheme," indicating narratives to come, namely, the *ecclesial* narratives. The function of this future tense is to be located at the level of narrator/readers (cf. above, p. 96). "Forever," "an unending debt (or: sin)": these indicate the duration of the earthly narratives in the "age" *(aiōn)*.

The addition of "for they were saying: 'He has an unclean spirit,' " situates the conclusion reached in J's reading: the scribes blaspheme against the Holy Spirit who guides the STR of J; he is the X, the adversary of Satan (S 2), the authority who explains the ACT narrative of J. To be unable to read this is an unending debt; in S 22, the scribes, the possessors of ideological power (SOC), will be shown, through a parable, to be on the side of Satan. At the narrator/readers level, the destruction of Jerusalem and the abomination of desolation are the sign of this "unending debt" of the ruling classes in Israel.

S 21

a. "Having heard this, his relatives": The narrative of J's practice reaches Nazareth, and his kinsfolk read it: "He is out of his senses," that is, he is mad. Madness and possession are the same thing among the Jews; J is thus classified as belonging to the field of pollution and curse. The reading made by J's relatives (SOC) is like that of the scribes, and this is why S 20 and S 21 are interwoven. "To lay hold of him": STR of J's relatives; like the STR of the AA, it tends to stop the narrative.

b. "His mother and his brothers": the kinsfolk of J are specified. "Send in to call him": in order to lay hold of him, of his body. They cannot draw close to him because of the C that "was sitting around him"; this is an index of their nonfaith (cf. S 12). J reads the STR of his relatives and compares it with that of the people around him: "Behold, my mother and my brothers!" He is here pointing to the BAS *circle*; those who follow him are the *new* "house" or kinsfolk of J, as opposed to those who are his kinsfolk in the SOC, this apparatus for the production of the codes of the social formation. We must observe, however, that the DD are not explicitly distinguished from the C; that distinction and separation will be the object of the next sequence.

"Whoever does . . . ": the addition of "sister" to the list of relatives seems to locate this ending rather at the narrator/readers level.

Read in the light of this sequence, the scene "Jesus came from Nazareth in Galilee" (S 2a) has the meaning of a *break* between J and his "house" (cf. S 27).[20]

S 22 (4:1-34)

a1 And again he began to teach by the sea, and a very large crowd
gathers to him, so that having entered a boat he sits down there, on
the sea, and the entire crowd was on the shore by the sea. And he
taught them many things in parables,

b1 and said to them in his teaching: "Listen! The sower went out to
sow, and it happened as he sowed that some fell by the wayside, and
the birds came and ate it; and some fell on the rocky ground, where
it did not have much soil, and at once it sprang up because the soil
was not deep; and when the sun rose, it was scorched and, for lack of
roots, it withered. And some fell among the thorns, and the thorns
grew and choked it, and it did not yield fruit. And some fell on good
soil; it grew and increased and yielded fruit, and it produced
thirty-, sixty-, and a hundredfold." And he said: "He who has ears to
hear, let him hear."

c2 And when he was alone, those around him with the twelve asked
him about the parables.
   And he said to them: "To you is given the mystery of the kingdom
of God; but to those outside everything happens in parables, so that
'looking, they may look and not see, and hearing, they may hear and
not understand, lest they return and be forgiven.'"

c3 And he says to them: "Do you not understand this parable? Then
how will you know all the parables? The sower sows the word.
There are those who are beside the road when the word is sown;
when they have heard, Satan immediately comes and takes away the
word that has been sown in them. And those who have been sown
on rocky soil are the ones who, when they hear the word, immediately accept it with joy, but they have no root in themselves
and last only for a little while; if tribulation or persecution because
of the word comes, they immediately fall away. And there are
others who are sown among thorns: these are the ones who hear the
word but the cares of the world and the attraction of riches and the
desire for other things come in and choke the word, and it becomes
barren. And there are those who are sown on good ground: they
hear the word and accept it and bear fruit, thirty-, sixty-, and a
hundredfold.

c4 And he said to them: "A lamp does not come, does it, in order to be
placed under a bushel basket or under a bed? Does it not come in
order to be set upon the lampstand? For nothing is hidden except in
order to be revealed, nor does anything remain secret except in
order to manifest itself. He who has ears to hear, let him hear."

c5 And he said to them: "Consider what you hear. According to the
measure with which you measure, it will be measured unto you and

more will be added to you. For to him who has they will give, and from him who has not they will take away even what he has."

b2   And he said: "The kingdom of God is like a man who casts seed upon the ground. He sleeps and rises up, night and day, and the seed sprouts and grows without him knowing how. By itself the earth produces fruit: first the stalk, then the ear, then the full grain in the ear. And when the fruit is ready, he immediately sends out the sickle, for the harvest is at hand."

b3   And he said: "To what shall we liken the kingdom of God, or in what parable shall we present it? It is like a mustard seed, which, when sown in the ground, is the smallest of all the seeds on earth, but once sown, grows and becomes larger than any other vegetable and produces large branches so that all the birds of heaven can shelter in its shade."

a2   With the help of many such parables he preached the word to them, according to their capacity for hearing, and without parables he did not speak to them;

c1   but privately he explained everything to his disciples.

a. "And again he began to teach by the sea," "a very large crowd," "having entered a boat": these elements bring us back to S 18. If we reread S 18, we see that there were two different structures for the crowd. One is for the C of Galilee (S 18a, b) in which the C follows J as he moves along the sea (as in S 13b). The other (in S 18 c-e) is for the C that comes from further off; this C is brought together by the narrative of J's practice, and it witnesses various powerful practices. The first structure is to be found in S 13b, S 20a, b, S 31a, b, c, and S 45d, and it always ends with a teaching to the C. The second structure is to be found in S 6e, S 7e, S 10c, S 11b, S 25d, S 26a, S 25e, and S 34b; in all these, except for the last, there is question of STR instructions relative to the C.[21]

On the one hand, S 18 lacks the teaching of the crowd, but it is found here in S 22 (a1, b). On the other hand, the boat is a strategic element that is deployed here (S 22 a1; S 23a1), as in S 31a, f, and S 39a. We are therefore justified in concluding that S 18–22 contain an enshrinement, in which S 19–S 21 are the sequences enshrined, and in which, strictly speaking, S 22 should have been marked as S 19h and following (we did not do this because it would have been too inconvenient).

In other words, from a structural viewpoint, S 18 and S 22 form but a single sequence that strategically identifies J's hearers as C, AA, and DD. The enshrined sequences show the following dominants: STR (DD/C) for S 19, and ANAL (AA/C, DD) for S 20 and S 21; this explains the enshrinement; S 22 draws the strategic conclusions.

J sitting in the boat/the C "on the shore by the sea": the edge of the sea is thus a line separating J from the C and excluding the C from the BAS circle. Entry into this circle requires crossing the line; that is what the DD have done by leaving their trade (S 4, S 13) and their place in the SOC and its codes in order to follow J (cf. S 49). The *boat*, like the "in private" (S 22c1) and the *house* (cf. S 35) then become strategic sites (TOP) for the BAS reading of the ACT narrative and the *space DD* (TOP-STR). The analysis of S 22 will show us why this is so.

S 22 presents a lengthy discourse of J, the actant-hearers of which are not the same from beginning to end.

In a1 and a2 J is dealing with the C; opening/closing of scene b, which is enshrined by a1 and a2.

In c1 and c2, with "privately" and "when he was alone, those around him with the twelve," we are in the space DD.

Evidently, b1 is addressed to the C, and c3 to the DD. We need only divide up the other parables. Two criteria come into play. The first is that c4 and c5 are introduced by "he said to them," while b2, and b3 are introduced simply by "he said." The second is that b1, b2, and b3 have to do with the same image, that is, sowing/harvest, while c4 and c5, with their opposition of secret or hidden/manifest, and their emphasis on hearing, refer to a mystery (c2) and to J's words at the beginning of c3. We have, therefore, the following order: a1, b1, c2, c3, c4, c5, b2, b3, a2, and c1, with c1 being the beginning of scene c, which is enshrined between b1 and b2.

There is still one difficulty. "And he said to them: 'To you is given . . . be forgiven' " is intercalated between the opening words of c2 and the beginning of c3, although the latter should evidently follow immediately upon the former. There is thus a second little enshrinement. It may be suggested that this enshrinement belongs primarily to the level of narrator/readers, but the enshrinement in fact turns the parabolic teaching in Mark into a general theory.[22] In summary, then, we are to read b1 (c3), b2, and b3, and then c1, c2, c4, and c5; the enshrinement of c in b in easily explicable by the concern to bring c3 into harmony with b1, the interpretation of the parable with the parable itself.

From the textual viewpoint, what is a *parable*? We can immediately answer that every parable is a narrative-fiction. What is its function? It is a technique for reading (ANAL) the ACT narrative; that is, the narrative provides itself with a narrative *mirror* so that it can be read where there is a lacuna in it (or where there is a "mystery," a "secret," something "hidden"). That is why there is so much insistence on "understand," "know," "he who has ears to hear, let him hear," and "according to their capacity for hearing"—words that all relate to the ANAL code. Parabolic narratives are thus keys for reading the ACT narrative. Let us read them in this light.

A single image dominates the three parables of S 22b: that of an agricultural production, with its two working seasons (sowing and harvest) and an intermediate season (the time when the seed is growing in the earth). How do the three parables differ? They differ because in each only one of the three elements is the object of special consideration: the soil that receives the seed, the man who sows and harvest, and the seed, respectively.

First season: "The sower went out to sow." To what does this correspond? "The sower sows the word": this relates back to S 12b and S 22a2 ("he preached the word to them"). The sower is J, and the first season in the parabolic narrative points to the practice of teaching of J himself, and thus to at least a part of the ACT. Second season: in the fertile ground the seed "produced thirty-, sixty-, and a hundredfold," which indicates a rather extraordinary fruitfulness and blessing. When linked to the other two parables that have the "kingdom of God" as their explicit referent, this fruitfulness permits us to read the harvest as the final eschatological narrative in which the blessing reaches its culmination. Note that in the phrase "the full grain in the ear" (b2) "full" is a translation of the Greek *plērēs*, and this word recalls S 3, "the time is fulfilled." "The birds of heaven" (b3) indicates the MYTH. Finally, the intermediate season of the seed's growth or sterility, its *toil*, is the season for the linking up of the two narratives, the ACT and the eschatological. Now that we have the key to reading the parables, let us take them one by one.

b1, c3 (we shall read them together, so as not to take too long): the usual title is "the parable of the sower"; this is in fact a more suitable title for S 22b2, whereas the title here should be "the parable of the soils." The soils are the hearers of the word, and the parable gives the reason for the *diversity* of their responses to a word which all alike hear. There are four little narratives, corresponding to the four types of soil or hearers. The first type are linked to Satan who, like the birds, comes and removes the seed-word. These hearers are J's adversaries,[23] the scribes, Pharisees, and Herodians, whose hearts are hardened (S 16). The lesson of the reading prolongs the lesson of S 20: Those who are "guilty of an unending debt" (S 20d) are the scribes, the people on Satan's side. Here J reverses their reading, as though what is involved is a negative transference in the Freudian sense: you say that I blaspheme (S 12) and that I am possessed by Beelzebul, but in fact it is you who blaspheme and are on Satan's side.

The last type of soil or hearers are those who believe in the good news (S 3; by being converted), break with the system (SOC; S 4, S 13c, S 49d), and follow J in a practice that is fruitful in its turn (S 28, S 49); in short, these hearers are the disciples. In the ACT narrative, then, J reads the two radically opposed practices of the readers of his practice and explains them in terms of their relation to the system (SOC). The two extremes are those who have a power function within the system (ideological power, in this particular instance), namely, the AA, and, on the other hand, those who break with the system, the DD (cf. S 49 and S 50).

When we come to the two intermediate types of soil or hearers, in whom the break starts but is not carried through, we cannot find any correspondence in the narrative up to this point. As we shall see, however, the correspondence is in fact to Mark's readers at Rome after the Neronian persecution.[24]

Before passing on to S 22b2, let us look again at the equivalence established between *seed* and *word*. I noted in the commentary on S 6 that J's teaching practice is not specified, that is, the text does not tell us the object of this teaching.[25] No such specification is made in S 12b (where the teaching is called "word") or in S 31c or in S 45d; while in S 56b there will be a reading of the practice of the scribes. The teaching is made explicit only here in S 22, where it is once again called "word" (S 22a2), and in S 55d, where there will be another parable given as a reading of the ACT narrative. On the other hand, in S 10, as we have seen, "word" designated the narrative of J's practice; similarly, in S 42c, it will designate the (anticipated) narrative of his passion; in both cases, then, "word" designates the ACT narrative itself.

In our present text, moreover, the teaching likewise proves to be a reading of J's practice and its effects. What are we saying? We are saying that the seed-word does not comprise only the teaching of J but his entire *practice,* which, in its textual form as narrative, is to be read, that is, seen and heard. In short, the word is the narrative of J's practice, the ACT narrative itself. For it is by relation to this that the various actants are differentiated and classified as AA and DD.

The first parable (S 22b1) is for practical purposes, then, a theory of the narrative of J as given by the text itself. More accurately, it is a theory of the reading of this narrative. That is why the text here shifts to the level of narrator/readers, for the theory of the reading of Mark's narrative *also* concerns his readers, and it will be important for the later reading by bourgeois exegetes as well as for the reading we ourselves are in process of producing. It develops for us a theory of evangelical exegesis: *people read the Gospel in accordance with the space they occupy in the SOC or in the BAS.*

b2. We are still in the same parabolic field; the sower, therefore, is J, and the word relates him to the work of his practice in the soil, the work being on the one hand the effect of the seed-word, and on the other the effect of the soil, that is, the hearers (during the season that lasts until the eschatological harvest). It is usually said that we have here a parable of the seed that grows by itself.[26] It seems to me, however, that the decisive factor is precisely the relation of the sower to this work, which is done *without* him ("he sleeps and rises up, night and day"), and the relation is explained in the words: "without him knowing how." The relation is one of ignorance: the sower J is confronted with a "secret," something "hidden," a "mystery" (S 22c4, S 22c2), namely, the underground work accomplished by his practice in the *hearts* of his hearers, where it leads either to sterility or to fruitfulness.

The parable thus provides us with an important element in the theory of the text's narrativity, by locating its secret element, the factor which causes the problem, and which therefore is the foundation of the ANAL code as such and causes the narrative to be one that has to be read after the event, or in its effects. This last part of the statement holds not only for the various actants (AA, DD, C, or II) but even for the sower, J, himself. If even he does not know *in advance* the effects of his practice but is himself involved in the narrative at the point where the outcome is still undecided, then we can see why, from the reading he makes of each fruit (ANAL), he must derive a strategy (STR). The logic of successivity proper to narrative is respected even in the part played by the actant J.

b3. "To what shall we liken the kingdom of God?": in what mirror are we to read it? "In what parable shall we present it?": what narrative (of what practice or production, of what work) can be the means of presenting it? "It is like a mustard seed": here the hidden work of the seed is taken as the object of the parable. It is not any seed that J takes, however, but "the mustard seed" as distinct from "all the seeds on earth." Here we are to read: the practice of J as opposed to all the human practices, his narrative as opposed to the narratives recounted in the great narrative text that is constantly being reproduced in the ideological instance of the social formation.

"The smallest of all the seeds": J's narrative, then, is a narrative of littleness. Are not its principal actants (J, DD) recruited from the classes of the little people, the people who are ruled by others? And its beneficiaries are little people who are sick, bodies that are despised. Evidently, the register of the parable at this point is that of the antithesis between the SOC and its class practices, on the one hand, and the BAS, on the other. At the level of narrator/readers, this means: our ecclesial narratives about little people who are poor and persecuted by the repressive imperial apparatus, as opposed to the narratives of the great people of this world.

But this narrative of a practice relating to the little will end in greatness: the mustard seed, "once sown, grows and becomes larger than any other vegetable and produces large branches." "The birds of heaven": the MYTH, with its earth/heaven opposition. Here we have the third element of the theory of Mark's narrative, namely, the link between the narrative of J and the final, eschatological narrative, between this earthly narrative that is one of many, and the narrative that will crown them all. What is the link? The practice of J is the only one that will reach its completion in the kingdom of God; all other practices, those proper to the kingdoms of this world, practices dominated by their codes (SOC), will have become small and will be excluded.[27]

The text of Mark is here reading the destruction of the temple and the capture of Jerusalem. Consequently, at the narrator/readers level, it is not only the practice of the Roman imperialists but that of the governing classes in Israel that is being excluded from the kingdom of God.

A final remark that will be useful later on: in what grows, becomes large, and produces (moving upward from earth toward the birds of heaven), the logic of the development of the seed is manifested, and it connotes, in the spatial scheme proper to the MYTH, an *ascensional* movement that the eschatological events will close. This will be the movement of the Son of man himself, contrasting with the *descent* of the Spirit, this bird (a dove) descending from heaven (in S 2) and inaugurating the narrative of J at the MYTH level. Here we have an index of the Spirit's function in the subterranean, mysterious work of the seed-word.

This parabolic image, which is also rooted in the ancient biblical texts (the vine of Isaiah, for example),[28] is a metonymy: in a social formation in which agriculture is the dominant production, blessing takes the form, first of all, of superabundant fruits and the satiety these bring. Metonymy: an (essential) *part* of the social formation expresses the *whole*.

a2, c1. ANAL and STR imply one another, as we have just seen. From the fact, then, that these three parables are given as schemes for reading the ACT, we can infer that the parabolic discourse has likewise a STR function. It is this that finds expression in S 22a2 and S 22c1.

"With the help of many such parables he preached the word to them, *according to their capacity for hearing*, and without parables he did not speak to them": these words mark a strategic innovation relative to what has preceded. We are being told that the reading will no longer be given to the crowd directly, and that the function of the parables is to be a kind of veil, limiting the reading to the *capacity* of the crowd *to hear* the narrative. Here is the reason for the line drawn between J and the C: on this side of the line, people are to consider the narrative as it unfolds, listen to it, and then, in the soil of the heart, decide whether or not to cross the line and enter the space of the DD. For "privately he explained everything to his disciples": it is in the space of the DD that the reading can be done fully, in the space of the BAS circle. This last designation, "BAS circle," can be justified at this point, for the space of the DD is the space of the followers of J that will be fulfilled in the kingdom; their space, then, is *basileic space*. The DD are on J's side of the line that separates him from the C.

c2. "When he was alone": that is, without the crowd. "Those around him with the twelve": the *circle* is once again textually drawn; within it the twelve are distinguished from the other DD, but they are not its sole occupants. "Asked him about the parables. . . . Do you not understand this parable? Then how will you know all the parables?" "This parable": it is the link with the interpretation of b1 that justifies the enshrinement of c2–c5 between b1 and b2. The reading of the parable is not obvious, even in the BAS circle, and this surprises J. This lack of understanding will continue in the J/DD sequences.

"To you is given the mystery of the kingdom of God": that is, to you who surround me in the BAS circle, you who have crossed the line. "The mystery": that is, the subterranean work of the seed-word, of J's practice, "of the kingdom of God"; this work is linked to the eschatological narrative and announces the approach of the kingdom by means of its readable fruits. It is thus a word-narrative that proclaims the kingdom, and the voice (S 3) that had proclaimed it is replaced by the narrative of J's practice. As a matter of fact, there is a shift here that must be assigned to the narrator/readers level: the kingdom of God, which elsewhere in the text is always and exclusively connected with the end, is also, and already, the narrative of J's practice in this discourse of S 22.

"But to those outside": the focus shifts from the BAS circle to those who do not cross the line (AA, C), that is, the kinsfolk of J in S 21, the scribes in S 20, and, here, the C as well. "Everything happens in parables": this is the *strategic* novelty of S 22, which was already to be glimpsed in S 20. Henceforth, there will be *two teachings*, depending on whether the space is that of the C or of the DD. "So that 'looking . . . and be forgiven' ": those outside can only look at J's practice and hear of it. The citation from Isaiah (6:9–10) is to be read at the narrator/readers level: they have not *seen* or *understood*, and therefore have not been forgiven; Israel has been destroyed as a social formation, and has been dispossessed of the SYMB field with which the promise of eschatological blessing was connected.

c4. "Lamp under the bushel basket, under the bed/on a lampstand": this is a metaphor for hidden-secret/manifest. What is now being strategically reserved to you and kept from those outside will be made manifest to the whole world when the kingdom of God, the harvest, comes. "He who has ears to hear, let him hear": this was the conclusion of b1; one must have ears to hear properly (that is, to be good soil for) the narrative which everyone hears (cf. c3). This is the condition (namely, entry into the BAS circle) for the eschatological blessing and the superabundance of fruits. In other words, there is a *hidden* (BAS) text that must be deciphered in the *manifest* ACT text; connected with this is the term *mystery* that already occurs in the apocalyptic language of the Book of Daniel (2:19, 29), where a hidden text must be read in the manifest text of a dream.

c5. "Consider [be attentive to] what you hear. . . . According to the measure with which you measure": according to your grill for reading and hearing the narrative. "It will be measured unto you": your practice will be read by the same grill. "And more will be added to you": you will have thirty-, sixty-, or a hundredfold according to the measure of your reading and practice. "For to him who has" produced fruits, "they will give," according to the logic of the debt system (give and it will be given to you), whereas "from him who has not they will take away even what he has," according to the same logic (if you do not give, you will lose what you have).[29] Here we have an indication of the place of the DD (and the twelve) in J's STR: they in their turn are to spread J's practice and be sent for the circulation of the ACT narrative, its expansion in space (cf. S 28).

Retrospective Reading of S 2-S 22

This theory of the reading of the narrative (ANAL) and of its interaction with the STR will enable us to reread some STR points of the narrative thus far. In S 2, the MYTH discourse "You are my beloved son, on you my favor has rested" is addressed to J as an election, which J reads (ANAL) as a sending; the Spirit "drives" him into the desert ("drive" being a term that elsewhere indicates the STR in regard to unclean spirits; therefore still in the MYTH) and inaugurates the STR of J. The MYTH is thus at the starting point of the narrative of J. Before this point there is no narrative of J, since his coming to the Jordan resembles that of other members of the C. The heavenly "voice" and the Spirit single him out of the C and make him the principal actant.

On the other hand, while the narrative imposes itself on J as object of reading, in which he will read the power (the divine "favor") for his practice, the mythical discourse short-circuits the narrative and contradicts it. The same holds for the confession elicited from the unclean spirits (S 6, S 7, S 18) who do not need a narrative in order to read "Who J is" (Q 1). It is in order to avoid this short-circuiting of the narrative by the "confession" of the demons, that J imposes silence (STR). Light is also shed on S 8: the prayer of J is a time of reflection on the narrative, as if the latter were *new* even for J, at least as far as his success with the crowd goes. His STR with regard to the C (S 10–S 11), including his imposition of silence on the former leper, flows from this prayer, which is the site of the ANAL-STR of J.

Similarly, in S 12–S 17, and especially in regard to the "anger" of J in S 16, the practice of the AA against him is a narrative which he reads and from which he derives his STR of withdrawal from the towns and of clandestinity (separation from the space of the F/AA). Finally, the new STR of the parables, that is, the distinction between the space of the DD and the space of the C, is also the result of the reading J makes of the fruits resulting from his sowing in various soils, and of J's astonishment (which comes up several times: S 23, S 33, S 35, S 40, etc.) at the inability of the DD to understand. His dominant STR concern will be the DD's reading of his practice.

The Practice of J

We have identified the seed-word with the narrative of J's practice. But what is this practice? It is threefold. It is practice of *power* in relation to the bodies of the IIc that have been afflicted with uncleanness. It is a practice of teaching, that is, of the *reading* of this practice of power, for the latter raises three questions (the hidden text): what is this power? (Q 2); that is: who is J? (Q 1); and: what relation does it have to the final, eschatological narrative? (Q 3), its proper site being the ANAL code. Finally, J's practice is a practice of *subversion* of the Israelite symbolic field and order, and a strategy, deriving from this practice, for dealing with the C and the AA, its proper site being the STR code.

It is then a threefold practice that is really a single complex practice. It is therefore *word*, since the word always plays a determining role in it, either as imperative or as discourse. The threefoldness enables the practice to be related to different sites of the body: to the *hands* that touch (cf. S 27), the *eyes* that read and the *ears* that hear (S 22c2), and the *feet* that move about. We will find this semantics of the body again in S 46.

S 23 (4:35-5:1a)

a1 And he says to them this same day, when evening has come: "Let us go over to the other shore." And sending the crowd away, they take him as he was into the boat, and there were other boats with it.

b   A fierce gust of wind comes up, and the waves were beating upon the boat so that it began to fill up. And he was in the stern, sleeping on a cushion. And they wake him and say to him: "Teacher, are you not concerned that we are perishing?" And awakening, he rebuked the wind and said to the sea: "Silence! Be still!" And the wind fell, and there was a great calm.

c   And he said to them: "Why are you so cowardly? Have you no faith?" And they were seized with a great fear, and they said to one another: "Who is this man, that even the wind and the sea obey him?"

a2   And they reached the other shore of the sea,

    a. "This same day": a link with S 22 (and S 18). "When evening has come": the sequence occurs during the *night*, which connotes darkness, the infernal, danger, and also *fear*. "Sending the crowd away, they take him . . . into the boat": The *boat* acquires a STR status, both as the means of distancing J from the crowd, and as carrier of the BAS circle, and (ANAL) space for reading ("Have you no faith?")

    b. "A fierce gust of wind, etc.": the sea as danger. "Sleeping/they wake him": SYMB (powerlessness/power of the body). "Teacher": the current reading of the ACT (S 46, S 54, S 55g, etc.) and the answering of Q 1 are taking place, since teacher = Messiah. "That we are perishing": the curse of danger (cf. S 6c). "He rebuked": cf. S 6 for this STR term (cf. S 42, S 51). "Silence! Be still!": cf. S 6; the sea is thus infernal and treated like the unclean spirits (MYTH). "The wind fell, and there was a great calm": the blessing; the awakened J is powerful.

    c. "So cowardly, no faith?": fear is seen as being, in opposition to *faith*, on the side of nonunderstanding; so in S 45 and S 73. "Who is this Man?": Q 1. "That even the wind and the sea obey him?": Q 2. Here we have a prolongation of S 22c2. The ANAL questions will henceforth be asked by the DD, until the high point in S 42 (confession of Peter). Q 2 relates back to S 20: J is the stronger in the conflict with the infernal.

S 24 (5:1b-20)

a1   the land of the Gerasenes. And as he was leaving the boat,

b   there came from the tombs to meet him a man with an unclean spirit. He had his dwelling in the tombs, and no one was any longer able to bind him even with a chain, for frequently they had bound him with fetters and chains, and he had broken the chains and snapped the fetters, and no one was strong enough to overcome him; and throughout the night and the day, in the tombs and on the hills, he was crying out and bruising himself with stones.

c   And seeing the Jesus from afar, he ran and prostrated himself before him and cried out in a loud voice: "What have I to do with you, Jesus, son of the Most High God? I implore you by the God not to torment me." For he was saying to him: "Impure spirit, go out of the man!" And he asked him: "What is your name?" And he says to him: "My name is Legion, for we are many." And he urgently appeals to him not to send them from the land.

d   Now there was there on the hillside a large herd of swine that were feeding. And they entreated him, saying: "Send us to the swine so that we may enter them." And he permitted them to do so. And the unclean spirits went and entered the swine, and the herd rushed down the steep bank into the sea, about two thousand of them, and they drowned in the sea. And their herdsmen fled

e   and told of the event in the town and hamlets, and people came to see what had happened.

f   And they come to the Jesus and see the demoniac sitting, dressed and in his right mind, the one who had the legion, and they grew fearful. And the eyewitnesses told what had happened to the demoniac, and about the swine. And they began to implore him to leave their district.

a2   And as he was entering the boat,

g   the man who had been a demoniac begged him to stay with him. He did not send him away, but said: "Go to your house and family and tell them all that the Lord has done for you and how he took pity on you."

h   And he went away and began to proclaim in the Decapolis all that the Jesus had done for him, and all were astonished.

a. "The land of the Gerasenes": Gerasa is in the Decapolis, a pagan area. The text indicates the pagan character by the presence of the swine, which were unclean animals and therefore not kept in Israel.[30]

b. "A man with an unclean spirit": his present state is described in detail, unlike his state after the demons have been expelled.[31] "Tombs": space of the dead. A man who cannot be controlled: therefore a danger to the town and to life itself; the man's strength links him to the parable of the strong man(S 20); his aggressiveness toward himself is a form of death and madness. The "cries" he utters (like the unclean spirits in S 6 and S 45) are evidence of madness as read in the MYTH. In contrast is "the demoniac sitting, dressed and in his right mind," and thus on the side of life. In short: Ic/Ib.

c. "What have I to do with you, Jesus, son of the most high God? I implore you not to torment me": as in S 6; the absence of the command to remain silent is explained by the absence of the C. "My name is Legion": cf. S 6, "to destroy *us*"; "an army of demons" is "working" in a given region (MYTH). "Unclean spirits," "the swine," "drowned in the sea": a series of pollutions.

e. "Told of the event, " "came to see": the narrative brings the C together. "Fearful": fear = nonfaith. The term "begged" ("appealed," "entreated," "implored") occurs four times in the sequence; when added to the prostration of the demoniac, it indicates that J is being recognized as "powerful," stronger in fact than Satan (cf. S 20).

g-h. "Go to your house and family": no break but a reintegration, yet also a "missionary" task, to "tell them all that the Lord has done for you." The narrative picks this up in "all that Jesus had done for him."

J is on the side of the Lord, and the Lord is at work in the narrative of J; J's power comes from God. Here again, no command to be silent, as in S 10, but, on the contrary, a command to broadcast the news; they are in pagan territory, where J is in no danger.

S 25a-d (5:21-24a)

a   And when the Jesus had once again reached the other shore,

b   a large crowd gathered around him, and he remained by the sea.

c   And one of the leaders of the synagogue, Jairus by name, comes to him and, on seeing him, falls at his feet and urgently begs him, saying: "My little daughter is at the point of death; come, lay hands on her so that she may be saved and live."

d   And he went with him, and a great crowd followed him

S 26 (5:24b-34)

a   and pressed in on him from all sides.

b   And a woman with a flux of blood for twelve years, who had suffered much at the hands of many physicians and had spent all she had to no avail but instead was becoming worse, having heard what was being said about the Jesus, came behind him in the crowd and touched his garment. For she said: "If I touch at least his garment, I shall be saved." And immediately the source of her blood was dried up, and she knew in her body that she was healed of the infirmity.

c   And immediately the Jesus, knowing in himself the power that had gone out from him, turned in the crowd and said: "Who touched my garment?"
   And his disciples said to him: "You see the crowd pressing on you, and yet you say, 'Who touched me?' " And he continued looking about to see the woman who had done it.

d   Then the woman, fearful and trembling, knowing what had happened to her, came and fell down before him and told him the whole truth. But he said to her: "Daughter, your faith has saved you; go into peace (abundance), and be free of this illness."

S 25 e-a2 (5:35-6:1a)

e   He is still speaking when they come from the home of the leader of the synagogue and tell him: "Your daughter has died. Why bother the teacher any longer?" But the Jesus, hearing what has been said, says to the leader of the synagogue: "Do not be afraid, only believe." And he allowed no one to accompany him except the Peter and James and John, the brother of James.

f   And they reach the house of the leader of the synagogue, and he sees the uproar and the people weeping and uttering loud cries. And entering, he says to them: "Why the uproar and weeping? The child is not dead but sleeping." And they laughed at him. But having ejected them all,

g   he takes with him the father and mother of the child and his own companions, and goes in to where the child was lying. And taking the child's hand, he says to her: *"Talitha koum,"* which means, in translation, "Little girl, I tell you: arise." And immediately the little girl stood up and walked, for she was twelve years old. And they were beside themselves with great amazement. And he sternly commanded them that no one should know of this, and he told them to give her food.

a2. And he departed from there,

Gr. *anakeimenon,* "lying" (S 25 g) is a variant reading of several manuscripts, but is not noted in Aland's edition.

S 25

a, b. "Again," "the other shore": Galilee → pagans → Galilee. The C gathers, but outside the two structures characteristic of it,[32] for its function here is not that of an actant; the crowd is simply part of the scenario.

c. "One of the leaders of the synagogue, Jairus by name": an actant who occupies a position of power (SOC), but whose name is given to show that it is the individual and not the function that is of concern here. This is an indication (as in S 49, S 55i, S 72) that "faith" is possible for such people of power when regarded as individuals; in other words, their class position does not necessarily exclude them. "Lay hands . . . be saved and live": SYMB.

(We shall pass over S 26, which is enshrined here, and return to it below.)

e. "Is at the point of death, come"/"has died, why bother?": the account asserts the death of the little girl, so that there is a "resurrection" and not simply a "cure." "Do not be afraid, only believe": fear/faith, cf. S 23; the individual is urged to overcome fear in the face of death (the supreme form of pollution), for faith is not halted even by death. "He allowed no one to accompany him": the C is eliminated from the scene. "Peter, James, and John": a more limited circle within the circle of the twelve.

f. "Uproar, weeping, cries": in the face of death. "The child is not dead but sleeping": J plays down (STR) the effect he is going to produce. "They laughed at him": the narrative heightens the impact of the "resurrection" that is to follow by repeating the theme of nonfaith that was enunciated in S 23 c.

g. "Father, mother, his own companions": STR of secrecy concerning the narrative, continuation of the playing down of the effect J will produce. "The child's hand": SYMB/BAS, *touching;* same for "lying/stood up." "*Talitha koum*": Realism by citing the Aramaic words and providing a translation; emphasis also on the importance of the imperative, of power. "She was twelve years old": the age at which marriage became possible.[33] The child is thus restored not only to life but also to *sexuality* and the table ("he told them to give her food"), or, in short, to blessing (Ic → Ib). "Beside themselves with great amazement": strong emphasis on the passage from death to life. "No one should know of this": STR of silence on the ACT, as in S 10. Note here what we might call the hesitation of the text: on the one hand, the power of J's practice is stressed as a "resurrection," but on the other hand it is attenuated by J's strategy. We will return to this point later on.[34]

S 26

a. "A great crowd followed him and pressed in on him from all sides": J is as it were bathed in the C. Note the "followed him" which elsewhere (from S 4 on) is almost always used of the DD.

b. "A woman with a flux of blood": and therefore unclean.[35] "For twelve years": this confirms the remark made with regard to the young girl and her reaching the age of twelve (in S 25 g), for here too the blessing of the woman will involve her restoration to her sexuality. "Suffered much . . . becoming worse": The description of the illness is emphasized; sequences 24–26 are distinguished from S 7, S 10, S 12, and S 16 by this abundance of detail. "Having heard": the narrative of J's practice is what brings her. "Came behind him in the crowd": the C is an obstacle, as in S 12; the woman's strategy for reaching the body of J will gain for her the response "Your faith has saved you."

"Touched his garment": this, according to the SYMB, makes J himself unclean. "For she said: 'If I touch him I shall be saved' ": this goes counter to the logic of the SYMB. "And immediately . . . she was healed": the narrative confirms this anti-SYMB logic. "She knew in her body": the body (SYMB) is the site of salvation; *touching,* which is mentioned four times (in S 25–S 26), links the body of the Ic and the body of J, but it works in reverse, subverting the Jewish SYMB field, as in S 10 and also in S 25 (where touching a corpse should make J unclean but instead raises the dead child to life).

c. "Turned," "the disciples," "the crowd pressing on you," "continued looking about": J is the center of the large circle formed by the C; the DD form a smaller circle of "bodyguards" for J. The woman has touched the center of the BAS circle.

d. "Fearful and trembling": because, being unclean and touching the clean, she subverted the SYMB. "Knowing . . . told him the whole truth": The ACT narrative, connoted as "truth"; previously, in S 10, it was connoted as "word," where the SYMB ("cleansed") was likewise emphasized. "He said to her": J reads the narrative (ANAL). "Saved": = healing. "Go into peace": blessing.[36]

"Be free of this illness": the imperative comes after the fact, since the illness has already been taken from the woman, thus giving the narrative something of the atmosphere of magic. It is the working of the "power" or might of J's body that has been shown in the narrative, and this comes through all the more strongly because of the absence of any word of command. J inquires into the narrative: a good example of the "without him knowing how" of the parable in S 22b2. His reading of the "truth" ("Your faith has saved you") links *faith* (the effect on the woman of the earlier narrative) with the effect of the work of the power that has gone out of J's body. This twofold work is the subterranean work of the seed-word, and exemplifies the articulation of what P. Ricoeur calls hermeneutics and energetics.[37]

S 27 (6:1b-6a)

a   and comes into his own country, and his disciples follow him.
b   And when the sabbath came, he began to teach in the synagogue; and the many hearers were amazed and said: "Whence does he get all this, and what wisdom has been given to him so that works of power are done by his hands? Is he not the carpenter, the son of the Mary and the brother of James and Joses and Jude and Simon? And are not his sisters here among us?" And they were scandalized (were caused to fall) because of him. And the Jesus said to them: "A prophet is not dishonored except in his own country, among his kinsmen and in his own house." And he could do no work of power there, except to heal a few sick people by laying hands on them. And he was amazed at their unbelief.

a. "Comes into his own country": Nazareth in Galilee (S 2). "His disciples *follow* him": "follow" is one of the terms that defines the place of the DD in the STR.

b. "Sabbath . . . synagogue . . . teach . . . hearers were amazed": link with S 6, which confirms the questions (ANAL) that follow: Q 2 (on his wisdom and the works of power *done by his hands*[38]) and Q 1 ("is this not. . . "). "The carpenter": the trade of J, which places him in the working class, the dominated class (SOC). "The son of Mary": J's mother is named here. "The brother of James . . . ": his brothers are likewise named. "His sisters": thus, the "house" of J (SOC). "They were scandalized because of him": literally, they were "caused to fall" (SYMB). The question (ANAL) is asked, but the answer is not given. If the answer were expressed, it would be: the carpenter, the son of Mary, etc., is a prophet. But the questioners are unable to read the passage from the one to the other (S 2 recounts this passage as the work of the MYTH).

"And the Jesus said to them": he reads their unbelief, which, according to the narrative, he did not expect ("he was amazed at their unbelief"). "A prophet is not dishonored . . . his own house": that is, in the place of the (ideological) production of the codes of the social formation. This means that the place of reading determines the unbelief: a place of repetition and custom, giving rise to an inability to read the new; the codes of the social formation are what prevents the reading of the narrative, and it is the blinding power of these codes that is the object of J's amazement.

"And he could do no work of power": this corrects the impression of magic given in S 26. Faith (reading of the narrative in the BAS) is decisive for healings and blessing ("your faith has saved you"). Here there is a clarification of the town/outside the town STR: the town is the place of domination by the ruling powers (TOP) and the place of unbelief; this will be true of Jerusalem. In addition, if we recall that the "house," or kinship, means the "same flesh" (SYMB),[39] we must conclude that the flesh, in the sense of blood relationship, prevents the BAS relation to the body of J; this is why there must be a break with blood relationships (cf. S 49 d).

S 28a-c (6:6b-13)

a   And he traveled through the villages round about, teaching.
b   And he called the twelve to himself and began to send them out two by two, and he gave them authority over the unclean spirits. And he instructed them to take nothing for the journey but a single staff: no bread or knapsack or money in the belt, but to wear sandals on their feet and not to wear two tunics. And he said to them: "Wherever you enter a house, remain there until you leave the place. And if a place does not welcome you and the people in it do not listen to you, depart from it and shake the dust from your feet as a testimony against them."
c   And going forth, they proclaimed that people should be converted, and they expelled many demons, and anointed many sick with oil and healed them.

a. "And he traveled through the villages": the villages (outside the towns), together with the shore of the sea, prolong the STR of S 11 and S 18; the villages will come up again in the narrative about Galilee (S 31, S 34, S 40, S 41). "Round about": the Greek *kuklō* literally means "in a circle." The figure of the circle once again is inscribed to characterize the movement of this scene; it marks the influence of the BAS circle and the expansion of J's circulation. "Teaching": his teaching is still not made explicit.

b. "He called the twelve to himself and began to send them out": link with 19; the present STR was announced there, and c, below, describes it being carried out. "Two by two": collective action (cf. S 4). "He gave them authority over the unclean spirits": the field of J expands by limiting that of Satan; so the parable of S 20 read the situation. Note that while the MYTH (S 2) opposed the Holy Spirit to Satan (evil spirit) according to the scheme taken over from the Persians,[40] the narrative (ACT) opposes J to Satan. The STR of

J reflects the STR of the Spirit, and therefore the practice of the twelve will do the same.

"And he instructed them": strategic instructions. "A staff": for a traveler. "No bread or knapsack or money or two tunics": travelers who are *poor,* unlike the merchants and unlike the pilgrims who are the usual travelers (SOC). The contrast with the system is accentuated, prolonging the "carpenter" of S 27 and the "leaving everything" of S 4 (cf. S 49); there is no *money* involved in the practice of the BAS circle (cf. D 31). "Sandals on their feet," "dust from your feet": as noted in regard to S 22, the *feet* signify, by metonymy, the strategic level of BAS practice, the practice of the traveler. "Two tunics": the bodies of the twelve are a prolongation of J's body to which they are related (cf. S 19: "so that they might be with him").

"Whenever you enter a house, remain there": counterpart of the STR instructions; the house being the (economic) site of the table, the twelve will be fed and housed by those who welcome them. "Welcome/not listen" (=not welcome): contrast of soils (S 22b1). "Shake the dust. . . as a testimony against them": one who welcomes washes the feet of the guests; the dust on the unwashed feet will be testimony of nonwelcome at the final narrative.

c. "Should be converted": cf. S 1, S 3; conversion (to welcome and listen) is the crossing of the line separating J and the twelve from the C. "Anointed with oil": an addition by comparison with S 19; the use of oil as a means of healing, in contrast to J's use only of his hands, shows the subordination of the twelve to J. "Healed them": their practice, too, bears fruit (c/b).

S 29-S 30

These two sequences are enshrined between S 28c and S 28d. The period of the sending represents a pause in the narrative, which will be set in motion again in S 31, but in a new direction. S 28 completes S 18–S 19, etc. S 29 takes advantage of the pause to prepare for S 31–S 42. S 30 is chained with S 29a, thus marking both the continuity with and the break between the practice of J and the twelve, on the one hand, and the practice of John the Baptist, on the other.

S 29 (6:14-16)

a1 **And the King Herod heard,**
b   **for his name was becoming well known, and they were saying: "John the Baptist has been raised from the dead, and that is why the powers are at work in him." Others were saying: "He is Elijah." Still others were saying: "He is a prophet like the other prophets."**
a2 **Having heard, Herod said: "The man I beheaded, John, it is he who has been raised."**

a1. "King Herod heard": the narrative reaches even into the court of Herod, which is the center of political power in Galilee.

b. "For his name": carried by the narrative. "And they were saying": the readings (ANAL) by the C in answer to Q 1, "Who is Jesus? This will be the dominant question in S 31–S 42; it was raised in S 23 in relation to the DD. "John the Baptist has been raised from the dead": along with a2, this marks S 30 as being retrospective. "That is why the powers are at work": Q 1 tied to Q 2; already then, in the text of Palestine, "resurrection from the dead" connotes "powerful practice."[41] "Elijah": cf. S 43. "A prophet": cf. S 27. None of these readings is correct, for S 1 has already indicated that J is "more powerful" than John, and "Elijah" connotes John as precursor of the eschatological Messiah (S 43). "Like the other prophets": indicates the rejection of eschatologism.

The C thus fails to read the narrative of J. It does read the power, and this fascinates it (cf. S 12; in fact, this is one reason for J's STR with regard to the narrative[42]), but it does not (according to S 16) read the liberation of the body (Ic/Ib) as a proclamation of the eschatological blessing, as a salvation that announces salvation (cf. S 42).

a2. Herod's reading follows that of the C. "The man I beheaded": guilt. Introduces S 30 ("For").

S 30 (6:17-29)

a   For it was Herod himself who had sent to arrest the John and bind him in prison, because of Herodias, wife of Philip his brother, whom he married. For the John told the Herod: "You are not permitted to have your brother's wife." The Herodias hated him and wanted to kill him but could not, for the Herod feared the John, knowing him to be an upright and holy man, and protected him; after listening to him, he was greatly perplexed, and it was with pleasure that he listened to him.

b   And a propitious day came when Herod, for his anniversary, held a banquet for his courtiers and officers and the leading men of Galilee. The daughter of this same Herodias came in and danced, and pleased the Herod and those reclining with him. The king said to the young girl: "Ask me for anything you want, and I will give it to you"; and he swore an oath to her: "Whatever you ask me I will give you, even if it be half of my kingdom."

c1 She went out and said to her mother: "What shall I ask for?" And she said: "The head of John the Baptist."

b2 Returning immediately in haste to the king she asked, saying: "I want you to give me immediately the head of John the Baptist on a dish." The king became very sad, but because of the oath and the guests he did not want to refuse her. And the king immediately sent an executioner and ordered him to bring his head;

d   and he went and beheaded him in the prison

b3 and brought his head on a dish and gave it to the young girl,

c2 and the young girl gave it to her mother.
e   And his disciples, having heard of it, came and took his body and
    placed it in a tomb.

a. A retrospect that links this sequence to S 1a2; it is difficult to see where
the narrative could have inserted this sequence except at this pause. Herod's
incest: in the logic of the Jewish SYMB, John denounces the king's pollution,
and is answered by the desire of Herodias to murder him (debt, SYMB).
Herod's ambivalence: he keeps John's body in chains, but listens to his word
with pleasure. "Perplexed": he is torn between the pleasure connected with
his desire for the body of Herodias and the pleasure connected with the word
of John, "an upright and holy man," one who is clean (SYMB); the SYMB
engenders the sense of guilt that dominates his reading of the narrative of J (S
29a2).

The circle ("the court") of political power is described as polluted (by the
interplay of desires), as repressive (of the body of John), and as ambivalent.
The following scenes will be circumscribed by this circle.

b1. "A propitious day": for setting in motion the interplay of desires and for
overcoming the obstacles opposed to this (the Law, and the pleasure derived
from listening to the word that conveys the Law: "you are not permitted").
"Banquet": the circle of the courtiers, officers, and leading men (SOC); the
banquet that will end in murder. "Danced and pleased Herod": the desire of
Herod and those present is directed to the body of the young woman; dance,
too, inscribes its circles. "Anything you want": Herod becomes an ac-
complice of the young woman's desire, but she draws back to let the desire of
her mother be effective; her mother is outside the circle, and now introduces
murder into the circle and the banquet ("on a dish").

b2. "Sad": the king is ambivalent now, just as he had been perplexed in the
face of the Law.

d. "Beheaded John": with the body's life the word too is extinguished, since
the head is the place where the two unite.

b3. "And brought his head": the head travels the circuit of desires in
reverse; the court is the site of desires focused on death. Note that all the
digressions of the narrative into the circle of political power (here, S 59, S 66,
S 68, S 71) are marked by this pursuit of *death*; this power (SOC) is thus
clearly characterized as repressive and murderous. Note, too, that Herod's
ambivalence will be matched by that of Pilate (S 68).

e. There is a contrast between the death of John and that of Jesus, a contrast
highlighted by the identification of the two men in S 29a2 and the allusion to
the resurrection. John's narrative will end in the tomb, while that of J will
begin again after the burial. Moreover, the disciples of John gather around his
tomb, while the "apostles" of J are returning from their mission (S 28d). The
fasting (absence of table) of John's disciples (S 14) contrasts with the
superabundance of the table of the apostles (S 31). The narrative of Mark
affirms the superiority of J over John, of the practice of J over the voice which

John has (not) ceased to be, and of the Messiah over his precursor, his Elijah (S 43): J is more powerful than John (S 1).

S 28d (6:30-31)

d   And the apostles (those sent) gather around the Jesus and told him all that they had done and taught. And he says to them: "Come apart to a desert place and rest a little." For the people coming and going were so many that they did not have time even to eat.

d. The "apostles": this is the only time the term "apostles" appears in Mark's text; it will later become a technical term for distinguishing the *function* of the twelve (proclaimers) from that of the DD (followers).[43] "Told him all that they had done and taught": the narrative of their practice as envoys; again, for the only time in Mark, the sender here becomes the listener. He does not become a disciple, but we are told of his reading (ANAL) of the fruits of his narrative and thus we are told of his ignorance (cf. S 22b2, S 26). "Come apart to a desert place": repeated in S 31a. The desert (S 8) is a place where distance can be had for reading/strategy, as in S 32 (the prayer on the mountain). The strategy in question is, first of all, STR in regard to the C; the narrative tells us the crowd is so large that it leaves no time for eating and resting.

S 31 (6:32-45)

a   And they set out in the boat for a desert place apart. And seeing them departing, many understood,
b   and from all the cities they came there on foot and got ahead of them.
c   And disembarking he saw a great crowd and pitied them because they were like sheep without a shepherd. And he began to teach them at great length.
d   Since it was already late, his disciples came to him and said: "This is a desert place, and it is late; send them away so that they may go to the farms and villages round about and buy themselves something to eat." But he answered them: "You give them something to eat." And they say to him: "Shall we go and buy two hundred denarii worth of loaves and feed them?" But he says to them: "How many loaves do you have? Go and see." And, having gotten the information, they say: "Five loaves, and two fishes."
e   And he bade them have them all sit down in parties on the green grass. And they reclined in groups of hundreds and fifties. And taking the five loaves and two fishes and looking up to heaven he said the blessing and broke the loaves and gave them to the disciples to distribute to them, and he divided the two fishes for all. And all

ate and were filled. And they gathered twelve baskets full of fragments of the bread and fishes. And those who ate the loaves were
five thousand men.

f   And immediately he compelled his disciples to enter the boat and
go before him to the other shore, to Bethsaida, while he himself
dismisses the crowd.

a, b. J's strategy is thwarted by the C, whose strategy (from S 8 on) is to *look
for* J (S 12, S 18, S 20). The parallel with S 8 suggests that S 28 marked the
close of the mission in Galilee (S 28 completing S 19) and that S 32 marks the
beginning (STR) of the circulation of J outside of Galilee. The strategy of the
C is particularly emphasized here; without it, there would be no place for S
31d and e, and yet this will be a key sequence in S 31–S 42; consequently, the
STR of the C is going to influence the course of the narrative.[44]

c. Seeing the crowd, J changes his STR and teaches at great length. "Pitied
them because they were like sheep without a shepherd": the STR of the C,
then, is to find a shepherd, a guide, perhaps a political leader; it is a STR in
which Zealotry may be discerned (STR Z).[45] This is precisely what the STR
of J with regard to the C has always sought to avoid; he tries to avoid it again at
the end of the sequence (S 31f). This will be confirmed in S 45i. In S 8, the
four disciples, and Simon in particular, are the spokesmen for the C; their
STR, then, prolongs that of the C and is also to be regarded as STR Z.

d. "Farms and villages": TOP characteristic of sequences S 31–S 42. "Send
them . . . buy": the C is hungry (Cc). "You give them something to eat": J sets
up an opposing STR that is inscribed in the logic of the debt system (SYMB),
by substituting "you" for "them," "give" for "buy." "Two hundred denarii":
the DD's answer remains within the framework of the monetary system
(SOC); they understand the first substitution but not the second. "How many
loaves do you have?": the correlative of *giving* is not *buying* but *having*. "Five
loaves and two fishes": note the emphasis on numbers throughout this
sequence (two hundred, five and two, hundreds and fifties, two, twelve, five
thousand); on the one hand, these numbers indicate the extent of the "multiplication" and thus the power and superabundance that can require such
numbers (as in S 38 and S 49); from another viewpoint, the numbers give an
air of reality and verisimilitude.

e. "In parties. . . . in groups": the C is arranged for the meal. (This arrange-
ment replaces the *table*; the scene is a desert place where there is a great deal
of room.) "Taking the five loaves": MYTH as in S 37 but not in S 38 or S 62.
"He said the blessing": instead of words of command; nowhere else (except in
S 37) does J "pray" before deeds of power; the sequences of power from S 31
to S 41 contain indications of "difficulty" felt by J (S 31, S 36, S 37, S 41).
"Broke the loaves": again, hands and loaves, the symbolic gesture in this
narrative (cf. S 40: "when *I broke*").

"Gave them to the disciples to distribute to them": the DD are connecting
links between the center of the BAS circle and the C. "And the two fishes": a

narrative equivalent to the one about the loaves, with the fishes being related to the "fishers" (S 4); this element will not occur in S 40 or S 62, and the narrative will not assign a value to the fishes as it will to the loaves, at the level of the ANAL code; the mention of the fishes, therefore, again lends realism to the picture. "And all ate and were filled": Cb; the blessing was invoked and has been granted (cf. S 40). "And they gathered": there is superabundance even beyond repletion. "Five thousand men": the effect of the multiplication is emphasized, but the narrative is one of "filling" rather than of "multiplication."[46]

f. Insistence (STR) on the sending away of the DD ("he compelled" them) and of the C (twice mentioned). The STR of J is clearly different from STR Z.[47]

S 32 (6:46)

And after taking leave of them, he went to the mountain to pray.

"He went to the mountain": place closest to heaven in the MYTH[48]; S 63 will likewise connect the mountain with prayer, a fact which indicates that S 19 and S 43 also imply prayer. "To pray": we noted that the STR of the C in S 31b has influenced the course of the narrative; consequently the narrative of the filling of the C has been forced on him as something unexpected. The sending away of the C and the DD (cf. S 8 and S 64) shows the strategic importance of S 31. This is why, as in S 8, S 19, S 43, S 64, J must read (ANAL) and decide (STR); in short, he must *pray*. The desert place (S 8; cf. S 28d) and the mountain are the privileged sites of prayer (ANAL/STR), outside the towns; the latter, privileged in the SOC, are sites where one cannot pray.[49] J's action is a further subversion of the TOP-SOC.

S 33 (6:47-53a)

a1   When evening had come, the boat was in the middle of the sea, and he was alone on the land.
b   And seeing them becoming exhausted from rowing, since the wind was against them, at about the fourth watch of the night he comes to them walking on the sea, and he was going to pass them by. But they, seeing him walking on the water, thought it was a ghost and they cried out. For they all saw him and were frightened. But he immediately spoke to them and said to them: "Courage, it is I (I am), do not be afraid." And he got into the boat with them, and the wind fell. And they were utterly astonished, for they had not understood concerning the loaves, but their heart was dulled.
a2   And, having made the crossing,

Gr.: *Egō eimi* (in b) here means "it is I" (as in S 58); in S 66 it will mean "I am."

a1. "Evening/night": As in S 7–S 8 (cf. S 23). "The boat . . . on the land": unlike S 23 where J is with them in the boat.

b. "Exhausted from rowing, since the wind was against them": sea connotes curse, as in S 23. "Walking on the sea": power of J over the sea, the infernal. "A ghost, and they cried out": the cries recall the unclean spirits (S 6, S 24, S 44), while the ghost (ANAL) puts J on the side of the demonic (cf. S 20–S 21). "Frightened . . . do not be afraid": fear = nonfaith; cf. S 23 which opened up, in the space of the DD, the Q 1: Who is this?

"It is I": in S 58 and S 66, the phrase connotes the Messiah; here, then, it indicates the ANAL code (reply to Q 1), and corrects the reading made by the DD (ghost/I, more powerful than the sea). "The wind fell": the sea connoted as blessing; however, it is the walking on the water that is decisive as ACT. "Utterly astonished . . . understood nothing": the ANAL. "Concerning the loaves . . . dulled": in the ACT of S 31, then, there was something that required understanding; the ANAL (Q 1) is related to the loaves (cf. S 40). "Heart dulled": like that of the AA in S 16 (cf. S 40).

c. "Having made the crossing": they sailed "to Bethsaida" according to S 31f, but they now land at Gennesaret (S 34a), for the wind has forced them to change direction. They will reach Bethsaida in S 41.

S 34 (6:53b-56)

a   They came to land at Gennesaret and dropped anchor there. And when they had debarked,

b   immediately those who recognized him ran about through that whole area and began to bring the sick on their beds to where they heard he was. And wherever he went into villages or towns or farms, they brought the sick to the public squares and begged him to at least let them touch the hem of his garment. And all who touched him were saved.

a. The crossing is in the opposite direction from that of S 31a. The C had made the journey on foot, and J intended to do the same, but the storm made him go by sea. Thus we are still dealing with the same C.

b. "Recognized him . . . heard that he was": the narrative once again brings the C together. The C brings the sick; this is the other structure for a C (cf. S 22a) as compared with S 31b, c. "Villages or towns or farms:" the TOP of this major sequence. "On their beds": cf. S 12. "Touch the garment": cf. S 26. "Touched . . . saved": Ic → Ib; touching (SYMB).

S 35 (7:1-24a)

a   And the Pharisees and some of the scribes came from Jerusalem and gathered around him,

b   and seeing that some of his disciples were eating bread with unclean, that is, unwashed hands—for the Pharisees and all the Jews

do not eat without first carefully washing their hands, thus observing the tradition of the elders, and they do not eat what comes from
the market without first sprinkling it, and there are many other
traditions they observe, such as the washing of cups, pitchers, and
copper vessels—

c   the Pharisees and the scribes ask him: "Why do your disciples not
act according to the tradition of the elders but eat bread with
unclean hands?" He said to them: "Rightly did Isaiah prophesy
about you hypocrites, as it is written: 'This people honors me with
their lips but their heart is far from me; in vain do they worship me,
for they teach doctrines that are precepts of men.' You set aside the
commandment of God and observe the tradition of men." And he
said to them: "You are clever at setting aside the commandment of
God so that you may observe your own tradition. For Moses said:
'Honor your father and your mother' and 'He who curses his father
or mother is to be punished by death,' but you say: 'If a man says to
his father or his mother, "I declare *korban,* that is, a consecrated gift,
anything with which I might have helped you,". . .' and you allow
him to do nothing more for his father or his mother; thus you annul
the word of God through the tradition you have passed on. And you
do many other things like that."

d   And having called the crowd to him again, he said to them: "Listen
to me, all of you, and understand! Nothing entering into a man
from outside can make him unclean, but it is the things that come
out of a man that make him unclean."

e   And when he had entered the house away from the crowd, his
disciples asked him about the parable. And he says to them: "Are
even you so much without understanding? Do you not realize that
nothing which enters a man from outside can pollute him, since
such things enter not his heart but his stomach and pass into the
privy?" Thus did he declare all foods clean. And he said: "What
comes out of a man, that is what pollutes him. For from within, from
the heart of men, come evil machinations: fornications, thefts,
murders, adulteries, avarices, wickednesses, deceit, debauchery,
the envious eye, blasphemy, arrogance, lack of sense. All these evils
come from within and pollute a man."

f   Setting out from there,

a. No link with S 34. "The Pharisees . . . Jerusalem: the search of the AA
for a way to get rid of J (S 17, S 20) goes on. No TOP is indicated.

b. "Seeing that some of his disciples": another practice subversive of the
Jewish SYMB field. "Were eating bread": this is part of the major sequence
(S 31–S 42) that has bread for its theme. "That is, unwashed hands—for the
Pharisees and all the Jews . . .": Level of narrator/readers, with the narrator
explaining Jewish customs; the readers, then, are gentiles.[50] "Do not eat":

pollution of food and table (twice). "Observing the tradition of the elders": in fact, this regulation is not found in the pollution system as it has been read in the Book of Leviticus.[51]

c. The question of the AA is answered by a lesson in reading (ANAL) their practice by comparing it with Scripture; the citation from Isaiah (29:13) introduces two distinctions that determine two different readings. The first distinction is that of "lips/heart," the second that of "precepts of men/ commandments of God."

"He said to them": the opposition here involves the first reading, in which the *saying* of Moses is contrasted with the *saying* of the scribes and Pharisees. Moses *says* to *do,* that is, to honor,[52] which amounts to not cursing (not male*dicting,* not evil-*saying*). By contrast, the scribes *say* (declare something *korban*) and *do nothing* "for (their) father or (their) mother"; instead, they leave father or mother in a state of wretchedness or curse. Conclusion: your tradition annuls the word of God, which you no longer *read.*[53] This first reading thus reduces the importance of the "tradition of the elders" and the casuistry of the scribes in their ideological discourse (SOC), in order to restore the debt system as "commandment of God," as writing.

"And you do many other things like that": a generalization from this instance to a significant portion of the practice of the AA in the SYMB; from the generalization J returns to the original question concerning cleanness of hands and food.

d. "Having called the crowd to him again": the C was not involved in the preceding scenes; its function here is to introduce the parable and its interpretation, according to the logic of S 22, and also to introduce the "house" as the space of the DD, "away from the crowd." "Listen to me, all of you, and understand": instruction marking the (ANAL) reading; a similar instruction accompanied the parables in S 22. Entering man/leaving man is the opposition of nonpolluting/polluting.

e. "The disciples asked . . . without understanding?": a clear reference back to S 22c2–c3; the same theory of the parables as a strategy for reading the narrative comes into play here. The interpretation of the parables contrasts two circuits of entering and leaving. The first is that of food: food (outside) → stomach (inside) → privy (outside); this circuit does not pollute a man. Therefore the narrator draws a conclusion for his readers: "Thus did he declare all foods clean"; this broadens the question from foods that are unclean through contact with the hands (at table, in the market), with cups, plates, etc., to that of foods that are unclean according to the pollution system generally. This last is one of the questions raised in the ecclesial communities in which Christians coming from Judaism and paganism are mingled.

The second circuit is that of the heart (inside) → evil machinations (outside), the things that really pollute humanity. The list of the evils belongs to the debt system (theft, murder, adultery, and avarice; the others are variants that can be easily inscribed in these four), a fact already indicated by the seat assigned to them, namely, the *heart.* The key to the opposition of the two circuits in which the components are not directly equivalent (foods and evil machinations) is to be found in the inside/outside scheme. The inside is the stomach in one case, the heart in the other. What comes from the stomach goes into the privy (a place of pollution and filth); what comes from the heart are *practices* involving debt (aggression). The first circuit, which belongs to the pollution system that is specific to the Jews, is a digestive circuit; J explicitly excludes and annuls it, thus once again subverting the Jewish symbolic field. That is how he *reads* the ACT narrative concerning the disciples who eat with unclean hands. At the same time he removes a frontier (SYMB) between Jews and pagans; this is the conclusion the narrator draws as he turns to his pagan readers: all the foods that travel this digestive circuit are clean.

In the second circuit, what is it that is *within,* in the heart? J. Derrida has taught us to distrust this particular contrast as found in the western philosophical text, but bourgeois exegetes do not pay heed to this and immediately read "a religion of the heart, of interiority."[54] We have already seen that the heart is the site of *readings* and misreadings of the narrative (which belongs to the outside and enters a person through the eyes or ears). In the present text, the heart is the site of machinations, of desire and its objects, and thus of the strategic choices that, in consequence of these readings, will give rise to practices (good or evil). The heart is thus the place in a person where readings and strategies, ANAL and STR, meet.[55]

The circuit itself shows that we must not *cut off* the inside from the outside, for the heart is the site of the text of the actant, and is interior only in this sense that it is not public and accessible to others. The distinction inside/outside thus has to do, in our context, with the possible dislocation between this (hidden) text and the (manifest) text of the practices (or, more accurately, of their narratives). It is this dislocation that makes possible the hypocrisy J denounces in his AA in the form of the opposition lips/heart ("deceit" also occurs in the list). As in his first reading, J is here reading the practice of the scribes and Pharisees. In doing so, he repeats, but also draws the ultimate consequences from, the action of the Deuteronomists and prophets in giving the debt system a privileged place over the pollution system. The pollution system collapsed when the temple at Jerusalem was destroyed; at the level of narrator/readers, the last barrier between Jews and pagans was thus eliminated.

S 36 (7:24b-31a)

a1   he went to the territory of Tyre.
b   And having entered a house he wanted no one to know it, and he could not remain hidden.
c   But immediately a woman whose daughter had an unclean spirit heard about him and came and fell at his feet. The woman was a Greek, a Syrophoenician by birth; and she asked him to expel the demon from her daughter. And he said to her: "First, let the chil-

dren have their fill, for it is not good to take the bread that belongs to the children and throw it to the little dogs." But she answered and says to him: "Lord, even the little dogs under the table eat the crumbs left by the children." And he said to her: "Because of what you have said, go, the demon has gone out of your daughter."

d And going home she found the child lying on the bed and the demon gone.

a2 And departing again from the territory of Tyre,

a1. "To the territory of Tyre": TOP, a foreign and pagan land. J leaves Palestine (STR), since his denunciation of the "tradition of the elders" and his subversion of the Jewish SYMB field have put him in danger.

c. "A Greek, a Syrophoenician by birth," "whose daughter had an unclean spirit": a twofold pollution, of the I and of the Ic. "Asked him to expel": petition. "First, let . . . little dogs": the opposition children/little dogs refers to Jews-pagans, and is therefore in the SYMB field. "Have their fill": link with S 31, where the C has its fill. "The bread that belongs to the children": a metaphor (in the major sequence dealing with bread), since the woman is not asking for bread but for a practice J has often engaged in in Israel and even, once before, in a foreign land (S 24). *Bread* is here a metaphor for the powerful practice of J, just as the *seed* in S 22 was. In other words, the "bread" too means the word-seed and its fruits of blessing. "Have their fill": cf. S 31, S 38, S 40; however, the sequence of the loaves (S 31–S 42) is not excluded from this powerful practice; on the contrary, the metaphor of the word-bread will provide the key to this major sequence.

"First": J explains his STR, a first stage of which aims at the filling of the Jews, and a second, after the circulation of J and his narrative have exhausted the space available among the Jews, at the filling of the pagans. "But she answered . . . the children": she accepts the children-dogs distinction and her own exclusion from the table at which the Jews are filled, but she finds something available for her in the metaphor J uses, namely, the scraps that fall from the table for the dogs; she thereby pursues her request. "Because of what you have said": J reads her persistence as "faith" and tells her it has been effective ("the demon has gone out"; Ic/Ib).

d. "Going home": the narrative (ACT) statement shows that J's discourse has had its effect. The STR of J has been influenced by the woman's word, and some pagans have been filled before the Jewish space has been completely traversed. In other words, the Jewish/pagan frontier has been opened, as in S 35. Note, too, that the powerful practice has been produced without J's body being present to the cured girl.[56] This prepares for S 62, if we connect this absence of the body with the metaphor of the bread.

S 37 (7:31b-37)

a he went by way of Sidon to the Sea of Galilee through the region of Decapolis.

b And they bring him a deaf man with a speech impediment and ask him to lay hands on him.

c And taking him aside, away from the crowd, he put his fingers into the man's ears and with his spittle touchèd his tongue. And having raised his eyes to heaven he groaned, and he says to him: *"Ephphatha!* that is, 'Be opened!' " And immediately his ears were opened, and the restraint on his tongue was loosened and he spoke correctly. And he ordered them to tell no one.

d But the more he ordered them, the more they proclaimed it. And they were utterly amazed and said: "He has done everything well; he even makes the deaf hear and the dumb speak."

a. "Sidon . . . Decapolis" (GEO): still in pagan territory.

c. "Fingers," "spittle," "touched": SYMB. "Eyes to heaven . . . groaned": difficulty of J's practice (cf. S 31). "Speech impediment/spoke correctly," "deaf/ears opened": Ic/Ib. "Away from the crowd," "tell no one": STR.

d. Instructions not obeyed, as in S 10 ("they proclaimed" the narrative). "Utterly amazed . . . done everything well": the narrative produces the amazement of the C, as in S 6, S 12, S 24, S 25. *"Ephphatha!* that is, be opened!"*: the translation of the Aramaic into Greek (level of narrator/ readers) is given here in order to emphasize the fact that the narrative has crossed the boundary of Jews/pagans (as in S 35 and S 36).

S 38 (8:1-9)

a In those days, when there was once again a large crowd and they had nothing to eat,

b he calls his disciples to him and says to them: "I have pity on the crowd because they have been with me for three days and have nothing to eat. And if I send them home fasting, they will collapse on the way; and some of them have come from a distance." His disciples answered him: "Where can anyone get bread to feed them, here in the desert?" And he asked them: "How many loaves do you have?" They said: "Seven."

c And he orders the crowd to take their places on the ground. And taking the seven loaves he gave thanks and broke them and gave them to his disciples that they might distribute them, and they distributed them to the crowd. There were also a few small fish. And having said the blessing over them, he told them to distribute these as well. And they ate and were filled, and they collected the leftover fragments, seven baskets of them. And there were about four thousand men.

d And he sent them away.

a. "In those days": CHR with absence of TOP; no link with S 35–S 37, while there will be a link with S 39–S 40.

a–d. Let us briefly compare S 38 with S 31. Here there is no STR of the C ("they have been with me for three days and have nothing to eat"), which is characterized simply by the lack of "anything to eat" (Cc) and the possibility of *death* ("they will collapse on the way"). To their situation J answers with "bread to feed them." Therefore, curse/blessing. "I have pity on the crowd": similarly in S 31, but there he taught them; here their need is for bread. As in S 36, the word is paralleled with bread, and the latter is also given a place in the ANAL code (as already in S 33; cf. S 40).

Lack of understanding (ANAL) on the part of the disciples, as in S 31, but without any reference here to buying bread. To have seven loaves/to give seven loaves. No "lifting his eyes to heaven" here. "He gave thanks" instead of "he said the blessing," but the latter phrase does occur in connection with the fish. Finally, all are filled (Cb), and there is even food left over. There are fewer numbers here than in S 31; the various figures (seven, four thousand, seven baskets) will be kept in S 40. Dismissal of the C: STR of J in relation to the C.

S 39 (8:10-13a)

a1 And immediately getting into the boat with his disciples he came to the region of Dalmanutha.
b1 And the Pharisees came
c   and began to dispute with him, looking for a sign from heaven from him and tempting him. And groaning in his spirit he says: "Why does this generation look for a sign? In truth (amen) I tell you, no sign will be given to this generation."
b2 And leaving them,
a2 and embarking again,

a. "Dalmanutha": TOP, unknown to the historians,[57] but a place of the AA and therefore in Galilee (GEO).

c. "Dispute," "looking," "tempting": here there is no subversive ACT narrative as earlier (S 12–S 16, S 20, S 35), but an initiative of the AA, as on later occasions (S 47, S 55) where the term *tempt* will recur, a term linked with "hypocrites" in S 55 (as already in S 35). Thus it is the strategy of the AA that is described as a *temptation* (compare with S 2 where Satan "tempts" J).

"Looking for a sign from heaven": in opposition to "coming from men"; cf. S 55. "A sign" (*sēmeion*): the AA thus come forward as readers, as semiologists of the practice of J (ANAL); they try to make heaven intervene (MYTH), as Elijah once did (1 Kings 18:20–40). But, as can be observed, the powerful practice of J has not invoked heaven (MYTH) as a factor in reading (ANAL) since S 12 (where "knowing in his spirit" corresponds to "groaning in his spirit" here). This fact enables us to read J's refusal ("Why does this generation look for a sign?"): you have signs enough in my practice here *on earth* (cf. S 12), signs which even the C has often read (S 12, S 24, S 25, S 36). The semiological grill is c/b: the lives that have been *saved* (S 16).[58] Read *these* signs, therefore; be readers, semiologists, of my narrative. The refusal thus refers the Pharisees to a reading of the narrative; this is a constant theme in the reading lessons (cf. S 12–S 16, S 20), but the "hardened hearts" (S 16) of the Pharisees will not let them do what J says. In any event, there will be no more signs from *heaven*, because there are signs on *earth*.

"In truth I tell you . . . to this generation": in S 42 the "generation" is the Jews (or possessors of power) who have known J's practice without believing in it ("unbelieving generation": S 44) and will also come to know the practice of his disciples. But the Jews have just been conquered by the Romans and killed or scattered. This final comment is thus at the narrator/readers level and relates the reading failure of these semiologists to the curse that falls on them; this, as we shall see, is one of Mark's "theses."[59]

S 40 (8:13b-22a)

a1   he set out for the other shore.
b   And they forgot to take loaves with them, and had only one loaf with them in the boat. And he gave them orders saying: "Look, be on guard against the leaven of the Pharisees and the leaven of Herod." And they said to one another: "We have no loaves." And knowing this he says to them: "Why do you tell one another that you have no loaves? Do you still not see or understand? Is your heart hardened? Do you have eyes but not see, and do you have ears but not hear? Do you not remember when I broke five loaves for five thousand men, how many basketsful of fragment you collected?" They tell him: "Twelve." And when I broke the seven loaves for the four thousand men, how many basketsful of fragments did you collect?" And they tell him: "Seven." And he said to them: "Do you still not understand?"
a2   And they reached. . .

a1. "Embarking again, he set out for the other shore": as we said before, the crossing in the boat is part of J's STR in relation to the C (S 22, S 28d, S 31, S 39); here it is related to the AA ("leaving them"). If we go back and reread the sequences, we will see that there are three sets (S 22–S 26, S 28d–S 34, S 38–S 41) which prove to be parallel and linked precisely by these crossings of the Sea of Galilee from one shore to the other. Beginning in S 42, however, J will undertake a new STR: he will set out for Jerusalem. Why does he not do this sooner? And why are the above-mentioned three sets of sequences interrupted by S 27–S 28 (Nazareth and sending of the twelve) and S 35–S 37 (detour beyond the borders of Israel)? These crossings from shore to shore are filled with strategic instructions and show an *expectation* of J in relation to the DD, for the sequences whose scene is the sea (S 23, S 33, S 40) are sequences in which the ANAL is dominant in the space of the DD (the boat): who is J? What is his practice?

b. "Loaves," "one loaf": we are still in the loaves sequence, which is connected with the ANAL of the DD. "He gave orders": a strategic instruction (S 25, S 37). "Be on guard against the leaven of the Pharisees": in Lev. 2:11, leaven is excluded from "the oblations that you offer to Yahweh"; it indicates "less cleanliness" and therefore has a pejorative connotation here. If bread connotes the word (S 36, S 38) and is therefore located in the ANAL, leaven, which is linked to bread by metonymy, connotes the discourses of the AA. The AA cannot read the word-seed, the narrative of J, because their leaven, that is, their ideology,[60] has hardened their hearts.

"They said to one another": The DD do not understand the metaphor. "He says to them: 'Why do you . . . but not hear' ": J addresses them as standing in the same site of nonreading as the AA (S 16, S 20c1). "Do you not remember?": a lesson in how to read (ANAL) the two sequences on the filling of the crowds (S 31, S 38). "Do you still not understand?": what is there to understand? Five loaves filled five thousand men and there was plenty left over, twelve baskets of fragments; seven loaves filled four thousand men, and there were seven basketsful left. The five loaves and seven loaves are related, in their respective sequences, to "how many loaves do you *have?*" The loaves are their *possession*. The ACT sequence is therefore to be read thus: what you *have, give* to them; they are *filled*; gather twelve and seven basketsful respectively. It is this power to *fill* by *giving* what one *has*, with the resulting superfluity, that the DD should read but fail to.

In S 42 Peter will succeed. "You are the Messiah" is his reply to the question "Who is Jesus?" which the narrative has raised from S 23 on and which it explicitly connects with the narrative of the loaves in S 23. Peter's response, then, as a first completion of the ANAL code of the DD, answers the questions of the present sequence: he who, by *giving* what he *has, fills* the C in a superabundant manner, is the Messiah; this kind of practice is the characteristic mark of his *messianity*, a fact they had not previously understood. This is the object of J's *expectation*: he is waiting for this reading as the *fruit* of his practice; once it is achieved, he will be able to undertake the journey to Jerusalem, which is his new STR.[61]

S 41 (8:22b-26)

a   to Bethsaida.
b   They bring him a blind man and ask him to touch him.
c1 And taking the blind man's hand he conducted him outside the village.
d   And when he had put saliva on his eyes, he laid his hands on him and asked him: "Do you see anything?" As he began to see he said: "I see men; I see them walking like trees." Then he placed his hands on

the man's eyes once again, and he saw clearly and was cured; he saw everything very plainly, even far off.

c2   And he sent the man away to his home, saying: "Do not even enter the village."

a. "Bethsaida": On the road to Caesarea Philippi (S 42).

b-c2. We shall pass over the "touching," "the saliva" (SYMB), the leading of the man "outside the village," and the instruction given to him after the cure (STR). The real interest of this sequence resides in the two stages of J's powerful practice, this last being shown to us in "slow motion."

"I see men; I see them walking like trees": an almost humorous reply that expresses both seeing and nonseeing (since trees do not walk) and therefore a stage intermediate between blindness and sight. The sequence thus anticipates S 42 in which Peter, being questioned, finally *sees*; the present sequence is also linked to S 40, where "having eyes, they do not *see.*"

"Asked him": in the text the verb "ask" almost always implies the ANAL code, with reference either to the DD (S 22c2, S 35d, S 43a2, S 44e, S 47c, S 58b), or to the AA (S35b, S 47b, S 55h, S 66c [twice], S 68b [twice]), or to II (S 49b, S 55i), or to J (S 24c, S 42b [twice], S 46a); the exceptions are S 38a, S 44b, S 72c. Only here, however, is the verb used for a question regarding the powerful practice of J; J *asks* about the fruits of his practice (for the reason, surely, that only the blind man can say whether or not he sees; but such a question is not asked in S 51). It thus indicates the *ignorance* of J regarding the fruits of his practice, and thus illustrates the "without him knowing how" of S 22b2.

S 42a-b (8:27-30)

a   And the Jesus and his disciples went out to the villages of Caesarea Philippi.

b   On the way he asked his disciples, saying to them: "Whom do people say I am?" They told him: "John the Baptist; but others: Elijah; and still others: one of the prophets." And he asked them: "But you, who do you say that I am?" The Peter answers and says to him: "You are the Messiah." And he rebuked them and ordered them not to tell anyone about him.

This sequence is of basic importance in the narrative and therefore the commentary on it will be somewhat complicated; the references back to what has gone before, the digressions on theory, and the multiplication of references generally may confuse a number of readers. But the text of Mark, like my own, is not linear; it can be read only by means of the analysis of codes, and this means many references to other parts of the text. Similarly, the theoretical formulation that controls the texts cannot be found clearly and definitively enunciated in any one passage of the text in a linear manner; the entire complex text is needed for a "reading of Mark," and it is only the fabric indicated by the many passages marked "cf. later," etc. that will provide the key to the theoretical formulation. The "reading" in question is not, as it might seem at first sight, a linear superposition of a text on the supposedly linear text of Mark, in a line to line, signified to signified equivalence; it involves rather the work of the weaver on the signifier, as Barthes has neatly defined it.[62]

a. "To the villages": TOP characteristic of the sequences after S 18. "Of Caesarea Philippi": a pagan area (STR); "Caesarea" connotes Caesar, while "Philippi" refers to Philip the brother of Herod (S 30). At the TOP level, therefore, S 29 (Herod in Galilee) to S 42 form a major sequence in which the main point is the announcement of the passage from Galilee to a pagan area (S 35–S 37).

b. "On the way": this phrase will recur frequently in the major sequence that begins here. The *boat* and the pattern of the *circle* are replaced by the pattern of the *way* or road, which is characteristically associated with the term *follow*. The disciples gathered *around* J will become primarily disciples who *follow* J.

"Who do people say that I am?": Q 1—How does the C read my narrative (ANAL)? The reply refers back to S 29 and shows that S 42 completes the major sequence begun in S 29, the sequence of the loaves. What the three answers here given have in common (John the Baptist, Elijah, one of the prophets) is the pre-eschatological character of the reading of the C; they see J only as a precursor of the final narrative.

"And he asked them": insistence on questioning; we saw in S 41 that this is inscribed in the ANAL code. The insistence also shows that J wishes to put an end to this period of *expectation* ("from shore to shore"; cf. S 40). S 42 thus proves to be the completion of S 18–S 42, with the twofold question distinguishing "the people" (the C) and "you" (the DD). Here we have the responses given to Q 1 in the space of the C and the space of the DD (spaces differentiated in S 18 and S 22).

"Peter says to him": Simon, the spokesman (S 8) who has become Peter, will read the ACT of J, and his reading will win him a place of preeminence henceforth among the DD[63] as their spokesman. "You are the Messiah": ANAL (response to Q 1). The term "Messiah" appears for the first time in the text, apart from the title (note the narrator/readers level in the title, indicating that the narrator is making his own the answer given by Peter[64]); whereas other answers have already been given: "Son of God" (MYTH; S 2, S 6, S 18, S 24), "Beelzebul, "out of his senses" (S 20, S 21), and the list here in S 42. All these answers have in common that they are inscribed in the semantic field of the Jewish ideological text of the period, and it is to this that the term *Messiah* is initially opposed. Admittedly, *Messiah* too belongs in the same field. But the fact that Peter's response is made in the space of the DD, in sequence with the terms of the ANAL code (a fact we have emphasized especially in S 40), shows how his answer has its own specific character. In Peter's mouth *Messiah* is a reading of the practice of J, of the ACT narrative (expulsion of the unclean spirits, cf. S 20; perfecting of defective bodies, Ic/Ib, cf. S 16; subversion of the Jewish SYMB, cf. S 12–S 16, S 35), and especially of the practice of the loaves, the major sequence concerning which ends here. In short, *J's practice is a messianic practice: that* is what Peter has just read. Consequently his reading announces the final narrative, since the Messiah is an eschatological figure.[65] The passage shows in what the MYTH/ACT narrative contradiction, which I mentioned in connection with S 6, consists.[66]

"He rebuked them": a very strong STR term, used in regard to the unclean spirits (S 6) and the sea (S 23b). "Not to tell anyone about him": this strategy of silence on the reading of J's messianity in the BAS field indicates how this reading differs from the current interpretation of the term Messiah, which exists prior to the narrative of J and carries a meaning that J must reject. The entire concern of the actant J in the major sequence that begins here will be to make the DD understand the difference and its strategic implications. He will do this through a confrontation with the STR Z, for it is the latter that shows the dominant meaning "Messiah" has in the Jewish ideological text, where the Messiah is to conquer and expel the Romans from Israel and establish his supremacy over the pagan nations. Bourgeois exegesis has grasped this point clearly, but it has fallen into the trap of setting over against such a Messiah a "spiritual Messiah" (political/spiritual in the bourgeois ideology).[67] But the fact that the confession of the Messiah occurs primarily as a reading of the sequences of satiation through bread shows the "nonspirituality" (in a bourgeois sense) of Jesus the Messiah; Jesus' messiahship is economic, political, and ideological, and thus in the last analysis he is indeed a "political Messiah." It is precisely within the category of the "political" that the two kinds of messiahship will be differentiated. J is a "political" Messiah but not after the manner of the Zealots.

Retrospective Reading of S 18-S 42b

Let us pause here and take the time to reread the major sequence S 18–S 42. What makes a major sequence of it is the *boat* that was introduced in S 18 and disappears in S 41. The crossings from shore to shore define three sets of sequences within the major sequence: S 22–S 26, S 28–S 34, S 38–S 41.[68] We noted how the narrative was stopped in S 28c, to permit the introduction of S 29–S 30. S 28 had been programmatically announced by S 19, just as S 29 opens what S 42 has just closed with (the three replies of the C to the question, "Who is Jesus?"). Thus the sequence of the loaves is defined, with the TOP of opening/closing being respectively Galilee (Jewish country) and Ceasarea (pagan country). Finally, S 35 and S 37 are not linked to S 34 and S 38 respectively, while S 35, S 36, and S 37 are linked to one another.

The result is the complex scheme which appears on the following page.

Let us read this scheme in the light of the ANAL/STR codes. The major question here is what has been called, since Wrede's time, the "messianic secret."[69]

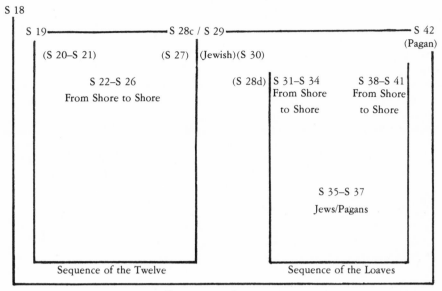

Sequence of the Boat

The sequences in which there are AA (S 20, S 21, S 27, S 35, S 40) are not relevant at the level of the major sequence; their place is justified by sequences that precede or follow the major sequence. The basic actants involved are the C and the DD, as S 18 and S 22 have already shown us.

S 19 and S 28 (sequences of the Twelve) tell of the completion of the "mission of J" in Galilee and the part played in it by the twelve as his envoys (*apostles*, S 28d). These two sequences thus deal with what had been programmed in S 18–S 19 (according to the logic of the closed text).

S 29–S 42 (sequence of the loaves) links the question "Who is Jesus?" to the two sequences dealing with the loaves (S 31, S 38), as we have seen. However, a difficulty arises: the mission of the twelve in S 28 takes place *before* they read the messiahship of J, as though this last were of scarcely any importance for their mission. Yet S 31 narrates the first sequence in which the C is filled with the loaves as having been "forced" on J by the STR of the C, so that the reading of Peter in S 42, which is a reading above all of S 31, depends on the new element introduced in S 31 (cf. the prayer of S 32). In addition, S 36 (the pagan woman, mother of a daughter with an unclean spirit) also narrates a modification of J's STR in relation to the pagans; the same idea is conveyed by the terminal points of the TOP in S 30–S 42, with S 35 having established, in the parable of the stomach/heart, the crossing of the frontier (SYMB) between Jews and pagans, a frontier opened by the insistence of the pagan woman.

Since the text is not more explicit, we cannot conclude, except as a hypothesis, that J's STR changes its course in this sequence of the loaves, in the direction of a widening of the horizon of his practice and that of the twelve to embrace what lies beyond the borders of Israel, a change, that is, in the direction of the pagans, with S 18–S19 having already indicated this programmatically. We will see that this is one of the decisive elements in the confrontation between the STR of J and the STR Z which will dominate S 42–S 58; the business of the loaves will come up again only in S 62, that is, precisely as the movement (STR) toward the pagan nations, by way of Galilee, is beginning.

We can now read the entire major sequence *S 18–S 42:* the separation (STR) between the space of the C and the space of the DD (boat, theory of the parables) leads the DD to a reading of J's practice as *messianic,* a reading opposed to the reading of the C; this is a result *expected* by J (sequences "from shore to shore").

The Strategy of the So-Called Messianic Secret

Let us reread the various elements in J's strategy. First, in relation to the AA: he avoids the towns, goes into them only secretly (S 18, S 36, even in a pagan region), leaves them and goes elsewhere (end of S 35, S 39). This STR is justified by the STR of the AA who are seeking to get rid of him (S 17). All the other elements of J's STR relate to the C. He makes the unclean spirits remain silent lest they short-circuit the narrative (S 6, S 7, S 18, but not S 24, since there is no C there) and cause it to abort by precipitating a messianism of the Z type. The same STR holds in regard to the Ib (S 10, S 25, S 37, S 41), though not in S 24 (a pagan region) and S 26 (where J brings out what had been hidden, in order to highlight the *faith* of the Ib). There seems to be a contradiction between S 24g (the former demoniac is sent to proclaim the narrative of J in a pagan area) and S 36b (secrecy of J's going into a pagan area); in fact, however, in the first of these sequences there is question of J's STR regarding the narrative, while in the second the secrecy bears on the very *presence* of J.

These orders given to people who have been cured that they should keep silent (about the *narrative*) have as their purpose to prevent the effect of the circulation of the narrative, to avoid great gatherings of the C, and, in the latter context, to avoid precipitating a messianism of the Z type. By contrast, the STR in regard to the C has to do with the *bodily presence* of J in their midst: he does not refuse to "heal," teach, and fill, but then he puts himself at a distance from the C; he *absents himself* (or sends the C away) because he does not wish to become a leader of the masses, especially in the cities (S 8, S 11, S 23, S 28d, S 31f, S 38d). Moreover, in S 22 he adopts, for the same purpose, the strategy of teaching in parables which no longer make clear the relation of his practice to the eschatological narrative. Let us also note the *prayer* in S 8 and S 32, which emphasizes this STR.

In S 8, however, Simon appears as the spokesman for the C; in addition there are former Zealots in the group of disciples (cf. S 19). The STR of the DD is inscribed in continuity with that of the Zealots and is in the same field (consequently the DD too are sent away in S 32). This is why the space of the DD as a field for the reading of the BAS code is separated from the space of the C. Peter's reading of the narrative of J is already BAS, but the term "Messiah" belongs in the Z field,[70] and therefore the DD must be silent about it. Meanwhile, the game has not yet been fully played out, for although J's messiahship has been acknowledged in the reading of the ACT, its differentiation in relation to the STR Z does not appear immediately. The DD, therefore, and especially Peter, will, in the major sequence S 42–S 58, be spokesmen for the STR Z. The *strategic differences* will be analyzed as the journey to Jerusalem progresses.

With this, we end our pause and return to the narrative.

S 42c-e (8:31-9:1)

c   And he began to teach them: "The Son of man must suffer much and be rejected by the elders, chief priests, and scribes and be killed and rise after three days." And he preached the word openly.

d   Taking him aside, the Peter began to rebuke him. But turning and seeing his disciples he rebuked Peter very severely and says: "Get from behind me, Satan, for your thoughts are not those of God but those of men."

e   And calling to him the crowd along with his disciples, he said to them: "If anyone wishes to come after me, let him deny himself and take his cross and follow me. For whoever wishes to save his life will lose it, but whoever loses his life because of me and the good news will save it. For what does it profit a man to gain the whole world and forfeit his life? What can a man give in exchange for his life? For whoever is ashamed of me and my words before this adulterous and sinful generation, the Son of man will be ashamed of him when he comes in the glory of his Father with the holy messengers." And he said to them: "In truth (amen) I tell you, some of those standing here will not taste death before they see the kingdom of God coming in power."

c. Gr. *Parrhēsia*—openly.[70a]

"And he began to teach them . . . and he preached the word openly": "began" marks a *turning point* in the teaching given to the DD. "Preached the word" refers us back to S 12 and especially to S 22, where there was a transition from an *open* word to a *parabolic word*; it is true that the "mystery" was given to the DD (S 22c2) but after S 31, since their minds were closed, J had to wait until they succeeded in reading the ACT of the loaves, which had become *for them* a parable they did not understand. They have now succeeded in reading it.

What is the object of this new teaching? The text tells us: "The Son of man must suffer. . . ." This seems crystal-clear; it is the "paschal mystery": J's STR requires a death so that he may win a resurrection.[71] Let us distrust this clarity, however, and practice what L. Althusser calls a "symptomatic reading," although we must adapt it to our situation since we are not reading a scientific text, as he is, but the text of a narrative.[72]

J's discourse in this scene is an *anticipation* of the ACT narrative (not, of course, in the narrative statement itself, like the backward look in S 30 at the death of John the Baptist, but in the discourse of J). J is here already in possession of the narrative *to come*, the narrative of his death, and this *contradicts* the "without him knowing how" of S 22b2, as well as the fact that the ANAL code applies also to the actant J, as the narrative has several times shown. This is a first symptom.

When the STR for the elimination of J by the AA (S 53d, S 55e, S 59) becomes concrete, we will see J adopting a STR of clandestinity in order to escape them, and the treason of Judas will be necessary in order to effect his arrest. Moreover, when J is close to death, he will cry out to the God who has abandoned him (S 71d). In other words, the narrative unfolds according to the logic of "without him knowing how," and therefore in *contradiction* of the prevision in our present sequence (if he *must* die in order to rise, why should he cry out that God has abandoned him when death comes?). This is the second symptom.

Finally—the third symptom—*must* says *necessity*, and this last, as linked to the anticipation, is not only contradictory to the narrative logic which the text has reflected in the mirror of the second parable (S 22b2), but also raises the question of its own status: to what code does it belong? Not to any of the sequential codes (ACT, ANAL, STR), for these are articulated in accordance with the narrative logic of the text. The presence of the "Son of man" seems to point to the MYTH code, and we will see that this is true enough. The most important index, however, is that the *must* introduces the *anticipated narrative* that is the possession of the *narrator*. The *must*, therefore, is to be read primarily at the narrator/readers level.

Since the text does (not) end with the narrative of the rejection and death of J and the declaration of his resurrection, all of which take place during the Passover, we shall give the provisional description *prepaschal* to the narrative of what takes place before this feast. The narrator who writes the narrative in the past tense is situated after the Passover; we shall call his anticipatory discourse *postpaschal*. The contradiction we are now analyzing is therefore a contradiction between the prepaschal narrative and the postpaschal discourse of the narrator. How is the postpaschal discourse to be characterized? It is a rereading by the narrator of the narrative which he possesses and which he inscribes in a plan external to the narrative, a plan that is marked by necessity and that foretells and foreordains the narrative to come. The postpaschal discourse is thus a discourse about *predestination*, and we shall call it *theological*, using a term we shall justify very shortly.[73] The contradiction is therefore a contradiction between narrative and theology.

Let us return now to this scene as a whole. It contains a new teaching and a clearly stated message, but the object assigned to them is not at the level of the narrative but of the postpaschal discourse. There is a strategic change on J's part in relation to the preceding narrative. In what does the change consist? In other words, what does this anticipated narrative *erase* in the text of the ACT narrative? Is it possible, by using the logic of the symptomatic reading, to restore what has been erased?

We shall attempt such a restoration in our commentary on the three scenes (c, d, e) of S 42, while leaving aside for the time being what belongs to the postpaschal discourse. One point we must emphasize: in speaking of prepaschal and postpaschal we are not reverting to the problematic that is dominant in bourgeois exegesis, namely, that of the historicity of the narrative of J. We are reading a text written at Rome after the year 70, and it is this text that we are analyzing. Nor is the *restoration*, by means of a symptomatic reading, of the prepaschal text an analysis of the history of the text, in the sense in which form history and redaction history would conduct such an analysis. The erasure of which we are speaking is in the text, and what we are calling "prepaschal" was (probably) never *written*. The narrator did the erasing in the very process of writing, and this process of writing is precisely the object of our reading.

c. "The Son of man": we shall speak of this below in connection with scene e.

"The elders, chief priests, and scribes": this group of actants, as a *group*, will intervene in the narrative only in Jerusalem (S 55b); in S 45f, which contains a parallel to our present prediction, we read: "Behold, we are going up to Jerusalem, and the Son of man will be handed over to the high priests and the scribes." The major sequence that begins here will in fact be about the ascent of J and the DD to Jerusalem. This, then, is the change in STR: they leave Galilee and take the road to Jerusalem. In addition, the three predictions (S 42c, S 45b, S 45f) present the actants who are the high priests, elders, and scribes as AA, and that, in fact, is what they will be. The "being rejected" enables us to read the ascent to Jerusalem as a *confrontation* between J and the AA; this can be foreseen from the strategic viewpoint, on the basis of S 17, S 20, S 35, S 39.

d. "Taking him aside, Peter began to rebuke him": the last term ("rebuke") is STR,[74] as is the "taking him aside"; a STR of Peter is here stated or rather it *begins*, in response to the new STR of J. What we see here is the *programming* of the major sequence which is *beginning* here and which has the confrontation of the two STR for its dominant note.

Let us suppose here that the STR of Peter is a STR Z; only our reading in its entirety can confirm the supposition in a decisive way. We shall see, moreover, that Zealotism, which is present throughout the Markan text but never named, is also an object of textual erasure.[75] In a proper symptomatic reading, then, we must try to restore the STR Z.

Let us assume, then, first of all, that Peter realizes that the confrontation should not be first and foremost with the AA but with the Romans (cf. S 45i).

Let us assume, secondly, that contrary to the command about remaining silent concerning J's messiahship, Peter intends to organize an armed contingent from the C that will go up to Jerusalem and fight against the Romans. There were four thousand and five thousand men respectively in the crowds whose hunger had been sated. Was it not in such armed combat that the Zealots were constantly engaged throughout this century?[76] "He rebuked Peter": a sure sign of a confrontation of STR.

Gr.: "Get from behind me," not "Get behind me" (Jerusalem Bible). The Greek text authorizes both translations, but the one I adopt is rendered necessary by comparison with S 4b, "Come after me." J is telling Peter here: Stop being my disciple. "Satan": the STR Z is located, like that of the AA,[77] on the side of Satan. "Your thoughts are not those of God but those of men": "thoughts" = "strategies"; the central debate in the text of Mark concerns the right strategy, the one that God will bless. As a matter of fact, the STR Z ended in a curse, in the "abomination of desolation" (S 58); it was therefore a strategy only of "men" (narrator/readers level).

  e. "And calling to him the crowd along with his disciples": the C is outside the framework of the sequence (on the road to Caesarea Philippi) and the space of the DD in which J speaks "openly." The C is introduced, however, to show that it represents the stake in the two opposed strategies. "His disciples": the following discourse lists the conditions for being a disciple of J, for "coming after me" and "following me," for sharing his STR in answer to a second call (second in relation to S 4). The discourse ends by evoking the final narrative ("The Son of man will . . . come in glory of his Father"); this in turn enables us to read the oppositions "save his life/lost it" and "lose his life/save it" as the opposition of the two (future) times of the narratives to come: the narrative which the STR of J involves ("because of me and the good news") and eschatological narrative.

"Save his life/lose his life": cf. S 6. "Saving," which is the result of blessing, operates here in the register of the two narratives (the ecclesial and the eschatological). The difficulty in reading here is due to the superposition of the narrator/readers level (which looks to the persecutions experienced by the community of Rome) on the level of the prepaschal narrative.

"Let him deny himself and take up his cross": the *cross* is the punishment the Romans kept for the Zealots; therefore the confrontation that will take place in Jerusalem involves the *danger* of the cross. On the checkerboard of (class struggle) strategies being deployed in Palestine, the STR of J is closer to that of the Zealots than to those of the ruling classes; that is why the text is so careful to distinguish the STR of J from that of the Zealots.

The same risk is indicated in the opposition lose his life/save his life, but in terms that belong to the narrator/readers level: those who have lost their lives in the Neronian persecutions will save them at the eschatological narrative, unlike those who are "ashamed of me and my words" and have denied J. "Gain the whole world": The goal of the STR Z was to expel the Romans and establish Israel's dominion over the pagan nations.[78] "Forfeit his life": In the logic of the debt system as pushed to its extreme, for he who *kills* will be cursed and forfeit his own life; the Zealots incurred this curse. "What can a man give in exchange for his life?": in the context of the opposition between the two STR (J/Z), the danger of loss of life that each individual accepts should obey the logic of the eschatological perspective; that is, a person should run the risk on the side of the "thoughts of God," not the "thoughts of men."

When all this has been said, we still do not know, despite the indices we have, what the goal of J's STR is, nor how the narrator reads his narrative as a whole in confrontation with the narrative of the Zealots who were conquered by Rome. When the time comes, we will have to reread all this.

"For whoever is ashamed of me": the opposition between the two times of the narratives to come is made explicit: narratives of the (ecclesial) disciples and eschatological narrative.

"Me and my words"/"The Son of man will . . . come in glory," "the kingdom of God coming in power": the "Son of man" (S 12, S 15) and the "kingdom of God" (S 22b2, b3) had already been mentioned, but then, in consequence of J's STR of parables, these expressions disappeared from the text, as did every reference to the *final narrative.* Now they return in the space of the DD; they are reintroduced by Peter's confession, since the Messiah is an eschatological figure. Now, the object of the ANAL in S 12–S 16 and S 22 was precisely to relate the practice of J to the final narrative; this was the "mystery" (S 22c2) given to the DD. The failure of the DD to understand (S 22c2, S 23, etc.) prevents them from reading the mystery; now that Peter has penetrated it, J proclaims it anew to the DD: "And he preached the word openly."

This analysis is not without its difficulties, which are due to the textual mixing up of the ACT level and the narrator/readers level. To resolve the difficulties, we must impose a reading grill regarding the "Son of man."

1. This *name* is used in the discourse of J (and not in that of any other actant, a statement that holds for *all* the Gospels), and it is always used in the nonpersonal verbal system.[79] Here as in S 66c, it is part of a discourse in which J speaks in the first person; here and in S 58b5 and S 66c, the term "Son of man" refers to the final narrative, while "the messengers" (angels), "the glory," and "the clouds of heaven" (in S 66c) inscribe it in the MYTH code. These three textual sites may be designated as "eschatological Son of man." There is nothing to indicate that J himself is meant; on the contrary, the I/he shift seems to show that there is no such identification. However, the link between the ACT narrative of J and the final narrative is evident in these sequences (except in S 58b5).

Elsewhere (at the beginning of this discourse in S 42c, as well as in S 44c, S 45b, f, S 50d, and S 62b, twice), in discourses which *all* belong to the postpaschal discourse, there is question of the future ACT narrative of J, and J himself is said to be the Son of man. These textual sites will be designated as "paschal Son of man." Finally, S 12 and S 16 are simply inscribed in the reading of the ACT narrative; these sites will be designated as "ACT Son of man."[80]

2. In the text of Dan. 7:13–18, the Son of man is, according to the interpretation verse 18 gives of him, a collective figure, namely, "the saints of the Most High," while at the same time being inscribed in the MYTH code ("clouds of heaven": v. 13). "The saints of the Most High," however, are the people of Israel who are persecuted by Antiochus Epiphanes, and the famous vision of the Son of man is an apocalyptic promise that God will take up Israel's cause and will soon come to see justice done.[81]

The name "Son of man" indicates the *earthly* origin of this figure, and the movement in Dan. 7:13, is not, as has often been said, *a descent,* with someone *coming* (from heaven to earth), but on the contrary an *ascent*: "the Son of man" comes to the throne of the one of great age,[82] from humanity to the clouds, or, in short, from *earth* to *heaven.* We find this scheme of *ascent* in some other texts of the Old Testament,[83] and also in one of Paul's earliest letters, 1 Thessalonians 4:17: ("then those of us who are still alive will be *taken up* in the clouds, together with them [the dead who rise first], to meet the Lord in the air"). In this text of Paul, the eschatological event, inscribed in the MYTH code, is recounted in the form of a *collective ascent* of the Christians who are found faithful at the final narrative or who are, in other words, "the saints of the Most High."

In this text of Paul, Christians admittedly go to meet Jesus, and they are not called "Sons of man." The important thing, however, is that we find the scheme of Dan. 7 in a (postpaschal) Christian text. We may therefore suppose that the scheme was operative in the text of Mark on the prepaschal level, but was *erased* by the postpaschal discourse. What erasures were made? First of all, the Son of man here is individual, even though the title is not applied to J ("of *his* Father" here; set over against the "elect" is S 58b5). Secondly, the name is applied to J in the "postpaschal Son of man" and "ACT Son of man" texts, and this influenced the "eschatological Son of man" texts: the Greek verb describing the movement of the Son of man *(erchomai)* can mean "go" as well as "come," which is already true in fact in Dan. 7:13. The other textual sites relating to the Son of man inevitably introduce the second meaning of the verb and thus a movement of *descent,* which erases the prepaschal meaning of "ascent." The *ascent* that is erased is the MYTH correlative of the "descent" of the Spirit; this descent opens the narrative of J, the ascent will close it. But since the movement is inverted,[84] the actual closure will be a descent of J who *comes* from heaven.[85]

Let us summarize. There is a change of STR and a new ANAL teaching. The new STR: to go up to Jerusalem with a view to a confrontation that is not of the Z type but does imply the danger of losing life. The new teaching that is given "openly": the narrative of J is linked to the final narrative, "the kingdom of God coming in power." How is the link established? The *ascent* of the "Son of man," that is, of J with his disciples (behind him, following him, risking their lives, and so on) and the Crowd of all those who have heard the word[86]: this is the ultimate (MYTH) horizon of J's STR.

In this STR there is no room for the *death* of J; on the contrary, it is excluded by S 35–37, which show the STR circulation of J's narrative among the pagans after the Jews: with the *twelve* he must go to the pagans after the ascent to Jerusalem. This is one of the factors opposing J's STR to the STR Z.

We can also understand (always *in the text,* not in historical reality) that when this STR was cut short (treason of Judas, arrest and death of J, flight of the twelve), the text should have been reworked in the light of the postpaschal discourse, that is, of the theological viewpoint and its discourse in which the death becomes necessary for the sake of the resurrection. Another point should be made clear: I am not claiming that it was "Mark," writing around 73 or 74 in Rome, who did this work of rewriting, or even that the rewriting was done in a formal, explicit way. The history of the transmission and transformation of the texts, as reconstructed by the history of forms school, will perhaps find nothing but texts (written or oral) that were *ever-already* revised by the postpaschal discourse.

There is one further question, and it concerns the link of the ACT narrative with the eschatological narrative. The question was raised at the narrator/readers level ("in truth I tell you"), for it had become a crucial question in the Roman community. Peter and Paul were dead, and the generation of those who knew Jesus was passing away. The eschatological kingdom would come—but *when?*

"Some of those standing here will not taste death before they see the kingdom of God coming": the kingdom is therefore very near at hand. This will be the thesis of S 58. This addition here in S 42 is not accidental: the second function of the postpaschal theological discourse is to justify this prediction, this thesis of "Mark."[87]

"In power": this recalls us to the *power* of the narrative of J, which thereby announces the final narrative in which the text of the kingdom, now hidden, secret, and mysterious, will become *manifest* ("the glory of his Father").

S 43 (9:2-14a)

a1　And six days later the Jesus takes with him the Peter, the James, and the John and brings them up a high mountain alone, by themselves.

b　And he was changed in form before them, and his garments became radiant, exceedingly white, to a degree that no fuller on earth can whiten. And Elijah appeared to them with Moses, and they were speaking with the Jesus. And the Peter answering says to the Jesus: "Rabbi, it is good that we be here, and we shall erect three tents, one for you and one for Moses and one for Elijah." For he did not know what to answer, for they were afraid. And a cloud came and cast a shadow over them, and a voice came from the cloud: "This is my beloved son. Listen to him!" And suddenly, looking around they saw no one but Jesus alone with them.

a2　As they were coming down from the mountain,

c　he commanded them to tell no one what they had seen, until the Son of man should be raised from the dead. They kept the word, while discussing among themselves what rising from the dead meant. And they questioned him, saying: "Why do the scribes say that Elijah must come first?" He said to them: "Elijah comes first and reestablishes everything. How then is it written of the Son of man that he will suffer much and be treated with contempt? But I tell you that Elijah too has come, and they did whatever they wanted to him, as it is written of him."

a3 And coming . . .

Gr.: "It is good that we be here, and we shall erect three tents." The Greek text resists the translation that some critics propose for the opening words of Peter: "It is good *for us* to be here," as though the spokesman for the disciples were voicing their happiness. In fact, he is only saying how opportune it is that they are here so that they may "erect three tents."[88] The text says that "they were afraid." How then could they be happy?

a1. "Six days later": link with S 42; the two sequences round each other out. "The Peter, the James, and the John": witnesses of the "resurrection" of the little girl in S 25; they formed the innermost circle around J. "Alone, by themselves": STR. "Up a high mountain": place close to heaven (MYTH) and place of prayer (S 32).

b. "Before them," "appeared to them," "This is . . . listen to him": The vision scene ("what they had seen") is meant for the three, not for J (who remains passive throughout), while S 2 was addressed to J himself ("he saw," "you are").

"He was changed in form . . . his garments . . . exceedingly white . . . on *earth* can whiten": the whiteness is inscribed in the MYTH code, it is *heavenly*. The garments stand, by metonymy, for the body (cf. S 26, S 34), so that the body of J (SYMB) is the real object of the vision, a body "touched" by heaven.

"Elijah, Moses": their appearance on the high mountain[89] evokes memories of Sinai and Horeb. Moses represents the first promise-fulfillment of Israel (cf. the Passover in S 62 and the new exodus); Elijah, the one who is to come before the Messiah,[90] represents the final fulfillment.

"The Peter answering [i.e. to the vision] . . . did not know what to answer": what Peter says is disavowed by the author and must therefore refer to the STR Z; *perhaps* the tents were to be for the three, while they, strengthened by the support of Heaven, would go and gather an army of Zealots (cf. Ex. 23:27-33).

"They were afraid": as unclean men in the presence of power, like the Israelites gathered around Mt. Sinai (Ex. 19:16-23; 20:18-21). "Cloud": MYTH (cf. Ex. 19:6); in S 58 and S 66 the Son of man is linked with the "clouds." "A voice came from the cloud": the voice of God (cf. Ex. 20:21: "the dark cloud where God was").

"This is my beloved son": cf. S 2; relates back also to S 42: "the Son of man . . . when he comes in the glory of his Father." According to the new teaching of S 42c-e, then, J is shown to *be* the Son of man, whose *body* is taken up into the clouds, into the "glory" of his Father. "Listen to him": the disciples are urged to *listen to* the new teaching; this confirms that S 42c represents a new call. At the postpaschal level, the MYTH urges men to hear the *prediction* made by J; it guarantees the theological discourse of the narrator, indicating that the latter, according to the text, has its ground in the divine voice. The necessity of the suffering, death, and Resurrection is a necessity created by the plan or STR of God. *Theology* is thus presented, not as words *about* God (that is what Greek theology will be), but as a discourse coming *from* God. In short, the contradiction theology/narrative is related to the contradiction MYTH/narrative, in which the latter is cancelled out by a knowledge of its unfolding that is acquired in advance. This *knowledge in advance* concerning the narrative will define the structure of the theological ideology in its relation to the narrative.[91]

"Suddenly": end of the vision. "Looking around": disappearance of the cloud. "They saw no one": disappearance of Moses and Elijah. "But Jesus alone with them": present, as before, are the carpenter of Nazareth and his disciples. The MYTH parenthesis is closed because the purpose of the vision has been achieved, and the ACT narrative resumes. The SYMB of the BAS is placed in relation to heaven (the MYTH has *touched* the body of J), J is placed in relation to the Son of man, and theology has received its guarantee.

a2. "As they were coming down from the mountain": they return to the sites of J's practice (on the "mountain" there is no narrative).

c. "He commanded them to tell no one": STR prolonging that of S 42b in regard to messiahship. Let us recall the ambiguity of the title of Messiah. In the Zealot text, Messiah = king, liberator of Israel from the Romans (cf. S 68–S 71); in the BAS, Messiah = Son of man, and brings about the completion of the BAS circle in Israel and, as we shall see, among the pagans as well (or, at the narrator/readers level, the completion or fulfillment of ecclesiality).

"Until the Son of man should be raised from the dead": the vision meshes with the postpaschal theological discourse (in the erased text, the terminus of the delay might have been the return to Galilee; cf. S 63). "They kept the word, while discussing": narrator/readers level.[92] A question (ANAL) has been raised for the DD, which has been erased in the prepaschal text and which related to the eschatological narrative; perhaps the question was how the Son of man would go up. "They questioned him . . . Elijah must come first?": that is, before the Messiah; therefore, what is the relation between his coming and your messiahship? "Come": as he went up (ascending movement; cf. Acts 1:11).

"Reestablishes everything": the Jewish SYMB code; Elijah is to make known those who are clean (pollution system) and just (debt system). "Elijah too has come": refers to John the Baptist who came to prepare the ways for one more powerful than he (S 1). "They did whatever they wanted to him": the death of John (S 30), compared with the coming death of J. Reference to Eccles. 48:10.[93] The identification of John with Elijah serves Mark's "thesis" that the final events are very close (cf. S 58): "As it is written of him": corresponds to "How then is it written of the Son of man?": postpaschal discourse.

S 44 (9:14b-30a)

a1   . . . the disciples,

b   they saw a great crowd around them and scribes arguing with them.

c1   And immediately the whole crowd, seeing him, were amazed and, running up, greeted him. He asked them: "What are you arguing about with them?"

d1   Someone from the crowd answered him: "Teacher, I brought my son to you because he has a mute spirit. Whenever it lays hold of him, it throws him to the ground, and he foams at the mouth and grinds his teeth and becomes stiff. And I asked your disciples to expel it, but they could not."

c2   But he, answering them, says: "Unbelieving generation, how long shall I put up with you? Bring him to me."

e1   They brought him to him. And seeing him, the spirit immediately convulsed him, and he fell to the ground and rolled around, foaming at the mouth.

d2   And he asked his father: "How long has this been happening to him?" He said: "Since childhood. Often, too, it even throws him into fire or water to destroy him. But if you can do anything, have pity on us and help us." And the Jesus said to him, " 'If you can?' Everything is possible for him who believes." Immediately the father of the child cried out and said, "I believe; help my unbelief."

e2   But the Jesus, seeing that the crowd was running together, rebuked the unclean spirit, saying to it: "Mute and deaf spirit, I command you: Go out of him and do not go into him again." And crying out and convulsing him greatly, it went out. And he became like a corpse, so that the people said, "He is dead." But the Jesus took his hand and lifted him up, and he stood up.

f   When he had returned to the house, his disciples asked privately, "Why were we unable to expel it?" And he said to them, "This kind cannot go out except through prayer."

a2. Having departed from there,

We shall make only a few comments on this text:

b. The C is around the DD, who are the center of the circle, although they are powerless to expel the spirit (unlike S 28). Correlative with this is f, below, that is, the question privately in the *house* (fictitious TOP): "This kind [a spirit that is mute; in S 24, J expels the spirit who is "legion" after having asked it for its name] cannot go out except through prayer."

c2. "Unbelieving generation": Who is meant? The scribes? The C? The DD? The text is vague; S 39 seems to point to the AA; this passage seems to mean the C. In addition, the event seems to take place in pagan territory, but the presence of the scribes[94] shows that it is Galilee. "How long shall I put up with you": that is, remain in your SYMB field, the field of unbelief and misreading. The perspective (STR) of a departure from this field to the pagan nations appears here. The "how long" indicates the ignorance (the "without his knowing how") of J about his own future, led onward as he is by the ANAL of the narrative.

d2. "Everything is possible for him who believes": faith in relation to power (cf. S 27).

e2. "He became like a corpse": as in S 25, the C asserts a death, while the narrative (in S 25 it was the actant J) plays down the "resurrection."[95]

Let us note that faith/prayer/power form a series in this sequence, at the beginning of the "ascent of Jerusalem" (S 45f); the series will return in S 53–S 54, which completes S 45. This ascent is used for teaching the disciples the *strategy of power,* the STR J. It seems that this is what justifies putting S 44 at this point in the narrative.

S 45 (9:30b-32)

a   they passed through Galilee, and he did not want anyone to know.
b   For he was teaching his disciples and telling them: "The Son of man will be delivered into the hands of men, and they will kill him, and when he has been killed, after three days he will rise up." But they did not understand what he said and were afraid to ask him about it.

a. "Having departed from there" (S 44a2): Link with S 42c–e, across S 43–S 44, and thus between the two postpaschal "predictions." "They passed through Galilee" (GEO): coming from the north (Caesarea Philippi). The strategic instruction that follows extends clandestinity to all of Galilee and no longer to the towns alone. The mission in Galilee is therefore finished: S 5–S 9 and S 18–S 28, after which there is a turning point (STR), messianic in character if any is, namely, the sequence of the loaves (S 31–S42). Here the ascent to Jerusalem begins, but S 45 is interwoven with several other sequences down to S 53. "He did not want anyone to know": clandestinity (STR).

b. "For he was teaching his disciples": ANAL in the space of the DD. "The Son of man": Postpaschal prediction. In the logic of S 42c–e the erased text sets up a confrontation of J/AA at Jerusalem (here the AA are simply "men") and a confrontation of STR J/Z. The clandestinity seems meant to keep the C from going up to Jerusalem with J while thinking he was a Zealot. The ascent scheme of the Son of man is on the horizon. "They did not understand": they are in the field of the STR Z. After their failure to understand his practice during the sequence of the loaves has been made up for by the confession of his messiahship in S 42, the STR of the messiahship now becomes in its turn the subject of their failure to understand. "They were afraid to ask about it": because of the confrontation (cf. S 45e)?

S 46 (9:33-10:1a)

a1 And they came to Capernaum.
b   And while he was in the house he asked them: "What were you discussing on the road?" But they were silent, for on the road they had been discussing with one another who was the greatest.
c   And sitting down, he called the twelve and says to them: "If anyone wants to be first, he must be the last of all and the servant of all." And taking a child, he stood him in the midst of them, and embracing him he said to them: "Whoever welcomes one of these children for the sake of my name welcomes me, and whoever welcomes me welcomes not me but the one who sent me."
d   And the John said: "Teacher, we saw someone who does not follow us expelling demons in your name, and we tried to stop him because he was not following us." But the Jesus said: "Do not stop him, for no one will do a work of power in my name and be able straight-way to speak ill of me. For he who is not against us is with us. For anyone who gives you a cup of water to drink in the name of the fact that you belong to the Messiah, in truth (amen) I tell you that he shall not lose his reward. And he who causes one of these little ones who believe in me to fall, it is better for him that a millstone be tied around his neck, and he be cast into the sea. And if your hand causes you to fall, cut it off; it is better for you to enter into life crippled than to have both hands and go into Gehenna, into the fire inextinguishable. And if your foot causes you to fall, cut it off; it is better for you to enter into life lame than to have both feet and be thrown into Gehenna. And if your eye causes you to fall, pluck it out; it is better for you to enter with one eye into the kingdom of God than to have both eyes and be thrown into Gehenna, where their worm does not die and the fire is not extinguished. For each one will be salted by fire. Salt is good, but if the salt loses its taste, how can you season it? Have salt in you, and be at peace with one another."
a2 And rising up from there,

a1. "And they came to Capernaum": echo of S 5 and of the definitive completion of what had begun then.

b. "And while he was in the house": the space of the DD in Capernaum (TOP). "He asked them": ANAL. J seeks to have the narrative of the DD, their discussion, read. "On the road" (twice): scheme of the *following* of J by the DD. This scheme, introduced in S 42a, will be dominant during this major sequence of the ascent to Jerusalem, just as the *circle* had been in Galilee. Especially to be noted is that the confrontation of the STR J/Z is connected with the road, the journey. The discussion here, following as it does on S 45a, is to be read in the context of the ascent to Jerusalem: in the new city (to be established at Jerusalem) what will the hierarchic place of the DD be (STR Z)? Who will be the greatest among them, according to the codes that are dominant among the AA?

c. "Sitting down": in the house, the circle takes shape again ("in the midst of them"). "The first/the last, the servant of all": overturning of the hierarchic code, subversion of the code of political power (SOC); cf. S 50. "A child": forms a series with "servant."[96] "He stood him in the midst of them, and embracing him" (SYMB): a reading lesson (cf. S 16). The child is related by metonymy to J, the two bodies being brought together in the center of the circle; thus the series becomes now: servant/child/Jesus (cf. S 50: "The Son of man has come . . . to serve"), and the subversion of the dominant political code is related to the body of J.

"Whoever welcomes" (cf. S 28): into his house and to his table, as a host; the reference is to the debt system, with the gift of the table being a condition for satiation and blessing. Another term is now added to the series: child/Jesus/the one who sent me (that is, God; cf. S 2, S 43), with his kingdom of superabundance and eschatological blessing. In the articulation of the three narratives (ACT/ecclesial/eschatological) their three centers are placed in series: Jesus, the child-servant, God.

d. John reads the narrative of another man who "does not follow *us*" (instead of: "does not follow *you*") and yet expels demons in *your* name, with power. "We tried to stop him because he was not following us": STR Z. J's reading: anyone who "will *do* a work of power in my name" will not be able "to speak ill of me," because his narrative is related to mine and the power in him is the power of *my name* in which the narrative is proclaimed.

"He who is not against us" (is not one of the AA) "is for us" (is a D). In a word, where there is a narrative of blessing, I am there. "Anyone who gives up a cup of water to drink": once again nourishment, this time in the line of drink, the gesture being the equivalent of "welcoming." The cup is given because "you belong to the Messiah," that is, because of your messianic practice and its power which is read despite the subversion it entails or, more accurately, because of that very subversion.

"In truth I tell you": narrator/readers levels. The future tense ("anyone who will give you") shows that it is *ecclesial narratives* that are meant. At Rome these narratives are narratives of persecution; anyone who "welcomes" another because he "belongs to the Messiah"[97] is dangerous. "And he who causes . . . to fall": by his practice.[98] "Cast into the sea": into the abyss of Satan (MYTH). "And if your hand, your foot, your eye causes you to fall": SYMB, according to the semantic system that articulates the body with practice at the three levels.[99] Meant here are Christians who have given in to persecution and whose practice (of hands, feet, or eyes) has thereby become nonecclesial (cf. S 22c3 and S 63: to fall, to be scandalized or to scandalize in relation to persecution).

"Life, kingdom of God/Gehenna": the final narrative, with which the ecclesial narratives are put in relation (cf. S 42e); the two consequences of the judgment are related as life/death, Gehenna being the place of uncleanness and death, and the kingdom of God being the place of blessing, fruitfulness, and *life.*

"Crippled, lame, with one eye/both hands, both feet, both eyes": a paradox based on the pollution system (SYMB) and on the effectiveness of J's practice (in restoring a man's hand, S 16; the power to walk, S 12, S 25; and the power to see, S 41). In the face of persecution, as in the face of unbelief, power is inhibited; nonetheless a man should not (cause to) *fall* but keep going, in search of the kingdom and life.

"For each one will be salted by fire": persecution has the function of purifying practices and hearts (cf. the judgment by purifying fire[100]).

"Salt is good": the meal again, assuring the linkup of the entire discourse of J. "The salt loses its taste": those who fall, whose practice is treasonable. "Have salt in you, and be at peace with one another": be true to ecclesial practice (welcoming children to your table, giving your bread; S 31); then the *ekklesia* will be at peace and be blessed, even in time of persecution. Here, then, we have a call to eccclesial unity; we are still on the narrator/readers level, where the ecclesial narratives in the difficult period of persecution are related to the final narrative that will come as an everlasting blessing before "some of those standing here . . . taste death" (S 42e). The alternative is everlasting uncleanness: "They will see the corpses of men who have rebelled against me. Their worm will not die nor their fire go out; they will be loathsome to all mankind" (Isa. 66:24). To assert this alternative is meaningful even at the beginning of the ascent to Jerusalem, since persecutions are predicted that will arise from the confrontation with the AA.

S 45c-d (10: 1b)

c   he comes into the region of Judea beyond the Jordan,
d   and again crowds go with him, and according to his custom he taught them again.

c. "Rising up from there, he comes into the region of Judea": (GEO) Galilee/Judea, programmed in S 2, announced in S 42, begun in S 45a. "Beyond the Jordan": Jordan—Jerusalem—Judea, a TOP series in S 2; in the present context, Jordan looks to Jerusalem.

d. "Again crowds . . . according to his custom . . . again": a double "again," plus "his custom." This is a Galilean structure[101] that will not come into play again until S 45i–S 53. As with the circle in S 46 and the tempting by the AA in S 47, the text seems to put these Galilean elements here *as a reminder,* as a kind of résumé of the Galilean narrative, thus on the one hand marking the contrast with the narrative of the ascent to Jerusalem, and on the other marking the continuity with it.

S 47 (10:2-12)

a   And some Pharisees approached him and asked him in order to tempt him: "Does a man have authority to dismiss his wife?" But in answer he said to them: "What command did Moses give you?" But they said: "Moses gave permission to write a bill of divorce and to dismiss." But the Jesus said to them: "It was because of your hardness of heart that he wrote that commandment for you. But at the beginning of creation he made them male and female; on that account a man will leave his father and mother and the two will become one flesh; thus they will no longer be two but one flesh. Therefore, what God has joined together, let man not separate."

b   In the house the disciples asked him again about this. And he says to them: "Whoever dismisses his wife and marries another woman commits adultery against her; and if she dismisses her husband and marries another, she commits adultery."

a. "Some Pharisees . . . to tempt him": as in S 39 the AA take the initiative. "Does a man have authority to dismiss his wife?": (SYMB). The debt system,[102] in which, since the man receives the woman as a gift from another "house," she belongs to the "house" of her husband; the latter has *authority* over her as over everything else in his house. In a class society such as Palestine, divorce is in fact a class privilege,[103] just as polygamy is,[104] since the poor cannot afford either (SOC).

"Your hardness of heart": that of the AA, as in S 16. The connection of the woman with the patrimony is being challenged. The repudiated woman is abandoned and returned to the "house" of her parents. Divorce is a means by which man holds sway over woman.

"But at the beginning of creation": J opposes the writing of the beginning to the writing of Moses; the Law and the covenant resulted from a degradation of the original writing (that the Law was required by men's hardness of heart is a frequent theme of the Pentateuch). "He made them male and female . . . one flesh": the flesh in opposition to the patrimony, to wealth (SOC).

"What God has joined together, let man not separate": J "corrects" the law of Moses and goes back to the beginning because the eschatological narrative is at hand, when blessing will be restored in its original superabundance (cf. S 58: the time between creation and the end is a time of tribulation and curse). Love, or the union of man and woman in *one flesh*, is restored over against the power-based domination of the rich (subversion of the SOC). In the ANAL, J reads Gn. 2:24 in order to bring the AA to read their own practice.

b. "In the house": fictitious space of the DD (TOP). "He says to them": the reading is expanded. To the dismissal by the man, which alone was admitted in Israel, he adds dismissal of the man by the woman, which was accepted at Rome (SOC).[105] Therefore, we are on the narrator/readers level. In the *ekklesia*, whose members belonged to the dominated class, the patrimony/ love opposition no longer has any meaning; man and woman are placed on the same level.

"Commits adultery": debt system (SYMB), site of desire as covetousness and even as madness. The *ekklesia,* in consequence of the conversion of their practice on the part of those who are now Christians, is seen as a site where the love of man and woman can continue to exist, rising above the madness of desire that is at the mercy of the principal equivalents of the SOC, and the woman becomes more than her vagina[106] and her blood. In short, the two fleshes can become one *flesh in the ecclesial context.*[107]

S 48 (10:13-16)

a   They brought children to him so that he might touch them, but the disciples rebuked them.

b   But seeing this the Jesus became angry and told them: "Let the children come to me, do not prevent them, for the kingdom of God belongs to such as they. In truth (amen) I tell you, whoever does not welcome the kingdom of God like a child will not enter it."

c   And embracing them he placed his hands on them and blessed them.

a. Gr. *paidion* includes children from eight days to twelve years old.[108] "They brought . . . touch them": his action is analogous to that done to the sick (Ic), as in S 7 and S 34. Here, however, the act of touching (SYMB) is perhaps to be read as a "promise of blessing" for a vaguely defined future, while in the case of the Ic it was a "fulfillment of blessing." "Children": like servants[109] and women (S 47), *children* are the *possession* of the father of the family and are subject to his sway in the "house" throughout the entire period in which the codes of the social formation are being produced (SOC).

"The disciples rebuked them": children/adults antithesis. Children, like women, are excluded from the STR proper to the place of struggle *for* political power (STR Z, which is regularly indicated by the verb "rebuke"; cf. S 42 especially).

b. "Jesus became angry": STR J, rare (S 16, anger). "Let the children . . . and blessed them": metonymy J/children (SYMB) as in S 46.

"Do not prevent them, for the kingdom of God": therefore, in the BAS space, there is room for children; the STR J is here opposed to the STR Z (children can take part in the struggle *against* power). "Belongs to such as they": the practice of children is the practice of play and pleasure, involving some aggressivity indeed but no relations of domination; that is how it will be in the kingdom.

"In truth I tell you": attention is now on the ecclesial narratives. "Whoever does not welcome the kingdom of God like a child will not enter it": ecclesial narratives should be narratives like those of children, that is, narratives of play and pleasure, without relations of domination. This is the condition for entering the kingdom (eschatological narrative), as will also be seen in the next two sequences, which likewise deal with entry into the kingdom of God. There is a continuity between ecclesial practice and the kingdom (cf. the parable of the seed, S 22b3). The kingdom of God is baffling to adults who belong to the system (SOC); it brings into existence another field of society.

"He . . . blessed them": the body-to-body relation with J (SYMB), which is a pledge of blessing for these children.

S 49 (10:17-31)

a   As he was setting out on the road,

b   someone ran up and, falling on his knees, asked him: "Good teacher, what shall I do so that I may obtain eternal life?" But the Jesus said to him: "Why do you call me 'good'? No one is good but the God alone. You know the commandments: Do not kill, do not commit adultery, do not steal, do not bear false witness, do not defraud, honor your father and mother." But he said: "Teacher, I have kept all these since my youth." Then the Jesus, fixing his gaze on him, loved him and said to him: "One thing you lack; go, sell what you have, and give to the poor, and you will have a treasure in heaven, and come, follow me." But he became gloomy at this word, and went away saddened, for he had great possessions.

c   And looking around him, the Jesus says to his disciples: "How hard it is for those who have possessions to enter the kingdom of God!" The disciples were amazed at his words. But the Jesus again answers and says to them: "Children, how hard it is to enter the kingdom of God! It is easier for a camel to pass through the eye of a needle than for a rich man to enter the kingdom of God." But they were even more dismayed and said to one another: "Who then can be saved?" The Jesus fixes his gaze on them and says: "For men it is impossible but not for God, for all things are possible to the God."

d   The Peter began to say to him: "Behold, we have left everything and followed you." The Jesus said: "In truth (amen) I tell you, there is no one who has left home or brothers or sisters or father or mother or children or fields because of me and because of the good news, who shall not receive a hundred times more, now in this time, of houses and brothers and sisters and mothers and children and fields along with persecutions, and in the time to come eternal life. Many of the first shall be last, and the last shall be first."

a. "On the road": this is the scheme that will dominate the entire sequence, which raises the question of the *following* of J.

b. "Falling on his knees": except for Jairus (S 25), only the unclean do this (S 10, S 18, S 24, S 26, S 36). The narrative statement shows the teacher/disciple relationship of which the discourses speak. "Good teacher . . . call me 'good'?": the man reads the narrative of J and the blessing it produces. "No one is good but the God alone": J relates his narrative to the God (ANAL).

"What shall I do . . . eternal life?": question on the *correct practice* in relation to the final narrative (in the field of the ideology of the SOC). "You know the commandments . . . father and mother": J refers to the Scriptures and specifically to the debt system. "I have kept all these": the man reads his own practice; his question to J shows that he feels the limitations of that practice in relation to the eschatological blessing. In short, his question is: how shall I *act* so that, *in the framework of the system (SOC)*, I may have a share in eternal life?

"His gaze . . . loved him": the narrative statement prepares for the call in the discourse; this is the only time that the text speaks of J's love for someone. This fact emphasizes the importance of the call. "One thing you lack": J offers him a messianic reading (BAS) of his practice, telling him that his practice is unfulfilled, that it is being carried on within the limits of the debt system, which, in a class society, is distorted.

"Go, sell whatever you have, and give to the poor": You *lack* one thing/whatever you *have*—(the poor *lack*)/whatever you *have* (give to them). "And you will have a treasure in heaven": you have/you will have, present narrative and final narrative (MYTH); this is the reply to the man's question.

"And come, follow me": be my disciple, I will be your teacher. Here, then, is the definition of a *disciple* according to two stages: *break* with the SOC/*following* after J, as in S 4 ("*leaving* their nets there . . . their father Zebedee/they *followed* him, they *went off after* him") and S 13 ("sitting at the tax office . . . standing up/he followed him"). The SOC is the site of the *desires* that are bewitched by the dominant codes, in this case the desire for *wealth* ("he had great possessions").

"He became gloomy at this word, and went away saddened": the scene ends ("He went away") with a refusal of the call; the dominant codes have gained the upper hand over him ("saddened" shows the *heart* is involved). The debt system as read in the class society (SOC) is being challenged here. The following scenes will develop this.

c. J reads the narrative of the rich man's *refusal* (ANAL, the circle is reconstituted: "around him") according to the opposition: be rich/enter the kingdom of God; this entry is said to be *difficult* and finally *impossible*. A metaphor emphasizes this point: the metaphor of the camel and the eye of the needle effects the passage from the "difficult" to the "impossible."

Note the various emphases in the text. Four times the key opposition is stated; in only one of them is there no allusion to wealth, but this lacuna is evidently supplied by the parallel statements. Twice attention is called to the gaze of J; the gaze in both cases echoes, as it were, the gaze he fixed on the rich man. Twice the amazement and dismay of the disciples is mentioned, which ends with the question: "Who then can be saved?" There is question still, as in b, of the relation between present practice and the final narrative; this emphasis is found nowhere else in the text of Mark, showing us that we are dealing with a key factor in the narrative, namely, the confrontation of the STR J/Z which dominates the ascent to Jerusalem.

Why are the disciples amazed? In the debt system, the system in which the STR Z is inscribed, wealth is a blessing from God and a mark of uprightness, if the wealth belongs to a follower of the Law, as is the case with the man invited to follow J. The fact that J once fails to mention wealth, in the statement: "Children, how hard it is to enter the kingdom of God!" and thus generalizes the difficulty, enables us to see that wealth is the determination of all the codes of the social formation, and that it is at the level of wealth that everything comes together in relation to the messianic narrative and to the kingdom of God.

"Who then can be *saved*?": "be saved" is parallel to "enter the kingdom of God," and thus to the final narrative. This program was already set forth in S 42e, where *save* (one's life) was opposed to *lose* (one's life), and this in the two registers of present practice and final narrative. Moreover, in S 16, S 25, S 26, S 34, and later on in S 51, *save* is used of the cure (c → b) of the Ic, which is an effect of the power of the practice of J (SYMB). Here, too, "difficult" and "impossible" indicate power ("who *can* be saved?").

"For men it is impossible": for men, like this rich man, who are in the framework of the system (SOC), it is impossible. This is J's reading of the rich man's refusal; once again, J *reads* the ACT narrative of the Ic (just as in S 16 his anger reads the narrative of the AA).

"But not for God, for all things are possible to the God": above, "No one is good but the God alone" had been J's reading of his own narrative; here again, this is *possible* to those who *follow* me, me whose narrative is the narrative of a practice of *salvation*, powerful and related to him to whom all things are possible. This turns the text toward the narrative of the disciples, which Peter now brings in.

d. "We have *left* everything and *followed* you": a narrative which is the opposite of the rich man's; we are still concerned with the definition of a *disciple* (break with the SOC/following of J).

"In truth I tell you, there is no one . . .": the text puts the answer at the narrator/readers level; it speaks not of "you who have left" but of "all who, in the *ekklesia*, have left" (first element in the definition of a disciple). "Home or brothers or fields": in short, the SOC in its sites of economic production and ideological codes. "Because of me and because of the good news": because of my narrative and because of the fact that it announces the final narrative (second element in the definition of a disciple).

"Who shall not receive a hundred times more, now in this time": as in S 22b ("a hundredfold") and in S 31, the practice of following J ("they hear the word . . . and bear fruit": S 22c4) is superabundantly fruitful. "Houses and sisters . . . and fields": as in S 21, the "house" (kinship) is replaced by the

BAS circle, in this case by the ecclesial circle, in which the family and its relations and its economic production (fields) are common to all and thereby multiplied. There is only this difference, that the *father* who has been left is not reacquired in the *ekklesia*, because in the latter there is to be no father but only brothers and sisters.[110] Similarly, one does not leave his *wife* or recover a multiplicity of *wives*; S 47 is inscribed against polygamy (*one* flesh). We may note, moreover, that the logic of the debt system is maintained: to him who gives (all that he has, being rich, to the poor) a material blessing is promised. The promise given to the disciple of J is not some kind of "spiritual, interior life," but the *satisfaction of the poor* (who break with the SOC) *who follow J.*

"Along with persecutions": this is what the *ekklesia* of Rome has just experienced. The persecutions are a response to the *subversiveness* of messianic practice (to save one's life is to lose it, S 42e).

"Now in this time"/"in the time to come": the text clearly shows that there are two times of blessing and life, and not a time of curse (now) that is recompensed by a time of blessing (later on). This contrasts with the *sadness* of the rich man after he has refused to be a disciple.

"Eternal life": an echo of the rich man's question. The whole sequence answers his question by means of a twofold reading: a reading of the rich man's narrative and a reading of the narratives of the disciples (and of the *ekklesia*).

"Many of the first shall be last": the first in the SOC, the rich. "And the last shall be first": you, the disciples, who are last in the SOC. "Shall be": in the kingdom of God. The conclusion clearly brings out the subversion which the BAS effects in the SOC.[111]

S 45e-f (10:32-34)

e   They were on the road, going up to Jerusalem, and the Jesus was going before them, and they were filled with wonder, and those who were following were afraid.

f   And taking the twelve aside again, he began to tell them what would happen to him: "Behold, we are going up to Jerusalem, and the Son of man will be handed over to the chief priests and the scribes, and they will condemn him to death and hand him over to the pagans; they will mock him, spit on him, scourge him, and kill him, and after three days he will rise."

e. "They were on the road . . . and the Jesus was going before them . . . and those who followed": The scheme of the *road* is clearly indicated by the text: "going up to Jerusalem . . . we are going up to Jerusalem." Sequence 45 finds its expression both in narrative statement and in the discourse of J. The scheme of the road and the ascent to Jerusalem (STR) are connected, which is an index that the scheme is predominantly STR, while that of the circle is predominantly ANAL (or is predominantly a matter of powerful practice).

"Wonder . . . fear": the wonder and the fear change depending on whether they refer to the *circle* (S 6d, S 12e, S 23, S 26, S 33, S 37, S 43, S 45b, S 49c, S 73c) or to the *road* (S 45e, S 64e). Here there is question of fear at the thought of the confrontation with the AA in Jerusalem, as the scene confirms. They are afraid because they are unarmed and unorganized (STR Z).

f. "Taking the twelve aside again": within the group of followers (including the women of S 71g) the distinction of DD/twelve has been becoming ever clearer since S 46, which follows S 45ab. The place of the twelve is STR (cf. S 19, S 28); it is stated therefore in a part of the narrative in which STR is dominant.

"Began to tell them what would happen to him": the contradiction is expressed at the level of the narrative statement itself, in the form of an indirect discourse that incorporates the theology of the narrator, the prenarration being antinarration in the narrative logic of the text itself.

S 50 (10:35-45)

a   And James and John, the sons of Zebedee, approached him,

b   saying to him: "Teacher, we want you to do for us the thing that we shall ask of you." He said to them: "What do you want me to do for you?" And they said to him: "Grant us that we may sit, one at your right hand and the other at your left, in your glory." But the Jesus said to them: "You do not know what you are asking. Can you drink the cup that I drink or be immersed in the immersion (baptism) in which I am immersed?" They said to him: "We can." But the Jesus said to them: "You will drink the cup that I drink, and you will be immersed in the immersion in which I am to be immersed. But to sit at my right hand or my left is not mine to give you, but it is for those for whom it has been prepared."

c   And having heard, the ten began to be indignant at James and John.

d   And having called them to him, the Jesus says to them: "You know that those who are regarded as the rulers of the peoples lord it over them and that their great men tyrannize over them. But it is not so among you. Instead, he who wants to be great among you must become your servant, and he who wants to be first among you must become the slave of all. For the Son of man did not come to be served but to serve and to give his life as a ransom for many."

a. "James and John, the sons of Zebedee": the mention of the "house" of Zebedee shows that the request to be made comes under the social codes produced by the "house" (SOC).

b. This sequence is akin to S 62–S 63, in which the postpaschal theology is likewise at work. Thus we find here three metaphors for the death of Jesus: drinking the cup, being immersed (baptized), and giving his life as a ransom; we shall analyze these later on.[112] However, the request for places of political power (STR Z)[113]—"Grant us that we may sit . . . in your glory," which is inscribed in the ascent to Jerusalem—belongs to the prepaschal *logic* of Z: they are going up to Jerusalem, and then the final narrative will come. The following dialogue, in which J already knows the future narrative of James and John is postpaschal and even more than simply postpaschal, since it supposes that the narrator knows of the death of the two brothers. This dialogue in which the brothers' request is rejected presupposes two things: that places in the kingdom depend on the narrative of each individual, and that J is not the master of these places (cf. S 58b7: "nor the Son"). The kingdom is not conquered but received (S 48).

"It is for those for whom it has been prepared": predestinational logic proper to the postpaschal theological discourse.

c. "The ten began to be indignant": jealousy showing that all were aspiring to the first places (I submit that such "rivalries" always play a part in strategies for the "acquisition of power" such as the STR Z was).

d. "Jesus says to them . . . lord it over them . . . tyrannize over them": such is the logic of the codes in the system (SOC) that the twelve share (J adds the nuance: "are regarded"). Z does not fall outside the SOC.

"But it is not so among you": subversion of the political code of class domination, in accordance with the opposition "great/servant" and "first/ slave." This is the lesson of S 46 and the end of S 49 (first/last).[114] The narrator/readers level is at work in this scene too; the conclusion illustrates this subversion of the codes by a postpaschal reading of the narrative of J, in which the word *serve* is clarified. Since it is a practice that moves people from a situation of curse to a situation of blessing (c → b), *serve* is equivalent to *save*. If we compare this sequence with S 49, we may say that in S 49 the disciple is defined in the first of the two constitutive moments, namely the break with the SOC, while here he is defined in the second moment, namely the *service* of fulfillment and salvation.

S 45g (10:46a)

g   They came to Jericho.

g. En route to Jerusalem.

S 51 (10:46b-52)

a   And as he was leaving Jericho with his disciples and a large crowd,

b   Bartimaeus, the son of Timaeus, a blind beggar, was sitting beside the road. And hearing: "It is Jesus of Nazareth!" he began to cry out and say: "Jesus, son of David, have pity on me!" And many rebuked him to make him be silent, but he cried out more loudly: "Son of David, have pity on me!"

c   The Jesus stopped and said: "Call him." And they call the blind man, telling him: "Have courage! Stand up, he is calling you." And throwing aside his cloak, he jumped up and came to the Jesus.

d   And in response to him the Jesus said: "What do you want me to do for you?" And the blind man said to him: "Rabboni, I want to see!" And the Jesus said to him: "Go, your faith has saved you." And immediately he saw

e   and was following him on the road.

   a. "He was leaving Jericho with his disciples and a large crowd": Outside the town (TOP), a scenario typical of Galilee (crowd; Ic who hears the narrative: "It is Jesus!"). Like S 45c,d, and S 47, the sequence is a reminder of the powerful practice of J, the only one since the departure for Jerusalem. Thus there is a contrast between the practice of J in Galilee and his practice in Judea.

   b. "Jesus of Nazareth": J, who comes from a small village in Galilee (SOC). "Jesus, son of David": prepares for S 45i, in which the C receives J as Davidic Messiah. The parallel with S 41–S 42 is inescapable. Here the C is compared to a blind man; there Peter was compared to a blind man who initially sees something but will see clearly only at a second stage. "Many rebuked him": this term, characteristic of the STR code (S 6, S 42, S 48) here indicates the STR Z (the cry of the Zealots is not to be used, for fear of the Romans, since the Zealots are not prepared militarily).

   d. "Your faith has saved you": as in S 12 and S 26, *faith* consists in the man's little strategy for getting through the C and reaching J.

   e. "Was following him on the road": the text returns to the scheme of the road.

S 45h (11:1a)

h   And when they draw near to Jerusalem,

   h. The goal of S 45, Jerusalem, is at hand. This is the moment to ask the question: what is the strategic purpose of this ascent? We have spoken thus far only of confrontation with the AA. The text gives a further indication in the parallelism which all the commentators note between S 52 and S 61. In these two sequences J takes the initiative in a small strategy (sending of the two disciples). The strategy leads to the temple sequence (S 53c), which will determine the STR of the AA for getting rid of J; in short, the confrontation takes place around the temple as scene. In this context, it will lead to the supper during the feast of Passover; in connection with this the (prepaschal) STR of J can be further explained.

S 52 (11:1b-7a)

a   at Bethpage and Bethany on the Mountain of Olives, he sends two of his disciples and tells them: "Go into the village ahead of you, and immediately on entering it you will find an ass's foal tethered there on which no one has yet ridden; untie it and bring it. And if anyone asks you: 'Why are you doing that?' say: 'The Lord has need of it, and will send it back here straightway.' "

b   They went off and found an ass's foal tethered near a gate, outside in the street, and they untie it. And some of the people standing there asked them: "Why are you untying the foal? They answered as the Jesus had told them, and the people let them go.

c   And they bring the foal to the Jesus,

a. Gr. *oros:* Usually translated "Mount (of Olives)," but the word elsewhere means "mountain," and because I want to be literal as possible, I translate it as "mountain" here. "Bethany . . . Mountain of Olives": until S 65, Jerusalem will be opposite them in the TOP code. Bethany and the Mountain of Olives are related to Jerusalem as "outside the town/town," as in the Galilean STR (S 11, S 18). These places outside Jerusalem will be indices of the space of the DD, a space of clandestinity (STR).

b. The narrative statement repeats the discursive statement of J, thus bringing out the STR character of the sequence. The purpose is to acquire the *ass's foal,* or colt, which in the semantics of transportation, is contrasted with the *horse,* which is the warrior's mount, and the *chariot,* in which kings travel.[115]

c. "And they bring the foal to the Jesus": J's STR is therefore not that of a warrior or a king. In this subversion of the Zealot code (STR J/Z), the contrast seems to be pushed to the extreme by the fact that on this foal "no one has yet ridden," that is, the animal has as yet not been trained to carry a rider. The contrast extends further: the scenario in S 45i will be that of the entry of a victorious king into Jerusalem; in other words, J's STR is deliberately messianic, but at the same time it eliminates the current semantics of the Zealots.

S 45i-j (11:7b-11a)

i   and they throw their cloaks over it, and he sat on it. And many spread their cloaks on the road, while others spread rushes which they cut in the fields. And those who went before and after him cried: Hosanna! Blessed in the name of the Lord be he who comes! Blessed be the kingdom that is coming, the kingdom of David our father! Hosanna in the very high places (save us from the Roman)!"

j   And he entered Jerusalem,

Gr. *Hōsanna en tois upsistois.* W. Vischer has noted that this exclamation is meaningless when translated literally: "Save us in the very high places!"[116] A translation of the Greek text back into Hebrew would give: *hsnn bmrm,* which can have the same meaning as the Greek, but can be translated in an entirely different way if we read *lmrm* instead of *bmrm:* "Save us! Blessed be he who comes in the name of the Lord! Blessed be the reign that is coming, the reign of David our father! Save us from the Roman!"[117]

i. "On the road": termination of the road scheme that runs through Sequence 45. "They throw . . . he sat": the STR of J, that of the DD, and that of the C all meet in this procession with its royal acclamations.[118] The ass's foal, the cloaks (of the people), and the reeds all show that the narrative is concerned with the people and the poor; everything that would point to the ruling classes is missing.

"Cried": the cry (Hosanna) is not translated, or is translated in a distorted way; we shall come back to this later on.[119] A blessing is invoked, in the Lord's name, on "him who comes" and on "the kingdom which is coming" and which is connected with David. "Save us from the Roman": the expectation of the C in Jerusalem is thus, on the one hand, messianic-Davidic, in accordance with the teaching of the scribes (S 56), but on the other, it is an expectation of national independence and the expulsion of the occupying forces, in accordance with the hopes of the Zealots. In short, the Zealot semantics of *messiahship* win the day around J and will dominate the coming sequences. Note the confirmation of the Zealot grill we have postulated for the C and the DD.[120]

j. "And he entered Jerusalem, into the temple": Jerusalem—temple, a metonymy that will be repeated in S 53 and S 55. This is to say that in Jerusalem the temple is the place of J's practice; to go up to Jerusalem is to go up to the temple. What will be narrated in the temple constitutes the first of the STR purposes of J, as indicated by S 52.

S 53a-b (11:11b)

a　into the temple. And after looking around at everything, since it was already late,
b　he went out to Bethany with the twelve.

a. "Into the temple": the temple is the center of the Jewish symbolic field (SYMB), the organizing principle of its geography (GEO), and the axis joining earth to heaven (MYTH), as we have already seen.[121]
b. "He went out to Bethany with the twelve": to a place outside the city, a space for DD (STR-TOP).

S 54a-c (11:12-15a)

a　The next day, as they were coming from Bethany he was hungry.
b　And having spotted from a distance a fig tree that had leaves, he went to see if he could find anything on it, but when he came up to it he found nothing but leaves; it was not the time for figs. And in response he said to it: "May no one ever again eat fruit from you." And his disciples heard it.
c　They reached Jerusalem.

Sequences 53a-b and S 54a-c are interwoven. The reason for this is simple: according to the STR begun in S 22, S 54 is the reading of S 53 that is reserved for the DD (Bethany, on the road). Here the scheme for reading is established (as in S 12 and S 16).

a. "He was hungry": The proximity of the references to David (S 51, S 45i) and the temple, the "house of God" (S 53c-e) suggests that we should refer back to S 15, in which we are told how David, when hungry, satisfied his appetite in the house of God.

b. "A fig tree": subject of parable in S 58b6; J finds only leaves on this tree.[122] The commentary, "it was not the time for figs," implies that there was no point in going to look; it thus shows the incoherence of the scene *at the level of the signified.* We are thus urged to read the *signifier* and to look for another *signified,* that found in the scene which is interwoven with this one; the fig tree is parabolic. L. Marin makes the point well: "Buyers and sellers are to the temple what the absence of fruit is to the fig tree: a negative sign of a food that cannot be consumed."[123]

"He said to it: 'May no one . . . from you' ": where there is no blessing, no fruits, a word of curse and judgment comes.

S 53c-e (11:15b-19)

c1 **Having entered the temple, he began to drive out the sellers and buyers in the temple, and to overturn the tables of moneychangers and the seats of the sellers of dove, and he did not allow anyone to carry anything through the temple. And he was teaching and saying to them: "Is it not written: 'My house shall be called a house of prayer for all the pagans'? You, however, have made it a den of robbers!"**

d **And the chief priests and the scribes heard of it, and they were looking for a way to destroy him. For they were afraid of him,**

c2 **since the whole crowd was amazed at his teaching.**

e **And when evening came, they left the city.**

c1. "Having entered the temple, he began to *drive out":* this is the STR term for the expulsion of unclean spirits; the narrative puts those expelled from the temple in the same category as the unclean spirits. "Sellers, buyers, moneychangers, sellers": the four terms show commercial practice that is regulated by the monetary system; this is what is being put in the same category as the unclean spirit. The term *temple* is written three times in this short scene. The money from commerce is connected with the temple, and this is why the temple bears no fruit. Money, the money of the traders, is master there.

"And he was teaching . . . den of robbers": the reading given by J opposes the blessing, the fruits that the temple should have produced according to Scripture ("is it not written") to the actual practice in the temple ("you, however, have made it"). Here is explicitated the confrontation that we said was strategically foreseen in the ascent to Jerusalem. If we recall that this trade was controlled by the chief priests,[124] we can conclude that they are the ones being challenged by the subversive practice of J.

"For all the pagans": in the Jewish eschatological perspective, the center of Israel was to be the place where the pagans, the non-Jewish peoples, would gather. There is nothing here which is alien to the STR Z, but this reference to the pagans shows an element in the STR of J which is in fact foreign to the Zealots and that the pagan readers of Mark could not fail to read.

d. "The chief priests": the text for the first time brings them in as actants, as though it were echoing the words "den of robbers." The chief priests were announced as AA in S 42. Now their practice takes shape: they hear the narrative of the practice of J (in expelling the traders from the temple and making it a site of his own teaching), and they seek for a way to destroy him. Like the scribes and the Pharisees, the chief priests are AA right off in the text, according to the first lesson of the parable of the types of ground (S 22b1, c3).

c2. "The whole crowd was amazed at his teaching": as on every occasion until now, the teaching takes the form of a reading (ANAL) of practice in relation to the temple. After being acclaimed as Messiah the afternoon before, J is listened to as the Messiah who teaches in the symbolic center of Israel. Down to S 56 inclusive, the C will always practice a favorable reception of J; this points to the game of STR that will follow between J and the AA. During the day, since the C is on his side, J is secure from the AA; he speaks and argues openly, and the AA are afraid of the consequences of his practice ("they were afraid of him, since the whole crowd . . .").

e. "When evening came": the C is now gone. "They left the city": therefore J and the twelve depart for Bethany or the Mountain of Olives, where they can find security outside the field dominated by the AA.

S 54d-f (11:20-27a)

d   Passing by early in the morning,

e   they saw the fig tree withered to its roots. And the Peter, remembering, says to him: "Rabbi, look! The fig tree you cursed has withered!" And answering, the Jesus says to them: "Have faith in God. In truth (amen) I tell you, he who says to this mountain: 'Be lifted up and thrown into the sea!' and has no doubt in his heart, but on the contrary believes that what he says will indeed happen, it will be done for him. I tell you, therefore, whatever you pray and ask for, believe that you have received it, and it will be done for you. And when you stand in prayer, forgive if you have anything against anyone, so that your Father who is in the heavens may forgive you for your falls."

f   And they came again to Jerusalem.

d. Morning/evening: CHR link with S 53f.

e. "The fig tree withered to its roots": the parabolic curse has been fulfilled. Peter *reads* the effectiveness of J's word. "Have faith in God": (ANAL) read the parable of the fig tree in what it signifies, namely the temple, which the Messiah has found to be without fruit. As God has withered the fig tree, so will he wither the temple, which has been cursed for being a den of robbers.[125]

"In truth I tell you": at the narrator/readers level, the parable takes on its full meaning after the destruction of the temple. "To this mountain": Mount Zion, on which the temple was built. "Be thrown into the seas": into the abyss of Satan (MYTH). "It will be done for him": in Mark's time it has just been done by the Roman troops. "He believes that what he says will indeed happen": as it has happened to the fig tree, so it will happen (has happened) to the temple. The reading of the parable is a reading about *faith*, a reading about the lack of fruits and about the curse that has fallen on the temple because it has become a place of trade and a den of robbers.

The contrast between J and the Zealots emerges with full clarity: the Zealots would fight on behalf of the temple, in order to free it from the Romans (and from the chief priests); J has something quite different in view: a house of God which "shall be called a house of prayer for all the pagans." The pagan readers of the Gospel read this fulfillment: the messianic communities in which they pray have replaced the temple. To this statement of J, therefore, we find linked a teaching to the *ekklesiai* on the prayer of these messianic communities: just as J's prayer, cursing the temple, has been fulfilled, so their prayer, if made with faith in God, will be fulfilled ("it will be done for him . . . it will be done for you").

"Has no doubt in his *heart*," "ask" according to the desires of your *heart*: *faith* and *prayer* are readings of practice; they are the desire of the heart and a forecasting of what will be done. The power of J's practice, which is being recounted throughout the narrative and has been set forth as a question in S 44 ("This kind cannot go out except through prayer"), is finally clarified by being related to faith and prayer. This will enable us to reread all the sequences telling us of J's prayer, and to work out the theory of it.

"Stand in prayer, forgive": an addition comparable to that regarding the salt in S 46; forgiveness, or cancellation of debts, is a condition for ecclesial unity which is threatened by the question of the *lapsi*.[126] House of prayer, house of cancellation (debt system) as condition of your forgiveness, or cancellation of your debts, by your Father. "Who is in the heavens": (MYTH) points to the eschatological judgment, which is announced by the mountain that fills the sea; overturning of the GEO code in relation to the MYTH code.[127]

One final remark: in the logic of "without his knowing how," the withered fig tree is *also* parabolic for J himself. For the first and only time in the text, the imperative based on J's power is not immediately followed by its effect. This will make it possible for him to predict the destruction of the temple in S 58a, as well as the replacement of the temple by the messianic communities made up of pagans, according to the parable of the vineyard, which now follows (S 55d).

S 55 (11:27b-2:34b)

a　And as he goes about in the temple,

b1　the chief priests and the scribes and the elders come to him,

c　and they said to him: "By what authority do you do this? Or who gave you this authority to do these things?" But the Jesus said to them: "I will ask you one word, and if you answer me, I will tell you by what authority I do these things. Was the immersion of John from heaven or from men? Answer me." And they said to one another: "If we say: 'From heaven,' he will say: 'Why then did you not believe in him?' But if we say: 'From men,' . . ." they were afraid of the crowd, for everyone maintained that the John was a true prophet. And answering the Jesus, they say: "We do not know." And the Jesus says to them: "Neither do I tell you by what authority I do these things."

d　And he began to speak to them in parables. "A man planted a vineyard, put a fence around it, dug a winepress, and built a tower; then he let it out to vine growers and went abroad. When the time came, he sent a servant to the vine growers to receive from the vine growers his share of the fruits of the vineyard. And taking him, they beat him and sent him away empty-handed. And again he sent another servant to them, and they struck him on the head and treated him shamefully. And he sent another, and this one they killed, and many others, some of whom they struck and others they killed. He still had one left, his beloved son. He sent him to them last, saying: 'They will respect my son.' But these vine growers said to one another: 'He is the heir; come, let us kill him, and the inheritance will be ours.' And seizing him, they killed him and cast him forth from the vineyard. What will the lord of the vineyard do? He will come and destroy the vine growers and will give the vineyard to others.

　　"Have you not read this that is written: 'The stone which the builders rejected is the one that has become the cornerstone; it was the Lord who did this, and it is wonderful in our eyes'?"

e　And they sought to arrest him, but they were afraid of the crowd, for they realized that he had addressed the parable to them.

b2　And letting him go, they went away.

f　And they send some Pharisees and Herodians to him in order to trap him in speech.

g　Arriving, they say to him: "Teacher, we know that you are truthful, and that you court no man's favor, for you regard no man's opinion but teach the way of God truthfully. Is it permitted or not to pay the tax to Caesar? Should we pay it or not pay it!" But he, knowing their hypocrisy, said to them: "Why do you tempt me? Bring me a denarius that I may look at it." And they brought it. And he says to them: "Whose image and inscription is this?" And they told him: "Caesar's." And the Jesus said to them: "What is Caesar's give to Caesar, and what is God's give to God." And they wondered greatly at him.

h   And Sadducees come to him, who claim that there is no resurrection, and they questioned him, saying: "Teacher, Moses has written for us that 'if a man's brother dies and leaves a wife behind and does not leave children, his brother is to take his wife and raise up children for his brother.' There were seven brothers. And the first took a wife and died without leaving any child. And the second one took her, and died without leaving a child. And the third one, and so on. And all seven left no child. Last of all, the woman herself died. In the resurrection, when they rise up, to which of them will she be wife, since the seven had her for wife?" The Jesus said to them: "Are you not in error because you do not know the Scriptures or the power of the God? For when they rise from the dead, they neither marry nor are given in marriage, but will be like messengers in heaven. But concerning the fact that the dead rise, have you not read in the book of Moses, with regard to the bush, how the God spoke to him saying: 'I am the God of Abraham, and the God of Isaac, and the God of Jacob'? He is not a God of dead men but of living men. You are greatly in error."

i   One of the scribes came forward after hearing their discussion and seeing that he had given them a good answer, and he asked him: "Which commandment is the first of all?" The Jesus answered: "The first is: 'Hear, O Israel, the Lord our God is the only Lord, and you shall love the Lord your God with your whole heart and your whole soul and your whole mind, and your whole strength.' The second is this: 'You shall love your neighbor as yourself.' No other commandment is greater than these." And the scribes said to him: "Well done, teacher! You have said truthfully that 'He is the only one, and there is no other besides him. And to love him with the whole heart and the whole mind and the whole strength, and to love the neighbor as oneself, is more important than all the holocausts and sacrifices.' " And the Jesus, seeing that he had responded wisely, said to him: "You are not far from the kingdom of God."

j   And no one dared ask him any more questions.

a. "In the temple": as Messiah (S 45i) who has taken his place there (S 53).

b1. "The chief priests and the scribes and the elders": whom S 42c has announced as about to reject J. For the first time here they are mentioned together as actants. Scene c will be the scene of rejection; the Sanhedrin will ratify it (S 66).

c. By what authority do you do this?": question Q2 which, in S 6, had been explicitly raised by the ANAL code in connection with the new teaching that so contrasted with that of the scribes. The same question is raised now in a decisive way, no longer in a Galilean synagogue but in the temple at Jerusalem (TOP). J has himself acclaimed as Messiah, drives the traders from the temple, and teaches there. "Or who gave you . . .?": Second formulation (same question or a different one?). The AA presents themselves as readers of J's narrative ("do you do this"). The question of *authority* is meant to be answered within the semantic system of the Jewish ideology. The question that J asks in turn seems to offer two possible answers: heaven/men (MYTH). The C's reading is: he came from heaven (S 45i: "in the name of the Lord"). "Men": at this level J lacks authority since it is the AA who have supreme authority in Israel (such an answer to the question would fit the Zealots to whom the AA deny any authority).

"Jesus said to them": he answers by asking a question of his own. The STR of J, in articulation with the ANAL, has always been to refuse to give answers within the established semantic code, and to refer the questioner instead to a reading of his narrative. In this case, however, it is to the narrative of John's practice that he refers the questioner, a practice which S 1 had recounted as taking place in Judea and as proclaiming the narrative of J himself. "Answer me" (twice): if you could *read* the practice of John, you could also read mine.

"They said to one another": the text shows them evaluating the STR consequences of the two possible answers; the stakes for which they are playing is the C. Both answers entail disadvantages for them, and they refuse to give any answer at all. It is their STR that dictates this refusal, rather than what the answers would signify. In a word, they bring themselves into disrepute as readers of J's narrative; they confess the site of their reading. But in doing so, they themselves give an answer to the question they have asked: "You are not the Messiah." *There you have their rejection of him.* This explains the conclusion J draws: "Neither do I tell you [openly] by what authority I do these things." However, he will give them an answer in the form of a parable, and the point of the parable is precisely to read their *rejection of the Messiah.*

d. "He began to speak to them in parables": a narrative that will make it possible to read the ongoing ACT narrative and its outcome. The parable is a metaphor that is located in the same figurative agricultural field as the metaphor in S 22b and the metaphor of the fig tree. But the vine is the most widely cultivated plant in Judea and ever since Isaiah, Chapter 5, has been an image of Israel itself with its abundance or its barrenness.[128] "Fence": the political-ideological frontier separating Israel from the pagan nations. The fruits are appropriated by those on the scene, that is, the ruling classes; there are no fruits for the true owner, Yahweh ("Asiatic" conception of owner-ship[129]). "Servant . . . servant . . . servant": the parable is a rereading of the history of Israel. The prophets called for conversion in accordance with the debt system, as a condition for fruits, blessing, and fulfillment, but the ruling classes always rejected them. The parable obeys a logic of a reading proper to the dominated classes; it dismantles the reading made by the ruling classes.

"His beloved son": according to S 2 and S 43, the beloved son is the equivalent of the Messiah. "Abroad": becomes the equivalent of *heaven* (MYTH), and the parable links up with the rejection in scene c. "The inheritance will be ours": since the Messiah is the final envoy, the rejection of him is equivalently a definitive appropriation of Israel and its fruits by the ruling class. "They killed him": postpaschal; the narrator/readers level is superimposed. "What will the lord of the vineyard do?": the parable indicates the outcome of the ACT narrative. "He will come and destroy the vine growers": narrator/readers level; Jerusalem has just been captured and the temple destroyed. "Will give the vineyard to others": To the pagans-readers.

"Have you not read this that is written": the reading lesson (ANAL) is finished, with the narrator/readers level always dominant. The metaphor of the vineyard slips over into a metaphor of a building (house). "The stone which the builders rejected": rejection of J by the AA (and in S 68 by the C as well). "Has become the cornerstone": in the pagan *ekklesiai*, which were *houses* for the sharing of bread.[130] Thus a new structure has been erected (the old tower and fence having disappeared) outside the symbolic field of Israel. The metaphor of the old structure rebuilt (elsewhere) is taken up again by the text in S 66.

"It was the Lord who did this, and it is wonderful in *our* eyes": the narrator links himself, in the "our," with the readers in this reading of their ecclesiality, the new space of the eschatological promise.

e. The reading we have just offered of this parable, while traditional in exegesis, may seem to force the text of the parabolic narrative. We, after all, are readers who are outside the ideological field of Israel and outside the inner logic of the metaphor of the vineyard. But the narrative immediately goes on to say that the AA read the parable quite well: "They realized that he had addressed the parable to them," and that it referred to their rejection of J and of John, just as their (class) fathers before them had rejected the prophets.[131]

"They sought to arrest him . . . but they were afraid of the crowd": the STR stakes in S 53 are indicated once again, with emphasis on the *political* character of the stakes.

b2. "And letting him go, they went away": STR.

f. "And they send some Pharisees and Herodians to him": (cf. S 17) the only mention of the presence in Jerusalem of those who, with the scribes, had carried on the ideological struggle in Galilee. They share here the STR of the chief priests, elders, and scribes.[132] "In order to trap him in speech": with a view to a future trial.

g. "Teacher, we know that . . .": the text replies: "knowing their hypocrisy."

"Is it permitted or not to pay the tax to Caesar?": J reads their question as a *temptation* (S 39, S 47). In what does the temptation consist? In the Zealot semantics of messiahship, which have been established in S 45j, to answer yes would cut J off from the C and allow the STR of the AA to win, since the principal obstacle to it would have been removed. On the other hand, to answer no would be to provide an argument allowing him to be accused before the Romans.[133] Let us immediately refute the reading current in official ecclesiastical discourses and in the discourses of politicians of the Right, which claim that the words "What is Caesar's give to Caesar" show J's respect for the "legality of the State" and assert the autonomy of the political order (a class system) over against the kingdom of God that would be concerned only with the interior life of individuals. If this reading were correct, the words "What is Caesar's give to Caesar" would be equivalent to saying: "Yes, pay the tax to the Romans," and J would have fallen into the trap by inscribing himself against the Zealots, something that the C would have no trouble in grasping. But the text in fact concludes: "They wondered greatly at him," which is to say that he did not fall into the trap. The current reading, then, is a nonreading of the narrative, an act of ideological blindness imposed by the interests of those who make it.[134]

"Bring me a denarius that I may look at it": J wants to read and analyze. "Whose image and inscription?": it is the reply, "Caesar's," that leads to the opposition Caesar/God, which is an opposition of their *images*. In the debt system (SYMB), it was forbidden to make images, "any likeness of anything in heaven above or on earth beneath" (Deut. 5:8); therefore any image either of God or of Caesar.

"Caesar's": the image and inscription of the political power on the signifier that regulates economic circulation (SOC). The coin enables J to read the very structure of the SOC system in its economic/political articulation. "What is Caesar's give to Caesar": this coin, with this image and inscription, does not belong to God or to Israel; on the contrary, it is the mark of the uncleanness inflicted on the country by the occupying power; what J is rejecting is the occupation.

"What is God's give to God": according to the parable that has just been read, the reference is to the vineyard Israel; according to the lesson in S 53c, it is the temple, the "house of prayer," that must be given to God. "Give to God": acknowledge me as Messiah, do not reject me, and you will be freed from the occupying power, in the logic of the promise of blessing that is attached to the debt system.

How then does J escape the trap set for him in the question? By shifting the question: his response is inscribed in the logic of the Jewish SYMB field, which the Pharisees, like everyone else, accept. J refers them to the reading of his practice as messianic, according to his constant ANAL procedure. In doing this, he does not evade the STR question, but locates it after the ANAL reading.

"And they wondered greatly at him": we must emphasize the narrator/

readers level. The readers have just endured persecution for their refusal to worship the divinized Caesar. For them the antithesis Caesar/God is as radical as it could possibly be; it is inscribed, so to speak, in their flesh and in the blood of their martyrs.

b. "And Sadducees come to him": (SOC) the two ideologically opposed classes are at one in their opposition to J. The latter's practice thus displaces the problematic of the ideological struggle. "There is no resurrection": a question regarding the final narrative, asked of him who sets himself up as Messiah. "Teacher, Moses . . . children for his brother": the purpose of the levirate law (SYMB) was to maintain the "house" in accordance with the promise of blessing given to Abraham,[135] and following a logic that is "materialist"[136] in the sense that it is of vital importance to the "house" of those who have no children and do not believe in the resurrection of the dead. But it is also of vital importance for the handing on of an inheritance— and the Sadducees are large landowners.

"There were seven brothers . . . left no child": a little narrative in which the law, though observed, is not fulfilled. "Last of all, the woman herself died": the "earthly" narrative ends, and another problematic is introduced that has to do with belief in the resurrection, which the Sadducees do not share but which J is regarded as sharing.

"In the resurrection . . . for wife?": the question is about a contradiction between the levirate law written by Moses and the unwritten belief in the resurrection. "The seven had her for wife": but not simultaneously, which would be incest and an abomination; the resurrection, however, implies the simultaneity of all the persons, and it is this that causes the contradiction to the law, inasmuch as the resurrection is conceived as the prolongation of the *same* earthly narrative.

"Are you not in error . . . power of God?," and, after his twofold answer, an insistent repetition, "You are greatly in error": if we advert to the words "Have you not *read?*" we see that the Sadducees' error is an *error in reading.* It is by the logic of the ANAL code, which articulates the reading of the ACT narrative of J (a powerful narrative that announces the eschatological power) with the reading of Scripture (therefore of a narrative, in fact), that we must read J's twofold response.

"For when they rise from the dead": to begin with, let us note that the objection of the Sadducees is well founded if there is question only of reading the Scripture. For, as we have seen, belief in the resurrection of the dead was introduced into the Jewish text in the second century B.C. by the Persian ideological textual production; the older Scriptures know nothing of it.[137] J will handle this difficulty in his second answer.

"They neither marry nor are given in marriage": first, J refutes the objection based on the levirate law, by denying that the eschatological narrative is to be conceived as *identical* with the earthly narrative. As a matter of fact, there will no longer be any question of "houses" or procreation or marriage.

"But will be like messengers in heaven": this seems to exclude sexual love as well, so that the eschatological narrative will be the affair of eunuchs. As a matter of fact, this reading is that of the Greek ideology in which the ideological discourse will speak of the "angels" as "pure spirits" without bodies. This is why I have translated *angeloi* as "messengers," in order to show that the body/spirit distinction does not exist in the Jewish semantic field any more than in that of the Persians. The "messengers" are *powers* that have to do with the cosmological order and thus with the material and the corporeal. This is to say that, while procreation and marriage are excluded, we do not see why sexual love, which is a power, should be a priori excluded.[138]

"Heaven": (MYTH) heaven is *other* in relation to earth. The eschatological narrative is therefore not identical with the earthly, but obeys only the power of God. It is characteristic of the kingdom of God to be *other,* beyond the *desires* of the agents who are ever-already marked by the dominant codes of the SOC. "Concerning the fact that the dead rise": J now gets to the bottom of the Sadducees' question. "In the book of Moses, with regard to the bush": in the narrative of the burning bush. "I am the God of Abraham, Isaac, and Jacob": in that narrative God presents himself to Moses as the God of the promise given to the patriarchs, the promise in memory of which he undertakes to free the Jews from Egypt. The promise was a promise of blessing to the posterity of Abraham, and it is on this that the Sadducees' objection is based.

"He is not a God of the dead": yet Abraham, Isaac, and Jacob are dead, and, according to the parable of the vineyard which has been given to other vine growers who are not Jewish and not descendants of Abraham, the promise had indeed failed according to the "materialist" logic which the Sadducees follow. In other words, the god of Israel, of the pollution system especially, and of the SYMB field that is centered on the temple, which has now become a "den of robbers," the god of the ideology of the system (SOC), is indeed a *god of the dead.*[139] At the narrator/readers level, for the readers who are located after the destruction of the temple, this is an evident fact: Israel has collapsed, its god has not saved it.

"But of living men": the text since S 16 has produced the inversion of the death/life opposition, with the BAS space being the *space of life,* in opposition to the field of the SOC, which is a space of death and Satan (S 20, S 22b1). This God whose power is at work in the ACT narrative that liberates the body is the *God of the living.* Thus J rereads the narrative of the bush in the light of his own narrative and takes sides in the question of the resurrection of the dead: this power that makes *lying* bodies *get up* (SYMB: S 7, S 12, S 25, S 44 . . .) is in the logic of the blessing promised to Abraham, Isaac, and Jacob, which is a logic of material blessing, even in relation to death. It matters little to J that faith in the resurrection is a borrowing from the Persian religious ideology. His argument is based on the reading of the ACT and the reading of Scripture. Abraham, Isaac, and Jacob must themselves also rise and share in the promised blessing even if it miscarries in the case of their descendants.

i. "One of the scribes came forward": a member of the scribal class (SOC) that the narrative places among the AA comes forward and distinguishes himself from his class. As in the case of Jairus, the leader of the synagogue (S 25), and later on, Joseph of Arimathea (S 72), class does not so determine each of its component members that he or she cannot hear the narrative of J. On the other hand, the exception does not prove that what determines the others, namely, their hardness of heart, is not the effect of class ideology.

"Seeing that he had given them a good answer": that J had given a good lesson in reading according to the logic of the Jewish SYMB field. These words also link the two problematics found in S55h and S 55i. "Asked him: 'Which commandment is the first of all?' ": how do you read the Scripture and its two systems of prohibitions, pollution, and debt? Which is primary? The question has to do with the site of confrontation between the priestly class, on the one hand, and the Deuteronomists and prophets, on the other.[140]

"The first is: 'Hear, O Israel . . .' ": the dominant formula in the Jewish liturgy.[141] "Hearing" acquires its structure in the ANAL code: Israel, the vine, is called upon to hear the Messiah teaching in the temple from which trade has been eliminated. This is in a way the definitive call of him who comes to fulfill the promise of the God of the living, the God of Abraham, Isaac, and Jacob, to an Israel subjected to taxation by the occupying Caesar.

"The Lord our God is the only Lord": there are no other lords, be they money (from trade), Caesar, or the god of the dead. A triple opposition is thus affirmed, which the text has already worked out: God/money,[142] God/ Caesar, God of the living/god of the dead. The last two of these are related to the first, since Caesar holds his position by means of the tax money, and the god of the dead is the god of the temple in which the trade is carried on and the treasury is located (S 57). What the practice of J has effected throughout the narrative is precisely the division between the field of Israel, which is dominated by these three "lords," and the BAS space which is that of God, the only Lord. "Hear, O Israel" is equivalent to "Read my narrative" (ANAL).

"You shall love the Lord your God . . . with your whole strength": on the basis of this reading work out your strategy at the level of your *heart* and your desires; let them not be bewitched by those other lords; rather let your practice, your giving of your life (STR), your intelligent reading (ANAL), and your acting with power (ACT), *break* with the system that those lords dominate (SOC). We are dealing here with the first moment or step in the following of J (S 49–S 50), the moment of break.

"The second is this: 'You shall love your neighbor as yourself' ": the second commandment is the second moment or step in the following of J, the love of the one who is near *you*, of the poor who are to be freed (for if you have broken with the system, the rich man has withdrawn from you; cf. S 49a2), of those who are marked by want and curse. "As yourself": give them what you have (S 31, S 49); what is yours is theirs. This is the logic of the debt system when the latter is radicalized and its ultimate consequences are worked out. "No other commandment is greater than these": the debt system, when radicalized, has primacy. All the prohibitions of the Decalogue (S 35, S 49) are summed up in this *gift:* the love of God and of neighbor.

"And the scribe said to him . . . holocausts and sacrifices": in turn he reads the response given by J ("You have said truthfully") and draws the conclusion; these two commandments of the debt system are "more important than all the holocausts and sacrifices" or, in a word, than the pollution system.

"Seeing that he had responded wisely": reading as the prophets had read. The words are a link with the beginning of the scene ("seeing that he had given them a good answer"). The narrative puts J and the scribe on the same side, over against the AA. Therefore the conclusion: "You are not far from the kingdom of God," you who have just stated the uselessness of the temple and its sacrifices and who have fully broken with your class.

j. "And no one dared ask him any more questions": the sequence of "questions" put to the Messiah is finished; the displacement, announced in the parable of the vineyard, from the Jewish symbolic field to the field of the pagans, furnishes the problematic common to the various discussion scenes (ANAL). In the latter there is first the political debate concerning the relations of the subasiatic mode of production to the slave-based mode of production, then the ideological debate on eschatology, and finally the debate on the "transformation" (reform) of the social formation that dominated the Old Testament, or on the relations between the pollution system and the debt system. Among the AA, however, only a single scribe succeeded in making the reading proposed by J.

S 56 (12:35-40)

a And replying, the Jesus was saying, while teaching in the temple: "How is it the scribes say that the Messiah is the son of David? David himself said in the Holy Spirit: 'The Lord said to my Lord: sit at my right hand, until I have put your enemies under your feet.' David himself calls him 'Lord.' How then can he be his son?"

b And all the people listened to him with delight. And in his teaching he said: "Beware of the scribes who like walking about in long robes, salutations in public places, and the first seats in the synagogues and the places of honor at banquets; they devour the houses of widows and for appearance' sake make long prayers. These people shall receive the harshest judgment."

a. "And replying": to the silence of those who dared not ask him any more questions. For there is in fact a further question beyond the three that have been asked. But it is not a question any person asks of J. Rather it is his practice that asks it, not of the AA, but of the C ("and all the people listened to him with delight") and, via the C, of the Zealots, actants whom the text manages not to mention although they are present and active throughout the narrative. As a matter of fact, the C has already asked the question in the form of its acclamations in S 45i; the question has to do with the ambiguity of the semantic system when it speaks of the Messiah.

"Teaching in the temple: '. . . the Messiah' ": the completion of S 55 is indicated, in the form of a prolongation of S 55i.

"How is it . . . son of David?": the dominant reading of messianism was that of a restoration of the kingdom of David,[143] and this by means of a blood descendant, someone of his "house." This constitutes a final objection to the messiahship of a "Nazarene," since the "house of David" was from Judea.[144]

"David himself": David will correct the scribal reading; the psalm cited was traditionally attributed to David. "In the Holy Spirit: 'The Lord. . . under your feet' ": the "lords" of the SOC, money, state-temple, god of the dead (at the narrator/readers level this subjection has already been achieved).

"David himself calls him 'Lord' ": refutation of the objection, for if the Messiah is called "Lord" by David, then he cannot be David's son. There can be no question, then, of a restoration of the "kingdom of David," which implies structures of subasiatic monarchic power in which David replaces Caesar, or, in other terms, a social formation that is reformed but nonetheless continues to be based on class exploitation. Just as the structures of blood kinship, or "houses," have been replaced by the fraternal relations proper to the BAS circle (S 21, S 49d), so too the "house of David" is replaced by a poor Messiah with a powerful practice. This is what was to be read in S 45i: the entry into Jerusalem on an ass's foal.

b. "With delight": the C seems won over to J, though this is contrary to its class interests.[145] Perhaps the delight is in seeing the oppressors confounded? In S 68, however, the C will line up with the chief priests.

"And in his teaching he said: 'Beware of the scribes' ": the opposition teaching of J/teaching of the scribes, which was enunciated at the beginning of the narrative of J's practice (S 6) and which has run through the entire text. Just as the teaching of J was, in the ANAL code, a constant referral to the reading of his own practice, so here he relates the teaching of the scribes to their practice in the SOC. We are dealing here with J's final teaching to the C; the Messiah is occupying the temple and holding a protest meeting against the dominant ideology.[146]

Do the scribes love the Lord their God with all their heart, and their neighbor as themselves? No, they love smart long robes, deferential greetings, the first seats, and the best places at table, and houses taken from widows who have no husband to defend them. In a word, read their habitual narrative and you will know how to read their teaching. "These people shall receive the harshest judgment": at the last judgment; it is the Messiah speaking. In the eyes of Mark's readers, the destruction of the temple had already fulfilled J's prediction.

S 57 (12:41-44)

a   And having sat down opposite the treasury, he was watching how
    the crowd was throwing money into the treasury; and many of the

wealthy threw in a great deal.

b   And a poor widow came and threw in two small copper coins, worth about a quarter of a penny.

c   And having called his disciples he said to them: "In truth (amen) I tell you, this widow, a poor woman, has thrown in more than all the others who throw money into the treasury. For they have all thrown in money from their surplus, but she in her indigence has thrown in all she had, her entire life."

a. "Opposite the treasury": the treasury, mentioned here three times, relates the temple to money, as did the trade spoken of in S 53. Thus this major sequence in the temple (S 52–S 57) begins and ends by emphasizing the temple-money relation.

"How the crowd . . . a great deal": J is here reading the economic functioning of the temple; the rich are contributing what the high priests will administer; thus, a class economy.

b. "A poor widow . . . two small copper coins": that is, *very little* in contrast to the *great deal* of the wealthy. "A quarter of a penny": translation, in terms of exchange value, for Roman readers; we are still in the economic register.

c. "Having called his disciples": lesson in reading by confrontation of narratives (rich/poor). "In truth I tell you": the lesson is immediately extended to the narrator/readers level, for it directly concerns these readers in their ecclesial practices. The issue now is not the treasury, but the contribution of Christians, and their possessions in the community.

In summary, the economy of the temple is compared with the economy of the BAS ecclesial field. The former, an economy of the ruling classes, is done away with, along with the barren temple-treasury, and replaced by the economy of the poor in the *ekklesiai,* that is, by a radicalized economic practice in which people share all the means of life they have as a condition for blessing.

S 58 (13:1-36)

a   And as he is leaving the temple, one of his disciples says to him: "Teacher, look, what wonderful stones and what wonderful buildings!" And the Jesus said to him: "Do you see these great buildings? Not a stone will be left upon a stone and not thrown down."

b1 And as he was sitting on the Mountain of Olives opposite the temple, Peter and James and John and Andrew asked him privately: "Tell us when that will happen, and what the sign will be that all those things are about to be accomplished."

b2 And the Jesus began to say to them: "Beware lest anyone lead you astray. Many will come in my name, saying 'It is I (I am),' and will lead many astray. But when you hear of wars and rumors of wars, do not be frightened; these things must come to pass, but the end is not yet. For nation will rise up against nation, and kingdom against

kingdom; there will be earthquakes in various places, and there
will be famines. These things will mark the beginning of the birth
pains.

b3 Look to yourselves; they will hand you over to tribunals, and you
will be beaten in synagogues, and you will appear before governors
and kings on account of me, to bear witness before them. And the
good news must first be proclaimed to all the nations. And when
they lead you away to hand you over, do not be anxious beforehand
about what you will say, but say whatever is given to you in that
hour, for it will not be you who speak but the Holy Spirit. For a
brother shall hand his brother over to death, and a father his son,
and children shall rise up against parents and kill them. And you
will be hated by all because of my name, but he who perserveres to
the end will be saved.

b4 But when you see the abomination of desolation standing where it
should not be—let the reader understand!—then let those who are
in Judea flee into the mountains, and let him who is on the roof not
come down or go inside to get anything from his house, and let the
man in the field not come back to get his cloak. Woe to those who
are pregnant or nursing in those days! But pray that this not be in
winter. For those days will bring tribulation such as there has not
been since the beginning of the creation which God created until
now, and will not be in the future. And if the Lord had not shortened those days, no flesh would be saved. But because of the elect
whom he has chosen, he has shortened those days. If at that time
someone says to you: 'Look! The Messiah is here,' 'Look! There he
is!' do not believe it. False messiahs and false prophets will arise and
perform signs and wonders in order to lead the elect astray if
possible. But you, be on guard. I have told you everything in
advance.

b5 But in those days, after that tribulation, the sun will be darkened,
the moon will no longer give its light, and the stars will fall from
heaven, and the powers in the heavens will be shaken. And then
they will see the Son of man coming in the clouds with great power
and glory. And then he will send the messengers and will gather his
elect from the four winds, from the end of the earth to the end of the
heaven.

b6 From the fig tree learn the parable: once its branch becomes flexible and it sprouts leaves, you know that summer is near. So too,
when you see that happening, know that he is near, at the doors. In
truth (amen) I tell you, this generation shall not pass away before all
that happens. The heaven and the earth shall pass away, but my
words shall not pass away.

b7 Concerning that day or hour no one knows it, neither the angels in
heaven nor the Son, but only the Father. Look to yourselves! Be

watchful! For you do not know when the time is at hand. It is like a man who is away on a journey, leaving his house and giving his slaves authority, assigning each one his work and bidding the doorkeeper to be on guard. Be watchful, then, for you do not know when the master of the house will come, whether in the evening or at midnight or at cockcrow or in the morning, lest he come suddenly and find you sleeping. What I say to you, I say to all: be watchful!"

a. "As he is leaving the temple": after his lesson in comparative economics, J leaves the temple, the center of the Jewish symbolic space that will be replaced by the practice of *giving* what one has.[147]

"One of his disciples. . . wonderful buildings!": the temple has been left behind but it continues to be a monument that fascinates when people think of the vast labor that went into its construction. This thought refers us back once again to David, who has wanted to undertake the building of it as a "house of God." But Yahweh had answered him with a refusal but also with a promise concerning the "house of David." Now J has refused the "house of David" (S 56), for the ecclesial *"house"* will replace the temple at the center of the BAS space.

"Do you see. . . thrown down": J's practice in relation to the temple has already been read parabolically in the withered fig tree; now it attains its fulfillment in the destruction of the "den of robbers" and its replacement by the "house of prayer for all the pagans." As L. Marin remarks, the temple will not be mentioned again in the TOP code in narrative statements, and when it does recur in discursive statements, it will be under the sign of its destruction (S 66, S 71)—this until the moment when its veil is torn as a sign prefiguring the destruction that will make it possible for Christian readers to turn their attention once and for all from Jerusalem and its temple to their own practices and what is promised to them.[148]

b. This is a single scene comprising the question of the four disciples and J's long discourse in reply to it. For convenience, we have broken this discourse into six sections (b2–b7), following pretty much the divisions suggested by J. Lamprecht who distinguishes three major sections, equivalent to our b2–b4, b5, and b6–b7.[148a] B2 and b3 are introduced by commands ("beware," "look to yourselves"), and b4 by "when you see" (the sum of all the signs preceding the coming of the Son of man). B5 is introduced by "in those days" (the coming of the Son of man on earth). B6 is introduced by the parable of the fig tree, and b7 by "concerning that day," which will be illustrated by another parable ("like a man who is away on a journey"); b6 and b7 deal with the "when" of the coming.

b1. "Sitting on the Mountain of Olives opposite the temple": the mountain of Olives (TOP) connects with S 52 and indicates the completion of the major sequence (S 52–S 58) on the temple; we shall go back over this major sequence after finishing our reading of S 58. In addition (cf. S 63 and the metonymy Bethany/Mountain of Olives in S 52), the Mountain of Olives is the space of the DD ("in private") and the BAS space, as opposed to the temple, which is the space of the AA. Located now in the BAS space, J reads the destiny of the Jewish symbolic field that is centered in the temple from which he has just come out. Since that destiny is its destruction, we may describe this coming out as an *exodus* and the completion of the *road* traveled in the ascent to Jerusalem-temple.

"Peter . . . Andrew": those who were present at the *beginning* of the road (S 4) ask the question about its *end*.

"Asked him": the verb points to the ANAL code. In fact, the entire discourse will be a complex reading in this code. Some indices of this: "beware" = look, see; "astray" = error in reading; "you see," "do not believe," "they will see," the parables, "let the reader understand," "you do not know," with several of these being repeated. In addition, both in the question and in the answer, *future tenses* punctuate the entire discourse, showing it to be an *anticipatory narrative.* But it is not therefore to be read in terms of prepaschal and postpaschal, for there is no mention in it of the death and resurrection of J. In fact, there are three indices that place the discourse, almost in its entirety, on the *narrator/readers level:* "let the reader understand!" "now" (b4), and "what I say to you, I say to all," the last of the three being an explicit extension of the range of hearers/readers from "you" to "all," but thereby also enabling us to read some elements of the text at the level of J's narrative, and thus justifying the placing of the discourse at this point in the text of Mark.

"When that will happen and what the sign will be": two questions (when, what sign) to which the discourse will reply in reverse order, b2–b4 giving the signs that must be read, and b6–b7 answering the question of the when. "That" and "all that" seem, moreover, to make the second question one that is implied in the first. "That" refers to S 58a, the prediction of the destruction of the Temple, while "all that," connected as it is with "accomplished" (the Greek verb *sunteleisthai* is built on the word *telos,* "end"), is connected with the final, eschatological narrative. Cf. b6: you will see "that" happening, therefore it will have happened; "all that," however, is still to come, and no one knows when. This implication, that is, the fact that the destruction of Jerusalem implies the eschatological narrative, will be found in the discourse, but it is also already present in the question of the disciples; the question, therefore, has to do also with the final narrative.

b2 (b4) "Beware lest anyone lead you astray": a warning that will be repeated at the end of b4. The DD (Christians) will be readers for whom error is possible, for J will not be with them, teaching them to read as he used to. The ANAL code, the code for practices of reading, is therefore constitutive of Christian practice or ecclesiality, as it is of the messianic practice of J.

Two kinds of signs: false messiahs and narratives of war, catastrophe, and famine; the two kinds of sign are taken up again in b4, but in reverse order. "Many will come in my name" is equivalent to "false messiah . . . will . . .

perform signs and wonders," since "my name" refers to power (S 46); "saying: 'It is I,' " is equivalent to "Look! There he [the Messiah] is!" The linking of false messiahs to wars makes us think of the messianic claim of the Zealots, or perhaps of Christians who have been seduced by other sects. The wars and famines, like the "abomination of desolation," refer to the Jewish War, news of which ("when you hear of. . .") has reached Rome.

Since the text is markedly apocalyptic in character,[149] we must not be overzealous in seeking a strict correspondence with narratives attested by history. Apocalyptic writing, a literature that has to do with the mysterious, is deliberately obscure in its allusions to contemporary events that its readers were reading elsewhere with full clarity.

"The end is not yet," "the beginning of the birth pains," "those days will bring tribulation": marks of the successivity of the various narratives within the single narrative; the various signs add up to but a single sign of what is awaited (b5). The metaphor of birth inscribes this single narrative in two periods: that of the pains (b2–b4) and that of liberation, the joy of birth, and salvation (b5). The narrative of the pains is precursive to and therefore predictive of the final narrative; the two, it is implied, are successive and also related as sign and fulfillment.

b3. "Look to yourselves": another kind of sign is enshrined between those of b2 and b4. The latter are exterior to the *ekklesiai*, while the new kind relates directly to the *ekklesiai*, the readers, "yourselves." The new kind of sign is persecutions: arrested, being handed over to tribunals, struck, with brother against brother, father against child and vice versa, and with this breakdown of "houses" being pushed as far as death and hatred from everyone involved. This describes the recent past of the Roman community (S 49d). The opposition between the practice of the BAS and the dominant practice of the SOC was very marked at such a time, as it is in the narrative of J.

The description of persecution itself enshrines two strategic instructions relative to the practice of proclamation in the *ekklesiai*. The first is: "The good news must first be proclaimed to all the nations." Here the *exodus* of the narrative of J, and of its bearers, the disciples, is indicated with perfect clarity. This exodus to the nations is the ultimate goal of the STR of J after the ascent to Jerusalem; it will come up again in S 59 and following. "Mark," who is at Rome, the center of the contemporary world, reads this as already accomplished, since *ekklesiai* have been everywhere established in the space of the Roman Empire.

"Do not be anxious . . . Holy Spirit": this is the second strategic instruction; we shall return to it later on.[150] "He who perseveres to the end will be saved": in reading this series of narratives about the curse we must realize that the curse is not the end and that the end will come as *salvation* and eschatological blessing (b6–b7 will take up this point). The logic of the metaphor of birth pains is still at work; that is, this narrative points to another that will soon follow.

b4. "The abomination of desolation": allusion to Dan. 9:27 (where a later addition of the words "of the temple" clarifies the location). In the parallel passage Luke writes: "When you see Jerusalem surrounded by armies" (21:20). The reference is undoubtedly to the capture of Jerusalem in 70 by the legions of Titus (this is the desolation) and the burning of the temple (this is the abomination). This superlative degree of curse inscribes the narrative in the semantics of the Jewish symbolic field. In other words, the narrator ("Mark") reads the destruction of Jerusalem and its temple *according to the Jewish codes:* the center of the Jewish symbolic field has been desecrated and destroyed as predicted in S 58a. Everything that follows confirms this reading, since the flight into the mountains, the not turning back, the distress of women who are pregnant or nursing describe the desolation that fell on Judea. Judea, Jerusalem, and the temple are the center of the world[151] for a Jew; their desolation is the worst of catastrophes according to the Jewish codes.[152] Once the Jewish symbolic field has been destroyed, people must abandon it and flee from it, for it no longer guarantees blessing (that is why to be pregnant or to be nursing becomes a misfortune). In short, this desolation represents the disorganization of the current codes, their upheaval, and the collapse of the symbolic field and the codes that inscribe it.

"Since the beginning of the creation . . . in the future": the code that defines Jewish chronology by a beginning *(archē)* and an end *(telos)* is cited, in order to emphasize the amplitude of this curse, which is utterly unparalleled in past or future, but also in order to bring out the fact that these days of curse will be shortened (by the Lord of the CHR code) as a condition for the salvation of the "elect," that is, of the readers in the BAS space.

"Let the reader understand!": this is the only time in the text that Mark's *reader* is explicitly mentioned; in our view, this is a key point in the structure of the text as such and gives an explicit key for reading it at its narrator/readers level.

"When you *see*": these words, with which the appeal to the reader is connected, show that there is question of being able to read something visible. The appeal to the reader is explained, on the one hand, by the fact that the visible event which is to be read is not named, and the reader will have to take this into account. On the other, and more decisively, since the term "understand" is proper to the ANAL code throughout the narrative, this imperative (often used by J: S 35d, S 40b, or its equivalent "Listen!": S 22c2, S 33b, S 35c, S 40d twice) marks the intent of the ANAL code as a textual structure of the narrative: *it is in order that this reading by the reader might take place that the narrative has been written.*

The practice of J has often been narrated as a process of subverting the Jewish symbolic field. S 55, in particular, has us read the replacement of the Jewish symbolic field among the pagans by the BAS space; J then leaves the temple and foretells its destruction. In other words, for Mark the event that has taken place is the *consequence* of J's practice; it was *announced* by him, *said-in-advance* by him. This is what the pagan readers must understand.

"Until now": here again the narrator takes the words, as it were, from the mouth of actant J, for the *now* is the now of his writing and also of the reading, *after* the collapse of the Jewish symbolic field.

After recalling the dangers of an erroneous reading by those who let themselves be led astray by false messiahs seeking to take J's place (the place precisely which the narrator, "Mark," occupies), b4 ends with a warning: "But you, be on guard. I have told you everything in advance." The narrator withdraws into the background, since it is the weight of J's prediction that is to guarantee the reading of what has happened.

b5. "But in those days, after that tribulation": a chaining with the narrative of the desolation of the Jewish field.

"The sun will be darkened . . . will be shaken": the MYTH code, the Jewish *heaven,* now collapses along with the Jewish symbolic field. The desolation becomes universal and no narrative is any longer possible: the final narrative is beginning, the time is fulfilled.

Let us go back to b4: this extraordinary event, unique in its tragic character, is the destruction of the temple or, in Jewish semantics, of the axis which is the center of the world and unites heaven to earth.[153] If the temple falls, the heaven has no support and will collapse in its turn. Thus it is the logic of the SYMB-MYTH codes that structures the text and allows the eschatological narrative to follow immediately upon the collapse of the Jewish symbolic field. This is the logic at work in the writing of Mark, which is situated in the "now" between the two.

"Will no longer": this is not a prediction but a logical consequence in the text of the codes that structure it. We do indeed find in the text the matrix—namely, predestination—in which the theological prediction is cast ("because of the elect whom he has chosen, he has shortened those days"), but this matrix itself is determined by the textual solidarity of the two Jewish codes. In the wilderness of desolation, "Mark," a Jew, can only await the final narrative.[154]

"And then": after the collapse of heaven upon earth, that is to say, after the disappearance of the difference that makes any narrative possible, there can only be the closure, the advent of the eschatological narrative.[155]

"They will see the Son of man coming in the clouds": cf. 42e. This is the *manifestation,* in the BAS space, of what the narrative had been keeping *hidden.* This is why no one must believe in a messiah localized here or there: there is no longer any possible practice for such a messiah, even if he does signs and wonders. There will be no more signs, no more predictions; the definitive blessing will be at hand, and all will see it.

"With great power and glory": no more authority or wealth, since the SOC codes have collapsed. The power and glory, for their part, are the fruit of "the smallest of all the seeds on earth" (S 22b3). In a word, the power and the glory are the ultimate justification of J's strategy, a "horizontal" justification (that is, in terms of what is "on the horizon"). In it, J's strategy and thus the practice of the poor—the carpenters, the fishermen, the tax collectors—reaches the apogee of its subversiveness of the power of "those who are regarded as the rulers of the peoples" (S 50d).

"Gather his elect from the four winds": all those who have heard the narrative and have believed in it, out of all the nations of the earth (for "the good news must first be proclaimed to all the nations": S 58b3), will be gathered in the great final circle, which has become the basileic circle, the kingdom of God, the court of God.

"From the end of the earth to the end of the heaven": earth and heaven are no longer opposed, for the two terms of the MYTH code have exhausted their separateness; the text of the narrative is closed, and all that is left is to give instructions.

b6. "From the fig tree learn the parable": the structure I/you which has marked the discourse as a whole (it has been interrupted in b5) returns with the parable that the readers are to understand; in short, the ANAL code returns. As always, it is the image of agricultural production that enables these elect to read the proximity of their destiny that will be superabundantly blessed with thirty-, sixty-, or a hundredfold. Unlike the fig tree (temple) that had become barren, the fig tree whose leaves emerge signifies the nearness of summer.[156] Therefore, when you see *this* happen (the temple—the withered fig tree), understand that he, the Son of man, is near, at the doors. We are still in the "now" between the two events.

"In truth, I tell you": in a discourse that is situated in its entirety at the narrator/readers level, this index confirms what has been said. It answers the question "When will this happen?" (b1), the decisive question for these communities that have already been so tried and tested. The response—"This generation shall not pass away before *all that* [the eschatological event] happens"—has already been given in S 42e ("In truth, I tell you, some of those standing here will not taste death before they see the kingdom of God coming in power"). This prediction is the only one in Mark that stands as a genuine prediction, since it concerns an event that has not as yet taken place in the "now" of the writing. It is therefore a prediction by Mark himself, in response to the problem raised by the *ekklesiai* of Rome. If we take account of the fact that the response already given in S 42e had been given in the context of the postpaschal prediction of the death-resurrection, and of the fact that what is at stake is the predestination of the readers, we discover one of the elements in the logic of Mark's theological discourse, namely, that the first prediction was an advance justification of the second, the two of them being put in the same mouth. Moreover, the words that issue from this mouth cannot be given the lie, for, if they have their roots in the MYTH code, they also transcend it: "The heaven and the earth shall pass away, but my words shall not pass away." The text has been closured by the MYTH code and attempts a demythologization.[157]

A parenthesis is in place here. A comparison with the text of Luke, who writes around 100 A.D., that is, at the moment of passage from the second to the third ecclesial generation,[158] throws light on the reading I am here proposing of Mark's text; the light comes from the transformations that Luke imposes on Mark. Though I have reservations as regards some of the positions adopted by J. D. Kaestli in his book on the eschatology of Luke, I can only make my own the thesis he takes over from H. Conzelmann. According to this thesis, "the chief reason for the change Luke imposes on his source proves to be *the delay of the Parousia;* this leads him to a complete reconsideration of the nature and unfolding of the last things" (p. 55). Thus, the change that Luke makes in the final logion of S 42e, which places the Parousia in the lifetime of the first generation of disciples, is due to the fact that "since the end has still not come, Luke renounces any and every attempt to fix the date for it" (p. 18). The same is true of the logion: "This generation shall not pass away before all that happens" (p. 53).

So too the substitution, to which we have already referred, of "when you see Jerusalem surrounded by armies" for "the abomination of desolation," "makes clear to us the completely new eyes with which Luke reads the prophecies in Mark 13" (p. 49). Himself a non-Jew and a pagan by birth, Luke separates the SYMB code from the MYTH code (here are his "new eyes"), as he is required to do by the logic of elimination of "the expectation of an imminent end." He "deeschatologizes" certain events such as the destruction of the temple, the fall of Jerusalem, or the persecution inflicted on the people of God, by taking from them their traditional status as signs anticipative of the end, and by reducing them to the rank of necessary stages on the road that leads to final salvation. This salvation is pushed back into a distant, indefinite future (pp. 55–56).

Therefore (Kaestli here invokes the authority of Käsemann), Luke lives in the "period of transition that leads from the primitive church to the early church. The sign of this passage is the gradual extinction of the eschatological expectation of an imminent end of the world, an extinction that can also be seen in the Gospel of John" (p. 97). Luke thus *reads* the narrative of the Temple differently, both because he is writing thirty years later and the *prediction* made by "Mark" has not been fulfilled, and because the play of the SYMB and MYTH codes is not the same in his text as in Mark's (this point would have to be analyzed, of course, for the Lukan writings in their entirety).

b7. The end of the delay in the eschatological closure is thus quite precisely determined: it is the lifetime of a generation now growing old (forty years have passed)[159] and of which many in fact are no longer alive. There remains the determination of the day and the hour, but at this point the text recalls that a predictive discourse contradicts the narrative logic that has been established. Therefore, "concerning that day or hour no one knows it, neither the angels in heaven nor the Son." J cannot be more precise because he is ignorant of the day and hour; "without him knowing how," the underground work produces its fruits and reaches the eschatological moment of the harvest.

"But only the Father": the ultimate secret of him who made heaven and earth, sole Lord of the MYTH. The importance of the secret is the requirement it imposes of vigilance to the very end: "Be watchful! For you do not know when the time is at hand."

"It is like a man who is away on a journey": a final parable that concerns not agricultural products (a metaphor for the field of Israel) but the *house*. A shift is made from the vine-Israel and fig tree-temple to the house-*ekklesia*. There is nonetheless a parallel between S 55d and this parable. In S 55d, as here, the owner, who is at a distance, will return; in S 55d the owner is the God of Israel, here it is Jesus, the Son of man (a postpaschal reading, therefore). The lesson of the reading is thus easily grasped: those in charge of Israel did not watch for the coming of the Messiah; you must not be caught by surprise by the coming of the Son of man.[160] "Be watchful, then."

"Whether in the evening . . . or in the morning": watchfulness is exercised during the night, that is, during the time of curse, which makes the watchfulness so difficult. The listing of the four watches of the Jewish night prepares for the narrative of the arrest and condemnation of J; the watchfulness demanded of the readers contrasts with the failure in watchfulness of the disciples, who will be "found sleeping" (S 64e, g).

"Watchfulness" is thus opposed to "sleeping," as *standing* is to *lying down*. Sleep is the absence of any narrative; consequently it is over the narrative of the practices of the *servants* that watchfulness is to be exercised. "Giving his slaves authority, assigning each one his work": watch therefore over your practice, your practice which is service, that is, a powerful practice, a practice of authority leading to salvation (c → b) (S 50).[161] The reason for this great emphasis on watchfulness is that the seduction of the SOC, "the cares of the world and the attraction of riches and the desire for other things" (S 22c3) still continue to be felt by the *ekklesiai*, just as do the "tribulation or persecution because of the word" (S 22c3) that is caused by those who hold the power in the SOC.

"What I say to you, I say to all: be watchful!": beyond Peter, James, John, and Andrew, the readers of J, the text once again looks to the readers of Mark.

Retrospective Reading of S 53-S 58

This major sequence is structured around the temple and the recognition/failure-in-recognition of the messiahship of J. The messianic practice of J subverts the dominant practice (of the AA) at the center of the Jewish symbolic field (S 53). His readings in discussion with the AA effect a displacement from this symbolic field to the (ecclesial) field of the pagans (S 55–S 57) on the basis of his own reading of the parabolic cursing of the fig tree (S 54). "Mark" reads the destruction of the temple as a consequence both of this subversion-displacement and of the rejection of the Messiah by the chief priests, elders, and scribes. Through the interplay of the SYMB-MYTH codes he announces the proximate coming of the eschatological narrative during the time of the first ecclesial generation, which is nearing its end.

Retrospective Reading of S 42c-S 58

Perhaps I could begin by advising the reader who is not in too much of a hurry to reread the commentary on S 42c—e in which the program of this major sequence is set forth; she or he will perhaps find those pages now easier to understand.

There was question, to begin with (in S 42c), of a new STR of J, the STR of his ascent of Jerusalem where a "confrontation," not yet defined, would take place between J and the chief priests, elders, and scribes. The text subsequently described the confrontation more fully: it took place in the temple, in the form, first, of the expulsion of the traders (S 53), and then of an ideological attack in which there is a shift from the Jewish symbolic field to the (ecclesial) field of the pagans; the parable of the vine announced this shift.

Next, in scene d (of S 42), there was question of an opposition between a STR Z and this STR J, according to the scheme "thoughts of men/thoughts of God." It is now clear that the destiny of the temple was the stake in this confrontation: the STR of J led him to abandon the temple as barren and to opt for an exodus to the pagans, while the STR Z focused on liberating the temple and Israel from the Roman occupiers. The question raised was: which of the two strategies will issue in the eschatological blessing ("thoughts of God"), and which in a curse ("thoughts of men")? The reading "Mark" gives of the destruction of the temple and the defeat of the Zealots shows the correctness of J's STR.

But not everything was thereby clarified, for there was also question of a new teaching, a message clearly announced in the space of the DD, and this was the object of scene e. The latter related this teaching, this (ANAL) reading, to the scheme of the *road* and the following after J. The teaching has to do with the structure of the practice that will lead to the eschatological narrative. This structure is defined in relation to the practices (or strategies) of the SOC system, and this is why the contrast STR J/STR Z will dominate the ascent, the road, to Jerusalem. Moreover, the perspective (STR) of the exodus to the pagans, in which the twelve will be sent two by two without the presence of J (we shall return to this point), commands the articulation of the ACT narrative with the Ecclesial narratives and of the latter in turn with the eschatological narrative, an articulation of which the words "In truth, I tell you," are the major index.[162]

S 46–S 50

The oppositions child-youth/adult, servant/master, first/last, rich/poor, define this messianic-ecclesial practice as an *inversion* of the codes that are dominant in the SOC[163]: *power is the inverse of authority*. This idea returns in S 55 with its oppositions God/money, God/Caesar, God of the living/God of the dead, within the larger opposition Jesus the Messiah/temple, as it does in S

56, which opposes the Messiah to David, and in S 57, which opposes the economy of the temple-treasury to that of the gift of all one has. In short, it is a question of "losing one's life" according to the codes of the SOC, in order to "gain" it according to those of the BAS, and of not "exchanging one's life" for a claim to "gain the whole world." It is not indeed a question solely of blessing *to come* in the kingdom of God and his glory, for within the *ekklesia* people already find a hundredfold more than they had abandoned (S 49d). It is true, however, that the hundredfold will come only accompanied by inevitable persecutions on the part of the classes who have authority (S 49d, S 50b, S 58b3), as the communities have learned by bitter experience. Nonetheless—and this is the final element in this new teaching—the messianic practice of J and the ecclesial practice of the disciples will lead, in the eschatological ascent of the Son of man, to the definitive blessing, and this last is drawing near, "Mark" predicts; it will take place in the lifetime of the first generation of disciples (S 42e, S 58).

Is it worth insisting that all this is readable at the level of the prepaschal text? We have thus found the text that was erased by the theological discourse, the text that was perhaps never written but that we must nevertheless know how to read. We can already glimpse what is at stake in this reading (which bourgeois exegesis has never succeeded in making), but it will emerge in full clarity only after the reading of the narrative of the paschal sequences, to which we now turn.

S 59a (14:1-2)

a   Now the Passover and the Feast of Unleavened Bread were two days away. And the chief priests and the scribes were looking for a way to lay hold of him by trickery and to kill him. For they were saying: "Not during the feast, otherwise there will be an uproar among the people."

a. "The Passover and the Feast of Unleavened Bread": prepares for S 61–S 62, and sets the narrative in motion again. "Two days away": (CHR) agreement with S 58a after the long discourse in S 58b; so too, "the chief priests and the scribes" picks up S 53d and S 55e. Thus, S 59–S 60 (with the latter enshrined in the former) serves as a connecting link between S 53–S 58 (the temple) and S 61–S 62 and following, under the sign of the Passover. We will have to return to this point in a retrospect.

"Were looking for a way to lay hold of him": the STR of the AA has for its object the body of Jesus ("to lay hold of him") and its death. "Not during the feast": the C is always the stake in the strategy; it has acclaimed J as Messiah, son of David, thus causing a first uproar (S 45i). This STR of the AA is met by a strategy of clandestinity on the part of J (S 53e). This makes it necessary for the AA to make use of a factor outside of themselves in order to have their STR be effective. This factor will be Judas the Sicarius.

S 60 (14:3-9)

a　And while he was in Bethany, at table in the house of Simon the leper,

b　a woman came with an alabaster vase containing a perfume made of pure nard, very expensive. Breaking the vase, she poured it over his head.

c　Some were displeased and said to one another: "Why this waste of the perfume? For this perfume could have been sold for more than three hundred denarii, and the money given to the poor." And they scolded her. But the Jesus said: "Let her be. Why do you trouble her? It is a fine deed she has done to me. For the poor you have always with you, and you can do good to them whenever you want; but me you do not always have. She has done what she could: she has perfumed my body beforehand for burial.

"In truth (amen), I tell you: wherever the good news is proclaimed in the entire world, what she has done will also be proclaimed in memory of her."

a. "He was at Bethany. . . in the house": space of clandestinity proper to the DD (outside the city: TOP-STR).

"The house of Simon the leper": this information, at the level of *signifier,* recalls S 7 and S 10, and reminds us that the object sought in the STR of the AA is the body of J, whose narrative of power (SYMB) began precisely in those early sequences. The focus now will in fact be on the *body* of J.

"At table": the scheme of the *circle* returns, with the powerful body of J at its center.

b. "A woman came": as in S 26b, S 36b, because she has heard the narrative of J's practice. "Very expensive": wealth, luxury (SOC). "A perfume made of pure nard . . . poured it over his head": narrative of an *anointing;* therefore, in the context (S 45i, S 56a), an acknowledgment of messiahship (Messiah = anointed).

c. "Some": the disciples, but no names are given. "Were displeased and said to one another": indication of a reading that does not comprehend (cf. S 12d, S 23c, S 43c, S 49c, S 55c) the narrative of the woman and proposes another narrative in its place.

"Why this waste of the perfume": this *loss,* in Bataille's terminology. *"Sold for more than three hundred denarii, and . . . given to the poor"*: a lesson in economics, as in S 57; the lesson is given by the disciples who recall S 49b: "Go, *sell* whatever you have, and *give to the poor.* . . come, follow me," but "forget" the final words: *"follow me."*

"And they scolded her": STR DD. "Let her be": counterstrategy of J, giving the disciples another lesson in reading the narrative of the woman. "It is a fine deed she has done to me": the reading restores precisely the element in S 49 that was omitted from the reading by the DD, namely, the "me."

"You have always": from the practice of the woman the reading turns to the practice of the DD. "The poor you have always with you": your practice, in the BAS circle, is carried on in the dominated, impoverished classes; it gives priority to them.[164] "But me you do not always have": the *me* is introduced again, but in opposition to the *poor*. To have the poor with you/not to have me with you; that is, *presence* of the poor with the DD/*absence* of (the body of) J from the DD. There is thus question here of the absence of J, his departure, his *exodus,* and it is this perspective of his exodus that commands the further reading J makes of the narrative of the woman. Since, moreover, this sequence is linked to S 62, we shall see that in the same perspective of his exodus the body of J is related to the bread that is to be given to the poor; the body of J is related to the poor by metonymy.

"She has done what she could: she has perfumed my body beforehand": before my messianic exodus (to the pagans) she has *anointed* my body as the body of the Messiah,[165] this body of mine that is a source of blessing ($c \rightarrow b$) for bodies to be saved.

"For burial": postpaschal, since it implies the death of J. Introduced here because of the episode of the women who want to anoint the dead body of J and cannot do so because he is no longer there (S 73), this theological interpolation is presented as an anticipation of J's resurrection (the absence of his body from the tomb) and *transforms* the exodus of J from an "exodus to the pagans" (prepaschal STR) into an exodus to God by way of the resurrection. In this shift or transformation the collective Son of man is individualized in the person of the actant J.[166]

"In truth, I tell you": the text is placed at the narrator/readers level and has in view the ecclesial narratives of the "proclamation of the good news." "In the entire world": the goal of the prepaschal STR of J is reasserted here, namely, the exodus to the *pagans* of the entire world, as in S 58b3. "What she has done will also be proclaimed": the good news is thus a proclamation not only of the narrative of J but also of the various actants in that narrative, "those who believe" and "those who do not believe." The narrative of the anointing of J by the woman—which marks the end of J's reading which highlights the value of his body as a source of blessing (SYMB/BAS)—therefore takes on an important significance, pointing to the place of the body of J in ecclesial practice (cf. S 62).

"In memory of her": as her narrative; the narrative is a memorial of the practice of messianic anointing, which it recounts. We glimpse here a reading I have not been able to make: what is the relation between women and the body of J (S 26, S 60, S 71c, S 72e, S 73a)?

S 59b-d (14:10-11)

b   And Judas the Sicarius, one of the twelve, went to the chief priests in order to hand him over to them.

c   And they, having heard him, rejoiced and promised to give him money.
d   And he was looking for a way to hand him over at a favorable moment.

b. "Judas the Sicarius": the former Zealot. "One of the twelve, went to the chief priests": from the BAS space (which is also the space of clandestinity) and the circle of the twelve, who had already been sent out with power over unclean spirits and were to be sent out in the same way to the nations, "to the whole world," Judas passes to the space of the AA and their strategy over the body of J. "In order to hand him over to them": cf. S 19 and S 62; the word that characterizes the practice of Judas is *hand over*, that is, to give the *body* of J.

c. "Rejoiced": the chief priests will have their own time of festival, for their STR has now found what it lacked: the man who has changed spaces. "And promised to give him money": the body of J will be exchanged for money, which determines exchanges in the SOC. J has opposed "giving" to "buying" as characteristic of the BAS space (S 31). In changing spaces Judas therefore returns from the BAS to the SOC.

d. "And he was looking ... moment": on his return to the space of clandestinity, Judas introduces into it (via the characteristic word "look for": cf. S 53d, S 55e, S 59a) the STR of the AA; (the promise of) money, the opposite of God, now works in the BAS space as a threat of death.

S 59a–S 60–S 59b-d: the enshrinement enables us to reread S 60 and its lessons in economics. The exchange that is proposed: perfume-money (DD)/ (DD) money-poor, is not effected, because the perfume is lost in the form of an anointing of the body of J which is destined to absent itself. Judas, one of the DD,[167] regains the money thus lost by stopping this absence, this exodus, of the body of J: body of J-AA/(AA) money-Judas. Since the body is destined for death, the perfume will be given to it again (S 73), but it will change its meaning, in the axis life/death, from a festive perfume to a perfume for burial.[168] So too, the festive uproar of the people (s 59a) will change into a festive execution (S 68c). In addition, the money from the temple will prevent the body of J from crossing the symbolic Palestine/nations frontier, and it is perhaps the despairing Zealotry of Judas the Sicarius that is here signaled, his opposition to the internationalist STR of J.

S 61 (14:12-16)

a   And on the first day of the Feast of the Unleavened Bread, when they were accustomed to sacrifice the Passover, his disciples say to him: "Where do you wish us to go and make preparations so that you may eat the Passover?"
b   And he sends two of his disciples and says to them: "Go into the city, and you will meet a man carrying a pitcher of water. Follow him

and, where he goes in, say to the master of the house: 'Where is my
room where I am to eat the Passover with my disciples?' And he will
show you a large upper room, furnished with cushions and prepared. There, make preparations for us."

c   The disciples left, went into the city, and found things as he had
told them, and they made preparations for the Passover.

a. "On the first day": (CHR) two days after S 59–S 60, a tie which is
confirmed by the repetition of "Passover and the Feast of Unleavened
Bread." "Unleavened Bread," "the Passover": citation of the text of the
narrative of the *Exodus*, that is, the passage (Pasch) of Moses and the Israelites
from Egypt, the land of slavery, to Israel, the land of fulfillment of the
promise given to Abraham, Isaac, and Jacob. "Unleavened Bread": narrative
of the bread eaten on the eve of departure. According to the logic of the shift
or displacement announced in S 55d and deployed since then, it is an *exodus in
the inverse direction* that is to take place, since Israel has in its turn become a
land of slavery because of money, the state-temple, the god of the dead; S 62
will tell how they ate the unleavened bread on the eve of this new departure.
The memory of the first exodus or going forth to the first fulfillment of the
promise is a narrative enabling us to read (ANAL) the ACT narrative and
attests this second exodus or going forth to the final fulfillment (cf. Moses and
Elijah in S 43).

It seems that the narrative of this sequence functions only through its
parallelism with S 52 and gives us at last the key to a question raised in S 42;
the response, which has already been supposed in the reading of the last few
sequences, is given by the narrative at the level of its structures. The question
is that of the goal of J's STR in ascending to Jerusalem.[169] These two short
narratives of the sending of two disciples to do what in S 52 the Lord, here the
Master, "had told" them in advance: what else are they narrating but the
outcome of this ascent to Jerusalem? The taking over of the temple and the
proclamation of the vineyard given to other owners, on the one hand, and the
exodus, on the other hand, to the field of these "other owners," the pagans, in
the atmosphere of the paschal remembering of the first exodus—*that* is what
J came to Jerusalem to do. That is the twofold goal of his prepaschal strategy.

This question (and the response to it) is situated only at the level of the
prepaschal text. The question has therefore been *erased*, and this is why
bourgeois exegesis has not been able to raise it, for, after all, did Jesus not
come to Jerusalem in order to die?! But, if so, why does he hide himself from
those who are seeking to put him to death? Why must one of the twelve
change camps so that death may come to him? Why does the text deal in
"politics" instead of "religion"?

b. "The city . . . the house . . . my room": as Marin has pointed out,[170]
Jerusalem becomes "the city," and the temple is replaced by "one house"
among all the houses of the city. This means that we are no longer in the
Jewish symbolic field and at its center, but in a space that is marginal to this

field and that is therefore anonymous in the Jewish text. This marginal, anonymous space is the place (TOP) of departure for the exodus to the pagan nations, to the field of pollution and curse whose houses will become, in the cosmopolitan anonymity of the Roman Empire, "houses of prayer for the nations." Anonymous houses in a field that no longer has a center: to identify them we must be able to read the narratives of the practices that therein proclaim the good news of the eschatological blessing. What practices are these? S 62 will give the answer.

S 62 (14:17-26a)

a1 And when evening has come he goes with the twelve.
b And while they were at table eating, the Jesus said to them: "In truth (amen), I tell you that one of you will hand me over, he who is eating with me." They became quite sad and began to ask one by one: "It is not I, is it?" But he said to them: "One of the twelve, who dips his hand with me in the dish. The Son of man is indeed going as it is written of him, but woe to the man by whom the Son of man is handed over! It were better for this man that he had not been born."
c And while they were eating, taking bread, he said the blessing, broke it, and gave it to them, and he said: "Take, this is my body." And taking a cup, giving thanks, he gave it to them, and they all drank of it. And he said to them: "This is my blood of the covenant, poured out upon many.
  "In truth (amen), I tell you, I shall never drink again of the product of the vine until the day when I drink it new in the kingdom of God."
a2 Having sung psalms, they went forth . . .

a1. "And when evening has come": the CHR has been clearly inscribed since S 53. "He goes": the trajectory is Bethany-city, repeating S 54a-c, d-g, and especially S 45i. The parallel S 52–S 45i/S 61–S 62 yields the contrast manifested Messiah/hidden Messiah (S 42b). S 62 will enable us to explain, in the BAS space, the strategy of keeping the messiahship hidden, a strategy that S 45i has apparently belied. It will enable us, in short, to penetrate fully the implications of the contrast STR J/STR Z.
b. "While they were at table eating": repeated at the beginning of c; the scheme of the *circle* is inscribed again in the form of a meal. City-house-room-table: this progressive narrowing of the circle to the point of focusing on the *practice of the bread* is thus opposed to another progressively narrowing circle: Jerusalem-temple-trade. The displacement of fields ends with the opposition trade (selling-buying)/practice of the bread (having-giving), which is the key to the opposition we found just above: temple/house. In all this complex play of topographies that the narrative has set up as a STR since its beginning, the point at issue is the subversive contrast of economic practices

that have their place in the two different spaces of the SOC and the BAS.

"Jesus said: 'In truth, I tell you' ": the narrator addresses the readers, and the scene is to be read at that level.

"One of you . . . who is eating with me. . . . One of the twelve, who dips his hand": the emphasis is on the *circle* and the threat that weighs upon its center ("will hand me over," "is handed over"), in accordance with the exchange in S 59. But the exchange is promised and not yet accomplished; J's discourse, with its future tense ("will hand me over"), is thus a narrative of anticipation, the two references to the Son of man being parallel to the references in the predictions of S 42 and S 45.

"Woe to the man," "better . . . not been born": these phrases belong to a discourse on predestination that refers no longer only to Jesus but to Judas as well. In a word, we have a real postpaschal discourse, with the theological discourse inscribed in its matrix, which is predestination.

"As it is written of him": we shall return to this later.[171] There is, then, a twofold predestination: that of J, who obeys a theological *necessity* that is related to Scripture, and that of Judas, which produces woe and belongs to the narrativity and its *element of chance (aléatoire)*. The contradiction narrative/theology can therefore be read: the death of Jesus will come as a disavowal of the STR long since established, as the failure of it, with the curse falling on a practice of power and blessing. What is the work of theological discourse, except to justify this failure and to lay hold of this death as something contradictory for which a meaning must be produced? This can be achieved, however, only by recourse to a predestination that renders necessary what, from the viewpoint of narrativity, is simply a matter of chance. If the Messiah has been put to death, then this *must* have happened by the predestining action of the one who sent him.[172]

"One by one," "It is not I, is it?": under the pressure of the "In truth, I tell you." But it is rather the Christians of Rome whom the narrator has in view. Judas is given as a contrast to Peter (S 63, S 67) for the readers of Mark; the two are opposed examples of betrayal, the one betrayal being unforgivable while the other is not. The examples make it possible to read the destinies of those who gave in during the persecutions.[173]

c. "And while they were eating": reprise of the scheme of the circle around the table. This situates scene b as something different (the postpaschal theological discourse; but also, at the prepaschal level, an indication of the threat [money] which one of the twelve causes to weigh on the circle and its center).

"Taking bread . . . gave it to them": the narrative rereads the double narrative of S 31 and S 38, but omits the "to distribute to them" (to the C for allaying their hunger); it thus recalls the practice, the reading of which (in S 40) led Peter to confess the messiahship of J (in S 42b). In the structural contrast of S 52–S 45i–S 53/S 61–S 62, the two readings of J's messiahship are evaluated: that of the C according to the Z grill, and that of the DD. The C and the DD were already opposed as readers in S 42b: "Who do people say I am?" "But you, who do you say that I am?" Here, in S 62, the C is absent from the room but present in the background of the exodus road. The term which is lacking here is thus brought in, via the narratives being recalled, as the term of the strategy of the twelve, the ecclesial strategy: what you have in the form of loaves, *give* them to eat and be filled. "And he said: 'Take, this is my body' ": a further reminder of the Galilean narratives; the center of the circle, namely, the body of J, the *touch* of which is a source of power for bodies subject to a curse (SYMB-BAS)—the body whose absence was announced in S 60 ("me you do not always have")—will be replaced by the practice of giving bread.

What does this mean? Let us proceed cautiously, since we must here invert the process followed in current exegesis. That is, it is not "the Eucharist" that enables us to read the bread sequences, which have already been fully read by Peter; on the contrary, it is the bread sequences that will enable us to read "the Eucharist."[174]

At the prepaschal level, at which the death of J is excluded, the STR goal of J is to go forth to the pagans (that is what Paul will do): *"first*, let the children have their fill" (S 36), *then* it will be the turn of the pagans. Let us note that this absence of the body of J because of his exodus to the pagans has been prepared for from the beginning by J's STR of clandestinity, which is still being pursued here, and especially by his constant STR of avoiding the crowd (cf. S 31a and f, which enshrine the first bread sequence, and S 38d, which terminates the second). His body is thus destined to become absent, and thus the circle is destined to *lose its center*, which will be replaced by the supreme messianic practice: what you *have, give*. To whom? *To the poor* (S 60), those who when filled are related by metonymy to the body of J.[175] This practice, then, is what becomes the *body* of J; as such, it therefore becomes the place of messianic power.

This decentering of the circle is also a refusal by J to become a leader of the masses. His messianism is not to be taken for Zealotry, but neither is it "spiritual." We shall return to this point, of course. To put the matter briefly: the temple, the center of Jewish symbolism, is replaced by the practice of *giving* one's bread to the poor, to the hungry crowds (Cc). This practice is to be read as *messianic*; that is why it is to be accompanied by the proclamation of the narrative of J, of the *good news* and the "This is my body," as J. Lacan would say.[176] The absent Jesus will be present only in the text of his narrative, the narrative of his practice-seed-word.

"And taking a cup . . . all drank of it": this narrative, unlike the one we just read, is without any equivalent in the reminder of the text. If we leave aside for a moment the words: "This is my blood of the covenant, poured out upon many," which are an anticipation of the death and a theological metaphorization of it, and therefore postpaschal, light is thrown on the narrative by what follows. "In truth, I tell you": narrative/readers level. "I shall never drink . . . kingdom of God": J is here depicted as a participant in the ecclesial narratives (therefore a prepaschal text); he abstains from wine in expectation of the new eschatological wine (cf. S 14), which will replace that of the vineyard of Israel that has become barren and no longer produces.

A point that would still require explanation is this fast of the bridegroom, since, in S 14, it is the fast of the friends of the bridegroom that was announced, as a metaphor for the persecutions they will have to endure. It must be admitted that in these sequences in which the theological discourse is so much at work, the reading runs into difficulties that it is not always possible to explain in a satisfactory manner.

S 63 (14: 26b-32a)

a1   they went out to the Mountain of Olives.

b   And the Jesus says to them: "You are all going to fall away, for it is written: 'I will strike the shepherd, and the sheep will be scattered,' but after my 'being raised up,' I will lead you into Galilee."

c   The Peter said to him: "Even if all fall away, I shall not." And the Jesus says to him: "In truth (amen), I tell you: today, this very night, before the cock crows twice, you will have denied me three times." But he repeated more emphatically: "Even if I must die with you, I will not deny you."

a2   And they come...

Gr. *elalei* = repeated (in c); followed as it is by direct discourse, the verb does not here have the sense of "preach."[176a]

al. "They went out to the Mountain of Olives" (TOP). Let us look back at the journeyings of J since S 52:

Bethany-Mountain of Olives

	S 52–S 45i, j	Jerusalem-temple
Bethany	S 53b	
	S 54a-c	Jerusalem-temple
Bethany	S 53f	
	S 54d-f	Jerusalem-temple
Mountain of Olives	S 58a-b	

If we take into account that the two nights spent at Bethany have no narrative, we can reduce this first journeying to an even simpler scheme:

Bethany-Mountain of Olives_____

                                                              Jerusalem-temple

Mountain of Olives _____

The second journey is equivalent to the first:

Bethany_____

                    (S 60a) S 62a1   city-house-table

Mountain of Olives   _____

                    S 63a1

What this means is that at the TOP level the journeys return to their starting point; the code is looped. Just as in S 58 J leaves the temple, intending never to return to it, so here he leaves the city intending never to return to it; his exodus is beginning. What is the destiny of J in his (prepaschal) STR? If we take into account that this sequence is entirely under the sign of predestination (that of "all" and more especially of "Peter," as well as of J as "shepherd") and that the theological discourse emphasizes this fact by "for it is written," we are able to retain as belonging to the prepaschal level only the "I will lead you into Galilee." There is, then, question now of reaching Galilee as a stage in the exodus to the pagans. Thus the TOP program of S 1–S 3 is fulfilled.[177] Let us insist once again: If J is going to death as to his destiny, why should he hide himself in the space of clandestinity?

Given this impress of the postpaschal theological discourse on the text (an impress we shall not analyze immediately), the problem of uncovering the erased prepaschal text becomes almost insoluble. Let us say only what the reading of the next sequence requires: that J has read the threat of armed confrontation (cf. here "strike," "scattered") that results from the betrayal by "one of the twelve."

S 64 (14:32b-43a)

a   to a place the name of which is Gethsemani,
b   and he says to his disciples: "Sit down here while I go and pray."
c   And he takes with him the Peter and the James and the John, and he began to be afraid and distressed, and he says to them: "My life is full of sadness, to the point of dying; remain here and keep watch."
d   And going a little distance, he fell to the ground and prayed that if it were possible this hour might pass from him. And he was saying: "Abba, Father, all things are possible for you; take this cup from me. But not what I want but what you want." He returns
e   and finds them sleeping; and he says to the Peter: "Simon, do you sleep? Did you not have the strength to watch for a single hour?

Watch and pray that you may not enter into temptation; the spirit is ready, the flesh is weak."

f   And again he went away and prayed, saying the same thing.

g   And coming again he found them sleeping, for their eyes were heavy. And they did not know what answer to give him.

h   And a third time he comes and says to them: "You sleep away the time that was left, and you take your rest. The worst has happened. The hour has come; see, the Son of man is going to be betrayed into the hands of debtors. Get up, let us be going! He who is handing me over is near." And immediately, while he is still speaking,

a. "Gethsemani": the place of the sequence is named, a sign that the narrative has reached a decisive point; the same holds for "Golgotha" in S 71.

b-c. "To his disciples . . . takes with him the Peter . . . going a little distance": access to the place where J prays is guarded ("keep watch") by two groups of disciples who act as bodyguards to ward off the threat that weighs upon the center of the circle.

c-d. "The Peter and the James and the John": the privileged witnesses of the power of the body of J (S 25, S 43) become the witnesses to its powerlessness. The latter is strongly emphasized: "afraid," "distressed," "sadness, to the point of dying," "fell to the ground," all of this in very striking contrast to *the entire narrative.* Until now, Jesus has always been master of his own narrative and reader and strategist in the face of the narratives of others, even the possessors of power and even in the temple, the place where they exercise their domination. The narrative to come, designated as "hour" and "cup," is a narrative that threatens *death*, the end of his practice and his strategy of exodus to the pagans, in short, the failure of his own narrative and therefore of the eschatological narrative that he has announced. "He prayed that if it were possible": he prays to God as the sole master of the narrative to come, the only one whose power ("all things are possible for you") can prevent the failure. "Abba, Father": the Messiah, powerless, stands before the Mighty One, whose voice (MYTH) had called him "my Son" and who had made his practice fruitful.

"Not what I want but what you want": the ignorance of J ("without him knowing how") is brought out very clearly, even to the point of contrasting the two wills, that of J and that of God, according to the scheme "thoughts of men/thoughts of God" (S 42d). This, then, is a narrative of *temptation* ("watch and pray that you may not enter into temptation"). The temptation does not refer to the ultimate goal, that is, the blessing (neither will is bent on death), but to the *strategic* means of attaining the goal. The two possible strategies are indicated by the spirit/flesh opposition; this opposition refers to the difference STR J/STR Z, and involves the power of the *body* of J, on the one hand, and the might of money and political domination (arms), on the other. In what, then, does the temptation consist? What strategic means offer themselves to J for going to the pagans, means which are not, however, the means proper to the messianic STR? The next sequence opposes the body of J (pointed out by the kiss, then arrested) and, first, the sword of one of those present, then the swords and clubs raised against J for teaching in the temple. Thus the power of the body, which saves lives, is contrasted with the force of arms, which kill lives (according to S 16). In a word, the *temptation* J experiences is that of defending himself by recourse to arms.[178]

Although influenced by the postpaschal theological discourse, this sequence places J at a clearly-prepaschal level, as one involved, through strategic reading-decision, with the narrative that threatens to come, and as one who is powerless before it. His prayer, then, is indeed a prayer of *petition* offered by the Messiah in accordance with the desire of his heart ("what I want"): the setting aside of this cup, this threat of death.

e. A whole series of oppositions marks the two strategies J/Z: sleep/watch, flesh/spirit, weak/strong (to keep watch), temptation/prayer, asleep/ready. Those who were all ready to die (S 63c) fall asleep; in S 65d, f, recourse to the sword and to flight will mark those who had thus slept.

"Says to the Peter: 'Simon' ": the narrative gives the name "Peter," the new name proper to the BAS space (S 19), to him whom J, reading his sleep, calls "Simon"; that is, J gives Peter the name he had as one who is in the SOC space and is subject to its codes, to the flesh and its weakness.

f-g. The contrast between watching-praying/sleep-temptation is emphasized by its being repeated thrice, despite the injunctions of J.

h. "You sleep away the time that was left": the time of reading/strategy, of petition (prayer), before the narrative that threatens ("the hour has come").

"See, the Son of man is going to be betrayed . . . while he was still speaking": after his prayer and after overcoming the temptation, J tells them of his decision (STR) not to struggle, but to let himself be "handed over" and to have recourse to no power but that of the body. The reference to the "Son of man," postpaschal though it is, indicates that J still retains the eschatological hope, although he "does not know how" the connection will be established between this narrative to come ("the hour has come") and the final narrative. For "all things are possible to the God" (S 49c); in the same context of the contrast STR J/STR Z, the issue remains undecided, but J is no longer master of the situation; he makes as it were an "absurd" wager.[179]

S 65 (14:43b-53a)

a Judas arrives, one of the twelve, and with him a crowd bearing swords and clubs, coming from the chief priests and the scribes and the elders.

b He who was to betray him had arranged a signal for them, saying: "The man I shall embrace is the one. Arrest him and take him away securely."

a2 And, having come,

c he immediately went up to him, saying: "Rabbi!" and he embraced him. And they laid hands on him and arrested him.

d   One of the bystanders, drawing his sword, struck the servant of the high priest and cut off his ear.

e   And the Jesus answering said to them: "Have you come out to take me with swords and clubs, as though I were a terrorist? I was among you every day, teaching in the temple, and you did not arrest me. But this is in order that the Scriptures may be fulfilled."

f   And leaving him, they all fled.

g   And a young man was also following him, who had a cloth wrapped around his naked body; they arrest him. But leaving the cloth, he fled naked.

h   And they led the Jesus away

Gk. *lēstēs* = terrorist. "The Greek term *lēstēs* was often used in a technical sense of a rebel."[180]

a. "Judas . . . one of the twelve, and with him": one of those who were in the BAS space has passed into the space of the AA. In S 59c Judas was put in a relation with money (SOC); here he is linked to *weapons,* the signifier of political power, and, once again, to the dominant classes ("chief priests and scribes and elders"). Since the work of J's practice effects, throughout the entire narrative, the clear separation of BAS/SOC, it is in this "return" of Judas that the scandal called "betrayal" consists, this "Get from behind me, Satan" that has already been hurled at Peter (S 42d). This return or betrayal is signified in the embrace or *kiss* which is a two-faced signifier: on the one hand, it signifies the disciple/master relationship ("Rabbi!") within the BAS circle; on the other, it functions as an informer's signal to the armed band.

c. "And they laid hands on him and arrested him": the power of the body of J (SYMB) is neutralized. Whereas individuals under a curse had touched him and been saved, the kiss, which touches his body without faith, arrests and binds him. In a word, it is the *power* of the body confronted by the *force* of arms.[181] Scenes d and g make this same point: the sword that strikes, in contrast to the *naked body* of the fleeing young man. Scene g evidently functions as a signalization of the SYMB code, a kind of hint to the reader: pay attention to the *body* and its destiny! (The "young man" will reappear in S 73 to signal the empty tomb, the absence of the body.) To this we may add the contrast with the temple, which has just been mentioned (and will be mentioned again in S 66b and S 71c): the contrast between the center of the Jewish SYMB and the SYMB/BAS. But nakedness, the separation of clothes from body, is also the sign of the body's powerlessness, if we bear in mind that in S 26, S 34, and S 43 clothes stood in a relation of metonymy to the body and its power. In S 71c the temple will in its turn become naked.

e. "Jesus answering": answering both the sword that cuts off the ear, and the arrest. "As though I were a terrorist": You arrest me as if I were a Zealot. And with irony: "every day . . . not arrest me," because the C would not have permitted it. There follows a theological clause, which we shall be reading later on.[182]

f-g. "They all fled": result of the *fear* during the ascent to Jerusalem (S 45f) and of the sleep and nonwatchfulness of S 64. After the attempt at armed resistance, those following J abandon him. The BAS circle is broken both in its center (arrested, neutralized in its power) and in its members who are scattered in accordance with S 63b. The STR of J is thus *vanquished* by the STR of the AA. The body of J loses all strategic initiative; all the shifts in locale that are to come will be indicated by the verb "lead away," of which J will be the direct object (S 65f, S 66f, S 69a, S 70a): he is caught in the STR of the AA.

S 66a (14:53)

a   **And they led the Jesus away to the high priest, and all the chief priests and the elders and the scribes gathered.**

a. "To the high priest": J is led into the space of the Sanhedrin (named in b), the place of economic power (the elders), political power (the chief priests), and ideological power (the scribes),[183] the seat of that which guarantees the unity and dominative role of the system (SOC). "Gathered": the circle of the SOC is drawn in order to judge (ANAL) the practice of J, his messiahship.

S 67a (14:54)

a   **And the Peter followed him from a distance, as far as within the court of the high priest, and he was sitting with the servants and warming himself at the fire.**

a. "Peter . . . the court . . . the servants": another circle (court), at a lower level, judges Peter, who has been the reader of J's messiahship in A 42b. The interweaving of S 66 and S 67 emphasizes the parallelism of the two "courts" and the two judgments, and the contrast between the proclamation by J and the denial by Peter.

S 66b-e (14:55-65)

b   **And the chief priests and the entire Sanhedrin were looking for a testimony against the Jesus so that they might have him put to death, and they did not find one. For many bore witness falsely against him, and the testimonies did not agree. Some stood up and testified falsely against him by saying: "We heard him say: 'I will destroy this sanctuary that was made by hands, and in three days I will build another not made by hands.' " But even so, their tes-**

timonies were not in agreement.

c   And the high priest, standing up in the midst, questioned the Jesus, saying: "Do you give no answer? What is this testimony they are giving against you?" But he remained silent and gave no answer. Again the high priest questioned him and said to him: "Are you the Messiah, the son of the Blessed One?" And the Jesus said: "I am, and you will see the Son of man sitting at the right hand of the Power and coming with the clouds of heaven." But the high priest tore his robes

d   and said: "What further need have we of witnesses? You have heard the blasphemy; what is your decision?" And all judged him deserving of death.

e   And some began to spit on him and to veil his face and to strike him with their fists and to say to him: "Play the prophet!" And the servants pummeled him.

b. "Were looking for a testimony . . . put to death": Since S 17 the "temptations" (S 20, S 35, S 39, S 46, and especially S 55) were attempting to find this "testimony."

"Many bore witness falsely . . . did not agree": a "summary," followed by an example. The "falsification" is an index provided by the narrator who is "justifying" J: the latter's practice is beyond reproach from the viewpoint of Scripture, for the subversions of J, which call the class society into question, are in continuity with the subversions of the prophets and the outlook of the debt system.

"I will destroy this sanctuary that was made by hands": the temple in which they now are, that was erected as a signifying center (overdetermined by the three levels) of the social formation, its symbolic center.

"And in three days": postpaschal, relating to the theological discourse (cf. "and rise after *three days*": S 42c, S 45a, f); contrast between the temple and the body of the risen J, which is the new "center" of the BAS. At the prepaschal level, the reference here *may* be to the sequence of the traders expelled from the temple, and, more generally, to the destruction of the temple and the SYMB field and the rebuilding of a house of prayer in the field of pagans, which destruction and rebuilding are announced in the parable of the dispossessed vineyard tillers and that of the stone that was rejected but became the cornerstone of a new building (S 55d). The text of these parables had made it quite clear that the listeners had understood what was really meant.

c. "The high priest, standing up in the midst": the center of the SOC circle. The AA are always in the plural and never have personal names, since it is the *class* that is the actant. Here, "high priest" stands for a function in the apparatus of the state. In short, there is no question of "the sins of individuals," as the ecclesiastical discourse is always saying.

"Questioned . . . gave no answer": J refuses to acknowledge their competence as readers of his narrative, which they travesty ("falsely"). "Again": the testimonies lead to nothing, the court is at an impasse.

"Are you the Messiah, the son of the Blessed One?": a return to S 45i and the acclamation of the C. "The Blessed One": (MYTH) introduces an alternative like that in S 55b ("from heaven or from men") where they refused to answer because of the C (the C is absent here, because it is nighttime).

Before reading the reply of J, let us look at its consequences: tearing of the high priest's robes, blasphemy, condemnation to death. The reply is read as subversion that *tears* the Jewish symbolic fabric, and shatters the semantic of the dominant ideological text, to the point of attacking even the god ("blasphemy") who guarantees it.

"Jesus said: 'I am' ": J *openly* says that his narrative is a messianic narrative; until now, this claim had been kept hidden in the space of the DD (S 42b). But this secrecy, as we have seen, had been justified by the fact that his messiahship differed from a messiahship of type Z, the very kind of messiahship that the C proclaimed in S 45i. What is J's new situation that prevents his reply here from being subject to the old semantic ambiguity? Not simply the fact that he was a Nazarean, a Galilean (S 67 will emphasize this), a carpenter, a rabbi to sinners and tax collectors (SOC), for all this was already legible in the past and had already hindered the reading by the AA. The new thing here is his situation as a prisoner, the *powerlessness* of his body, the stopping of his practice by the forces of the SOC.

"You will see the Son of man . . . clouds of heaven": the narrative that has been arrested and silenced is related to the final narrative of *heaven* (MYTH), that is accompanied by definitive *power*, a narrative that will take place and which "you *will see.*" The thing that provokes scandal and is incompatible with the text of the SOC is precisely this passage from powerlessness here and now (ACT) to eschatological power, from the present situation of curse to superabundant blessing, as well as the denial of the power of the rulers of Israel to stop the messianic narrative, and, consequently, their expulsion from this messianic realm. This is the point, is it not, of the "mockeries" of the chief priests and scribes in S 71b? Is it not also the reading we are compelled to by the parable of the mustard seed (S 22b3)? In short, we have here the mystery of the kingdom of God, at the prepaschal level; the death/resurrection will not annul it but on the contrary will radicalize it. This is what bourgeois exegesis has never been able to read, and with good reason.

J thus speaks openly and proclaims what he had hidden in parables. He does so at the very moment when his STR of an exodus to the pagans has just been defeated. Of course, this raises the problem of how J, in his situation of powerlessness, can hope for a real connection between the ACT and the eschatological narrative; we will learn the answer in S 71d.

d. "And all judged him deserving of death": if we compare the silence of J with that of the AA (S 16, S 55b), we understand the strategy of referring to the reading of the narrative "do good," "save a life." The words of the AA here proves to be a discourse of *murder* and a repression through force (SOC); this is their only reply to the practices of salvation and *life*.

e. Force is thus unleashed against the body of J, which is defiled by spittle and has blows rained on it. "To veil his face": J thus blinded becomes the reflection of the blindness of those who "look but do not see"; the laughter of the AA at his words ("Play the prophet!") becomes the reflection of the deafness of those who "hear but do not understand" (S 22c2).

S 67b-e (14:66-72)

b   And while the Peter is below in the court, one of the serving maids of the high priest comes. And seeing the Peter warming himself, she stares at him and says: "You too, you were with the Nazarean, the Jesus." But he denied it, saying: "I do not know or understand what you are talking about."

c   And he went outside into the forecourt. And the serving maid, seeing him, began again to say to the bystanders: "That man is one of them." But again he denied it.

d   A little while later, the bystanders again said to the Peter: "In truth, you are one of them, for you are a Galilean." But he began to curse and swear: "I do not know the man you are talking about."

e   And immediately the cock crowed the second time. And the Peter remembered the words the Jesus had spoken to him: "Before the cock crows twice you will have denied me three times." And going out he burst into sobs.

b-d. "Below in the court": the judgment of Peter, in a lower court, by "one of the serving maids of the high priest." "You too . . . with the Jesus": not "with the Messiah" but with the prisoner from Nazareth in Galilee. "He denied it": he who had confessed to the Messiah "is ashamed of him before this generation" (S 42e). "He went outside": fleeing from the pursuit of the prisoner's accomplices; as a matter of fact, he has just definitively *gone out* of the circle of the DD, who are now scattered.

Note the parallel with the questioning of J: direct question to those accused ("Are you the Messiah?"/"You were with the Nazarean"; "I am"/"He denied it"); question to members of the circle (to the Sanhedrin: "What is your decision?"/to the bystanders: "That man is one of them"); verdict of the gathering (the Sanhedrin: "All judged him deserving of death"/the bystanders: "You are one of them"); contrast between the two outcomes of the two responses (confession/denial), namely: scene of Jesus being tormented/Peter going out to escape arrest.

e. "The cock crowed . . . Peter remembered": he had denied knowing the narrative of J, the cock refreshes his memory. "He burst into sobs": sadness, a sign of the trip of the SOC (cf. S 49b: "went away saddened, for he had great possessions"; S 62b: "they became quite sad" at the possibility of *their* betrayal of J: "It is not I, is it?"; S 64c: "My life is full of sadness" at the temptation to do "what I want").

Retrospective Reading of S 59–S 67

We are not dealing here with a major sequence in the strict sense, but rather with a series of sequences that raise a certain number of difficulties. If we compare S 59 with S 60–S 61–S 62a, c,[184] we observe that the two opposing STR are being paralleled: that of J, the goal of which, as we have shown, is the exodus to the pagans, and which is localized in a space of clandestinity (TOP-STR), which is the space of the BAS; on the other hand, the STR of the AA, which aims at arresting J in order to have him killed and which is localized in the space of the SOC. In addition, the actant Judas passes from the one space to the other and becomes a participant in the STR of the AA within the BAS space (S 59d), thus permitting a collusion of the two strategies (joined in the figure of betrayal), a conflict, a confrontation between the group J + DD and an armed band sent by the AA.

This conflict is recounted in S 65, where it issues in success for the STR AA and a defeat for the STR J. S 66 brings J back into the space of the SOC, as an actant "led away," deprived of strategic initiative at the political level, and doomed to death by the judgment of the Sanhedrin. However, his silence and his confession of messiahship show that at the level of his discourse he retains a certain "strategic hope," which looks to the eschatological narrative and to which we will return in S 71.

S 62b, S 63–S 65 thus prove to be a kind of *hinge* on which the narrative turns until the confrontation in S 65, and it is precisely in this section that we have experienced real difficulties in reading according to the grill we have chosen to use ever since S 42. Throughout this section the postpaschal text has been superimposed on the prepaschal in such a way that the restoration of the erased text is hazardous and open to challenge. But this is a sign that this hinge-section posed intensely felt problems for the narrator; the major symptom of this fact is precisely the work done here by the theological discourse. This work is done in two ways.

First of all, on three occasions (if not four) the theological discourse appeals to the Scriptures as justification for the failure of the STR J: "The Son of man is indeed going *as it is written of him*" (S 62b); *"It is written:* 'I will strike . . .' "' (S 63b); "But this is in order that *the Scriptures* may be fulfilled" (S 65c); to these passages we may add: "The hour has come; see, the Son of man is going to be betrayed" (S 64h). Now, together with S 43c, these are the only times in the entire text of Mark that *the Scriptures* are cited with this function of providing justification (a function we shall analyze later on). Are we not right to see a symptom of the validity of the postpaschal/prepaschal grill in the fact that such an operation takes place precisely in this hinge section of the narrative, where J is robbed of his strategy by the element of *chance,* of which Marin speaks, that is, by this betrayal that must, after the fact, be justified and made *necessary*?

In the second place, we twice find the words "In truth, I tell you," which, as we have seen, are addressed directly to the readers. On both occasions—and again, these are the only two occurrences in Mark—they are in the theological discourse of predestination regarding the two decisive actants, Judas and Peter. I am here making partial use of L. Marin's analyses.[185] The two discourses of predestination relate to the two betrayals by the two actants who are participants in the BAS circle, and the two betrayals are contrasted. On the one hand, Judas is not named in S 62b ("one of you," "one of the twelve," "he who is eating with me," "who dips his hand with me in the dish"); this lets a feeling of doubt weigh on each of the twelve. When it comes to Peter, however (S 63b), the specifics are multiplied: "today," "this very night," "*you* will have denied me," "three times." But the overdetermination of Peter weighs only on a *negative word,* a *verbal rejection* which can be repeated three times without causing harm, whereas the overdetermination of "Judas" has to do with a *positive action,* a real *giving,* which can take place only once.[186] In short, the "betrayals" are being contrasted as "handing over" is contrasted with "denying" and "doing" with "saying."[187] And the narrative, as we have seen, will tell how each of the betrayals comes to pass.

Mark enables us to go a little further and, on the basis of "In truth, I tell you" as an index, to read the ecclesial situation of the readers.[188] Having endured persecutions, the *ekklesia* of Rome is divided over the attitude to be adopted toward those who have given in to persecution,[189] just as it will be later on, at Rome again (Hippolytus) and at Carthage (Cyprian). Here we have a decisive problem of the early *ekklesiai:* the problem of the *lapsi.* This, along with the question of the proximity of the eschatological event, forms the *problematic* proper to Mark.[190] If we accept the tradition, Peter underwent martyrdom at Rome about 64–67, and Mark wrote at Rome some five to ten years later. The question of pardoning or not pardoning the *lapsi* (cf. the endings of S 46 and S 54) is answered through the figures of Judas and Peter, according as the betrayals of the *lapsi,* their changes of space (BAS → SOC) have been at the level of *doing* ("it were better for this man that he had not been born") or of *saying.* Peter had repented ("he burst into sobs") and now, as an old man, he has been faithful to the pledge he had given as a young man of dying rather than deny Jesus; he has, then, been pardoned. The criterion for pardon is thus established by the reading (ANAL) of the narrative.

Our conclusion: the narrative itself, at the level of the narrative statement and not simply of the discursive statement, has been rewritten from the postpaschal perspective; that is why it resists our reading.

S 66f-g (15:1a)

f   And as soon as morning came, the chief priests held a consultation with the elders and scribes and the entire Sanhedrin; having bound the Jesus,

g   they led him away

f. "Morning": (CHR). "A consultation . . . Sanhedrin": a repetition of what had been done during the night in the absence of the crowd. "Having bound Jesus": the powerlessness of the body is emphasized.

S 68 (15:1b-15)

a1 and handed him over to Pilate.
b1 And the Pilate questioned him: "Are you the king of the Jews?" And he answered and said to him: "You say it."
a2 And the chief priests were accusing him very loudly.
b2 Again the Pilate questioned him, saying: "Do you give no answer? See all that they are accusing you of." But the Jesus gave no answer, so that the Pilate was astounded.
c   At each feast he used to release a prisoner to them, the one they asked for. Now there was a prisoner called Barabbas, who had been arrested with the insurgents who in the course of the insurrection had committed murder. And when the crowd had come up, they began to ask him to do for them according to the custom. But the Pilate answered them by saying: "Do you want me to release the king of the Jews to you?" For he realized that it was out of jealousy that the chief priests had handed him over. But the chief priests roused the crowd to ask rather that Barabbas be released to them. But the Pilate again said to them in answer: "What then shall I do with him whom you call king of the Jews?" And they again cried out: "Crucify him!" And the Pilate said to them: "But what evil has he done?" But they cried more loudly: "Crucify him!"
d   The Pilate, wishing to satisfy the crowd, then released the Barabbas and after scourging the Jesus handed him over to be crucified.

Gk.: *tē stasei:* "the insurrection" (not: *an* insurrection).[190a]

a1. "handed him over to Pilate": "hand over to the pagans" according to S 45f. This is the second transfer in space, from the Jewish AA to the pagan AA; the sequel indicates that "the Pilate," whose name alone is mentioned at this point, is possessor of the *power to kill,* the representative of the *imperial power of Caesar.*[191]

b1. "Questioned him": a second trial, still focusing on the messiahship, but in terms of opposition to Caesar. "Are you the king of the Jews" is a question asked from the *Roman site,* the site of pagans who are occupiers of the country (in 71b the chief priests and scribes will say "the Messiah, the King of Israel" and not "the king of the Jews"). The difference between the question put to J by the high priest and the question put to him by Pilate is not therefore the difference between a religious semantic and a political semantic, for this distinction is absent from the Jewish semantic system. The difference is rather the difference between *Jewish power* and *Roman power*: in regard to the former, the "Messiah" stands in opposition to the politico-ideological function of the high priest; in regard to the latter, the Messiah stands in opposition to the political function of Caesar. In other words, the question Pilate asks J is a more direct version of the question the Pharisees and Herodians had asked him about the tax (S 55g),[192] the question of how J stands in relation to Zealotism. As the sequel will show, what interests Pilate, as it does the chief priests, is the relation of J to the C that had acclaimed him Messiah in the Zealotic logic of the kingdom of David (S 45i).

"You say it": J's answer is an accusation against the site of the reading Pilate makes of J's narrative, and in accord with the logic of the STR J (my dealings are with the ruling classes of Israel, not with you). Pilate grasps this point, according to the narrator: "For he realized that it was out of jealousy that the chief priests had handed him over."

a2. "And the chief priests were accusing him very loudly": because of their place in the SOC, which along with the temple has been called into question.

b2. "See all that they are accusing you of. . . . But the Jesus gave no answer": because he had already answered them, according to the messianic semantics of the Son of man, who is a personage completely outside Pilate's ken. J's silence is therefore a rejection both of a Zealotic messianism and of the negation of messianism. In the space occupied by Pilate, there is no semantic that enables J to bring this out, since while the Zealotic messianism is accepted by the C, it also calls Pilate's power into question.[193]

"Pilate was astounded": like the Pharisees in S 55g; this is emphasized by the parallel drawn above (in S 68b1). The answer and subsequent silence of J do not give Pilate reasons for condemnation; he therefore has recourse to a stratagem (STR): to split the AA and the C, for it is the latter that interests him; the C is the actant that replaces the chief priests in c ("when the crowd had come up, they began to ask").

c. "Barabbas . . . the insurrection": Barabbas is therefore a Zealot who is offered to the C as an alternative to J. In addition, however, *"the* insurrection" (with the definite article) must refer to something of which there has been question in the text and which can only be the messianic sequences relating to the entry of J into Jerusalem and into the temple.[194]

"Do you want me to release the king of the Jews to you?": from the viewpoint of the Roman authorities, as opposed to the viewpoint of the chief priests, Barabbas the Zealot is the more dangerous of the two men. Pilate's formulation of the question takes this into account.

"But the chief priests roused the crowd": the STR of the AA, hitherto opposed to that of the C, which supports J, is to change the outlook of the C and make the latter join the chief priests against J. This change on the part of the C is not, however, without its own logic, as has often been believed. The crowd has in fact always been on the side of the STR Z, and regards Barabbas as a hero. The text therefore plays on the opposition STR J/STR Z, which differed on the place of Jerusalem and the temple in relation to the promise. Now, the C of Jerusalem depended *economically* on the temple and the pilgrimages, and it was this that made it decide *against* the man whom Pilate in his strategem presented to them as "him whom you call king of the Jews," thus calling S 45i to mind once again. "And they again . . . more loudly: 'Crucify him!' ": the narrative emphasizes the change in the C; Pilate's question recalls the narrative of J in the key of doing good/doing evil (S 16). The emphasis does not exculpate Pilate, who still occupies the site of Roman power ("wishing to satisfy the crowd"), and represents rather "Mark's" reading of the destruction of the temple which he connects with this "guilt" on the part of the C.[195]

d. "The Pilate . . . then released . . . to be crucified": the three strategies—that of the Jewish authorities, that of the Roman authorities, and that of the C—*coincide* in the end: not by way of a narrative based on *chance* and involving "individuals," but in accordance with the strict logic of class struggle that also commands the STR J (a point to which we shall return later).[196]

"After scourging": as in S 68e and f, the sequence ends by calling attention to the *body* of J that has been rendered powerless.

S 69 (15:16-20a)

a   The soldiers led him away inside, into the court, that is, into the praetorium, and they call the entire cohort together.

b   And they dress him in purple and place on his head a crown of thorns they have woven. And they began to salute him: "Hail, king of the Jews!"And they kept on striking his head with a reed and spitting on him, and bending the knee to him, they kept paying him homage. And when they had done with mocking him, they stripped him of the purple and put his own cloak back on him.

c   And they lead him away

a. "The soldiers": still the force of arms (SOC). "Into the court, that is, into the praetorium": again a circle proper to the SOC; in this case, however, the narrator interprets for the readers by pointing out the element of "Romanness,"[197] supplied by the *cohort* (SOC of the slave-based mode of production).

b. "They dress . . . crown of thorns": throughout this scene (in which the body of J is dressed and undressed at the whim of the soldiers, thus calling attention continually to its powerlessness in this space that is dominated by the force of arms), we have a parody, a carnival.[198] The action proceeds through the contrast between the real situation of the condemned man, signaled by the blows on the head and the spitting, and the signifiers belonging to the power of the SOC.

"Hail, king of the Jews": the emphasis on this title throughout sequences S 68–S 71, which take place in the Roman space, seems meant here to be read as a parable. This narrative with its carnival atmosphere is a narrative of a nonreading by the soldiers of J's narrative (a nonreading that will have its contrasting echo in the centurion's confession after the death of J, the centurion's apprenticeship in the ANAL), and, at the same time, a narrative of how to read J's messiahship: his "kingship" (and therefore the "kingdom of God") is such that it can only be an object of mockery ("when they had done with mocking him") for those who serve the kings of the SOC,[199] those whom money, weapons, and the dominant ideology bewitch and render blind and deaf.

What is enunciated here, then, is the work of rereading the narrative of J and his STR at the level of the narrator, for the inversion of the SOC codes which this strategy required is here brought to its extreme form.

S 70 (15:20b-22)

a   And they lead him outside to crucify him.
b   And they press into service a passerby returning from the fields, Simon of Cyrene, the father of Alexander and Rufus, so that he might carry his cross.
c   And they lead him to the place called Golgotha, which is translated "place of the skull."

a. "Outside": outside of the city (TOP), the latter not being named, because the Jewish symbolic field has lost its meaning by its rejection of the Messiah.

b. "That he might carry his [Jesus'] cross": once again, the powerlessness of J's body is emphasized. "Simon of Cyrene, the father of Alexander and Rufus": by this abundance of proper names (the last two, given as a way of identifying Simon, must have been known to the readers) the text establishes its authenticity in the eyes of the readers (reality effect).

c. "The place called Golgotha": like Gethsemani (S 64a), the TOP of J's death is indicated, as the translator multiplies his signs by translating Aramaic terms into Greek.

S 71 (15:23-41)

a   And they gave him wine mixed with myrrh, but he did not take any of it. And they crucify him. And they divide his garments, casting lots to see who should take them. It was the third hour and they crucified him. And the inscription of his indictment was inscribed: "the king of the Jews." And with him they crucify two terrorists, one at his right and the other at his left.
b   And the passersby were blaspheming, shaking their heads and saying: "Ha! Destroyer of the temple and rebuilder of it in three days, save yourself and come down from the cross." The chief priests were likewise mocking him, saying: "He saved others, and he cannot save himself! Let the Messiah, the king of Israel, come down now from the cross, so that we may see and believe." And the men crucified with him were insulting him.

c   When the sixth hour came, there was darkness over the whole earth
     until the ninth hour.

d   And at the ninth hour the Jesus cried out in a very loud voice: "Eloi,
     Eloi, lama sabachthani," which means in translation: "My God, my
     God, why have you abandoned me?" Some of those present said
     when they heard him: "See, he is calling on Elijah." Someone ran
     and filled a sponge with vinegar, and, placing it on a reed, made
     him drink it, saying: "Let us see whether Elijah comes to take him
     down." But the Jesus, crying out with a very loud voice, expired.

e   And the veil of the sanctuary was torn in two from top to bottom.

f   The centurion who was standing there facing him, seeing how he
     died, said: "Truly, this man was a son of God."

g   There were also women looking on from a distance, among them
     Mary of Magdala and Mary, the mother of James the younger and
     Joses, and Salome, who used to follow and serve him when he was in
     Galilee, and many other women who had ascended to Jerusalem
     with him.

a. "Wine . . . did not take": in accordance with S 62c. "Crucify him": living,
left in *agony* and expectation. "They divide his garments": the *naked body* of J;
in a short scene that echoes that of the young man who fled naked, the SYMB
code is indicated. The point is still the *fate*—powerlessness and curse—of the
body whose narrative has told at length of its power to bless.

"It was the third hour": the CHR punctuates the sequence in periods of
three hours. The first of these periods is occupied by the "passersby" and
their reading of the death of J; the second is occupied by the MYTH; the third
by the death itself and the reading of it, first by J and then by the centurion.

"The inscription": writing (the sole instance, at the level of narrative
statement, in the entire text) of the "Roman" reading of the death of J, in the
historical text of the SOC. "The king of the Jews": that is, a Zealotic Messiah.
This phrase, along with *crucified,* has occurred frequently since S 68. This last
term *(crucified)* is absent from the various postpaschal "predictions," in which
we find the idea that J will be *killed (apokteinein)*, as an object of *murder* and
therefore according to the logic of the *debt* system and not the logic of
pollution in which there would be question rather of *"death."*[200] The death of
J is indeed a political murder,[201] for his narrative has been read as the
narrative of a Zealot, like that of the two men crucified with him. The latter
"were insulting him"; the text of Mark is always concerned to distinguish the
STR J from the STR Z. Despite this distinction, this political murder is part of
the picture of the class struggle in a Palestine occupied by the Romans, with
the Jewish ruling class "collaborating" with the Romans in this particular
matter.

"One at his right and the other at his left": refers us back to S 50:
emphasizing, on the one hand, the absence of James and John who have fled
(contrast cross/glory), and, on the other, relating "cup" and "immersion"
(baptism) to this death on a cross.

b. "Were blaspheming": misreading of the narrative of J; this last is more truly grasped by the chief priests and scribes who speak of it as a narrative of power ("he saved others") in contrast to his present powerlessness ("he cannot save himself"). As in S 20 when related to S 12, the accusation of "blasphemy" in S 66 is here turned against the accusers. "Destroyer of the Temple": reference to S 66b. "Were likewise mocking him": the failure of J is their revenge for S 45i and S 53 ("the Messiah, the king of Israel"). The themes of the mockery refer us back to the trial before the Sanhedrin, just as "king of the Jews" and "crucify" refer us back to the trial before Pilate, in accordance with the opposition prophet/king.

"Come down now from the cross, so that we may see and believe": the ANAL code, with the challenge to produce a spectacular sign being parallel to the challenge in S 39c. S 22c2, at the narrator/readers level, answers the challenge with the fall of Israel in 70: "So that looking, they may look and not see . . . lest they return and be forgiven." The judgment upon Israel, its ruling class, and the Jerusalem C (S 69) is now being executed.

"The men crucified with him were insulting him": the two Zealots, who are on the same side as J in relation to the spectators, nonetheless move over to the side of the spectators, and J is strictly *alone.*

c. "When the sixth hour came, there was darkness over the whole earth": the second period in this narrative of agony belongs to the MYTH whose words had confirmed J as the beloved son on whom the favor of *heaven* rested (S 2). Here the MYTH too is silent, causing the "passersby" to be silent and emphasizing the solitude of J. In the darkness the ANAL fades out definitively, since no reading of any sign is possible any longer. Even J no longer *sees* anything or understands anything. He who had taught his DD to read the fruits of his powerful practice is reduced to total powerlessness.

d. "At the ninth hour J cried out": J, who since S 65 has not been an "actant" (except for the two "replies" to the courts) but has been "passive," "led out," and silent, becomes once again an *actant.* "In a very loud voice": responding to the silence of heaven, whence the "two voices" had come (S 2, S 43).

"My God, my God": not "Father" now, as in S 64, just as he himself is no longer "Son" or "Messiah," because he has been "abandoned" (his sheep are scattered; he is alone, powerless, in agony, close to death). His *prayer* is a final *hopeless* cry, as he sees the defeat of his practice, his strategy, his reading of the announcement of the final narrative. "Why?": He had still retained some hope, as his confession in S 66 showed. What hope had he kept? The text indicates it. "Eloi . . . calling on Elijah . . . comes to take him down": the text plays on the Aramaic *Eloi* to introduce "Elijah" who is the "form" of the ascensional closure of the messianic narrative (MYTH), since he is the one who is to come before the Son of man does. Is J's last hope, then, based on the text of current apocalyptic, that is, the hope of a final intervention by God and his kingdom at the very moment of supreme distress,[202] a hope signaled at the prepaschal level by the "you will see" of the messianic confession before the Sanhedrin? The answer of heaven is darkness; J cries out at God's abandonment of him. This "why have you abandoned me?" thus corresponds to the *choice* of S 2 ("You are my Son"), just as the darkness and the nakedness of the body correspond to the extreme "whiteness" of the garments in S 43. What began there as a promised success ends here in failure.

The practice of J terminates in a question, a "why?" that seeks to break through the darkness and prolong the narrative that is now ending. There is no answer to this final question, this supreme illustration of the parabolic "without him knowing how." The second cry emphasizes this. Nonetheless, this "why?" is what will engender the theological discourse by metaphorizing the "death" as "cup," "immersion," "life given as a ransom for many" (S 50), and "my blood of the convenant poured out upon many" (S 50), and inscribing it in the necessity proper to a predestination. Where the narrative stops, the theological discourse begins.

"Made him drink it, saying": a little force is applied to the exhausted body amid its expectation of Elijah. The answer to this action is expressed in the "but" of "But the Jesus, crying out with a very loud voice, expired." The cry is the final cry of life as it rejects death, rejects the violence that triumphs at last over the body and its power to give life.

e. "The veil of the sanctuary . . . top to bottom": in the practice of giving bread, the death of the naked body of J replaces the temple, which is the den of robbers. Therefore the nakedness of the body entails the nakedness of the temple (and, earlier, the nakedness of the high priest at the center of the Sanhedrin) and manifests the emptiness of the temple's interior. The text does not deny that which the practice of J has effected; the tearing of the "veil," which matches the tearing of the heavens in S 2 ("from top to bottom," according to the same descending movement of the Spirit-dove), indicates the death of the symbolic field of Israel; the destruction of Jerusalem and the temple, some decades later, will be the simple consequence of this death. The witnesses proved in the end to be speaking the truth: the dying J has indeed destroyed the temple.

f. "The centurion. . . seeing how he died": this final struggle, this paroxysm in which the power of life cries out against the violence of death,[203] this ending of the narrative is *read* by the very man who has put J to death. Once the darkness has passed, the braiding of the ANAL codes continues; the text gains control again and opens a new possible field for the narrative, beyond the frontiers of the temple-barren fig tree, namely, the field of the pagans.

"Truly, this man was a son of God": in contrast to Peter ("I do not know *the man you are talking about": S* 67d), the centurion reads the overturning of the codes of the SOC as a sign of the "son of God," and the carnival scene as a parody that was not a true sign.

g. "There were also women looking on from a distance": new actants are introduced; they are a remnant from a now closured narrative and will permit that narrative to start again in S 73. Proper names are given once again that have meaning for the readers. "When he was in Galilee. . . to Jerusalem with him": the completion of the narrative of J, the two great stages of which—the Galilee stage and the ascent to Jerusalem—are recalled, as is the disillusioning of the women when confronted with its failure. The text thus swings back and forth between the completion of the narrative and its new beginning.

S 72 (15:42-47)

al   Evening had already come, and, since it was the preparation, that is, the eve of the sabbath, Joseph of Arimathea, a wealthy member of the council and a man who likewise was waiting for the kingdom of God, came and entered boldly in to the Pilate and asked for the body of Jesus. The Pilate was astonished that he was already dead,

b   and calling the centurion, he asked him if he had been dead for long. Informed by the centurion,

a2   he gave the corpse to the Joseph.

c   And having bought a shroud, he had him taken down, wrapped him in the shroud, and placed him in a tomb that had been hewn out of rock; then he rolled a stone against the door of the tomb.

d   And Mary of Magdala and Mary, the mother of Joses, observed where they had laid him.

a1. "Joseph of Arimathea, a wealthy member of the council": an actant who belongs to the ruling class from an economic and political standpoint. "Who likewise was waiting for the kingdom of God": but not after the manner of a disciple of J; his waiting is expressed after the death of J and is thus not harmonized with his narrative. "Entered boldly": he breaks with the practice of his peers, as did the scribe in S 55i.

b. A short scene that emphasizes the death of J; the centurion who confirms the death thus becomes a "witness" to the "empty tomb" of S 73 and a guarantor of the fact that the man had really been dead.

c. The fate of the body is sealed by the stone that finally closes the narrative.

d. Here as in S 71g the women are presented as a "remnant" that makes it possible for the text not to close and the narrative not to end. Their *observance* of the body, which is repeated emphatically here, signals that the ANAL code is not closured.

Nonetheless, S 72 does bring an end to the major sequence that opened in S 65: the sequence of the circulation of the body of J, which is "led away" into the space of the power proper to the SOC until it exits from that space into the tomb. It is a major sequence of the "victory" of the STR AA and of the defeat of the STR J and therefore of its announcement of the eschatological narrative.

S 73 (16:1-8)

a   When the sabbath was over, Mary of Magdala, and Mary, the mother of James, and Salome bought spices in order to come and anoint him.

b   And very early in the morning, on the first day of the week, they come to the tomb at sunrise. They were saying to one another: "Who will roll the stone from the door of the tomb for us?" And looking up, they see that the stone has been rolled away; now it was very large.

c   And having entered the tomb they saw a young man sitting at the right side, clad in a white robe, and they were afraid. But he says to them: "Do not be afraid; you are looking, are you not, for Jesus the Nazarean, the crucified? He is risen, he is not here. Here is the place where they laid him. But go, tell his disciples and the Peter 'He goes before you into Galilee. There you will see him, as he told you.' " They went out

d   and fled from the tomb, for they were trembling and beside themselves. And they said nothing to anyone, for they were afraid.

a. "When the sabbath was over": agreement with S 72 ("the eve of the sabbath"); in the CHR this is the third day after the death. "Mary of Magdala . . .": The "remnant" of S 71–S 72, recalling the narrative of Galilee and of the ascent of Jerusalem. "Bought spices in order to come and anoint him": once again a small completion of S 72; the narrative has trouble closing. And yet, after the death of the hero, what further narrative is possible?

b. "Very early in the morning, on the first day of the week, . . . at sunrise": the CHR contrasts with that of S 72 ("evening . . . the eve of the sabbath"), which closed both the day and the week. Here, on the contrary, a new day and a new week begin with the emphasis on the sunrise.

"Who will roll . . . for us?": a question aimed at completion: in order to anoint him. "They saw that the stone had been rolled away": the stone that has closured the narrative by burying the body is reopened. Since S 71c, after the death of J, we note this swinging of the text between the narrative that is ending and the elements that constitute a sequel and bring a reprieve as it were, a small postponement of the ending. Here the back-and-forth ends with a movement that denies the closure of the tomb. The narrative starts up again.

c. "Having entered the tomb": desire for the body of J. "A young man sitting at the right side, clad in a white robe": in contrast to the young man who fled naked in S 65g, thus signaling the SYMB as powerlessness of the body. The SYMB, which has been closured by the stone, starts up again as a body that is clothed and powerful; this inversion provokes the fright of the women.[204]

"You are looking, are you not, for Jesus the Nazarean, the crucified?": the narrative of J is called to mind by referring to its beginning (J came from Nazareth: S 2) and its ending ("the crucified": S 71) and by referring to the identification marks of his class (a carpenter from a little town in Galilee, executed as a Zealot by the ruling class) and not to his "messianic titles." "He is risen": the young man recounts the narrative (ACT) that has proceeded according to the logic of J's practice (sleep/rise up). "He is not here": the absent body; the rolling back of the stone enabled the body to go forth and the narrative to start up again.

"Here is the place where they laid him": the empty tomb is the sign to be read (ANAL) of this narrative that was unhoped for and was without witnesses.

"But go, tell his disciples and the Peter": go and proclaim the continuation of the narrative; this proclamation will reconstitute the BAS circle that has been scattered by the flight of the disciples and the denial of Peter. "He goes before you into Galilee": the STR of the exodus (to the pagans) by way of Galilee (S 63) (TOP) is renewed ("as he told you"). The braiding of all the codes begins anew; the narrative did not end and death did not get the better of it. The narrative starts up again in order to extend to the pagans; its harmony with the final narrative is asserted once again.

"There you will see him": the BAS circle will be reestablished in full force. This future narrative, announced now, of the rendezvous in Galilee will confirm in your eyes (ANAL) the narrative I am recounting to you now. Now, this future tense, "you will see," is used elsewhere in Mark only for the future vision of the Son of man coming on the clouds (S 58b5, S 66c); therefore, this narrative in Galilee refers to the final narrative, *as if* Galilee were the place where the elect will be gathered "from the four winds" (S 58b5).[205] At the level of the GEO, therefore, the text of Mark effects a subversion of the Jewish text: Galilee, from which J hails, is the theater of his power, while Judea, the theater of his death, is the land of unbelief.

"As he told you": the "paschal" narrative has been recounted; the distinction prepaschal/postpaschal is no longer in place.

d. "Fled from the tomb . . . trembling and beside themselves": the narrative of the power of the rising body over the powerlessness of the dead body renders its hearers powerless and dumb; the narrative is nonnarratable. "They said nothing to anyone": the circulation of the narrative stops; the BAS circle is not called together. "For they were afraid": the narrative being halted once again, the text ends abruptly with "fear" as its final word.

Chapter 3
A Rereading of Mark

INCOMPLETENESS OF MARK

Everyone is agreed that Mark 16:9–20, the so-called canonical ending of Mark, does not belong to the text and is a later addition.[1] The question has often been asked whether the abrupt ending is due to an accident, either in the transmission of the text (loss of the final part of the manuscript) or in its writing (the author unable to finish it). According to Kümmel, "there is an increasingly strong inclination to the view that 16:8 is the intended ending of Mark."[1a] However, it is not the author's "intention" that interests us in this matter but the text itself, and it is to the text as it has come down to us that we must put our questions.

The title of the text describes it as the "beginning" of the narrative of Jesus the Messiah, a narrative summed up as "good news." According to the prepaschal STR of J, this good news must be "proclaimed to all the nations" (S 58b3), to "the entire world" (S 60c). On the other hand, the "programing" of the text, according to the TOP code, says the narrative of J is to end in Galilee.[2] The "young man" repeats this in S 73: "He goes before you into Galilee. There you will see him." Finally, S 73 brings the new start, the rebraiding, of the codes of the narrative. In short, at the textual level, the narrative is incomplete; more accurately, there is an interruption of the *circulation* of the narrative of J, because of the *fear* of the women who have been charged with this circulation. This is what we must try to account for.

As a matter of fact, the writing of "Mark" is itself a *moment* in the continued circulation, and this at Rome, after the year 70. Thus there has indeed been a circulation of this narrative, at first orally, until it was *written* down; the written state gives witness to the *journey* of the narrative.[3] Let us digress and then come back to this point.

RETROSPECTIVE READING OF S 42c-S 73

S 42c–S 58 form a major sequence, that of the ascent to Jerusalem, which continues in S 60 and S 61–S 62a, c. S 59 and S 65–S 72, which prolong S 54 and S 55e, form another major sequence, that of the success of the STR of the chief priests, scribes, and elders, and the elimination of J by his murder on the cross. Between these two sequences we recognized a *hinge* of narrative hesitation, in which the theological discourse is strongly at work, namely S 62b, S 63–S 64.

We have, then, the following schema:

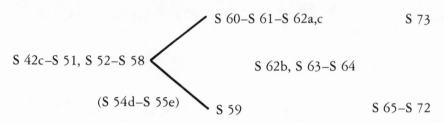

S 60–S 61–S 62a,c   S 73

S 42c–S 51, S 52–S 58

S 62b, S 63–S 64

(S 54d–S 55e)   S 59   S 65–S 72

Let us read the schema. Before S 42c, there is the narrative of the circulation of the powerful practice of J and his narrative in Galilee, with the setting up of the ANAL and STR codes that lead to the reading of this practice as *messianic* by Peter: "You are the Messiah" (S 42c). S 42c–S 51 (and S 45h) are the narrative of the ascent to Jerusalem as a new STR, with the ANAL code establishing a confrontation between STR J/STR Z. S 52 signals the first objective of this ascent, the confrontation J/temple and its occupants (AA), and the major sequence ends with the destruction of this temple, which "Mark" reads as a sign of the imminence of the final, eschatological narrative, since the destruction is the narrative of the *failure* of STR Z. S 60–S 61–S 62a, c, establishes the second objective of the ascent to Jerusalem, namely, the *exodus* to the pagans. The latter is opposed by the STR of the AA who, by means of the betrayal by Judas, one of the twelve, frustrate this strategic goal. S 65–S 72 recount the *failure* of the STR J, with the episode of Barabbas reactivating once again the J/Z contrast, to the temporary advantage of the Z. Finally, S 73 is inscribed in the renewal of the STR J that had been cut short. This renewal takes place after the narrative of the resurrection, and the very writing of Mark bears witness to the success of this STR, that is, to the proclamation of the good news in the whole world, as far even as Rome, the center of this world.

In a word, then, the second part of Mark shows the confrontation between the two STR and their respective failures. At this level, no doubt is any longer possible as to the validity of comparing STR J with STR Z and the Zealots. The latter were the ones who caused the Jewish War and in their defeat brought about the destruction of the temple and the collapse of Israel. We may ask, however, why Zealotry is not more clearly signaled, especially in S 45i, where the Zelotic acclamation is concealed (at the level of the Aramaic narrative itself), and in S 58, where we do not find any explicitation of "the abomination of desolation." It seems that "Mark" in his turn utilizes a STR of clandestinity, for fear that if his text fell into the hands of the Roman conquerors, it would supply new excuses for persecutions against the *ekklesiai* (Mark thus follows the norm for apocalyptic writings[4]).

It is more important, however, to read, at this narrator/readers level, the function of the postpaschal theological discourse, and this first of all in relation to the narrative of J. A first function is *apologetic*; this is to say that the postpaschal theological discourse explains and tones down this *failure* of the Messiah who was killed on the cross, this *curse* that came instead of the anticipated eschatological blessing, this *scandal* in the Jewish codes. In other words, the postpaschal theological discourse answers the question *"Why?"* which J asked when he was at the point of death, and it does so by inscribing it in the *necessity* proper to predestination: "The Son of man *must* suffer much . . . and be killed" (S 42c). In this necessity the sequel too is inscribed: "And rise after three days."

The same necessity is also *predicted* three times by J during the ascent to Jerusalem. Thus the readers are prepared *beforehand* for the failure. The latter, consequently, is to be read not as a failure but as part of God's plan for his Messiah. The murder occurs according to a preestablished plan and is therefore no longer a defeat that causes the narrative to end in desolation; instead, the murder is one sequence in a narrative that continues by means of the resurrection. This plan unfolds at the level of the narrative and thus involves the element of chance that is part of an unfinished process. Judas is the one who plays the role assigned to chance, as L. Marin has satisfactorily shown.

All this, nonetheless, was *written in advance*: "How then is it *written* of the Son of man that he will suffer much and be treated with contempt?" (S 43c). This *writing in advance* is cited in an emphatic way in the hinge sequence in which the element of chance in the narrative of betrayal is connected with the necessity proper to the theological discourse: "The Son of man is indeed going *as it is written of him*" (S 62b), *"It is written*: 'I will strike the shepherd, and the sheep will be scattered' " (S 63b), and "Have you come to take me with swords and clubs? . . . But this is in order that *the Scriptures may be fulfilled*" (S 65e).

THEORY OF THE READING OF MARK

Let us now reread the entire narrative, but still at the narrator/readers level. Beyond the confrontation of the STR of J/Z there looms another confrontation: between the destiny of Israel and the destiny of the *ekklesiai* of the pagans. This, as we insisted, was the problematic of S 55, in the parable of the vine growers who refuse the emissaries of the lord of the vineyard and kill his son, thus announcing the passage of the vineyard into the possession of the pagans, and in the discussions that follow upon the parable and give explanations in terms of the oppositions God/money, God/Caesar, God of the living/god of the dead. The curse to which Israel is destined is thus explained by the *rejection* of the Messiah and his practice by the chief priests, scribes, and elders (S 55b) as well as by the C (S 68c). All these—chief priest, etc., and crowd—have passed judgment on themselves by the STR they have followed. They stand in contrast with the disciples-readers, according to the opposition of the SOC/BAS spaces and the practices proper to each of these spaces. It is the opposition of "those outside"/"you": "To you is given the mystery of the kingdom of God, but to those outside everything happens in parables, so that looking, they may look and not see, and hearing, they may hear and not understand, lest they return and be forgiven" (S 22c2). This accounts for "the abomination of desolation standing where it should not be," and for these days of tribulation that have been shortened only "because of the elect whom he (the Lord) has chosen" (S 58b4).

This is what the text gives us to *read*: "Let the reader understand!" (S 58b4), at a second level, which is no longer that of the narrative of J but that of the narration of it by "Mark" in the space of J/DD. At this level Mark is to be read by putting "Mark" in the place of J, and the readers in the place of the disciples: "What I say to you, I say to all" (S 58b7). Most importantly, the discourses that are introduced by the words: "In truth, I tell you," function expressly as a connective between the narrative of J and the ecclesial narratives, a connective that is marked by the future tense (except in S 57c).[5] In this textual articulation of the different narratives we find two kinds of *future*, according to three narrative times that are articulated as: narrative of J/ecclesial narratives/final narrative, in a linear way, according to the succession of times.

The first *future* is located at the level of the narrative of J and looks forward to the ecclesial narratives. It articulates the *first* time with the *second*: "In truth, I tell you, there is no one who has left . . . who shall not receive a hundred times more, *now in this time*" (S 49d), where "this time" is the second or ecclesial time. The second *future* articulates both of these times with the final time: "and *in the time to come* eternal life. Many of the first shall be last, and the last shall be first" (S 49d).

What happens between the first two times, that is, the time of the narrative of J and the time of the *ekklesiai*? The exodus to the pagans takes place. Now, if we trust the narrative in Luke's Acts and Paul's Letters, it seems that this *exodus* came about through the ecclesial narrative of Paul, but also that this narrative-exodus of Paul was the site at which was structured the *theological discourse* that we see at work in Mark. In other words, what happens *between* the first two narrative times of Mark is the *writing* of Paul.

And what occurs between the second time and the final time? The *writing of Mark*. This fact will enable us to specify the second function of the theological discourse in this writing: it articulates the two *predictions* of J and exercises thus a *predestinatory* function. Just as J predicted his death and resurrection, and these came to pass, since the element of chance was contained within the plan of God, so too his prediction of the coming of God's eschatological kingdom during this generation will be fulfilled: "In truth, I tell you, this generation shall not pass away before all that happens" (S 58b6). Here we have Mark's *thesis*: "when you see that happening" (S 58b6), that is, "when you see the abomination of desolation" (b4), be able to read it: "let the reader understand!" "know that he is near, at the doors" (b6). The two predictions cancel the failures: the failure of J, his death, brought his resurrection; similarly, the failure of the Zealots will bring about the eschatological event.[6]

RESURRECTION AND ESCHATOLOGY

Let us go back to the first question we raised in this chapter: the question of the incompleteness of Mark. If Mark is textually incomplete, the reason is that the work is *open* to a sequel. What is the sequel? The *final narrative*. "You are looking, are you not, for Jesus the Nazarean, the crucified? He is risen. . . . He goes before you into Galilee. There *you will see* him," said the young man in S 73c. That is precisely what people are waiting for. "They will see the Son of man coming in the clouds with great power and glory. And then he will send the messengers and will *gather* his elect from the four winds" (S 58b5), and this gathering will take place in Galilee.

Here is the evidence. Ennio Floris[7] has analyzed the narratives of the apparitions of the risen Jesus in Matthew, Luke, and John, by comparing them with two types of mythic structures. One of these is the *apparition narratives* of the gods or their messengers, the "angels," in which "the apparition shows the divine origin of the message."[8] Floris works out the basic model for such narratives. The second type of mythic structure is the *recognition narratives* that "are part of the cycles of returning heroes."[9] Comparison of the Gospel narratives with these other structures enables him "to conclude that the apparition discourses [in the Gospel] are articulated according to a literary structure that results from combining the divine apparition narrative with the recognition narrative. Thus Jesus plays the role of the angel but at the same time that of the returning hero."[10] This returning hero is not immediately recognized and must therefore either produce signs proving his identity or declare his identity in a discourse or appeal to things remembered, etc."[11]

We can therefore draw this conclusion: that the final narrative of the *return* of the Son of man is what will complete the narrative of Mark and closure the text in accordance with the logic of the MYTH code that was programed at the beginning, whereas, *because this final narrative is delayed*, the other gospel texts will have to end with the narratives of the (provisional) return of the risen hero.[12] "Mark" sticks to the logic of his ANAL code to the very end; he gives his readers the "signs" that will enable them to "understand" that the Son of man will return as a hero "with great power and glory" (S 58b5) and not any longer in secrecy. For "nothing is hidden except in order to be *revealed*, nor does anything remain secret except in order to *manifest* itself. He who has ears to hear, let him hear" (S 22c4). Once again: "Let the reader understand!"

What all this comes down to is this: The text of Mark is given as an *immediate reading*, or the *time of reading* coincides for practical purposes with the *time of writing*. When the distance between these times becomes too great, others will feel obliged to closure this ongoing openness to a narrative that has not yet taken place. They will not be able to endure any longer an incompleteness in which the last word has to do with *fear* of carrying the narrative to the disciples, and they will add the canonical "ending."

THE MESSIANIC AND THE THEOLOGICAL

In order to read Mark from S 42 onward, we were obliged to posit the grill of a double writing, with one writing producing a text we called prepaschal, and the other partially erasing the first and producing in its turn a text in which the paschal narrative is predicted and which we called postpaschal. This terminology (prepaschal, postpaschal) was provisional. We are now in a position to give a better definition of the textual contradiction between *narrative* and narrator's *discourse*. Upon the narrative entitled "good news of Jesus the Messiah," and therefore upon the *messianic* narrative (the prepaschal text), the narrator's work has begotten the *theological* discourse (the postpaschal text). What we must do here is reach the *how* of this contradiction; later on we will ask about the *why* of it.

It is the logic of narrativity, which is expressly stated in the words "without him knowing how" of the parable in S 22b2, that posits the ANAL and STR codes as, respectively, the reading of the narrative that has already taken place and the decision concerning the narrative to come. Beginning with Peter's reading of the messianic narrative (S 42b), the strategy of Jesus led to the exodus to the pagans; this exodus implied the absence of the body of J from the BAS circle during the movement of worldwide extension that would constitute the narrative sequel (sending of the twelve, together with J). But because of the treason of Judas, the messianic narrative was halted by the murder of the crucified Jesus. The first function of the theological discourse, therefore, was to delete this strategy to some extent (only partially, because the symptoms have enabled us to restore the erased text) by making the murder and the ensuing resurrection the "necessary" (*he must*) goal of that very strategy.

However, despite this "necessity" proper to a specifically theological "predestination," the STR of the messianic narrative is not denied. We saw throughout the major sequence of the ascent to Jerusalem that the STR of J was distinguished from the STR Z by its inversion of the dominant codes of the SOC. The major sequence of the arrest, condemnation, and killing of J *radicalized* this inversion, and the parody of the "king of the Jews" (S 69) made this clear by contrasting the power(lessness) of J and the force exercised by the AA, a "king" condemned as a Zelotic terrorist and those who exercised the power of the state. So too is the absence of J's body radicalized, for it is first put into the tomb, but then proves to be "absent" even from the tomb ("he is not here. Here is the place where they laid him": S 73c). There is also a strategic continuity in the reprise of the "rendezvous" in Galilee ("as he told you") prior to the exodus to the pagans.

MARK AND THE OTHER GOSPELS

The messianic/theological contradiction sets us a problem: the how and the why of this contradiction. We shall speak of this at length in Part IV of this book, but we must advance cautiously. It may be that my use of a "symptomatic reading," which is borrowed from a Marxist who himself refers to Freud, has led me to force the text of Mark and to extract from it a problematic that is not really proper to it. Can we, then, find confirmation of the validity of my procedure? Let us look to the other Gospels for such a confirmation.

Let us take as our starting point the theory of the two sources,[13] according to which Matthew and Luke were produced on the basis of the text-narrative of Mark and the so-called Q source that gives the "sayings" of J. Let us then ask what happened, in this textual transformation, to some of the indices of the narrative logic of the messianic narrative in Mark. We shall look for the answer to this question even in John.[14]

The *indices* in question have to do with the textual sites in which Mark sticks fast to the logic of successivity that is proper to a narrative, by implying that even the actant J is ignorant of what is going to happen. To begin with, the parable of the "without him knowing how" (S 22b2) is not taken over by Matthew or Luke. The effort to find a trace of it in John 12:24[15] shows very clearly the influence of the theological discourse, for which the seed becomes a parable of the death-resurrection of J.

S 8 disappears in Matthew, while in Luke it has dropped the narrative of the prayer as well as the indication of a strategic change on J's part; in Luke it has also dropped the narrative of Simon's STR which is an extension of the STR of the C. So too, the indications of a change of STR on J's part because of the C in S 28d–S 31, disappear in Matthew (omission of S 28d) and in Luke (omission of S 31f, S 32, and the *entire sequence of the loaves*). Similarly, those sequences concerning J's powerful practices that involve "difficulty" (S 38, S 41) are omitted by Matthew and Luke.

It would take too long to analyze what Matthew and Luke have done with the numerous indications Mark gives of J's STR. It will be enough to point out that Matthew and Luke systematically play down (or simply omit) the strategy of the "Messianic secret" and its correlate, which is the establishment of a space of the DD as opposed to the space of the C.[16]

Finally, there are two symptomatic indices of the fact that Jesus "did not know" the *failure* of his STR. The cry of abandonment on the cross (S 71c) disappears in Luke, and the narrative of the "temptation" in Gethsemani (S 64) disappears in John, although his narrative of the "passion" is pretty much parallel to that of the three synoptic Gospels.

Now, this articulation of the STR and ANAL defines the very narrative logic of the narrative in Mark. Must not the attenuation and progressive elimination of it by the other three evangelists, and the corresponding invasion of these three texts by the theological discourse, be therefore an index of the progressive inversion of the relations between the messianic and the theological, with the latter erasing the former more and more?[17] Admittedly, the ACT narrative remains dominant in Matthew and Luke, but it is disarticulated from the STR and ANAL codes as far as actant J is concerned. J becomes one who already possesses the narrative, one "who knows *how*." Consequently the narrative becomes a narrative that is wholly focused on *predestination*; it becomes a theological narrative. The high point of this shift is reached perhaps by John when J speaks of himself in these terms: "I have *come from heaven*, not to do my own will, but to do the will of the one who sent me" (John 6:38). Here he does away with the difference between the two wills that are clearly manifested at Gethsemani (S 64d). In fact, the Jesus of John no longer prays except in a discourse dominated by predestination (John 17).

The ACT narrative thus becomes a succession of narratives that is programed by *heaven*; in other words, a mythologized narrative. The theological discourse has restored the narrative to the MYTH code in which the theological discourse itself originates, and has installed it in a kind of heavenly *timelessness* that is, according to M. Eliade, characteristic of the structure of the MYTH code: a sacred or primordial time.[18] The *Christology*[19] thus developed will culminate in the idea of the *incarnation* of the Word of God in Jesus Christ; the narrative, fragmented to fit a liturgical framework, will become ensconced *in illo tempore*, to use a favorite phrase of Eliade that is intended precisely to designate this "sacred time" in contrast to the time of profane chronology.[20]

The history of forms, the method of which presupposes that liturgical catechesis is the *Sitz im Leben* or "vital context" for the textual production of the Gospels, will take for granted the domination of the messianic by the theological and will make no effort to deal directly with the messianic narrative. The problematic of the narrative proper will be replaced by the problematic of "the historicity of Jesus" and the effort to determine what happened *historically*. Here again, however, priority will be given to the "words," the *logia* of Jesus, the *ipsissima verba*, while the narratives of his powerful practice will become secondary as a result of the rationalist expulsion of the miraculous from "history." The exegetes have never managed to escape the grip of the theological discourse.

All this assures us that the problematic we have produced as that of Mark is indeed to be validly regarded as his. It justifies us in moving on to clarify the *why* of this contradiction that ever-already exists between the MYTH code and theological discourse, on the one hand, and the messianic narrative, on the other.

Part IV
An Essay in Materialist Ecclesiology

THE PROBLEMATIC OF A MATERIALIST ECCLESIOLOGY

"Materialist ecclesiology": surely a barbarous pairing that will startle many an ecclesiologist and many a materialist! What theoretical purpose can be assigned to such a pairing? "Ecclesiology" refers to a site of the theological discourse, the site at which it takes the church for its object. But is not theology the very matrix of western logocentric discourse, the idealist discourse par excellence in the view of historical materialism? And has not historical materialism, from Marx to Althusser, staked out its ground by means of an epistemological break first with the economic region, then with the entire systematicity of the philosophico-theological discourse? In thus pairing two terms that designate two contradictory discourses, which term takes control of which?

I cannot refute this legitimate suspicion in advance; you must rather make your judgment depend on what I do with the two terms. On the other hand, I can state here the goal I have in view when I set up a materialist ecclesiological discourse. First of all, the adjective "materialist" is to be taken as meaning historical materialism; the very fact that my text began with an exposition of the concepts of historical materialism showed that this text was to be produced in the epistemological field opened up by Marx. Second, since the church or, better, the churches, and Christianity are a historical phenomenon, they are an object of historical science and therefore of historical materialism; consequently, a materialist ecclesiology will simply be one region of historical materialism. A materialist ecclesiology is thus to be regarded as an analysis of Christianity, one of the ideological forms of the western social formations.

But why analyze Christianity? After all, historians of Palestinian Judaism will not be as interested in one of the many movements that stirred Palestine before 70 A.D. as they will be in the Zelotic insurrection that started the "Jewish War" and led to the destruction of the temple, the ruin of Jerusalem, and the collapse of the Jewish subasiatic social formation. Historians of the Roman Empire during the two or three centuries after 70 will pay a certain attention to the growth of this Jewish heresy that managed to take root outside Jewish circles in the Diaspora. They will be interested, first, because Christianity was one of the most important forms of the sectarian religions of "Asiatic" inspiration that swarmed in the urban milieus of the empire; and second, because the persecutions that the Roman state inflicted on Christians seem to have been a symptom of the transformations which this state was undergoing and which would have well-known consequences in the fifth century.

On the other hand, historians of the European "precapitalist sequence" will be very much interested in the genesis and transformations of these sects which were structured as churches and became the apparatus that produced the ideology which dominated that sequence for a good ten centuries.

The few times, from Engels to Casanova, that historical materialism has tackled the question of the "origins of Christianity,"[1] it has done so by approaching Christianity as being ever-already a *strictly* ideological (religious) phenomenon and by relating it (as is proper) to its economic and political preconditions. Well, here is where my essay retains its suspect character: I think that the procedure just described combines disparate elements and that we must be more cautious in our reading of the texts that bear witness to the genesis of Christianity.

We are in the presence here of a textual whole that has three parts. One is the "authentic" letters of Paul, the man who effected the passage of Christians from the Jewish milieu of Palestine and Syria to the Jewish milieu of the Greco-Roman Diaspora and, above all, to pagan milieus. These letters are the site of an intense theological work that defends and assures the success of this passage, this exodus, this new "Passover."

A second part is the Apocalypse attributed to "John." Communist historians have a fondness for this work, and with good reason. Nonetheless I have left it aside, as I have Paul, because the narrative of the "events" in Palestine plays little part in it. Finally, there are the three "synoptic" Gospels, the chief object of which is precisely the *narrative* of these "events" that have to do with the "Jesus Christ" with whom Paul and the Apocalypse deal.

The choice of Mark was dictated by the discovery in this Gospel of a *structural contradiction* between a theological discourse that belongs wholly to the ideological instance, and an X that belongs rather to the three instances. We shall produce the concept of this X (which is recounted by the narrative as *messianic*) as the concept of a *practice that is articulated at three levels;* the result will be one of the major concepts of our materialist ecclesiology (the choice of the term "ecclesiology" will be justified later on). The other decisive concept will be that of the structure of the *theological* discourse in its contradictory relation to the messianic narrative; the proper object of the theoretical discourse that we shall endeavor to establish here will be the *contradiction* between these two concepts.

All historians whether communists or believers[2] agree that the vast majority of Christians in the first centuries were recruited from the popular classes of the Roman Empire. In addition, many critics (including some theologians for the last twenty years or so) have rightly seen in the "conversion" of Constantine and his edict of toleration in behalf of Christians[3] and in the official status given Christianity by Theodosius (379) a decisive factor in the transformation of a popular sectarian religion into a state religion, such as Christianity would continue to be throughout the period of the European feudal mode of production.

And yet this transformation of the ecclesiastical apparatus and its ideology raises certain problems. True enough, during the fourth century, the so-called golden age of the patristic church, an extensive theological work was carried on, of which the Councils of Nicaea (325) and Constantinople (381) were the outstanding moments. Nicaea was convoked at the urgent bidding of Constantine to the bishops in order to meet the threat of the "Arian heresy," and it began the formation of *Christian dogma.* Patristic theology and conciliar dogma can be analyzed to find indices of the *class transformation* of the ecclesiastical apparatus, but it is likely that we would find no clear break in relation, for example, to the theological texts of the third century, although these were produced when Christians were still undergoing terrible persecutions at the hands of the Roman state.

Something must therefore already have been at work shaping Christianity so as to make possible this class transformation of the apparatus, something that was in contradiction to the messianic practice of J as a practice of poor people such as we read in Mark and such as we might also read in Matthew, Luke, or Paul. To put it briefly: the theological discourse must be at work in the Christian texts from the very beginning, so that even after the class transformations of the apparatus a certain kind of reading (admittedly, a deformed reading) of these texts might continue to be made. Here we have the reason why the messianic/theological contradiction can legitimately become the first object of a materialist ecclesiology.

How shall we proceed in order to appropriate the historical *knowledge* of this contradiction? We shall follow L. Althusser's theory of the "theoretical."[4] The reading of Mark which we have just effected will serve as a *raw material,* and we shall put to work on it the theoretical concepts of historical materialism in its formal generality,[5] on the one hand, and the concept of the subasiatic mode of production as found in first-century Palestine[6] (and the concepts producing the knowledge of the situation of the *ekklesiai* in the slave-based mode of production after the 70s), on the other. The concepts produced by this theoretical work will then enable us to make an epistemological break with the theological discourse by disassembling the latter and establishing a specific field within the larger field of historical materialism. This process will evidently require a later theoretical reprise in regard to other texts and other "ages" of Christianity, if the theoretical status of a materialist ecclesiology is to be fully assured.

In what follows, we shall often go back to and develop our "reading of

Mark." We shall not always be taking pains, however, to mark carefully the boundary line between this "reading" and the ecclesiological discourse. Otherwise, the difficulty of writing and reading our text would be too great.

THE PRACTICE OF THE HANDS OR CHARITY

Mark's narrative recounts the practice of J. In this practice we have distinguished *three levels,* each corresponding to one of the sequential codes. Furthermore, in S 46 we read a semantics of the regions of the body; this enables us to articulate body with practice. Thus a practice of the *hands* corresponds to the ACT code, a practice of the *feet* to the STR code, and a practice of the *eyes* to the ANAL code.[7]

We may say that this work of the hands, which *transforms* bodies,[8] consists in a practice that is operative at the *economic level.* The objection of the AA in S 16 suggests this correlation, for they argue that healing is a *work* forbidden on the sabbath. We shall return later on[9] to the "powerful" (miraculous is the usual word) character of this practice; for the moment, we shall take the text as it yields itself to reading, a text that "alien" to our modern outlook.

Let us analyze first the question of the loaves. The strategic opposition between J and the DD[10] is based on the BAS/SOC codes, for to *buying,* which refers to the circulation of money, J opposes *giving* the loaves which *"you have."* He thus rejects the seizure of products by the monetary system so as to attach an *exchange value* to them, and makes the *use value* of the loaves and fishes the controlling factor. Exchange value is thus eliminated from the BAS economy. In S 49 it is the *rich* who are refused admission to the BAS space: "Go, *sell* whatever you have, and *give* to the poor . . . and come, follow me" (S 49b). Here, *selling* functions solely as a means of *giving,* and "go" (as a rich man) is opposed to "come" (as a poor man) because a person can enter the BAS circle only if he has left everything. The code that dominates the economic instance of the SOC, namely rich/poor, is thus reversed and subverted (first/last); the emphases laid by J in S 49 are unparalleled elsewhere in Mark.[11]

In S 57, the *exchange value* of what people give in the economy that is tied to the temple is cast out by another, ecclesial economy in which people share whatever they have as means of life. As Acts 2:44–45 and 4:32–37 show, the ecclesial rule is the economic practice of sharing "according to what each one needed," after the sale of what people had.

In S 60 J praises the *waste* (or "loss") of the perfume by its being poured out on his body.[12] He is not denying the rule we just analyzed, but allows the action in preparation for S 62c. As we saw, S 62 completes the various lessons in the BAS economy, by replacing the body of J (the center of the BAS circle, but a center that will absent itself) with the practice of sharing loaves in order to allay the hunger of the C of *poor.* The latter are thus established in a relation of metonymy with the body of J, as Matthew 25:40 makes explicit. The two kinds of practice of the hands, dealing with the bodies of the IIc and with the loaves, are thus drawn together into a single practice; the practice of sharing replaces the body of J as the source of power and fruitfulness, according to S 49d ("a hundred times more"). The primacy of this practice of sharing had already been emphasized by the fact that it was the reading of the corresponding sequences which, throughout the *major sequence of the loaves,* made it possible for Peter to read the messianic narrative.

If we take into account the fact that the narrative often brings out the *utopian* longing of the crowds ("outside themselves") in the face of the powerful practices relating to the bodies of the IIc and that the object of the practices of the loaves is the *filling* or satisfaction of the C, we can describe the movement of J's practice, at its *economic level,* toward the utopian horizon of the subasiatic mode of production.[13] The movement is that of the BAS circle of DD, which is delineated for the first time around a table (S 13), just as its final delineation also takes place around a table (S 62). In S 31 this *table* is extended to the entire crowd, which is arranged in an orderly way "in parties" and "in groups." The movement of the messianic narrative at the economic level consists in the extension to the whole world of this *circle* as a *table* at which the poor are filled, a pooling and sharing of all one has, and consequently a hundredfold multiplication of the announced blessing. This multiplication of the blessing and of the movement proper to it finally brings in its train the final, eschatological blessing.[14]

Let us observe that this practice bears not on the productive forces themselves (unless we want to compare the "healings" to the practice of medicine today, which aims at restoring the bodily power to work) but on the circuit of circulation and consumption. All this is summed up elsewhere in the opposition God/money, which is not an opposition between two generic equivalents (ideological and economic) but between the messianic narrative with its power and the monetary equivalent of this; we shall return to this point later on.

This *economic practice* is inscribed in the gift-debt system, and this is why J takes the "second commandment," "You shall love your neighbor as yourself," from Leviticus.[15] There is only this difference between the commandment on Jesus' lips and the commandment in Leviticus: that "neighbor" is no longer only the Jewish neighbor but embraces also the poor pagan neighbor. Now, to love the poor person as yourself amounts to seeing to it that he or she is filled as you are. This practice of economic love has a name in the messianic tradition; its name is *charity.*[16]

THE PRACTICE OF THE FEET OR HOPE

What is the practice of the feet but the *movement from place to place,* according to the TOP/GEO codes, that makes J and his practice circulate through the space of Israel,[17] in a process that parallels the circulation of his narrative? If we reread S 8–S 11, we see that a twofold movement is implied there: that of the geographic extension of the BAS circle and that of clandestinity, which in turn is also twofold, being both an *absence* from the crowd and a taking refuge from the AA (S 18).

The schema that directly relates to the *feet* as a bodily region of practice is the schema of the *road,* which belongs as such to the STR code. Galilee is the region of the first period of J's circulation, and the whole of Palestine is designated as the first goal pursued in the STR of J: *"First,* let the children have their fill" (S 36c). Judea and, more particularly, Jerusalem, will be the region of the second period of the narrative. Finally, the ultimate goal of the STR J, which will elude him but will be taken up again by the twelve (the eleven), is the field of the pagans. What practice is to be articulated with this geographical displacement? *"Let us go* elsewhere into the neighboring towns, so that I may make proclamation there too" (S 8d). What is given here as the definitive strategic goal is the *proclamation* of the final narrative or the approach of God's kingdom, and therefore the utopian eschatological horizon. This is what dictates the choosing of the twelve who are gathered into a narrower circle ("he made twelve, so that they might be with him") but are destined for the *road:* "and he might send them" (S 19b). The sending is recounted in S 28 as a first step to the goal; the horizon of the pagans (the crowds of Tyre and Sidon as early as S 18c) continues to be the justification for this setting apart of the twelve as "apostles" (S 28d).

This means that the establishment of the STR code cannot but end in a *displacement* from the Jewish SYMB field to the ecclesial BAS field that is to be opened up among the pagans. The displacement is geographical, since the Jewish SYMB field is inscribed geographically, with its center in the temple at Jerusalem. But the displacement is also the effect of the subversion, by the BAS practice, of the political codes that govern the SOC of the Palestinian subasiatic mode of production.

There is also a subversion of the relations of blood kinship: the "house" of mother, brothers, and sisters (S 21b), of father and children too (S 4, S 49d), is replaced by ecclesial relations of *brotherhood* ("a hundred times more . . . of houses and brothers and sisters and mothers and children": S 49d). A subversion, too, of the relations of political domination (this includes economic domination as well, since the relations of production are directly political relations in the subasiatic mode of production): unlike "the rulers of the people" who "lord it over them" and "their great men" who "tyrannize over them," "it is not so *among you.* Instead, he who wants to be great among you must become your *servant"* (S 50d). There is thus a reversal of the master/servant code, with "masters," like "the rich," being excluded from the *ekklesia;* "servant" changes its meaning and is no longer opposed to "master," but indicates, by way of the term *service,* the specific character of the intraecclesial political level of the BAS practice (not "to be served" but "to serve").

The relations parents/children, adults/children, fathers/children (the young) are likewise subverted ("let the children come to me . . . for the kingdom of God belongs to such as them": S 48b). The subversion operates, once again, by the exclusion of *fathers* and a semantic change in the term *children* (youth), thus expressing the absence of fatherhood (S 49d) and the *fraternal* character of ecclesial service in the *play* (lacking in domination but not in aggressiveness) that is proper to children.

Finally, there is also the exclusion of a kingship based on blood relations, such as the kingship of David: the Messiah is not a king, the son of David (S 56) (the theatrics of S 69 bring this out very clearly), but one whose strategy has placed him in the ranks of the condemned.

On the other hand, man/woman relations, though stripped of the relations of domination that are established by the "patrimony" of the "house" (S 47), will prevail in the *ekklesia* (S 49d); but man and woman will now be two in one *flesh* (S 47). Here, then, is how the STR of J leads to the establishment of a space of DD, of a BAS circle, in which relationships are not measured by those proper to the SOC but according to *fraternal service*. Access to this *circle* is had only by way of a *conversion* that is articulated according to two times: a time of a *break* with the SOC and its codes (S 4, S 13, S 49), and a time of *following* J and taking over his practice of service and salvation (S 50).

Let us now turn to the other movement in the STR J, the movement of clandestinity, and first insofar as this movement takes the form of the *absence* from the C that we have noted on several occasions. What brings the C together around J is the narrative of his powerful practice and the way in which the C reads it. Their utopian hope, which is stirred to life by the acquisition of this blessing, is often described in terms of the people being "beside themselves" ("out of themselves") in a state of fear that follows upon this irruption of power into a closured text of repetitive daily practices. The power enthralls the utopian hopes of the C and focuses their attention on the body of J, which thus becomes a *center* that is fixed, as it were, by the *great circle* of the surrounding multitude. This limitation of the practice of J is the primary goal of the STR of the C from S 7–S 8 on ("everyone is looking for you"). It is to this that J's STR of absence is a response; his STR thus avoids the closure that the fascination of the C would impose on his narrative.

In the context of the Palestinian class struggle, this quest of J by the C would have a direct political consequence: the setting up of J as a Zelotic Messiah, a leader of these crowds against the Romans. Such a leadership, however, would reinscribe the hierarchy of the codes of the SOC in the BAS circle and thereby do away with the difference which the practice of J is delineating throughout the narrative. (When the ecclesiastical formation reincorporates the codes of the SOC by way of a *hierarchy,* this is an effect of the christological discourse that turns J into Lord.) It is this difference that is indicated by the strategic ass's foal of S 52, but the C does not succeed in reading it.

A second effect of this "quest" of J by the C would be the political closure of J's practice within the frontiers of Palestine and thus a negation of the displacement from the Jewish SYMB field to the pagans. The STR of *absenting* J's body from the C will thus end in its *exodus.* In S 62c, as we could anticipate from S 60, the absence of the body of J is made definitive, and consequently the BAS circle, which was hitherto centered around the body of J, is radically *decentered*. This means that there will no longer be a body to attract utopian hopes and to closure strategies, since the only signifier given for the reading of the BAS practice will be the practice of sharing bread, together with what this practice implies, namely a break with every closure and a limitless extension throughout the space of the entire world. The absence of J's body is, in the final analysis, a refusal to let that body be established in the political instance, and, consequently, it means a liberation from the utopian horizon in the form of a possession of the whole world,[18] but with the exclusion of all domination, even that of Jews over pagans. This is why the temple must disappear: Jerusalem (Zion) will no longer be the center of the eschatological gathering of the nations around the Jews. The gathering, according to Mark, is indeed to take place in Galilee,[19] but it will be a gathering of the *elect,* among whom, in Paul's formula, there will be "neither Jew nor pagan" any longer (Col. 3:11), nor rich nor poor, nor masters nor slaves, nor males (dominating) and females. In short, there will be only brothers, with everyone a child, everyone last, everyone a servant.

Finally, we must analyze the STR movement of clandestinity in relation to the AA, the ruling classes in Israel. This movement is the narrative consequence of the radical subversiveness of J's practice and of the fascination it exerts on the crowds. The clandestinity is marked in the TOP by the avoidance of towns, which are the centers of political power. The narrative is handed over to the aleatory logic of relations between forces, and since power, threatened by the practice of J, seeks to get rid of him, the STR of the BAS will be to flee from the danger of death, the definitive curse, so as to make possible, when the moment comes, the *exodus* to the pagans and the issuance of the utopian hope in the eschatological blessing.

We can understand why the theological discourse, which inscribes the death of J in the predestination of a death he himself has predicted beforehand, would tend to obliterate the STR code, neutralize it, and reduce it to a provisional strategy that will end when "the hour" has come.[20] At the level of the messianic narrative, on the other hand, the treason of Judas, which will frustrate this strategy of a clandestinity that is directed to an exodus, can only be the aleatory effect of the interplay of forces between the SOC and the BAS, with "one of the twelve" being recovered by the codes of the SOC, from which he had previously broken away. Displacement of bodies, subversion of political codes, play of the relations of forces: does not all this put us in the sphere of the *political,* as we defined this earlier?[21] The code of the strategic *choices* that establish the constellation of actants in relation to J (C, DD, AA, MM) refers, in this messianic practice, to the *political* level.

Let us try to pin down further the logic of this STR code, in its relation to the ANAL and ACT codes. It is indicated by the "without him knowing how" of S 22b2: J knows *only* what happens as an effect of the ACT code; it is on the basis of his reading (ANAL) of the *fruits* of his practice that he makes a STR decision, in a movement of which the best example is that in which he waits, "from shore to shore," for Peter's messianic reading in order that he may decide on the ascent to Jerusalem as the final stage before the exodus. This movement is constantly repeated in response to each new effect of the ACT narrative, while the horizon of the STR code is always the coming of the eschatological narrative by way of the various geographical stages of the *road* that is to be traveled (Galilee, Jerusalem, Galilee, pagan nations, the whole world).

The movement is that of the *road* followed by the BAS *circle:* the road of a progressive extension of the practice of blessing bodies that are freed (c → b) and satisfying the crowds (Cc → Cb) through the sharing of bread; meanwhile, these provisional blessings announce the final blessing. This movement of the *messianic* narrative of the BAS circle as it undergoes geographical extension *proclaims* the collective Son of man; this political strategy aimed at a worldwide table at which the poor are filled also has a name in the messianic tradition: the name is *hope.*

THE PRACTICE OF THE EYES OR FAITH

The practice of the eyes and/or the ears is inscribed in the ANAL code. One *sees* (with the eyes) the practice being done, one *hears* (with the ears) the narrative of this practice as it circulates. And yet, having eyes, one may not see; having ears, one may not hear. This practice and narrative, then, raise a question: what is this? Who is it that does it? It is this problem of *reading* the narrative that articulates the ANAL code. "Do you not understand?" (S 22c3); "Have you no faith?" (S 23c); "Do you still not see or understand? Is your heart hardened?" (S 40b). To read the narrative is to grasp and understand the question; not to read it is to be hard of heart.

The parable of the four soils (S 22b1) enables us to read that seeing or not seeing, hearing or not hearing, depends on the space in which a person is situated. The strategy of the parables result from this factual situation and effects a separation of spaces: the space of the AA and C, and the space of the DD.

The AA are ever-already under the control of the SOC system; the dominant ideology causes them to read "through the eyes" of the principal equivalents: money, the state-temple, Caesar or the god of the dead. From this site, the subversive practice of J can be read only as a form of violence that threatens the entire system, and therefore as a curse. According to the semantic grill of the AA, J's practice belongs to Satan ("It is through the prince of demons that he casts out demons": S 20c). The parable of the soils turns this reading around and posits that this blind reading, this nonreading, is itself rather an effect of Satan's activity. This reading by J, which is determined by the MYTH code, provides the key for the reading of the narrative of his murder: those who have the power of the SOC in their hands are the very people who are located in the site of *death.* This is why they are blind and why their hearts are hardened; this is why no other signs will be given them except the signs of the power that saves and gives life. In short, the (primary) factor that determines the reading or nonreading of the messianic narrative is an effect of the class sites of the readers. This is especially evident in the counterreading J gives of the teaching practice of the scribes in S 56b, where he relates this practice to the entirety of their class practices.

The reading J proposes of his own narrative has its site in the struggle against this dominant ideology, which he endeavors to dismantle. The stake in this dismantling is first of all the C, to which the key is given, namely, save one's life/lose one's life (S 16). However, the C also becomes an object of the strategy embodied in the parables ("With the help of many such parables he preached the word to them, *according to their capacity for hearing,* and without parables he did not speak to them": S 22a2). For the C too is under the control of the codes of the SOC, and only if there is a break with these codes will a reading become possible. Admittedly, the C, unlike the AA, is awakened from its utopia by the practice of J, but the awakening itself remains prey to the fascination and fear caused by the power of J's practice in relation to the god of the ruling semantic. This fascination draws the C along in quest of J, but it also closes their eyes and prevents them from reading. We are speaking here of Galilee, since in Judea it is exclusively the Zelotic grill that comes into play and finally causes the C to take the side of Barabbas. How could a C that depends economically on the temple subscribe to a messiahship that would turn them from the temple?[22]

There are some, however, who do break with the SOC and follow J: his *disciples.* The space of parabolic interpretation that opens up in their behalf in the form of the BAS circle is not, however, automatically free of the Zelotic grill, and we have seen that the failure of the DD to understand (a failure frequently emphasized in the text) is due to the grip that the STR Z, closured by the subasiatic mode of production, still has on them.

The dismantling of the ideology of the ruling classes is accomplished by means of what we have called the "schemas for reading" the ACT narrative. These schemas are of several kinds. In S 12 and S 16, for example, J establishes a reading grill according to the schema of blessing/curse and the power connected with it. He expresses this power in the form of a question ("which is *easier* to say?": S 12d; "Is it allowed [or: has anyone the power] on the sabbath . . . to save a life rather than kill?": S 16c2). He thus overturns the semantic implicit in the accusation brought against him, and only *after this* does he do the practice of blessing which men may read. Elsewhere (S 13e, S 35b, S 55f, g) he replies to accusations or to questions expressly asked in order to test him, by a similar semantic reversal; at times he calls on the scriptures in order to justify this reversal. Finally—and this is the most frequent of the schemas for reading—he recounts a *narrative,* for example, that of David (S 15) or, preferably, a parabolic narrative, and sets this up as a parallel to his own narrative; the correspondence between the various elements of the two narratives then functions as a reading grill.

With the help of these several types of schemata, one and the same structure gradually emerges. For what the schemata always have in view is the semantics of the two systems of uncleanness and debt, both of which relate to the blessing/curse pair. The artfulness of J is to show that the power of his practice always has a *material blessing* as the fruit to be read, in contrast to the curse that is the fruit of the practice of the ruling classes. Consequently, it is from the *materialist site* of this blessing that the reading must be made: from the site, that is, of the salvation of the body and the feeding of the hungry.

Let us take a further step and discover another constant in these schemata for reading. J never makes the reading himself; the grill is always set up so that the hearers-witnesses will *make it by themselves.* This is why, although the text often refers to a practice of teaching by J, the teaching is never expressly stated except precisely in the form of a schema for reading (S 22, S 56, S 58). The absence of teaching reflects this "tradition" of supplying a grill for reading the ACT narrative: the reading is to be done by those who have eyes and ears. It is for them to *break* with the SOC and to decide whether or not to *follow* J; in other words, it is for them to decide on their own *conversion.* In a word, the reading is to be *taken* (as we might speak today of students or the proletariat "taking the initiative and speaking out"); the first moment in conversion is simultaneously a break with the codes of the SOC and a "taking" of the reading. This "taking" is a necessary condition for the circulation of the narrative, for its *proclamation,* and for the setting up of a *strategy.* Thus it is that on the three occasions when J (or the text) speaks of IIc having *faith*, his statement follows on a little strategy that enables them to reach the body of J despite the barrier of the C (S 12, S 26, S 51); similarly, the relatives of J remain outside, for their wrong reading makes them incapable of this strategy for gaining access.

In this reading that is to be taken by the actants themselves, what is going on is precisely the reversal of the scribes/disciples code. Those who have acquired the reading grill no longer need scribes and doctors; the latter are excluded from the BAS circle,[23] which contains only "disciples" in the sense of "readers who know how to read." There is thus a subversion of the practice of the scribes (a subversion announced as early as S 6 and completed in S 56b); the practice of the scribes, for its part, constantly reproduces the scribes/disciples relationship. J has disciples, but only as a temporary expedient: he is to absent himself in his exodus, and the twelve will no longer need him to do their reading.

What reading must be made, then, in order to answer the questions "What is this?" and "Who is he that does this?" It is necessary to read the practice of J as a practice of saving lives and bodies and especially as a practice of feeding the poor by sharing bread with them. This is the reading Peter makes: "You are the Messiah" (S 42b), your practice is *the* messianic practice; and he makes a success of it in the BAS circle by breaking with the SOC (which is the first step). The second is that of harmonizing this practice of a carpenter who is followed by fishermen, tax collectors, and sinners (in other words: a poor man followed by the poor), with the eschatological narrative. This messianic practice, like "a mustard seed . . . the smallest of all the seeds on earth" (S 22b3), will lead to the manifestation of the Son of man and his glorious power, "larger than any other vegetable" and producing "large branches so that all the birds of heaven can shelter in its shade."

To sum up: the messianic practice *at the ideological level* consists in the successful reading of the ACT narrative of J as a messianic narrative of blessing that leads to the eschatological narrative; the name of this practice is *faith*.

THE CONCEPT OF MESSIANIC PRACTICE

We have brought out a triple element in the narrative of the messiahship: a practice of the hands according to the ACT code, a practice of the feet according to the STR code, and a practice of the eyes according to the ANAL code. It will be recalled, however, that at an earlier point[24] the STR and ANAL codes were posited as subcodes of the ACT code (go, proclaim, see, hear, say, etc. are terms proper to this code). The triplicity is therefore that of a single code, and the articulation of ACT, STR, and ANAL constitutes the ACT narrative in the widest sense. In addition, this ACT code is articulated with the parametric code SOC, to which the Jewish SYMB (as Jewish "symbolic order") is likewise linked as a subcode; the articulation consists in this, that the ANAL code evaluates the ACT narrative in relation to the SOC. What is the SOC, after all, but the text of the codes of the social formation, which codes, through their parametric relations, evaluate all the narratives that are textually produced in the social formation? It is this parametric evaluation that is overturned by the play of the ACT, which produces a BAS code that excludes the dominant terms of the SOC (wealthy, lords, scribes) and shifts the dominated terms of the SOC (poor, servants, disciples) into *another* semantic field which is messianic or basileic.

In order to define, by way of a first theoretical approach, the practice that the narrative recounts as messianic, we will have recourse to Althusser's concept of "practice." The messianic practice is therefore to be articulated according to three levels (economic, political, and ideological) as a practice of charity, hope, and faith, and the articulation makes of all this *a single complex practice*. What is the object that this practice *produces*? The object is a new system of relations between the actants in the BAS field; we shall give this *new* system of relations the name *ecclesiality*.[25]

These new relations, which are produced by the powerful practice of J, or by his charity, are read by faith, and move from place to place along the road followed by the BAS circle and in accordance with the strategic hope. What does faith read? It reads, first of all, the healing and satisfying of bodies at the economic level; ecclesiality thus implies *salvation* (in the first of its two senses[26]) or the liberation of bodies. Faith then reads the inversion of the SOC code, that is, of the relations of power which are controlled by the principal equivalents: money (or gold), the power of the state, the god of the dead, all three of which, along with the Caesar of the slave-based imperial system, overdetermine the temple.[27]

How do the strategic choices that hope makes work out in the concrete? They take shape in the *following of Jesus* along the roads of the geographical extension of the BAS circle, as well as along the roads of clandestinity and the avoidance of the death-dealing power of the actants AA, so that the followers of Christ become *servants* (without masters).

Finally, what is the effect produced by this BAS circle? A fructification in blessing that is superabundant (thirty, sixty, a hundred times more, according to S 22b1; a hundred times more according to S 49d), as one becomes one of the *poor* by sharing their bread (without any rich people). Break, following, fruitfulness: these are the three components of a messianic or ecclesial *conversion*.

This articulation of the three levels of practice also allows us to produce a *theory of messianic* (or ecclesial) *prayer*. It contains these elements: a reading by faith of the fruits (blessing) that are brought about by charity; a strategy of displacement and proclamation of the eschatological blessing as a harvest whose fruits ever-already are and yet are also announced as still to come; a petition for new fruits that will set in motion once again (the narrative of) the messianic or ecclesial practice. The site of prayer is the site of a new fructification that comes without anyone knowing how; this site requires a topographical distancing (desert place, mountain, Gethsemani) and a new strategic choice. Prayer is thus articulated as a *moment* in the messianic practice; this is why it is, as such, an object of the narrative, as one of that narrative's sequences. There can be no prayer without narrative, without practice. Admittedly, since prayer is eschatological because of the very movement of hope that is turned toward the final narrative, it does not avoid the closure of the MYTH code, any more than does messianic practice itself. This means that we cannot obtain a concept of messianic practice that will be operative for our current practice, without analyzing this MYTH code from a de-mythologizing standpoint.

Let us turn again to the concept of practice that is articulated at three levels, and reread it according to the classic definition given by L. Althusser.[28] Thus understood, messianic practice is a process of *transforming* a given raw material (economic, political, and ideological relations, or, in summary, the social relations that constitute the bodies of the agents in the SOC system) into a product (new ecclesial relations in the BAS circle), a transformation effected by human labor (the practice of the body of J), using certain means of production (this raises the question of the "power" of bodies; to this we shall return at some length later on).

This definition has to do with the ACT code and does not enable us to grasp the logic of the ANAL and STR codes, although these play a decisive role in defining the "labor" and the "means of production." We must therefore expand Althusser's definition so as to introduce the elements of "reading" (of a text-narrative recounting the practice in question) and "strategy" (according to the evaluation of the means of production or transforming power and of the interplay of the relations of force that comes into existence around this power).

It seems to me that this expansion of the definition gives it a greater theoretical scope.[29] Althusser's definition is limited because of its origin, namely, in the concept of the practice of economic production (in the strict sense of the term), and must be expanded if it is to apply especially to *subversive practices*. It is for this reason that, in defining the relations of productive forces, ordering forces, and inscriptive forces, we were careful to introduce a *textual element* as constitutive of them. It is also why we spoke of a "seminal dialectic" (readings/strategies) in connection with the concept of "subversive practice."

At the same time and for the same reason, we can anticipate a theoretical expansion of the theory of narrative insofar as a narrative is a text recounting concrete practices. It is possible, for each narrative, to evaluate the place of the ANAL and STR codes, as well as the narrative logic, implicit or explicit, of these codes, and perhaps to elaborate a theory of narratives based on the place the aforementioned codes occupy in them. The degree of obliteration that the narratives undergo will make it possible, in addition, to detect the *work of ideology* in a narrative, according as this work contradicts the narrative logic. Similarly, with regard to the process of writing-reading narratives, an analysis of the relation between the degree of subversion of the SOC code of a social formation and the place occupied by the ANAL and STR codes will possibly open the way to a typology of narratives from the viewpoint of a theory of practice.

In summary: in this expanded concept of "practice" (and of its narrative), the elements of reading and strategy will enable us to conceive of the narrative of a practice (a class-struggle practice) as a practice articulated according to the three instances of the social formation.[30]

What is it that undergoes or is the subject of this messianic practice? Two kinds of answer may be given to this question. It may be taken as referring to the body of J; an answer from this viewpoint will be given in the next section. On the other hand, since as early as S 4 (and thus before S 6, in which we saw the beginning of the narrative of J's practice) J called four fishermen to come after him, the practice in question is also that of a circle of which the body of J is the center; therefore, the subject of the practice is a collectivity, a group.

This group will expand to form two circles: the more limited circle of the twelve (S 19) and the wider circle of the disciples. In Mark, all members of the group are recruited from among the dominated classes of the subasiatic mode of production (as S 49 shows); consequently the circle is inscribed among these classes. In addition, the narrative is the narrative of a subversion of the political field and the codes of social formation; it is also a narrative of confrontation with the ruling class. We can conclude that the messianic practice, inasmuch as its subject is the circle of J + DD, is a practice belonging to the dominated classes and—scandalous though this may be to pious ears—*a practice of class struggle.*

Precisely because the messianic practice is the practice of a class struggle, it must submit to comparison and confrontation with the Zelotic practice; we have been able to discern this confrontation going on throughout the Markan narrative, like a watermark repeated on a sheet of paper. For the Zelotic practice too, as we have seen, is a practice involving the struggle of the dominated classes in Palestine against the ruling classes and the Roman occupiers. However, if we are to make the comparison successfully, we must first go further in analyzing the other answer to the question we asked two paragraphs back: the answer that looks to the body of J and the power at work in it.

PRACTICE AS SEED-WORD

Although the messianic practice recounted by Mark is the practice of a circle and thereby of a class, it is also, and in a privileged way, the practice of the body of J, who is the principal actant in the narrative. His body, located at the center of the BAS circle, is the primary *subject* of the messianic practice.

What is a body, and how can it be the *subject* of a practice? This, of course, is one of the main theoretical questions raised in the *Ecrits* of Jacques Lacan: who is the subject of a discourse (of a discursive practice)? Lacan answers by using his concept of the *fractured subject* who has disappeared from the discourse and been replaced by a "proper name" and specifically by the pronoun I, but who can be spotted in the chain of signifiers by the symptoms (metaphors, metonymies) of distortion in this chain. It is the symbolic (in Lacan's terminology) that has ever-already provoked this fracture in the body that is the carrier of discourse, a body that is to be understood as the locus of desire that is deprived of its object.[31]

The body, as locus of desire, is spatiality; it is the difference interiority/exteriority that is produced by the work of the symbolic word, a work that Derrida calls writing or difference (French: *différance*).[32] (In writing this sentence I am shifting away from Lacan's discourse toward the philosophy of Nietzsche and anticipating my brief exposition of this philosophy below in the discussion of the kerygma of power or the apostolic affirmation, pp. 267–277). The body is materiality, differentiated complexity, the site of a play of forces that is determined by the system of organs. Upon this organic complexity the work of language inscribes another complex system (likewise determined) that permits a discernment and evaluation of the bodily interplay of active and reactive forces or of life and death.

The question of the subject thus turns into another question: *which* force carries the day in this interplay that makes the body an agent? Consequently, *who* is the power, whose the will possessing victorious power? In this second formulation, what does the proper name (Jesus, Peter, Pilate, etc.) or the subject of the practice designate?[32a] It designates the instance in the body whose *function* is that of watchfulness, discernment, reading, and elaboration of strategy; this instance is called the *heart* in the Markan text (in S 35, the opposition interior/exterior is related to the heart). Among other things, the heart is the place of prayer, which is watchfulness: "Watch and pray that you may not enter into temptation" (S 64e).

In reading Mark, we observed, as early as S 6, that the circulation of the narrative (of the practice) of J was itself the object of a narrative, one of whose functions is to call together either the C or the IIc. This means that the circulating narrative produces a *textual work* in those who hear it. This is what the three parables of the seed are saying: the narrative, the practice, is a word.

Let us look more closely at this work of the seed in the second of the three seasons depicted in the parabolic narratives, the season between the sowing and the harvest.[33] The season or time of sowing is the season for hearing; the season of harvest is that which results from the sowing and proves fruitful or barren; the intermediate season is the time when the word does its underground work in the hearts-soils. The work is said to be hidden, secret, mysterious, and it goes on without the sower knowing how; the sower's ignorance is the counterpart of the mysteriousness of the work, which can be glimpsed only when we see the fruits or lack of them.

Why is this? It is because the hearts of the agents are ever-already being worked upon by the unlimited text of the narratives that circulate in the social formation. The effect of these narratives, which are closured by the codes of the SOC, is not at all mysterious, for it is simply the reproduction of practices that are harmonized with the reproduction of the social formation and that depend on the place the agents have in the social formation, that is, on their class situation.[34] If there is any mystery, it is due to the interaction of the seed-word with the texts of the SOC and to the ideological struggle within hearts between two types of contradictory narratives. The effect that the sower looks for is the break of the agents from the dominant text of the SOC, their crossing of the line separating the C and J.[35] There is thus a struggle between two powers: that of the might of money, the state-temple, Caesar, and the god of dead men, and that of the ACT narrative, which is read according to the text of the Scriptures and the grill blessing/curse.

The messianic narrative is thus the *key* to the reading of the unlimited text of the narratives of the social formation; it is the textual site that enables hearts as the instance of watchfulness to evaluate the power at work in the narratives of their own practices. This evaluation thus takes place in the heart, which is the *hidden site*, in the body, where a text is elaborated (the writing of the texts of the SOC, and of the BAS text of the ACT), read, and written anew (the manifest, visible fruits). To anyone standing outside (like the sower in relation to the soil and the seed), the heart belongs to the interior of the other as a body, as a spatial being; the fruits of this work is the heart, however closured it may be, are therefore unforeseeable. Which power will win the day? This, then, is the reason for the "without him knowing how." The ignorance of the sower is correlative to the mystery of the working of the seed in the hearts of human beings.[36]

What is it that is to be read about the heart? On the basis of the barrenness of the body: the hardening of the heart (S 16) and its unbelief (S 27). On the basis of the body's abundant fruits: the faith of the heart. Hardening and unbelief, on the one hand, and faith, on the other. Which force carries the day, which power is working in the heart? This is the decisive question that commands the entire ANAL code. What authority does J possess: the satanic power that tempts, or the messianic power? (S 6, S 20, S 23, S 55b, etc.).

The text of Mark provides a sequence of special value for the analysis of this work of the practice-seed. It is S 26 that is marked out as a detailed narrative of the practice of the hands, because it contains four mentions of "touching."

The sowing is narrated first ("having heard what was being said about the Jesus") as an effect of the circulation of the ACT narrative. Next, the text allows the reader to read the heart of the woman who is being worked on by this narrative: "For she said: 'If I touch at least his garment, I shall be saved.'" Finally, the harvest: "Immediately the source of her blood was dried up, and she *knew* in her *body* that she was healed of the infirmity." Curse → blessing. The healing is the fruit of her reading and her touching, after the little strategy for getting through the crowd.

The text then moves on to the sower ("And immediately the Jesus, knowing in himself the power [*dynamis*] that had gone out from him") and his ignorance (he tries to find out who touched him). In this practice of the hands by touching, a *power* goes out from the *body* of J in order to work in, and heal, the *body* of the woman. Power from body to body: this is the index of a narrative that is to be learned. The woman "came and fell down before him and told him the whole truth"; this last word, *alētheia,* is used in Mark only to designate the practice of J (S 55f, i). The woman undoubtedly recounts the whole of the narrative, from sowing to harvest, and it is this narrative that Jesus then reads: "Daughter, your faith has saved you." In his response, the term "faith" indicates precisely the work done by the narrative that was sown in the woman's heart, and the term "saved" indicates its fruit. The work of faith in the heart has made possible the salvation of the woman's body; faith, as a reading of the power of J, has released the energy that passes in a powerful body-to-body contact. "Go into peace" (*eirēnē,* the peace of abundance), into blessing. The power of J (S 27, S 29, S 46) is related to the eschatological power of the Son of man, at whose coming all this hidden work will be manifested in transfigured bodies and open hearts.

Faith, as the practice of the eyes, is thus the reading of the power of the practice-seed of J as the good news of the eschatological power, a reading done according to the movement of hope. The hardening of the heart, on the contrary, is an error in reading: "Are you not in error because you do not know the Scriptures or the power of the God?" (S 55h). Of what do the Scriptures speak if not of the power of bodies, according to a logic that leads to resurrection from the dead? And what are the Scriptures if not the narrative of this messianic power that works from the body of J into bodies subject to the curse, and that thereby announces the resurrection of bodies?

This is why the narrative of J, this seed-word, will be given the title of "good news" or evangel (*Godspel*). Once again, we find ourselves led to S 62, where "this is my body" is equivalent to the replacing of J's body, which is destined to absent itself in its exodus, by the practice of sharing bread as the site of power and as ecclesial narrative. There is no question here, then, of a "liturgy" in the modern sense of the term, but simply of practice itself at the three levels, economic, political, and ideological. This practice becomes the source of power and of liberation for bodies, after the model of the body of J. The *ekklesia* is the site for reading this messianic power, this seed-word that announces the eschatological narrative. In short, the practice in question is the Gospel of the resurrection of bodies.

If we reread S 30, we see now that this sequence has to do with the closure of bodies in the circle ("the courtiers") of the SOC; it is the narrative of the desires that have free play there, of their working and their fruit, which is the *murder* of John. Then there are other circles: the tribunal of the Sanhedrin (S 66); the tribunal of Pilate (S 68); the praetorium (S 69); the court of the high priest ,which works on the heart of Peter to make him deny Jesus (S 67); and Golgotha (S 71), which produces the murder of J. The SOC thus defines the space for the working of money and for the power of Herod, the Sanhedrin, Caesar, the god of dead men and his temple ("he is blaspheming": S 12d) as a space of barrenness (the fig tree) whose fruit is murder. The AA are indeed on the side of Satan, as S 22c3 had given to read.

Let us return now to the key question regarding power. The ultimate criterion for reading and evaluating it is to discern between the power of life and the power of death, between life and death. Is this not the grill which S 16 establishes: "Is it allowed [=has anyone the authority, the power[38]] . . . to save a life rather than kill?"

A further point remains to be decoded with regard to the power of life. If we look beyond J, who has this power? (Just as, beyond human beings, Satan has the power to murder.) Consequently, who is J? In the MYTH code S 2 names the one whose "adversary" Satan is. That one is the *Spirit,* a holy Spirit in opposition to the evil or unclean spirit (as already in Persian ideology). In S 20d the reading the scribes make of J's practice is called a "blasphemy against the holy Spirit"; therefore the holy Spirit is the bearer of the practice or the seed-word. In S 56a, the text of Scripture (the subject of which at this point is David) is said to be a discourse of the holy Spirit. Finally, in S 58b3, when J is giving the disciples advice about how to comport themselves before the tribunals, governors, and kings of the SOC, he says to them: "Do not be anxious beforehand about what you will say, but say whatever is given to you in that hour, for it will not be you who speak but the holy Spirit."

In the three cases cited, the Spirit is linked with either narrative or discourse. The third case is especially interesting because the advice given amounts to refusing a discourse in self-defense according to the codes of the SOC and turning instead to a discourse given at the moment, and therefore to a discourse in power, a proclamation. What discourse is meant here? What is meant is the narrative as proclamation, that is, as a word that sows a seed, a narrative that engenders new narratives.

In fact, it was the Spirit who, in S 2, ushered in the STR J (in the MYTH code), by "driving" him into the desert to meet Satan. The Spirit is thus the ultimate bearer of the *entire* practice of J: of his powerful practice as well as of his strategy, and even of his reading of the writing of David. It is the Spirit who is at work in the narrative of J and is the key to his power, and it is the Spirit who is given back *(exepneusen)* when J dies on the cross (S 71d).

What work does the Spirit do? His effect at the strategic level is to bring about the very opening of the BAS field in the form of ecclesiality, as this field differentiates itself from the SOC space. This opening of a space different from that of the SOC, this opening of the site of the *ekklesia* as a practice-seed-word that announces the eschatological narrative, causes a rending of the text of the SOC (cf. the tearing of the veil of the temple, echoing the rending of the heavens in S 2) and brings into being a field of new possibilities: the field of the power of the practice of sharing loaves as an *alternative* to the now subverted social formation. Is it not this same *alternative* that we are seeking to open up today, in the revolutionary struggle to break with the capitalist mode of production? How are we to describe it, how are we to proclaim it? As the space of resurrection, as the open space of former tombs, which the young man of S 73 proclaims when he says: "He is risen!" In short, we are to proclaim it as the space of the *rising of bodies,* the rising of life, to use the happy phrase of Clavel, prophet of the Spirit who was at work in May '68.

We shall come back later on to the demythologization that the text of Mark requires, but are we not already in a position to point out the site of the entrapment and blinding of the bourgeois exegetes in their reading? For, which of them has really *read* Mark? The site to which we refer is the *heart.* In the theological ideology which is ever-already at work in bourgeois exegesis, the heart is the locus of *interiority,* that is, of intimate experience of the god, of the intercourse of soul with spirit. What these exegetes lack in their reading is the *body* as exteriority. Where they read only a narrative of hearts as purely interior, they should be reading a narrative of the power at work in bodies. From what standpoint do they read? From the standpoint of a text that ever-already refuses the openness of a revolutionized space; from the standpoint of the text of the dominant ideology of the capitalist mode of production that is commanded by the god or by reason; in short, they read from the idealist site. But this site in Mark is the site of the scribes! And we, as readers of Mark, are warned against this misinterpretation of the Scriptures and of the power of God (S 55h): "Beware lest anyone lead you astray" (S 58b2)!

Let us repeat the conclusion of the previous section. Messianic practice is the practice of a dominated class, but it is such in a specific way: the conversion of hearts is the condition that is especially required if this practice is to be powerful and able to liberate bodies. While it is a practice of the dominated classes, it is not simply to be identified with *all* the practices of these classes. The moment has come to compare it with the practice of the Zealots.

JESUS AND THE ZEALOTS IN MARK

The reading of Mark has shown that the practice of J was to be distinguished especially from that of the Zealots, just as the failures of the two practices were compared to the advantage of J. Our aim here is to try to understand, *at the level of Mark's narrative* (therefore at the level of *his* reading of the STR J and *his* reading of the STR Z), the historical reasons why the two strategies were distinct. I say "historical," in the sense that I am going to bring into play the concept, which I produced earlier, of the subasiatic mode of production as integrated into the slave-based mode of production; I shall therefore be supposing that the SOC code of the Markan text is that of this particular subasiatic mode of production. The comparison of J/Z can also be undertaken on a broader scale by taking into account the other New Testament texts and the textual transformations that are operative in them; in any such comparison, however, it must be borne in mind that no claim can be made to have constructed "the historical account" of the "real" practice of Jesus.[39]

The subasiatic mode of production peculiar to Israel came into existence because of emergence of an apparatus of the state (David) as a condition for defending the tribes that had formed an alliance in the face of "foreigners." The centralization of worship that Deuteronomy and King Josias had brought about turned the temple at Jerusalem into an element in *national identity* for the whole of the social formation; the temple came into play as an overdetermined element at the level of the three instances, thus allowing the priestly caste, in alliance with the great landowners of postexilic Judaism, to take over the power of the state. The temple and the closured Scriptures were the decisive factors in the permanence of this national identity (even for the Jewish Diaspora) throughout the several occupations by foreign nations.

We saw that the strategic goal of the Zealots, as of the Maccabees before them, was the restoration of the subasiatic mode of production. They sought to attain this goal by means of a twofold struggle. On the one hand, a struggle against the ruling classes that were collaborating with (and being manipulated by) the Roman occupiers; the goal here was to replace these corrupt holders of power with others who would not be corrupt (reformism). On the other hand, a struggle against the Romans; the goal here was to drive them from the nation's territory (nationalism). In the light of our Hypotheses 46 and 47,[40] this twofold struggle can only be described as a twofold *revolt,* since there could be a revolution only if the Zealots were aiming at a *transformation* of the dominant mode of production and therefore of the subasiatic social formation itself. This, however, was not the case, for possession of the temple was a decisive factor in the struggle. The reformist movement did not challenge the codes of the SOC, even though it did seek to adjust the interplay of classes in favor of the economic interests of the dominated classes. Then, too, nationalism could come into play only thanks to the temple and the sacred Scripture, which were the emblems of national identity. In short, the temple was the index of a *subasiatic closure* that made any revolution at all, to say nothing of a communist revolution, impossible. The Zealots were therefore not revolutionaries; they could not be such.[41] They were "men in revolt," and their revolt failed because the slave-based mode of production overclosured the subasiatic mode of production.

What, now, were the strategic goals of the messianic practice? On the one hand, the goal was the radical subversion of the codes of the SOC as well as of the Jewish symbolic field that was centered on the temple, and of the political segregations caused by the Law. The strategy therefore challenged the relations of production (subasiatic mode of production; large-scale ownership of property), the political authorities, and the ideological relations (exclusion of the rich, the masters, the scribes, and the priests). The strategy thus has all the markings of a *radically communist strategy*.

On the other hand, this strategy could not lead to the transformation of the subasiatic mode of production because of the overclosure of the latter by the slave-based mode of production. We are dealing, then, with a *nonrevolutionary strategy*.

This may seem paradoxical. But what is communism? It is a political program that seeks to eliminate relations of power between the classes at the three levels, and therefore to eliminate the class system itself. And what is revolution? It is a strategic process for taking power. Consequently, there can be a noncommunist revolution (for example, the bourgeois revolutions, the Russian revolution) and a nonrevolutionary communism (for example, the hippie communes whose marginality is an index of the nonrevolutionary nature of their strategy).

There was only one way to secure the extension of J's nonrevolutionary communism which had no desire to be marginal (unlike the Essenes): the way of internationalism, which Mark attributes to Jesus as the second goal of his strategy, namely, the exodus to the pagans.[42] It is at this intersection of communism and internationalism that the privilege of *conversion* (to which we shall return) is located, the privilege of transforming the practices by which a break with the SOC is made, the privilege of following J, the privilege of each agent bearing fruit in regard to the liberation of *bodies* (hands, feet, eyes) through the powerful work of the Spirit.

We can now explain the semantic difference in the use of the term *Messiah*. According to the Zealots, the Messiah is a "king," a leader bent on assuming political power. According to J, the Messiah is the one who produces the space for the collective Son of man. This latter title (to which we shall return) is the one that corresponds to a *communist ecclesiality:* to the gathering in the BAS circle of poor people without any accompanying rich people, servants without masters, disciples without scribes, young people without adults, brothers without fathers, or, in a word, sons of man outside any relations of domination and kinship.

Was this break with the Jewish symbolic field and with a nationalism that gave a privileged place to ties of blood, a symptom of non-Jewishness on J's part, as compared with the Jewish Zealots? If we are to answer this question,[43] we must compare messianic practice with the gift/debt system that we analyzed in the early part of the present text.

According to Luke, the Palestinian *ekklesiai* were, at least to some extent, driven from Jerusalem by the persecution that Herod Antipas launched against them.[44] A number of Christians took up residence at Antioch, in a pagan country, and it was because of this already taken step that Paul undertook a mission to other pagan cities, especially those that were Greek. He justified his action by pointing out that his method was to address first the Jews of the Diaspora and only then, when the majority of these hearers rejected him, to proclaim the good news to the pagans.[45] It was thus the reading of his practice and that of his hearers that dictated his strategy, in the logic of the ANAL and STR codes that we find in Mark. According to the parable in S 55d, the rejection by the ruling classes in Israel dictated the proclamation of the giving of the vineyard to other vinegrowers, transferring it from the Jews to the pagans. So too the rejection by the Jews of the Diaspora, again as a result of the dominant codes, dictated the STR of Paul. In other words, given the reading of the J's practice as messianic and therefore as proclaiming the eschatological narrative to be imminent, it was the very play of the relationship between the various practices involved that led to the exodus to the pagans.

Let us repeat our question: was the price of this exodus an infidelity to the Jewish Scriptures? The reply comes from the analysis we made in the first chapter of the second part of this text: the Scriptures are not "unitary"[46] but shot through with a dialectic that depends on the class struggle. And the exodus to the pagans, at the historical moment when it actually occurs, is in keeping with the logic of Deuteronomy and the prophets.

We have already laid sufficient emphasis on the fact that at the economic level the practice of J radicalizes the logic of the debt system; a good example is the statement in S 22c5, when read at this level: "For to him who has they will give, and from him who has not they will take away even what he has"—a statement that is thoroughly Deuteronomistic.

Similarly, at the ideological level the opposition God/money, God/state-temple, God/Caesar, God of living men/god of dead men sends us back to the Deuteronomistic opposition between Yahweh, on the one hand, and gold and silver, chariots and horses, idols, on the other.[47] In both cases, the narrative of power is the decisive factor in the challenge issued to the signifiers of class powers.

At the political level, however, it seems at first sight that the practice of J is a rejection of the gift/debt system as we read it in Deuteronomy. The

Deuteronomistic levites, after all, were nationalists, whereas J reverses the Israel/pagan nations relationship and denies Jewish preeminence. The two factors previously analyzed join forces here: the closure of the subasiatic mode of production as overdetermined by the slave-based mode of production, and the Jewish rejection of the messianic narrative. However, the order of J's strategic priorities (which is the same as Paul's) as voiced in S 36: "First, let the children have their fill," is already a sign that J's STR of exodus to the pagans (according to Mark) is only a reprise, but radicalized in this factual situation, of the very logic of the gift/debt system.

We analyzed this system according to two principles: the principle of extension and the principle of restriction. But what is J's STR if not the prolongation of this *extension* of gift, table sharing, service, and reading to the whole of the inhabited field of his day? The messianic time, according to the prophets, was to be precisely a time when the Jewish Law (the gift/debt system) was to be extended to the pagans. If we bear in mind that J made his own the prophetic gesture of reversing the relations between the pollution system and the debt system, we are justified in concluding that J was in no way unfaithful to the Scriptures but, on the contrary, brought them to their fulfillment. This is what his AA were unable to read, but it is also what J's recourse to the Scriptures gave them to read in the ANAL code.

This is true, for example, of the discussion on the first and greatest commandment (S 55i). The sentence "You shall love your neighbor as yourself" is a messianic rereading of the gift/debt system. The rereading amounts to saying: Love the poor person, the servant, the disciple, as yourself; be poor and a servant and a disciple with him or her; there are to be no more rich people, masters, or scribes. In short, we have here the *gift* of the messianic practice and its radical subversiveness.

This enables us to understand better the difference between the Zealots and Jesus as Mark sees it: while the eschatological urgency leads the former to commit suicide in the Jewish War of 66–70, it leads the latter to a mission to the pagans as the condition required for not halting the principle of extension that is at the basis of the gift/debt system.[48]

What is the meaning of this principle of extension? This is a crucial question when it comes to the political scope of an ecclesial practice. On the utopian horizon of the debt system lie *blessing,* happiness, pleasure. But the blessing is not assured when one encloses oneself within a closed community whose narrative too becomes self-centered; in the terms used by Mark, the blessing comes to the *circle* only insofar as circle is articulated with *road* or extension. This means that according to the promise, pleasure or blessing is assured to the rock, the "Amen," only when the blessing is sustained by the utopia of the dominated classes. The liberation of bodies can be accomplished only in the extension of this liberation to *all* the bodies that are held captive by the codes of the social formation. This structure proper to an unclosured narrative and its unlimited extension has the paradoxical effect that because its subversiveness is extended, persecutions will be mixed in with the "hundred times more" of houses, brothers, sisters, mothers, children, and fields (S 49d).

Here too we have the explanation of the fact that the individual's conversion holds a privileged place in messianic and ecclesial practice. This conversion is required as being a break with the codes of the SOC and a revision of objects and desires that are ever-already determined by the general equivalents of the social formation. For example, conversion implies a break with the "attraction of riches" (S 22c3), with money and exchange value, in a process by which objects of desire are revised and desire is led to attach itself to use value and the possession of products in their material bodies.[49] In the messianic tradition, this change and new attitude is called *poverty,* and it is the condition for charity.

There is, then, no place in ecclesiality for either asceticism or a Manichaean, masochistic desire for persecution. On the contrary, the aim is always to seek, in clandestinity if need be, the blessing that will be acquired or, more accurately, given, only when it is extended, in tendency, to the dimensions of utopia. Whenever the circle ceases to expand and closes in on itself, the grasp of the SOC codes begins again, and power is *tempted* to revert to force.

The point we have just been making explains why J refused to put up a struggle in Gethsemani and overcame this temptation (we shall be returning to this point later on). Does this mean that "Christians" must systematically adopt a strategy of the kind called "nonviolence" in our time? To draw such a conclusion would be to *deduce* from the Gethsemani narrative a "moral principle" that would theologize and nullify in advance the play of narratives. In addition to the difficulty we had in reading the prepaschal text that had been erased in S 64,[50] there is the fact that the closure of the subasiatic mode of production/slave-based mode of production affected the STR J according to the aleatory play of the relations of forces. Today, in the context of a quite different social formation—one in which the play of determinations resulting from technological transformations of the productive forces can perhaps make a communist revolution possible—the question of whether or not, and when, to have recourse to weapons is a matter of concrete strategic choices and concrete analyses that cannot be nullified in advance. For example, who will deny that power was being used against force in the clandestine struggle of the various resistance movements against the Nazi occupation? Or in the struggle of North Vietnam against the crushing military superiority of American imperialism?[51]

THE *EKKLESIA* AS PRACTICE

In the preceding sections we have been reading Mark *at the level of the* messianic *narrative* in a theoretical materialist analysis. We shall now continue the analysis but shall take Mark instead *at the narrator/readers level,* where the text articulates the messianic narrative with the ecclesial narratives.

The parametric codes that come into play will no longer be those of the subasiatic mode of production but those of the Roman slave-based mode of production, but in a Greek linguistic framework. In fact, we have already noted at several points in the text of Mark the signs of the Aramaic/Greek translation the text is effecting, a *translation* (or carrying over) that is a *tradition* (or handing on) of the messianic narrative to ecclesial readers whose language was Greek. Our concern now is to find out how this translation-tradition, as a process of writing, articulates the narrative of J with the narrative of the readers of Mark.

A first requirement would be to make clear the social situation of the peoples gathered in the *ekklesiai*. Since I cannot cite authoritative historians and exegetes on this point,[52] I shall limit myself to emphasizing here that the vast majority of Mark's readers belonged to the exploited classes of the Roman Empire, and I shall leave to a later point a sketch of the corresponding political and ideological context.[53] This kind of class membership is, of course, in the logic of the Markan text, which has meaning only if "the poor you have always with you" (S 60c).

What, in the last analysis, does the narrative of Mark recount? First of all, it puts in place the messianic practice that is articulated, according to the three codes, as charity/hope/faith (S 6–S 28). Next, it recounts the reading of this messianic practice by the DD (S 31–S 42b, the "sequence of the loaves"). Then it gives the strategy of the ascent to Jerusalem and the ANAL reading of this ascent (S 42c–S 52). Finally, it tells of the confrontation J/AA in its first phase, which is centered in the temple (S 53–S 58), and in its second phase in which the exodus is aborted and J is murdered (S 59–S 72). In this messianic narrative, what Mark enables his ecclesial readers to read is the ANAL question: *"Who* is Jesus?,"* which runs through the entire narrative as a question about the *power* of his body and about the struggle between this messianic *power* and the *force* of the SOC. S 73 looks beyond the failure of J's death and announces the resurrection from the dead as the victory of power.

We shall return to this question at some length later on; for the moment let us look only at the articulation of the messianic/ecclesial narratives. The narrative of J is recounted as the *good news* of the fruits of the power that is at work in the body of J. Now that this body has been replaced by the practice of sharing loaves as the *determining practice of the ekklesiai* (S 62), Mark's narrative is given as a *reading grill* for ecclesial practice. What is this last-named practice? It is the extension, into the field of the pagans, of the same BAS practice as that of J; consequently, it is the effect, in this new field, of the *same* power that was at work in the body of J. "What I say to you, I say to all: be watchful!" (S 58b7). Therefore, read this narrative; the reading of it will enable you to achieve *watchfulness* in your hearts! The *ekklesia*, as an extension of the BAS circle, is thus the site of watchfulness over the power that is at work in desires, over the ecclesial utopia. Since the *ekklesia* is always subject to *temptation*, it is the site of the pursuit of conversion, that is, of the revision of the objects of the desires by means of the practice of charity, hope, and faith. These desires must be turned away from the *fiction*[54] of the principal equivalents of the SOC to find their fulfillment in satiation, in the possession of the earth, in the consummation of the kingdom of God that is coming.

When all is said and done, what does the term *ekklesia* designate? It designates a site, a space, anonymous houses, but without any specific topography. It designates a "community" (to use a popular word), a set of new relations between the "brothers"—but what is a community? As a matter of fact, the term *ekklesia* can become a *concept* that makes knowledge (in Althusser's sense of the word) possible, only if it designates a *specific practice articulated at the three levels of this circle.* (Therefore it is a concept comparable to the one we produced in the section on the messianic practice.) In short, just as "messianic practice" is the concept of the powerful practice of the body of J, so *ekklesia* is the concept of the powerful practice of the BAS circle once the body of J has become absent ("but me you do not always have": S 60c). The latter concept thus becomes one of the concepts proper to a materialist ecclesiology. By the same token, the term "ecclesiology" is given its justification.

However, the term *ekklesia* is missing in the text of Mark! Where do we get it from, and how do we justify our importation of it into a discussion of Mark? It comes from other New Testament texts, and the legitimacy of importing into the discourse of a materialist ecclesiology depends on the reading of those texts.

The word occurs in Matthew 16:18, in the sequence of the "confession of Peter," which is parallel to S 42. The movement of this Matthean text opposes the reading of the messianic practice ("you are the Messiah") to the reading of the future practice of Simon and the other disciples ("you are Peter and on this rock I will build my *ekklesia*"); the assignment of a new name to Simon is the index of the change of his practice from SOC to BAS.

The word also occurs in St. Paul. If we follow the semantic transformations that the word undergoes in his letters, as analyzed by L. Cerfaux,[55] we will find justification for the conceptual content we are attributing to the term here.

1. First of all, in Pauline usage, the expression "the *ekklesia* of God" (with the definite article) designates the primitive Christian community of Jerusalem by itself.

2. Paul next gives the name *ekklesiai* (in the plural) to the local communities that he founds.[56]

3. Finally, the word *ekklesia* (in the singular) designates the totality of all the Christian communities, both that of Jerusalem and those emerging from pagan milieus. We must inquire, as Cerfaux fails to do, into the reasons for these transformations.

How was the passage effected from the first usage to the second? If we look carefully at Paul's manner of proceeding at the "council" of Jerusalem (Acts 14:27–28; 15:4, 12), we see that he produced there the *narrative* of his practice among the pagans and of the fruits this practice had yielded in the practice of the pagans themselves. It was, then, the *reading* of the extension of the ecclesial practice, an extension sustained by the same power, the same Spirit, that produced the first semantic transformation of the term *ekklesia*. The same Spirit who was at work in the *"ekklesia* of God" was at work also in the *"ekklesiai"* of the pagans.

And what brought about the passage from the second usage to the third? Cerfaux tells us, but without drawing all the inferences from it that he should.[57] The pagan *ekklesiai*, at Paul's urging, collected a large sum of money to meet the needs of the *"ekklesia* of God" at Jerusalem. Paul *reads* this economic practice of charity as having effected the unity of all the *ekklesiai* in a single *"ekklesia."* In other words, the narrative of the collection as a practice as the determining level of ecclesiality is read by Paul as an effect of (messianic) power that is at work in his strategic (missionary) practice, his practice of hope.

We are justified, therefore, in concluding that the *ekklesia* is not simply the community as a gathering but also designates the *practice* specific to this community, a practice that is articulated at the three levels—economic, political, and ideological—in the form of charity, hope, and faith.

We must therefore put the question of *Christian identity* to ourselves in terms of ecclesiality and no longer in what I may dare call the inevitably subjectivist form of "Do I have the faith?" We must find out whether our personal practice, when read by the grill of the messianic narrative, is being played out according to the structure of the *ekklesia.*

If it is then above and beyond the materialist or, if you prefer, political analyses we must make in order to elaborate our strategies, the Gospel will make us hear the promise of blessing: the promise of a radically communist social formation that stakes everything on use value, on the corporality of the agents, on the textual materiality of the signifiers of the various processes of writing. It is a promise, however, that is not to be awaited as a pure wager on a distant utopian horizon, but that is to be read as already realized in the fruits of blessing from a practice according to the debt system, a practice that is international or "catholic" in scope, and undergoing constant conversion, a practice that is the pledge of a revolution that goes on indefinitely.

THE KERYGMA OF POWER OR THE APOSTOLIC AFFIRMATION

Let us return to the question of how the messianic narrative is articulated with the ecclesial. We saw, reading Mark, that from S 6 on, there was an intense circulation of the narrative of J, first in the geographical space of Galilee, then as far as Jerusalem and even as far as Tyre and Sidon, beyond the frontiers of Palestine (S 18). In S 24, for example, J bids the cured demoniac, who "begged him to stay with him," to return to his home and tell them all that the Lord had done for him. This circulation of the narrative, despite the restrictions placed on it by the strategy of the "messianic secret," corresponds to a STR of J, and we saw him choose twelve of his followers "so that they might be with him and he might send them to proclaim" (S 19b), the proclamation being carried out a first time at the end of J's practice in Galilee (S 28c). It is on their return (S 28d) that the twelve are called, for the only time in Mark, *apostoloi* (apostles) when they *tell* J "all that they had done and taught," that is, when they recount their personal narratives to him.

At the ACT level, this is the only time that there comes into play this articulation between the narrative of J and the narratives of the other members of the BAS circle as a geographical extension of the messianic narrative by the *sending (apostellein)* of the twelve.[58] The narratives of the twelve are likewise narratives of powerful practices, according to the c→b schema. In other words, we have the articulation, in the ACT code, of the messianic and the *apostolic* practices.

Now, what else is the writing of Mark but the *proclamation* or *kerygma* of the messianic narrative at Rome? This writing thus depends on a practice analogous to that of the twelve, and we shall call it an *apostolic writing.*

Let us reread S 22c4–5: "He who has ears to hear let him hear"; understand therefore how to evaluate what you hear, for "according to the measure with which you measure, it will be measured unto you" in your own bodies. What is it that persons are to *measure* or evaluate when they hear the messianic narrative? They are to measure the power that the narrative recounts, the power of the body of J and, according to the measure of the reading, the power of the bodies of the ecclesial readers themselves, which is fruitfulness or barrenness according to the parable that has just preceded (S 22b1, c3), "for to him who has they will give, and from him who has not they will take away even what he has."

The question of the articulation of the narrative of J with the ecclesial narratives is, then, the question of the articulation of the power/powerlessness of J's body with the power/powerlessness of the bodies of the disciples-readers. The writing of Mark is the reading of the question of the power of J ("Who is J?") and of the response to this question ("you are the Messiah"), which is given to the readers as a key to their own narratives, their own bodies, and the power/powerlessness at work in them.

Evaluation of the power: this is terminology that evokes the text of Nietzsche and his philosophy of the body, according to the reading of it that is suggested by G. Deleuze in his *Nietzsche et la philosophie.* Before pursuing my own argument I must spend a few pages explaining the main concepts of this philosophy.

1. According to Deleuze, Nietzsche's philosophy is a symptomatology and a semiology. That is, it discerns the symptoms we call "phenomena," and *interprets* their *meaning* through a knowledge of the force that appropriates for itself the reality of the phenomenon.[59] The "phenomena" on which I shall concentrate here are bodies and practices, which are accessible to a semiological analysis only in a text recounting these practices, that is, in a narrative. The short exposition that follows will set forth the principles for the interpretation and evaluation of a narrative.

2. "What is the body? . . . There is no quantity of reality, but every reality is already a quantity of force. There are only quantities of force 'in a relation of tension' each with the others. Every force is related to other forces, either obeying these or commanding them. A body is defined by this relation between dominant and dominated forces. Every relation of force constitutes a body: chemical, biological, social, political.[60] Any two forces that are unequal constitute a body as soon as they enter into relation with one another. For this reason, a body is always the result of *chance*."[61] Thus we represent ever-already the play of the chance forces that constitute us, and it is this chance, which we may call primordial, that creates the problem of our destiny and our narratives. The narrative in question is the narrative of the chance play of forces in the body, and the chance defines a limitless symbolic field of possibilities for the body.

3. The forces differ in quantity, and "the difference of quantity is the essence of the force." This difference is the irreducible element *of* quantity, irreducible *to* quantity. Quality is nothing but "the difference in quantity."[62] "According to their different quantities, forces are called dominant or dominated. According to their quality, forces are called active or reactive."[63] "Inferior forces are defined as *reactive* . . . : they lose nothing of their quantity of force, and they exercise this quantity by assuring the operation of mechanisms and finalities and by providing the conditions needed for life and the functions of life and carrying out the tasks of conservation, adaptation, and utilization. This is the starting point for the concept of reaction."[64]

"What does it mean to be 'active'? It means to tend toward power. . . . The power of transforming, or the Dionysiac power, is the first definition of *activity*."[65]

Therefore, "the body is a *multiple* phenomenon, being composed of a plurality of irreducible forces."[66] "There is no *whole*; Nietzsche says we must crumble the universe and lose our respect for the whole."[67] The symbolic field of the body's possibilities is a field of differences and diversity; it is pure multiplicity.

4. The forces are unequal and different; "no balance of forces is possible," no terminal state, no beginning. "If the universe were capable of permanence and fixity, and if there were in its entire course a single instant of being, in the strict sense, then there could no longer be any becoming."[68] Chance and multiplicity therefore imply that there is only *becoming*; this is to say that everything is narrative and the play of narratives is limitless, without beginning or end.

5. "The will to power is the element from which there flows both the quantitative difference in the forces that are set in relation to one another and the quality that belongs to each force in this relation." The will to power is "the genealogical element in force, the element that both differentiates and generates."[69] The will to power, as "that which wills," is inseparable from, yet not identical with, the force or "that which can."[70] To *interpret* a narrative is "to appraise the quality of the force that gives it [the narrative] a meaning and

thus to measure the relation of the forces that are operative." "What is it that does the interpreting? The will to power." In order to do the interpreting, "the will to power must itself have qualities": "*affirmative* and *negative* designate the primordial qualities of the will to power."[71] To *evaluate* is to determine which quality of the will to power gives the narrative a *value*.[72]

6. What is the will to power as negation? That is, what is nihilism? Nihilism means to deny chance and to say that everything is necessary; it means to deny multiplicity and to say that the whole is one and uniform (with the uniformity of flocks); it means to deny becoming and to say that there is only being, permanence, a single whole. In short, nihilism *denies the play of narratives* and sets up canons or dogmas for them.

On the other hand, what is the will to power as affirmation? In the presence of the limitless play of narratives, the will to power as affirmation affirms the eternal return of the active. That is, it affirms *chance* and, in a second step that does not abolish but confirms the first, it affirms *the necessity in chance* (as its combination[73]). It affirms *the one as the many*; it affirms *the being of what becomes*, and this precisely is *becoming*. "The correlation of the many and the one, of becoming and being, forms a game."[74] To compare narratives in order to interpret and evaluate them and to affirm their play is the aim of philosophy and the supreme form of affirmation.

7. At the same time, however, no matter where Nietzsche looks in order to interpret and evaluate, he finds the triumph of reaction and nihilism commanding every evaluation. By means of "fictions," the reactive forces cut the active forces off from what they can accomplish; masters are replaced by slaves who do not cease to be slaves.[75]

Before raising the decisive strategic question: "How are we to overcome triumphant nihilism?," let us pause for a moment. Is our action in having recourse to the text of Nietzsche compatible with the materialist field inaugurated by Marx, in which I am attempting to produce this essay in ecclesiology? I shall make five remarks on this point.

1. First, I deny that Nietzsche has elaborated a "philosophy of history," as Deleuze claims.[76] We need only point out, I think, that Nietzsche ignores the text of the economic instance, the very text that Marx was decoding during the same second half of the nineteenth century. Then we can understand that as for the Greeks whom Nietzsche so greatly loved, so for Nietzsche himself, work and production (the concept of "mode of production") lack their discourse. But history is not decodable apart from the economic instance.[77]

2. Nonetheless, Nietzsche does have a critique of philosophy (he was working, after all, on philosophical texts), which already decries what Derrida would later call logocentrism.[78] Similarly, Nietzsche's philosophy of the body, which is put to work on the narrative of his own body as healthy/ill, can, I think, be taken over by a materialism that lacks such a philosophy. We must remember, however, that materialism maintains the thesis of the *determination* of bodies and their practices (and of philosophy) by economic, political, and ideological structures.

3. Let us try to gauge the implications of Nietzsche's theory of interpretation for the Marxist text and, more broadly, for the historico-materialist text. If we bear in mind Althusser's thesis regarding the reading Marx made of the liberal economic discourse,[79] we cannot but be struck by this fact: the empty page in this discourse which Marx fills in (and by so doing transforms the problematic of the idealist discourse on the economic instance into a materialist one) is filled in by the missing concept of "labor power" *(force de travail)*. Where the liberal economists spoke (and still speak) of "labor" and the "value of labor" (the first term belonging to philosophical idealism, the second to economic idealism), Marx changed everything by speaking of "labor power" (thus bringing out the value of the *body* of the productive agent) and "value of labor power" (thus doing the same for productive value, or the quasi-use value of the labor of production).[79a]

Now, when the economic instance is thus stated in terms of forces and production (or transformation, which is referable to a will to power), it can be interpreted in the Nietzschean manner. In the latter framework, we would say that in the capitalist mode of production the (active) labor power is separated from what it *can* make and that this separation is the doing of those who do not produce,[80] that is, of reactive forces that make the labor power itself reactive.[81] How is this separation produced? By means of a "fiction"[82]: directly by a monetary fiction (the fetishization of gold), indirectly by a juridical and ideological fiction of the subject. These fictions allow the economic appropriation of the means of production by the capitalists. The latter are thus reactive and, in Nietzsche's sense of the word, "weak." In the last analysis, this is the reason why they must have *weapons* (police) to keep the "strong" separated from their power, to keep them in a state of obedience as an exploited class. This analysis can be extended to what we called "autonomy" (in the relation of ordering forces) and "writing power" (in the relation of inscriptive forces), which are also bodily forces that become reactive when separated from what they can do by the "fictions" of the political and ideological apparatuses.

When the relation of forces is interpreted in this way, it becomes possible to evaluate the "wills to power" and to elaborate strategies for bringing about the liberation of the active forces (of work, autonomy, and writing) through the abolition of capital, the state, and so on. Here we find what was lacking in Nietzsche's philosophy because it failed to take the economic instance into consideration; Nietzsche's evaluation did not lead to a strategy of liberation, but remained confined in the closure which is denounced in the famous eleventh thesis on Feuerbach: Nietzsche, too, was simply "interpreting" the world in his own way, whereas the important thing was to "transform" it.

4. But Nietzsche makes a further valuable contribution (this is really why I go to him) that will eventually be useful in dealing with the old question (a badly formulated question, and with good reason) of the objective conditions and subjective questions of revolution. Historical materialism, for its part, makes possible only the knowledge of the limits set by the structures of the

social formation on the practices of the agents, as well as on the determinations and closures (but it can in principle produce this knowledge in a concrete analysis of a concrete situation, according to Lenin's formula). The question that is very often a stumbling block to revolutionaries is precisely the question of the bodies of the agents, the forces that produce them, and the wills to power that work upon them. Admittedly, Nietzsche does not make it possible for us to know these, since they are the site of mystery (of subversiveness or conversion), but he does give—in principle—the means of interpreting and evaluating the concrete narratives of the agents and therefore of elaborating strategies or, more precisely, tactics that take into account the concrete bodies of these agents. In order, however, actually to do this, one must be at their side, with them, part of them; one must change camps. This is the lesson to be learned from the Chinese cultural revolution; it is the Maoist "secret" of "invincible confidence in the forces of the people."

5. My final remark seeks to account for the ambiguity of Nietzsche's text that allows it to be used as it was by Nazism and yet be rejected as it has been by Marxism.

The ambiguity is first of all semantic. Take the sentence that is a favorite of Deleuze: "One must always defend the strong against the weak."[83] In Nietzsche's philosophy of the body, this comes down to saying: the active forces must be defended against the reactive, because the latter are able to separate the former from their possibilities. We have already seen how this idea can be applied to labor power and to capitalists: the strong are the producers, the weak are the capitalists (at the level of the body, of course).[84] But there is a semantic shift in Nietzsche when he speaks of "masters," meaning the "strong," and of "slaves," meaning the "weak."[85] Again, he distinguishes between "hatred"[86] and "aggressiveness,"[87] rejecting the former as negation and claiming the latter as affirmation, which is a good thing. But he identifies the "struggle" with the former and rejects "class struggles" as if they could not be embodiments of aggressiveness. He often reads history in this manner, and is therefore so hostile to democrats and to socialists.

What produces this ambiguity? It is produced by the extension of his philosophy of the body and of philosophy itself to a philosophy of history, as I pointed out at the beginning of these remarks. This is all the more striking since Nietzsche saw very well that profit,[88] political apparatuses (states, churches, class organizations, etc.[89]), developing ideology, progress, the common good, morality, truth, etc.,[90] are the means by which reaction triumphs!

The question that Nietzsche asked himself after the "revelation" of "the thought of the eternal return" was the question of the strategy for this return: "How is nihilism to be overcome?"[91] What is needed is a "transmutation," and "transvaluation," "a change in the factor from which the value of [established] values derives."[92] Deleuze sums up in six points what this transvaluation consists in.[93] For our purposes we may note only that there is need to effect a "conversion from heavy to light, from below to above, from sorrow to joy: this trinity of dance, play, and laughter effects at once the transubstantiation of nothingness, the transmutation of the negative, and the transvaluation . . . of the power of negation. It is what Zarathustra calls the Supper."[94] What is needed, in other words, is the production of another space in which only affirmation and the activity of forces reigns; this affirmation, being preceded and followed by a negation, by a destruction of established values, will make room for the creation of play. The dancer, the player, the laugher: such is the man of affirmation, the superman Dionysos.

But is there a strategy for attaining this goal? I am afraid there is not, except perhaps at the level of the individual. (Nietzsche is hardly concerned with utopia.) If power is a matter of "transformation" and if transformation takes place first at the economic level, how could the transformation fail to go on being determined by the economic instance? How could it fail therefore to be elitist, since others must produce for the sake of the superman? The eternal return is a "thought"; we reach it through a "revelation." Does Nietzsche's writing not remain, therefore, if not in the realm of theological discourse, as the term "revelation" suggests, then at least in the realm of the philosophical as understood by the Greeks and in the sense denounced by the eleventh thesis against Feuerbach? What I am saying is that Nietzsche's intolerable contempt for "humanity" (see the preface to *The Anti-Christ*) seems to me to be that of a *scribe* who has admittedly subverted in a radical way the closure of his field of problems, but has then remained proudly isolated therein.

Let us return now to Mark and attempt to take up again the question of the articulation of the messianic and ecclesial narratives in the light of Nietzsche's philosophy. We see that in Mark too a central affirmation is preceded and followed by a negation of the "established values" of the SOC: money, state-temple, Caesar, god of dead men. There is antecedently the break involved in a conversion, and subsequently the subversion of the SOC and confrontation with the temple on the way to an exodus. The first affirmation is that of the messiahship: "You are the Messiah." The key to this messiahship is twofold: saving life, on the one hand, and filling with bread, on the other. J's practice effects the opening of a space of salvation, a space of liberated bread, liberated bodies, and the word that is liberated by the action of reading. This triple liberation can be correlated with the Nietzschean trinity: charity leads to play as the liberation of labor power, hope leads to the dance[95] as the liberation of autonomies, and faith to laughter as the liberation of inscriptive forces. These are precisely the "beatitudes" of Matthew 5 and Luke 6 (which really should be treated in detail): "Happy you who. . . ."

The apostolic affirmation thus has to do with the messianic narrative. As kerygmatic, the affirmation proclaims this narrative to be "good news of Jesus the Messiah." This gospel or good news is addressed to the readers as to *chosen* people, and we saw how the scheme of ANAL reading is repeated as the narrator/readers level, where "Mark"/"readers" replace J/DD.[96] In this way the articulation of the two narratives is effected.

According to the two parables in S 22b2 and b3, the practice of J inaugurated the kingdom of God, which it proclaimed. (The kingdom or, in Greek, the *basileia* of God gave us the adjective basileic to describe the space of the messianic circle.) Now both J and the narrator say: "To you (DD, readers) is given the mystery of the kingdom of God" (S 22c2). The kingdom that is to come is *already-there*; the power of the Spirit that sustains the practice of J *also* sustains the *ekklesia*. This power of blessing and life, a power that leads to the definitive power of the Son of man: this it is that in the last analysis articulates the messianic and ecclesial narratives.[97]

This affirmation, however, runs up against a stone wall in the ending of the narrative, namely, the murder of J. When power stands up to force (the force of the SOC), the latter triumphs. That is, the might of the SOC, which is sutained by the power of negation and malediction, wins the victory. We must therefore look more closely at how the apostolic affirmation is made in the narrative of the "passion."

We interpreted the Gethsemani sequence (S 64) as a narrative of *temptation*. What is it that does the tempting? Negation,[98] or reaction: the active body of J is tempted to become reactive, that is, to allow weapons to separate it from its own possibility, and to engage in armed conflict, thus situating itself at the level of force, where the outcome can only be either to conquer or be conquered and where the stakes are those proper to slaves.[99] This is why the body of J is connoted by fear, anxiety, and sadness; it is tempted by the will to power proper to the "flesh," which is "weak"—"what I want"—but his prayer raises the question of the will to power proper to the "spirit" which is "ready" and therefore "strong"—"what you want."

That the temptation was overcome is recounted first in the sequence of the arrest, where the body in its nakedness (signaled by the young man who is naked) is contrasted with the "swords and clubs" (S 65); then in the silences and *affirmations* of J before the high priest and Pilate (S 66, S 68); and finally in the narrative of Golgotha, the place of the skull (S 71).[100] There is, on Golgotha, the refusal of the "wine mixed with myrrh" (a drink meant to anesthetize the victim), the silence before the "blasphemers," and then, above all, the outcry at his abandonment by God and his dying cry. Does all this indicate anything but *the death of one who is active*?[101] That is what the centurion reads: "Seeing how he died, [the centurion] said: 'Truly, this man was a son of God.' "

Let us see how the apostolic affirmation looks at this "death of one who is active"; we shall examine the affirmation in accordance with a triple movement that we will read according to the triple Nietzschean affirmation of the eternal return.

1. The young man of S 73 announces the outcome of this narrative, that is, the *becoming* of the power of an active body until the latter is murdered: "He is risen." On the basis of the becoming of the body, the living *being* is affirmed. "There [in Galilee] you will *see* him," in a future which we have seen to be that of the eschatological proclamation of the Son of man. This amounts to an

affirmation that Jesus *is* the Son of man,[102] an affirmation that will allow us to reread the entire narrative that has been *confirmed* or has been *amen*-ed ("Amen, I tell you"). The Hebrew etymology of *amen* links the word to the solidity of *rock*; the narrative is therefore as firm or solid as a rock on which the ecclesial narratives with which it is articulated can rest; at the same time, the becoming of the narrative is not annulled. We may note in passing that this affirmation is also the object of the mythological sequence to which we give the name "transfiguration" (S 43).

2. The *death* of J is read as *sacrificial* in the sense that I have given to this word[103] and that is not very different from that which Nietzsche also gives it: the death of an active man as a "surplus of life"[104] or as life given. (Recall S 50: "The Son of man did not come to be served but to serve and to *give* his life as a ransom for many.") According to a contrast signaled as early as S 1 by the Baptist, who immersed the C in water, J was immersed in the Spirit. J picks up this idea again in his words to James and John: "Can you . . . be immersed in the immersion in which I am immersed?" (S 50b). Similarly, the refusal of the cup of wine in S 71a leaves room for the "hour" of death as a "cup to be drunk" (S 64: "that . . . this hour might pass from him"; "take this cup from me"; "the worst has happened. The hour has come; see, the Son of man . . . "). Recall, too, the words to James and John: "Can you drink the cup that I drink?" (S 50b).

Now, in this same S 50, the murders of James and John are recounted under the same metaphors: "You will drink the cup that I drink, and you will be immersed in the immersion in which I am to be immersed." Their own (ecclesial) narratives are announced at the level of the narrative and recounted at the level of narrator/readers. Thus the *multiplicity* of the ecclesial narratives that are subjected to the test of persecutions by those who possess armed force is here affirmed to be *one* with the narrative of the murder of the Messiah. The *many* are affirmed as *one*.

3. The murder of J came to pass because of the aleatory element of Judas's treason, in accordance with the factor of *chance* in the relations of forces. The third movement of the apostolic affirmation is inscribed in the discourses on the "paschal Son of man,"[105] in order to express the *necessity* of passing through death as a condition for resurrection: "The Son of man must suffer much and be rejected by the elders, chief priests, and scribes and be killed and rise after three days" (S 42c). This necessity is *read a posteriori* according to the Scriptures: "How then *is it written* of the Son of man that he will suffer much and be treated with contempt," in the context of the command to be silent about the "vision" until "the Son of man should be raised from the dead" (S 43c). Moreover, the entire hinge sequence (S 62b, S 63–S 65) is influenced, we will recall, by this "it is written" and, finally, by "this is in order that the Scriptures may be fulfilled" (S 65e).

What is it that the Scriptures announce? They announce the resurrection of the dead in the eschatological narrative of the definitive blessing as fulfilled (S 55h). The *necessity* that the kerygma affirms is therefore that of the fulfillment by the Son of man of the victory over death, humanity's last enemy as Paul calls it,[106] so that all the elect may then share in the power of that victory. The apostolic affirmation is therefore not mistaken when it reads the Scriptures and the power of God[107] and affirms the resurrection of the dead. The resurrection of J, which is affirmed by the young man of S 73, is thus articulated with the resurrection, which is promised to the readers-elect as the outcome of their narratives as persecuted people, of the cups they must drink and the immersions they must undergo. Since this is an *a posteriori* reading, in a second phase, the necessity in question does not annul the factor of chance that plays in the narrative.

Let us sum up this lengthy section. The articulation of the messianic narrative with the narratives of the *ekklesiai* is effected by the apostolic affirmation that Jesus is the Messiah and that he has been raised from the dead and is the Son of man. This individualization of the collective Son of man in the sole person of Jesus ends with the announcement of his *return*[108]: "They will see the Son of man *coming* in the clouds with great power and glory" (S 58b5); "I am [the Messiah] and you will see the Son of man sitting at the right hand of the Power and *coming* with the clouds of heaven" (S 66c). The text of Mark is left unfinished after this announcement, which is the supreme affirmation of the entire narrative: The Son of man will *come back* to gather the elect—*that* is the good news.

It will be evident that I have italicized the word "return" because of the implicit analogy with Nietzsche's final affirmation, that of the eternal *return*. These two "affirmations" should be compared in order to try to show their possible common ground and the differences between them as well. At issue is the philosopher's attack upon Christianity.

A comparison should be made between the place of the Scriptures as a reading grill for J and of the Gospel as narrative-rock for us, on the one hand, and the place of pre-Socratic Greek philosophy as a reading grill for Nietzsche, on the other. Inasmuch as the Scriptures are the textual site of the promise and thus render possible the affirmation of the resurrection of bodies, we would perhaps find ourselves surprised at how small a place the question of the death of bodies has in Nietzsche and at how the question of repression and murder is entirely absent.

The next section will show that there is more than one point at which Nietzsche and a materialist ecclesiology converge in their critique of "Christianity" and the "theological discourse." Nonetheless, the interpretation which *The Anti-Christ* offers of Jesus as a "pure interiority"[109] represents a blindness to the messianic narrative—although Nietzsche was able to see that "it is false to the point of absurdity to see in a 'belief,' perchance the belief in redemption through Christ, the distinguishing characteristic of the Christian: only Christian *practice,* a life such as he who died on the Cross *lived,* is Christian."[110] In addition, the semantic shift from "strong/weak" to "master/slave," which we observed in Nietzsche, plays a part in his reading of the Gospel.

Finally, let the reader go back to what we wrote about Zarathustra in the early part of this book.[111] It is hard to keep back a loud laugh when we reflect that the "instruments of torture," the "forms of systematic cruelty by virtue of which the priest has become master," that is to say, "the concepts 'Beyond,' 'Last Judgement,' 'immortality of the soul,' the 'soul' itself,"[112] were introduced into the Christian texts by the very Zarathustra whom Nietzsche turns into the proclaimer of superman!

In any event, it would be very interesting to approach the collective figure of "the Son of man" in the light of superman.

THE DISCOURSE OF POWERLESSNESS
OR THE THEOLOGICAL NEGATION

After reading the preceding section, the reader may be tempted to think that the contradiction I thought I had uncovered between the messianic as narrative and the theological as discourse at the level of the narrator is beginning to disappear. After all, a number of elements I had attributed to the theological discourse have been taken back, as it were, and made constitutive elements of the apostolic affirmation and therefore continuous with the messianic affirmation itself. The reason for this is that in the course of writing I have been led to discriminate more carefully among the elements that I had initially attributed without qualification to the theological discourse. We are now in a better position to grasp the structure of this discourse.[113]

What the *apostolos* affirms and proclaims, namely, the kerygma, turns out not to be the whole of the narrator/readers level, but to have undergone the influence of what I have called the theological discourse, and this in such a manner that we can analyze this discourse as a triple movement of negation that contradicts the triple structure of the kerygmatic.

1. Necessity is predicated of chance, but it is done in the form of an *advance* prediction by the actant J himself or in the form of *predestination.* But the "without him knowing how" of the parable is essential to the play of chance in the narrative and to the logic of the narrative; advance knowledge of the outcome of the narrative (the murder of J) contradicts this logic. Predestination, then, affirms necessity as annulling chance; predestination is *negation. In relation to the narrative,* predestination is indeed the matrix of the theological discourse.[114]

2. The movement of individualization of the Son of man, which is produced in the narrative itself as a foreseen *anticipation* (the "ACT Sons of man" and the "paschal Sons of man"[115]), entails two other structural theological transformations.

The risen Son of man, according to the ascensional schema in which he is inscribed, has "ascended" to heaven.[116] Being "absent" from the ecclesial narrative, he is thus *established,* in the framework of the MYTH, as "Son of God," and the centurion already calls him this (but without the definite article). It is a name that only the MYTH (the heavenly and demonic "voices") had elsewhere used (but with the definite article: "*the* Son of God") to express what was specific to J's practice.[117] In this establishment, Jesus is *recentered*, in the BAS circle of the *ekklesiai, at an imaginary level.* The result of this contradicts the STR of absence, which we saw to be the strategy of J by fixing him as *Christ,* as *signifying image* with which the readers can identify; this theological fiction separates them from their possibility. This act of fixing annuls the *becoming* of the messianic narrative as it does that of the narratives of the *ekklesiai* themselves. The process of fixing will only continue,[118] and I may be permitted to oppose the decoding of J's practice as messianic in the narrative to the result of this act of theological establishment by using the distinction *Messiah/Christ.*[119] This second structure of the theological discourse will therefore be named the *christological,* and I claim that the development of the theological discourse in the form of Christology will increasingly obliterate the messianic and its narrative in the other Gospels, thus carrying still further the messianic/theological contradiction.

3. In consequence of the individualization of the Son of man, another theological transformation becomes articulated with the christological. The apologetic function of the theological discourse is to reduce the element of failure in the death of J by making this death a necessity within a matrix of predestination according to the Scriptures. The theological discourse must therefore work on this "death" in order to give it a *prewritten* meaning.

We noted earlier that the term *save* was used in the narrative to designate the transformation effected by the practice of J on defective bodies; salvation is the passage from the curse of illness to the blessing of its cure ($c \rightarrow b$).[120] Beginning in S 42, the term *save* acquires a further meaning: the future entry of the elect into the kingdom of God.[121] The work of the theological discourse will consist in *metaphorizing* the death of J in order to relate it to this coming *salvation,* which will be effected by the *return* of the Son of man when he comes to save the elect ("if the Lord had not shortened those days, no flesh would be *saved.* But because of the elect whom he has chosen"— predestination—"he has shortened those days": S 54b4).

Two metaphors will be produced. "For the Son of man did not come to be served but to serve [and serve = save, as we have seen] and to give his life as a *ransom* for many" (S 50d). It is no longer in accordance with the aleatory element that J is killed; rather, he himself gives his life according to the preestablished plan, and this as a ransom *for many,* for the sake of the salvation of the elect. The metaphor of ransom is taken from the debt system, as is clear from the fact that J's life is *given* (sacrifice), and then from the fact that it is a "ransom" that must be paid for the liberation of a slave. The future *salvation* of the elect, their passage from a state of slavery to a state of liberation in the kingdom of God, will be possible because Jesus has given his life. Here is a meaning for the murder of J: instead of being a failure, it becomes a *saving work,* according to the theological discourse.[122]

The other metaphor is borrowed from the pollution system; the metaphor of ransom is *political,* this second metaphor is *religious.* "And he said to them:

'This is my blood of the covenant, poured out *upon many*' " (S 62c). The blood of the murdered man is read according to the blood of the Passover lamb and, more generally, according to the purification that the blood of victims procured for the sacrificers who were polluted or debtors.

Despite the difference of register in the two metaphors, the same work is going on to establish a cause-effect relation between the death of J and the salvation of *many* or a multitude. In the context of the persecutions and of the lapses these caused among the members of the *ekklesiai*, the salvation of the members and the future outcome of their narratives become a question. The death of Jesus answers the question and assures them of salvation. We shall call this movement of the theological discourse the *soteriological* movement (Greek *sotēr* = savior). Through this movement, the narrative of J's murder acquires a privileged position in respect to the ongoing ecclesial narratives. The *multiplicity* of these is annulled in the *unicity* of the death of one man "for many."[123]

Predestination, Christology, and soteriology: here we have the threefold structure of the theological discourse in Mark. The other New Testament writings should also be read however, especially the letters of Paul, in order to confirm (or invalidate) and better define the genesis of this structure, in which the act of death/resurrection, which is connected with heaven by predestinative knowledge, is proposed as *exemplary* and *salutary* for all Christians, with Christ becoming their *general equivalent*.

What is going on in this triple movement that *reduces* the ecclesial narratives to the messianic narrative or, more accurately, to the paschal narrative alone (since the prepaschal is also erased), is the transformation of J's *murder* into a *death*. Now murder, as we will recall from Part II of our text, was the most important form of violence in the gift/debt system, while death was the most important form in the purity/pollution system. The practice of J, as we have seen, resembled that of the Deuteronomistic levites and the prophets in constantly affirming the primacy of the debt system over the pollution system, which was destined to disappear (cf. S 35e: "thus did he declare all foods clean") along with its symbolic center (the temple of the god of dead men). The theological discourse, on the contrary, tends to reestablish the primacy of the pollution system. Admittedly, the metaphor of ransom belongs to the debt system and affirms the liberation of "converted" slaves, but it will be absorbed by the metaphor of the "blood poured out," which is directly religious and cultic and depends on animal sacrifices. This reestablishment of the pollution system is accomplished by means of the christological and soteriological movements: a person "shares," at the imaginary level of the christological fiction, in the cultic death of the consecrated victim, a death which makes it possible to contain the violence of death and to insure oneself against it.

The murder of J, which is an effect of chance and yet is necessary, is changed into a death that is predestined and therefore willed as such. To will death, even as a source of salvation, depends on negation, in the Nietzschean sense. J's STR of clandestinity tended precisely to reject death, in the logic of the messianic practice that affirmed life; the theological discourse negates this messianic aim.[124]

By thus changing J's murder into a "death" and transferring it to the pollution system, which is a religious system, the theological discourse "ideologizes" the narrative. The theologized messianic narrative is inscribed *first of all* at the ideological level, and from there, in accordance with a logic that will not be halted, it will become *Christianity*, a practice in which the ideological instance is dominant. Charity as a practice of the hands will cease to determine the *ekklesia* (the economic level), but will instead be simply a "consequence" of the ideological practice; this is the root reason why the word "charity" has lost its power.

The question we must now ask ourselves is *why* the kerygmatic became thus overdetermined by the theological, the affirmation by the negation. For the answer, we must analyze the political situation of the *ekklesiai* in the slave-based mode of production.

I can only refer the reader to Antoine Casanova's study of early Christianity. He looks first of all to the crisis that was beginning to overtake the Roman Empire, "the basic reason for which is the fact that the slavery system, which had long since been introduced and developed in Italy, is an obstacle to the development of the productive forces."[125] This led "in the second century to the difficulties that the entire imperial system had to face at the level of its political functioning." The crisis was thus economic and political and would lead in the fifth century to the collapse of the western empire. The crisis also had ideological effects on the ruling class itself, which showed a "clear tendency to take refuge in private life."

Of more interest to us here is the fact that the crisis also had ideological effects on the "working classes," which consisted, says Engels (whom Casanova cites), of "all sorts of people, like the 'mean whites' of the southern slave states and the European beachcombers and adventurers in colonial and Chinese seaports, then of emancipated slaves and, above all, actual slaves; on the large estates in Italy, Sicily, and Africa of slaves, and in the rural districts of the provinces of small peasants who had fallen more and more into bondage through debt."[125a] These people, says Casanova, were "henceforth integrated into a single system of mercantile circulation and subjected to an administrative machine, while the system of slave-based enterprise was everywhere introduced and developed."

Now, all "these sufferings of the people were not accompanied by any hope of an earthly solution" (Casanova). Engels writes: "For all of them paradise lay lost behind them; for the ruined free men it was the former *polis*, the town and the state at the same time, of which their forefathers had been free citizens; for the war-captive slaves the time of freedom before their subjugation and captivity; for the small peasants the abolished gentile social system and communal landownership."[125b] In other words, the thing that characterized these people, in addition to the intolerable economic exploitation, was their *political powerlessness* to transform the slave-based mode of production.

All this produced an ideal soil for the development of religious forms of the third type,[126] that is, sects (which attracted the ruling classes as well) that attempted to provide, *solely at the ideological level,* a religious salvation that was more or less universalist in tendency inasmuch as ethnico-social differences tended to fade into the background before a common fate within Roman cosmopolitanism. "Every notion of 'fatherland' had thus disappeared. Upon the ruins of the old nationalisms there had been developed an international state of soul that tended to bring people together. The great intermingling of clans and tribes that the Romans had brought about led to a confused mix of traditions that were utterly diverse and even contradictory," says P. Alfaric.[127]

The situation was different, however, with the Jewish communities dispersed throughout the Roman Empire, for they had long been devotees of a strongly held ideological nationalism. It was within these communities that the Christian *ekklesiai* acquired an increasingly distinct existence because of the theological work of Paul. This nationalism, on the other hand, remained very dependent on relations with the Palestinian subasiatic mode of production and its temple, and therefore suffered a terrible blow when Jerusalem was captured and its sanctuary burned in 70.

Now, as we have seen, Mark's writing is the reading that "Mark" makes of the narrative of this fall of the temple; it is determined, in addition, by the social situation of the *ekklesiai.* This situation in turn is characterized, on the one hand, by economic exploitation (in the face of which the practice of sharing must have proved a rather barren exercise) and by the political powerlessness that was common to the exploited classes but was aggravated by the persecutions undergone during the 60s; and, on the other hand, by the ideological relation to the dominant codes of Palestine. It is this relation, as we have seen, that explains the logic of the eschatological discourse (S 58): the overturning of the Jewish symbolic field and its center brings with it, at the level of the text of Mark, the "certainty" of the collapse of the MYTH code of which the temple was the heaven/earth axis.

It is possible, in this light, to understand the reasons for the play of determinations in Mark's text, which remains within the Jewish ideological closure. The key to this play is the situation of economic exploitation and political powerlessness, the latter being aggravated by the fact of persecutions.

It is this situation that renders so urgent and heart-gripping for the *ekklesiai* of Rome the question of *when* the eschatological return will take place, now that many of those who had known Jesus are already dead. To this question "Mark" replies with the prediction that is put on J's lips, that the return will take place during this generation (S 42e, S 58b6) and therefore soon. The prediction is assured by the prediction that the same J made of the fall of the temple and, in the last analysis, by his prediction of his own death and resurrection. Here we have the ultimate justification for the predestinational matrix of the theological discourse.[128]

On what textual site is the theological discourse possible? On the one hand, it functions as a short-term prediction in the MYTH code; on the other, the theological discourse is possible, as predestination, only because the "heavenly voice" of the MYTH guarantees it: "Listen to him!" (S 43b).[129] This voice, which is already in possession of the narrative ever since S 2, is necessary, for who can predestine but heaven? Who has the exact answer regarding the day and hour of the final narrative "but only the Father" (S 58b7)? At the level of the narrative "no one knows it, neither the angels in heaven nor the Son." The "advance knowledge" that structures the theological discourse and contradicts the "without him knowing how" of the messianic narrative is the "heavenly knowledge" in which the predestinative plan is regarded as having been established. In short, *it is the mythological closure of the text that textually determines the theological discourse.*

In another connection, we saw that the *ekklesiai* of Rome were divided over the attitude to be taken toward those of their members who had denied and betrayed during the period of persecutions. Mark's text, by contrasting the narratives of Judas and Peter, claims to provide a key for decoding this problem.[130] The same problem may be in view in the discourses of S 46 and S 54 with their references to falls and to practices that "cause to fall," as well as with their calls for peace ("salt") and forgiveness.

We are thus led to read the theological discourse as a discourse that aims at the *unity* of the *ekklesiai.* This is, in fact, the need met by the christological and soteriological movements that lead to a reduction of the diversity and *multiplicity* of ecclesial narratives by establishing J as Christ and Son of God at the center of the ecclesial space, and by transforming the narrative of his murder into a narrative of salvation "for many." We may submit that during the stage of geographical expansion of the *ekklesiai* the scheme of the *road* or apostolic sending for the proclamation of the good news remained dominant over the scheme of the *circle*; but now that the "whole world" had heard the good news and the "eschatological gathering" was imminent, the circle took priority over the road.[131]

What, then, is the *political* site of the theological discourse in Mark? Its site is the ecclesial gathering and its center, and this at the moment of transition from the first Christian generation to the second, that is, the moment when the *apostoloi* were being replaced by the *episkopoi.* The very name of the latter is significant, for they were "overseers" in charge of the *ekklesiai,* like the doorkeeper whom the master of the house has bidden keep watch (S 58b7). They were in charge of the circle and its unity; they were thus established in a relation of authority to the ecclesial disciples and constituted the political order in the *ekklesia.*[132] The political site of the theological discourse may now be given its true name: the *episcopal site.*

It was political powerlessness, which in the last analysis is a powerlessness of bodies, that thus determined both the various cults propagated in the

Roman Empire and the theologization of the messianic narrative. This latter, in turn, was the first moment in the transformation of the ecclesial narrative into "Christianity" as a religion of the third type. *Theology is the discourse of the powerlessness of bodies.*

The narrator/readers level in Mark has thus two occupiers: one is the *apostolos* who affirms the kerygma (and thereby produces the ecclesial narrative; this is the very definition of apostolic practice as proclamation of conversion, cf. S 28c), and the other is the *episkopos* who denies the messianic narrative in the theological discourse.

A final remark: the *episkopos*, who renews the postexilic priestly action[133] of giving primacy to the pollution system over the debt system, reserves for himself a *priestly function* in relation to the cult that will go on developing in the church. *The episkopos is the priest.*

That the messianic narrative should thus be denied by the theological discourse raises a question that is fundamental for us. For, the fact that in a situation of economic and political powerlessness the messianic narrative should be unable to assure the transformation of the slave-based mode of production, implies that the messianic narrative was operational only to the extent that the social formation furnished it with the *codes* and the economic, political, and ideological means for it to become a revolutionary practice. As I believe I have shown, the messianic narrative does not *of itself* have these codes and means; it is not *of itself* revolutionary. The apocalyptic catastrophe in Mark is precisely the result of the lack of codes. The Jew "Mark," after the destruction of Jerusalem and of the Jewish subasiatic mode of production, finds himself in a desert as far as codes are concerned. His imminent apocalyptic expectation functions as a kind of *textual suicide* that can be compared with the collective suicide of the Zealots at the moment of defeat.[134] Nonetheless, his *process of writing* itself overcame this "suicide" by assuring the tradition or passing on of the messianic narrative to the Greek codes of the slave-based mode of production. The history of the church furnishes several similar examples of the transformation of social formations, during which the "return" to the evangelical messianic narrative (or to the "sources," as they say) operates as a condition for its translation-tradition.

It seems to me that we are now in one of these periods. This is what justifies our recourse in this text to the analytic concepts of historical materialism, to codes that seem to me capable of playing the game of effecting a revolution of the capitalist mode of production. Why was the messianic narrative not revolutionary? Because revolution was impossible or doomed to failure, as 70 shows. On the other hand, since for us revolution is the order of the day, why should Christians be hesitant to involve themselves in a revolutionary process aimed at a radically communist social formation?

There is a further question: what is the effect of ecclesial practice on this political practice? In order to analyze this effect, we must first tackle the question of the demythologization and detheologization of the evangelical narrative.[135]

THE POLITICAL STAKE IN DEMYTHOLOGIZATION

The reader will perhaps recall that in the first pages of our reading of Mark we spotted a MYTH/narrative contradiction that was prior to the other contradiction, that of theological discourse/messianic narrative, which we have just analyzed as being textually determined by the first. The MYTH (heavenly and demonic voices) short-circuited the narrative, but the narrative in turn thwarted the MYTH by setting in place the ANAL code and decoding the practice of J and the question "Who is J?" It achieved this decoding by reference to the reading of the narrative itself as a discourse of power, on the one hand, and to the reading of the Scriptures as text of the promise, on the other. Thus the ANAL was able to relate the messianic practice of J to the eschatological narrative, which was proclaimed as being near and indeed already at the doors.

The MYTH/narrative contradiction implies two things: the closure of the text by the MYTH code and the work of demythologization being carried on by the ANAL code.

We can see this work of demythologization going on in the major sequence, S 1–S 3, which gives the program of the text. While the coming narrative of J is guaranteed in advance by the heavenly voice: "You are my beloved son, on you my favor [my power] has rested" (S 2c), the proclamation of John the Baptist is guaranteed by the writing of the prophet Isaiah, which makes John the "messenger" of J. What is indicated here is the role of John as precursor, a role he himself proclaims: "There comes after me one who is more powerful than I" (S 1b). In this circuit of voices the Scriptures are cited at the very beginning, and although the heavenly voice is more important for the moment (it opens the narrative of J) because of the dominance of the MYTH, the opening with the Scriptures is nonetheless part of a process of demythologization.

This process, however, is easier to read once the initial circuit of voices is replaced by the narrative of the practice of J and by the geographical circulation of this narrative. The result is that the narrative is readable without any appeal to the heavenly voice. Thus Peter has read it before the second voice (S 43), although he had not yet come on the scene at the time of the first voice in S 2. The narrative is therefore self-sufficient as *word* (S 22), without the "revealed truth" that comes from heaven.

Similarly, the Spirit, who in S 2 was a component of the MYTH, will henceforth be related only to the discourse of the practice-seed or the Scriptures.[136] The Spirit too has been demythologized and takes his place in a narrative semantics that lies outside the mythological code.

What is the role of the Scriptures in this work of demythologization? They are cited according to two reading registers. On the one hand, they are quoted as the site of the two systems of pollution and debt and of the relation of these to the narrative of the power of Yahweh (the pollution system dominates this narrative, while the debt system affirms, on the contrary, the narrative of the exodus from Egypt and of the gift of the land of Canaan as the primary gift). Thus, for example, in S 35 the Scriptures enable J to affirm the primacy of debt over pollution. On the other hand, the Scriptures are the site of the promises, which are articulated both with the narrative of the power of Yahweh and with the symbolic code (blessing). The text that best exemplifies this meeting of readings from Scripture with the messianic practice of J is in S 55h: "Are you not in error because you do not know the Scriptures or the power of the God?" The text is exemplary because in it we see how, in the very movement of demythologization, J nonetheless accepts the belief in the resurrection of the deal, which had been imported, as we have seen, from the Persian MYTH code,[137] and reads it as a fulfillment of the promise made to Abraham, Isaac, and Jacob, and therefore as already *inscribed* in the old narrative of Moses, or in the Scriptures themselves. On the one hand, it is the narrative of the power of his own body, working on bodies subject to the curse of illness and death, that enables J to *reread* the Scriptures and the promise, and, on the other hand, it is the Scriptures and the promise that enable him to proclaim the eschatological fulfillment of the work of the power present in his own narrative.

The reading of the Sadducees is diametrically opposed to the reading of J. Since they are unable to read the narrative of the messianic power, they are also unable to read the promise in the Scriptures. They have fallen into the error that consists of hardening their hearts before the narrative of the power and, consequently, of blinding themselves to the Scriptures.

The movement of demythologization remains partial, however, for the text of Mark is closured by the MYTH that sets the heaven/earth difference and the genesis/eschatology *(archē/telos)* divergence as limits to the narrative, to all narratives. In Mark the MYTH is so bound up with the Jewish SYMB that the narrative of the destruction of the temple brings in its train the prediction of the imminence of the eschatological narrative.[138] This prediction is also determined by the political powerlessness of the *ekklesiai* of Rome, a powerlessness that brings in its wake the theological discourse as discourse precisely of this powerlessness. The theological discourse thus introduced by the MYTH code reinstates the MYTH code in turn and annuls the demythologization effected by the messianic narrative. By situating J in the heaven of the MYTH because of his predestinational knowledge, Christology will increasingly hinder the very movement of the ANAL code, that is, the self-examination of the ecclesial narratives in the mirror of the Gospel.

There are a number of paths that would have to be followed for further work on a materialist ecclesiology that will handle either the other New Testament texts or the later Christian text.

It would be necessary, for example, to see how the theological discourse will find in the mythological "voice" the idea (in the Greek sense of the term) of a "revealed truth" from heaven, an idea that will ground the whole development of dogmatic orthodoxy. How the so-called Apostles' Creed took shape as a mythologized narrative. How the theological discourse will set itself up as theo-logy, a discourse on God, and replace the powerful ecclesial practice that alone is word and alone can proclaim God. How the mythological code is related to the theology of the interiority of souls, a theology of which modern Christocentrism (faith having as its object the "person of Jesus") is the most recent avatar. How baptism-immersion in water will be reintroduced, which Mark clearly opposes to immersion in the Spirit; and also how the practice of baptizing infants was introduced and made general, thus doing away with the break involved in conversion. How the movement of replacing the temple with the body of J and the latter, in turn, with the practice of bread has been turned completely around: the bread disappears in the "host" (signifier of the signified "body of Christ") that is placed in the tabernacles of the temples-churches, so that the latter finally came to give symbolic orientation to the space of the cities and towns of the Middle Ages. How, finally—last but not least—the subversion of the codes of the social formation by ecclesial practice has been annulled. The ANAL code located this subversiveness on the side of the God of the living, while the god of the dead was located in the field of the satanic and death, so that Satan became the symbolic emblem of the chief equivalents of the SOC: money, Caesar, god of the temple. One of the clearest symbols of the remythologizing work done by the episcopal or ecclesiastical theological discourse will be the annullment of this subversion, for heaven will once again connote the powers of the SOC in which the church has installed itself, and it will instead be subversiveness that is repressed as satanic and infernal, something cursed, in accordance with a semantic that has prevailed down to our own day. In short, it would be necessary to examine how, and by what decisive transformations, a theocentric religion has been able, more or less with impunity, to appeal for its authority to the "good news of Jesus the Messiah" and even to go so far at times as to murder the "heretics."

Bourgeois exegetes, working on the basis of anthropocentric logocentrism, have sought with varying success to undo the closure of the MYTH codes that plays in the New Testament texts. The name of Bultmann especially is connected with this attempt at demythologization. For a symptom of the fact that the attempt is being made on the basis of bourgeois logocentrism I need point out only the appeal to "the modern consciousness," to scientific reason, and to advancing modernity that seems always to be the ultimate argument in texts aiming at demythologization. This effort at demythologization fails to understand the Scriptures and the narrative of power (the messianic narrative). This bourgeois form of the theological discourse ends up in *interiority* (even if it be called spiritual experience or a spiritual attitude), and it makes no difference whether or not the exegete be a "believer," as Bultmann is. These exegetes may talk about "the history of salvation," but in fact history has been dissolved into the timelessness of consciousness and interiority and its relation to the "eternity" of God.

You can see the point I am trying to make, namely, that it is only with the concepts of historical materialism and in a discourse of materialist ecclesiology that we will have any chance of effecting a consistent demythologization, as we take into account the fact that the nonindustrialized social formations are under an ideology that is dominated by the MYTH code.

Why does the theological discourse of Mark announce the eschatological narrative as an imminent *catastrophe* that is coming upon the slave-based mode of production? The reason is that the STR goal of the messianic narrative and of the *ekklesia* is the *transformation* of the social formation.[139] In the situation of powerlessness in which the dominated classes of the Roman empire found themselves, this goal of transformation is affirmed by the catastrophic aspect of the eschatological narrative as destruction of the power structures of the slave-based SOC[140]—an affirmation that can come into play only at the ideological level.

In Mark, however, the movement of demythologization that we have discerned there opposes to this catastrophic *break* a *continuity* between the powerful practice of J and "the kingdom of God coming in power" (S 46e). For the kerygma has affirmed that J is the Son of man, and this affirmation works on certain sites of the text.

The two statements about the "ACT Son of man"[141] give the practice of J as the practice of the Son of man ("In order that you may know that the Son of man has authority to dismiss debts *on earth*": S 12d; "The Son of man is lord even of the sabbath": S 15b). This identification is echoed in the metaphor of the spouse of the messianico-eschatological marriage in S 14. The two parables in S 22b2 and b3 likewise connect the final narrative about the kingdom of God with what is *already* going on in the practice-seed ("The kingdom of God is like a man who casts seed *upon the ground*"; "To what shall we liken the kingdom of God . . .? It is like a mustard seed, which, when sown *in the ground* . . ."). Similarly, the "added piece," the new cloth, which is the practice of J (S 14b), is a *"plērōma,"* as is the seed which yields "the full grain in the ear" (full = *plērōma*) (S 22b2). The kingdom of God, which is to *come* at the end as the fulfillment *(plērousthai)* of time (S 3), is said to be *already there* (because J is already the Son of man); it is the harvest from what J sows, and it is already growing and bearing fruit. The metaphor of childbirth ("the beginning of the birth pains") in S 58b2 is especially interesting because it expresses both a break (the passage from the womb to the light of the world[142]) with its pains and a continuity (it is the same child before and after).

The *continuity* thus refers us to the *figure of the collective Son of man* at the level of the erased text; this figure, though wholly inscribed in the MYTH code, nonetheless functions in the register of a continuity that is indicated by the ascensional schema in which *the starting point is earth*.[143]

Let us demythologize this figure. That is, let us take into consideration the relation between the heaven/earth opposition and the social formations in which empirical agriculture was dominant, and the fact that, in consequence, that code is no longer ours. What will be left of the figure of the collective Son of man will be the communist program of his practice, his subversiveness, and his ultimate STR goal of radically transforming the powers of the SOC of the capitalist mode of production, or, to put it briefly, the communist program and the transformist strategy. The purpose of demythologization is, then, to make manifest the utopian horizon of an ecclesial practice for today, or the liberation effected by a *radical communist utopia* as the liberation manifesting itself on the horizon of our practice.

This enables us to understand why bourgeois exegesis has failed in its effort at demythologization and also why the effort can be successful today. On the one hand, the utopia that was liberated in May '68 has made possible for us a break toward the material site of reading. On the other hand, for some years now there have been increasing signs of cracks in the various apparatuses of the capitalist mode of production in its present stage of the monopolistic, imperialist state: financial crisis; crisis of the political apparatuses of enterprises in the face of wildcat strikes; crisis in the dominant teaching and codes of logocentrism (progress and scientific knowledge in regard to pollution and waste; reason coming to grips with the analysis of the structure of madness); crisis in the apparatus of the state (Vietnam War, the prison problem, unrest in the army, scandals of the Nixonian state, repression in the Soviet state, etc.); crisis of sexual morality; crisis of the bourgeois symbolic code; and finally, crisis in the ecclesiastical apparatus after Vatican II: beginning of declericalization, and the spectacular decline of the seminaries, as we await the de-episcopalization that cannot be far behind. We may think that this last-named process is already beginning in Brazil, for it is desirable, in my view, that it should take place by way of the repression, by the political power, of bishops who take the good news seriously. And some day, we may hope, there will be a devaticanization and then a depapalization.

We must not expect, however, that this demythologization will come about simply as the result of theoretical texts like this one. A theoretical discourse cannot read concrete ecclesial narratives or evaluate their power; this is the task of the *ekklesia* itself, of its practice of faith, and of the strategies of hope that flow therefrom. But if this task is to be possible and if ecclesiality is to be liberated for the sake of the next generation (among the "pagans" as contrasted with the "church of the Christians"),[144] we must be able to take into consideration the question of the *power* of our own bodies and our ecclesial practices, and to disconnect it from the bourgeois process of demythologization.

RESURRECTION: A QUESTION ABOUT THE BODY

I would wager that many readers have felt as a stumbling block the way in which I have thus far read the sequences concerned with what are usually called the miracles, along with the resurrection of J, as though they were self-evident. After all, for the last century at least, have not reservations with regard to the Gospel texts become more and more widespread?

But how do Levi-Strauss and the ethnologists read the myths of the "primitive" social formations? They take them as *alien texts*; they do not look for a modern "signified" in them but read them as they present themselves in their material meaning. Similarly, we here—as you have just seen in the discussion of demythologization—are simply reading Mark as a text that depends on the codes of a subasiatic mode of production of almost two thousand years ago. We must therefore now ask whether and how a text, which is so alien to us, can overlap with the readings we make of our own narratives and our own current economic, political, and ideological practices. Shall we demythologize the sequences just referred to?

Let us resume our reading of Mark and emphasize first of all the fact that these "powerful practices" of transforming sick bodies belong not to the MYTH code but to another code that we have called the SYMB.[145] Now while the MYTH code, which closures the text, is set forth in Mark *naively*, as it were, and causes no problem for any of the actants or for the narrator or his readers (this despite the process of demythologization, since this process does not annul the MYTH code), the situation is quite different for the sequences we are discussing here. Not only does the narrative several times recount the astonishment and fear of the Crowds at these powerful practices, but it is also the reading of this power as an ANAL question ("What is this?" from S 6 on) that runs throughout the text and leads the actants to take sides.

Neither is the resurrection of J self-evident. We noted that in S 25 and S 44, which are two narratives that apparently have to do with "resurrections" (since on both occasions the C speaks of the children as dead), the text introduces a doubt about the death that is taken as certain ("The child is not dead but sleeping," says J in S 25; "And he became *like* a corpse" is what is written in S 44). This is all the more striking since such a doubt is carefully eliminated from the narrative of J's own death; the formal attestation that J is truly dead is the primary function of the "centurion" (S 71, S 72). In S 73 (a sequence that shows hardly any mythologization, in contrast with the parallels in Luke and John), the young man's announcement, "He is risen, he is not here. . . . He goes before you into Galilee," is received with doubt by the women who hear it: "And they said nothing to anyone, for they were afraid." It is on this note of doubt that the narrative ends (does not end). Admittedly, the resurrection of J is certainly affirmed in the apostolic affirmation, but, apart from the young man's announcement, the affirmation is found only at sites that depend on the theological discourse as predestination. In S 43c, moreover, the prediction of J's resurrection is followed by this remark: "They kept the word, while discussing among themselves what rising from the dead meant" (cf. S 45b).

In these sequences there is question only of the resurrection of an individual, namely J, but in S 55h, to which we referred in the previous section, there is question of the eschatological resurrection of all the dead. In affirming this resurrection, however, J refers not only to the reading of the Scriptures but also to the reading of the power of God and to the narrative of his own practice regarding bodies that are saved. The belief borrowed from the

Zoroastrian texts thus changes to the extent that it is no longer taken for granted but depends instead on readings of practices regarding bodies that are played out in the SYMB field. It is precisely because, beginning with Peter's mother-in-law in S 7c, bodies kept *prostrate* (recumbent) by illness have *stood up* (been raised up) and because one of the effects of J's practice is the raising of bodies, that it becomes possible to hope that all the bodies of the dead *prostrate* (recumbent) in Sheol will *stand up* (be raised). In addition, S 29 had already connected the powerful practice of J with the resurrection of John the Baptist.

The announcement of the resurrection of J himself is thus likewise connected with the logic of his practice of raising bodies that are prostrate (recumbent). Since, however, this resurrection is not an object of the narrative experience of the actants, the kerygmatic affirmation of it continues to be accompanied by the question: "What does 'rising from the dead' mean?" The resurrection of J is *affirmed as a question*, and only the reading of ecclesial practice can, through recognition of the power at work in it, engender both faith in the resurrection of J and hope in the eschatological resurrection of the readers themselves.

We can see, then, the justice of the distinction between the MYTH and SYMB codes, and how the text itself resists any hasty demythologization of the SYMB-BAS practice. To "naiveté" in the face of the MYTH code is opposed a questioning that might be called "critical" in the face of the SYMB-BAS code.

Consequently, it is by an abuse of reading that "progressive" bourgeois exegesis has extended the process of demythologization to these sequences. A result of this procedure—usually implicit but nonetheless clear in *Formgeschichte*—has been to accord greater importance to the *discourses* of J or his *"logia,"* as they are called, and to reduce the narrative element as far as possible, thus turning the Gospel almost exclusively into a "teaching." *What* is it that caused this abuse of reading? Rationalistic logocentrism, which is a form of nihilism, and its search for the historical authenticity of the Gospel narrative.[146] Logocentrism supposes the antecedent impossibility of "miracles" and the resurrection, and regards them as dependent on the irrational and therefore on the later work of writing in the ecclesial communities. Consequently, it is forbidden, in logocentrism, to define a MYTH code carefully, as we have done. We can see the importance, even for this question, of having recourse to the concepts of historical materialism.

It must be added that such a logocentric reading,[147] which demythologizes on an *a priori* basis, cannot account for the text of Mark, which has long been the poor cousin among the synoptics, for it becomes fragmented to the point of meaninglessness when all the sequences dealing with powerful practice are eliminated.[148]

By way of introduction to Nietzsche's philosophy of the body, Deleuze cites Spinoza as "opening a new path for the sciences and philosophy, for, Spinoza said, we do not even know what a body's possibilities are."[149] Spinoza's argument is that our experience of the body is very limited and that "no one has as yet had a sufficiently accurate knowledge of the construction of the human body as to be able to explain all its functions." He appeals to the often astonishing behavior of the brute animals and the "many things sleep-walkers do that they would not dare, were they awake." He concludes: "All of which sufficiently shows that the body *can* do many things by the laws of its nature alone at which the mind is amazed."[150] We may add that even today science cannot explain unusual bodily phenomena such as magnetism, telep-athy, levitation, or even acupuncture. Our experience of the body, because the body has been repressed, especially by class apparatuses, is very limited, and no one can *predict in advance* (a claim to do so would depend on the theological discourse!) what active forces will be liberated on the day when a radically communist social formation comes into being.

If bodies are no longer fascinated by gold and silver, what kind of produc-tion will follow upon the liberation of the forces of work? What kind of *play*, in Nietzsche's sense of the term, will they manifest? If they are no longer repressed by a king or by the power of the state, what order will follow upon the liberation of the forces of autonomy? If they are no longer deflected by a god or the logos, what kind of writing and science and art will follow upon the liberation of the forces of writing? What kind of sacrifice, what kind of *laughter* will be theirs? What profane/sacred relation, what festivals, what tragedy too (always in the Nietzschean sense of these terms)?

Here, then, is what I dare propose: that the question of the power of bodies in the BAS circle according to Mark is precisely our question today; more than that, it is the question that will be the *final question* in a radical com-munist revolution. By what right, and on the basis of what practice, can anyone claim today that the power that will then be manifested will have no relation to the power of which Mark tells? This *alien* text, then, can lay claim to a new relevance in the future, for it only opens up this future as something of which we have no knowledge, as something *other*, as something which, in St. Paul's words, "no eye has seen and no ear has heard."[151] I will even go so far as to say that the affirmation, *as a question*, of the unheard-of possibility of the resurrection of the dead can, even today, indicate the utopian horizon of a radically communist social formation.[152]

But does not such "boldness" as this make this present text, with its materialist purpose, collapse into idealism, just as it is about to end? Cer-tainly, the suggestion is liable to awaken the suspicion acknowledged at the beginning of this fourth part of the text. Let us therefore proceed slowly. How are we to articulate the question and the affirmation, so that the latter does not already contain the answer and thus annul the question?

We must here digress into the question of the "question," which, according to Derrida, grounds philosophical discourse as a "discipline of the question," the "question" that this discourse must preserve as "question."[153] He adds that there is a "difference between the question in general and philosophy as a determined (finite or mortal) mode and moment of the question itself," a "difference [which] is better thought out today."[154]

"The question in general," I would say while referring back to the use I made of Bataille's text in my first chapter, is the question about the original violence that is to be discerned in language. I have made both language and the perception of the life/death question to be constitutive of the infra-ideological, of the ideological instance as such.[155] This question would be "the first word of language," and not the "yes" or "no" of an answer.[156] Language, however, constitutes "a horizon of finiteness"; it is ever-already enclosed in the "finitude of the horizon,"[157] and it is not possible to discourse outside (this side of or the other side of) this horizon in which life/death are a question.

This is why no answer can be given to the question of the resurrection. For, in this horizon, the final fact is always death as the very condition for the continuation of life, as Bataille shows so well.[158] Neither can any answer be given to the question shouted on Golgotha: "My God, my God, *why* have you abandoned me?" (S 71d). It is not possible to say, "Yes, there is a resurrection of the dead," because our last experience is of death, but neither is it possible to say, "No, there is no resurrection of the dead," for that would be to annul the decisive question of language itself—"Which of the two, life or death, wins the day?"—and to fall back into "an absolute violence that would not even be the contrary of nonviolence; it would be nothingness or pure meaninglessness."[159]

Every positive response to the question would abandon the horizon of finitude that is proper to language and to our practice; it would be to locate oneself at an imaginary level comparable to a dream. This leap into the imaginary is constitutive of the theological discourse in its response to the "why" of the abandonment of Golgotha, which is the question of the ipseity of the body of the dying Jesus; that response is made by Jesus himself as he *anticipates* his own death. The theological discourse is possible only as a "christological identification": the *murder*, read on the basis of the "ego" that is killed, is thus changed into a *death*.

On the other hand, the distressed *ekklesiai* of Rome, themselves doomed to abandonment of God, could express their own experience by means of the question asked by J in his abandonment; they could make his question *their own*. This repetition of the question of the messianic narrative by the ecclesial narratives is the result of the apostolic or kerygmatic affirmation. The question "What does 'rising from the dead' mean?" is therefore very much the question also of Mark's readers; it concerns them in their own bodies as men and women who have drunk the same cup as Jesus and been immersed in the same immersion as he. The people killed in the Neronian persecutions have likewise undergone the death of active people, without falling. That this question is difficult to tolerate is something signaled to us by the fear of the women as they leave the tomb (S 73), a fear that echoes the fear of Christians who survived the persecutions.

But by what right do we ask a question about resurrection that cannot be simply identified with the "question in general" about life/death?[160] It is not possible to "invent" this question ourselves. Here is the place for recourse to the Scriptures as site of the promise and of the articulation of the ACT narrative with the narrative fabric of the Scriptures; the kind of bold recourse that J has in S 55h.

For, if the question of the resurrection were being put in the gnoseological text or even in that of the Persian "beliefs," it would be correct to say with Nicholas of Cusa [161] that the question would already contain the answer and that the dice would be loaded in the absence of the narrative and the element of chance it contains.[162] But the situation is entirely different if it is the ACT narrative, now unfolding and still open to its ending, that puts the question to the text of the narratives concerning the power at work in bodies.

But the bodies in question, those of Abraham, Isaac, and Jacob, are dead, death has had the final word with regard to them. We rediscover, therefore, the logic of J's reading in S 55h, which presupposes the logic of the Jewish SYMB code itself: the power of blessing must engender life, not death. Either death has the last word, and the God of Abraham is a god of the dead, or the narratives of Abraham and the others are not yet finished, and we can reread them: that is, a God of the living can be posed as a question.[163] Posed by *what*? By the power at work in the body of J, as articulated with the power that worked in the aged body of Abraham to render fruitful the equally aged womb of Sarai. The "cures," the salvation produced by the narrative of J: this is what affirms the resurrection of the dead. The raising up of the bodies of IIc announces a definitive raising up.

J was killed, however, and therefore this affirmation or announcement can be offered only in the form of a question. The affirmation remains always a *mystery*, that is, a question to which the answer remains open and dependent on the sequel of the narrative. The mystery attaching to the work of the power on the body, a mystery that is due to the opaqueness—the spatiality —of body and heart, is thus linked to the mystery of the eschatological resurrection.

The question is thus linked to the MYTH code in which the eschatological narrative is inscribed. Nor is this accidental, since the narratives concerning Abraham also have mythic status. Thus we can see the limitations of the demythologization that scholars have effected as a condition for tackling anew the question of the power in our text and our current codes. We must therefore inquire into the function of the MYTH code in the text of Mark and in the text of the Scriptures generally. Its function is precisely to pose, *as a possibility in the play of narratives*, the shattering of the horizon of finiteness in which the question is necessarily inscribed. It is of this shattering that S 43 tells us: "His garments became radiant, exceedingly white, to a degree no fuller *on earth* can whiten." The whiteness achieved by fullers is produced within the horizon of our finiteness, while the "radiant whiteness" of the garments here opens the door to the shattering of the finite horizon. The same holds for the dividing of the heavens in S 2. And if the darkness in S 71c means the closing of heaven and the horizon, like "the stone rolled against the door of the tomb" of J (in S 72c), then the rolling away of the stone and the whiteness of the young man's robe in S 73 effect once again the opening of the horizon.

We can see that the question about the God of the living, the "Father who is in the heavens" (S 54e) beyond the finite horizon, can never be separated from the question about the resurrection of the body and, consequently, from the question about the power that works in our bodies *on earth*. This shattering of the horizon by the MYTH code must therefore have its correlative in the practice of bodies. This correlative is *subversion*, on which in the last analysis the question of the resurrection depends. The resurrection can be posed as affirmation, as kerygma, as proclamation only on the basis of the work done on bodies in subversion of the dominant codes of the SOC: the powerful, liberating work of the Spirit. In the logic of the ANAL code we are referred to the concrete work of the *ekklesia*, "the smallest of all the seeds on earth" but one that "produces large branches" (S 22b3).

We are now in a position to determine the meaning of the problematic with which our text opened: that concerning the relations between the pollution system and the debt system. The primacy of the pollution system is the result of the theological discourse, which excludes the working of the power as well as the possibility of transforming the social formation, that is, revolution. The primacy of the debt system, on the other hand, means the opening of this other field as a possible field. But, according to Mark, J goes further and excludes the pollution system itself.[164] For it is only at the level of the debt system, enlarged in an internationalist manner to include the pagans, all the poor, and all the oppressed, and radicalized to the point of excluding every relationship of domination and every putting to death, even for blasphemy,[165] and therefore only through the work of radical subversiveness that the violence native to humanity will be overcome and the dead will arise. Thus there are not "two" native violences, for aggression is correlative to the prohibition of the violence of sex and death, the violence that alone is native and primary. To the secondary violence of this prohibition, a violence overdetermined by that of class power, there corresponds a third violence: that of messianic or ecclesial subversiveness, which opens the field of the question of bodily resurrection.

Let us conclude, which is to say: let us open the debate. The Gospel narrative is articulated with the indefinite play of the narratives of its readings, a play that must not be closured, even in the name of reason, even in the name of God. The debate thus opened concerns the evaluation of the power at work in the practice of the bodies which we are. It is in dependence on the extent of this power that we will be able to affirm, as an open question, the resurrection both of Jesus and of our own bodies: "According to the measure with which you measure, it will be measured unto you and more will be added to you" (S 22c5).

What we must do is *practice* in the direction of the liberation of bread, of the body, of reading, "like a man who casts seed upon the ground. He sleeps and rises up, night and day, and the seed sprouts and grows without him knowing how. By itself the earth produces fruit: first the stalk, then the ear, then the full grain in the ear. And when the fruit is ready . . ." (S 22b2). The hope of the kingdom of God passes by way of bodies. The god who is spoken of in the discourses which the ecclesiastical discourse reproduces endlessly is a god of souls; if there is a God, God can only be concerned with bodies and their power.

Let us add one final detail. The resurrection of Jesus is affirmed as following upon his murder. Would there be any point whatever in affirming the resurrection of a Jesus who had grown old and who had happily died the "good death" of which a certain type of piety speaks? The resurrection becomes a question on the basis not of his death but only of his murder, which is a con-sequence of the powerful, liberating subversiveness of a practice that breaks with the SOC. In a similar way, the Maccabees had already raised the question of the combatants who had been roused to insurrection against the Syrians. When the theological discourse changes the murder of J into a simple death, it *reduces this site* of the question.[166] *The resurrection can only be the fruit of insurrection*.

Is this not true in our day of the murder of a Che Guevara or a Camilo Torres? And even more of the many anonymous heroic combatants in the Russian, Chinese, Vietnamese, Algerian, Cuban, Chilean, etc., revolutions? How can materialists avoid asking themselves the meaning of the murder of the Russian revolutionaries, for example, when he sees how, fifty years later, state capitalism has been installed in Russia? There is no question here of a defense of martyrdom, for the (erased) messianic narrative sought to avoid martyrdom. It is when we accept as our site the repression of the bodies of so many who rebel against the ascendancy of money or the force of arms or a god or reason, it is when we accept the supremely materialist site of the daily violence exercised against the bodies of the poor, that we cannot fail to posit the affirmation-question of the resurrection.[167]

A COMING DEBATE

The materials for analysis by a materialist ecclesiology, such as I have attempted to sketch here, are vast, ranging from the New Testament down to the "theology of the death of God." As a result of such an analysis, the entire history of the relations between the church and the *ekklesiai*, which follow the changes of the transformations in modes of production, will take on a new look. In the phases of expansive reproduction, ecclesiality is in the background; the breaks characterizing conversions are often reduced to the narratives of individuals who go against the current, sometimes in a seemingly reactionary manner.[168] In phases of accelerated transformation, on the other hand, phases that are rich in ecclesial excitement and marked by the rebirth of the eschatological utopia, the relations between the church and the *ekklesiai* are more strained; the result is often ruptures of a shattering type, but the ecclesiastical apparatus recovers its ground by absorbing the parts that have broken off, and drawing therefrom new strength that enables it to survive.

The great shock of the bourgeois industrial revolution that fully established the capitalist mode of production, and the fierce ideological struggle between logocentrism and theocentrism, caused the church for a solid century to withdraw into its "ghetto," the refuge of "rightist souls" from Pius IX to Pius XII, from Vatican I to Vatican II.

This latter council, which had been prepared for by thirty years of efforts at "renewal" in the church of France, a church that had been driven to separation from the state, represented the reconciliation of the theological and clerical apparatuses with the progressivist ideology of monopolistic state capitalism. Despite a silent rightist majority, the energetic efforts of numerous clerics and laypeople, most of them from the middle level of the bourgeoisie (the liberal professions, the middle cadres in teaching, public service, and capitalist enterprise) won the day for the *aggiornamento*, or updating, that is associated with the name of John XXIII. Concerned as it was to meet the "religious needs" of this militant clientele that was looking for a *supplément d'âme* [addition of soul, i.e., to body] for daily activities that were chiefly those of the political center,[169] the old ecclesiastical house managed after a fashion to revamp its facade.

Toward the end of the sixties, monopolistic state capitalism, after a phase of very accelerated expansive reproduction, seemed to enter a new phase, one of transition, the outcome of which is still problematic; May '68 in France was one of the clearest symptoms of this shift. From the schools all the way to the army and the prison system, there is not a single one of the state's major apparatuses that has not shown the preliminary signs of possible crumbling. In this general unsettling of the bourgeois codes, the new space for a *different* social formation is beginning to open up. In the clerical apparatus, too, serious cracks are showing; the ecclesiastical "temple" seems destined to proximate destruction. Is it not time to reread Mark, in the year of his nineteenth centenary? If I had to describe the present essay in a few words, I could say that I in my turn am offering a translation-tradition of the Gospel narrative in a new epistemological space. Like Mark's, my writing is an unpolished writing, done apart from the ruling circles; it is the writing of a poor man (whose poverty consists in his being what they call in high places "self-taught"). What fruits, what blessings will the power that works in this text announce?

The emergence of a revolutionary fringe in the space of the churches is seen by many in a fact that is now beginning to be irrefutable: the fact that in this space too the class struggle goes on. After a period when a few pioneers tried to enter into a dialogue *with* the Marxists, a new generation is claiming to be Marxist *and* Christian. This claim raises, of course, the question of Christian identity. For what is left of Christianity when people manage to take their stand in a field in which analyses and strategies are worked out with difficulty and amid polemics? Is not the faith to which people still lay claim being reduced to a rather meaningless subjectivism? Here is the site for the debate to which this essay hopes to stimulate the reader. The claim to be both Marxist and Christian implies that the claimant has leaped over the wall that separated the two, just as in their day Paul and Mark leaped over the wall of hatred that separated Jews and pagans.[170] At the theoretical level, the claim implies the possibility of analyzing the Christian phenomenon in the epistemological field of historical materialism. We have taken as the object of such an analysis a crucial text regarding the messianic exodus.

As the reader may remember, our chapter on historical materialism began with the Althusserian thesis that there exists an invariance common to all the structures of the various historical social formations. If I have endeavored to apply this thesis to the formalization of the concept of "mode of production" itself, I have done so because I think that only this method will allow the transposition into the capitalist mode of production of a narrative dealing with a subasiatic mode of production. The agent of this transposition is the concept of *ekklesia* that we have produced. Will it not be possible to make this concept function as a means of comparing our current practice within/against capitalism with the narrative of the messianic power? The good news of Jesus the Messiah will then be the *grill* that enables us to read the narratives of our own practices with the freedom that its very alienness assures,[171] and to judge the power that works in our bodies, the curse from which our bodies are shaking loose (namely, the grip of the capitalist codes), and the blessing toward which they are moving.

Notes

INTRODUCTION

1. [The original has an unreproducible wordplay here, since *Eglise,* "church," and *crise,* "crisis," rhyme in French.—Trans.]

2. L. Althusser, *For Marx,* trans. Ben Brewster (London and New York, 1969), pp. 24, 33. [I have used throughout the Vintage Books edition of 1970.—Trans.]

3. L. Althusser and E. Balibar, *Reading Capital,* trans. Ben Brewster (New York, 1970), p. 204. [The English translation combines the two volumes of the French original—*Lire le Capital* I and II—and omits (by decision of the French editors, for an Italian edition) contributions by other writers, retaining only two essays by Althusser, "From *Capital* to Marx's Philosophy" (pp. 11–69) and "The Object of Capital" (pp. 71–198), and an essay by Balibar, "On the Basic Concepts of Historical Materialism" (pp. 201–308).—Trans.]

4. Balibar, p. 216.

PART I

1. L. Althusser, *For Marx,* trans. Ben Brewster (New York, 1970), p. 166. For the why and how of this "essay in formal theory," see the foregoing pages on the problematic. The essay was originally longer but has been condensed into a set of definitions of concepts, interspersed with "hypotheses." The latter offer propositions I believe to be my own (although they inevitably exert some influence on the definitions of concepts).

2. Products of writing, the latter term being taken in a broad sense (found in Derrida's works) that includes spoken language.

3. These are the three instances that Althusser, following Engels, regards as basic (*For Marx,* pp. 231–32).

4. For example, the theoretical region *within* the ideological instances.

5. For a definition of "structure," cf. J. Guichard, *Eglise, luttes de classes et stratégies politiques* (Paris, 1972), pp. 181ff.

6. The terms are from Marx; cf. E. Balibar, "The Basic Concepts of Historical Materialism," in L. Althusser and E. Balibar, *Reading Capital,* trans. B. Brewster (New York, 1970), pp. 209–10. On p. 230 Balibar seems to validate this thesis in advance.

7. Cf. L. Althusser and E. Balibar, *Reading Capital,* trans. Ben Brewster (New York, 1970), pp. 104–5.

8. The logics specific to each instance (and its regions and fields), their articulations, dominances, distortions, dislocations, survivals, and determinations-in-the-last-instance constitute the object of historical materialism as a science of history.

9. Italicized in Bataille's original French text.

10. Italics added.

11. Italics in Bataille's original French text.

12. G. Bataille, *Eroticism,* trans. M. Dalwood (London, 1962), pp. 40–41.

13. The term "symbolic field" is borrowed from R. Barthes: "The symbolic field is occupied by a single object from which it derives its unity. . . . This object is the human body" (*S/Z,* trans. R. Miller [New York, 1974], pp. 214–15). The symbolic field provides one of the codes for Barthes's reading of Balzac's story *Sarrasine.* This is no accident, since the symbolic field can be located only in narratives. The term "symbolic order" I have borrowed from J. Lacan in whose work it designates language as the place or site of the Law that "fractures" the Subject; cf. A. Rifflet-Lemaire, *Jacques Lacan* (Brussels, 1970): "The term 'order,' moreover, designates a dimension apart that is defined and specified solely by its internal articulations" (p. 127).

14. J. Lacan, *Ecrits* (Paris, 1966), p. 94 (italics added).

15. Ibid.

16. According to Stalin's well-known thesis.

17. According to Bataille, "the transition from animals to man is reflected through work, taboos, and the awareness of death" (pp. 30–31).

18. "Mode of production" has its strict sense here. In a second and broader sense, "mode of production" designates the system with its three instances, and, in a still broader sense, the whole social formation as seen from the viewpoint of its dominant mode of production (in the second sense).

19. According to the diversity of the forms of products (and of their use values), the *technical division* of labor and the *specialization* of the agents will be more or less extensive.

20. In an analysis that depends on Balibar (pp. 212–16), I introduce in this Hypothesis an element that he does not consider and that is inspired by Th. Herbert, "Réflexions sur la situation théorique des sciences sociales et, spécialement, de la psychologie sociale," *Cahiers pour l'analyse,* no. 2 (1966): 134 ff., and "Remarques pour une théorie générale des idéologies," *Cahiers pour l'analyse,* no. 9 (1968): 75, 77. Cf., however, Balibar, pp. 246–47, 302–5.

21. As distinct from "juridical ownership," which is an element in the political instance (cf. Balibar, pp. 216–17).

22. As muscular energy is intrinsic to "labor power."

23. Juridical texts, regulations, etc.

24. The authority/power distinction corresponds to that given by N. Poulantzas, *Pouvoir politique et classes sociales* (Paris, 1968), p. 112. My definition of the political instance, however, differs from his p. 45: "relation between political practice and the state"), since his definition, by his own admission, "is generally valid for social formations that are divided into classes" (ibid.) but not for classless social formations. The relation of authority is analyzed by E. Terray, *Marxism and "Primitive" Societies: Two Studies,* trans. M. Klopper (New York, 1972), pp. 130 ff., in relation to the "functional power" possessed by the elders among the Guro; the limits of their authority show in the fact that "it would be very difficult for the elders to transform their functional authority into the power to exploit" (p. 132). Terray's further inquiry leads him to the conclusion that we cannot rightly "speak of exploitation or class antagonism" because "the consent of the junior is a real condition of the power of the elders" (p. 172). In other words, the consensus is evidence of autonomy.

25. In the term "autogestion" as currently used the distinction between autogestion

and autoproduction is not taken into account; this causes confusion.

26. Called "primitive societies."

27. Cf. Terray, pp. 137–62, for a discussion of the Guro.

28. I prescind here from writing that is not linguistic (pictographs, etc.).

29. It is common knowledge that modern linguistic science has managed more or less successfully to analyze syntactic structures. It has failed, however (I include Chomsky), when it comes to semantic structures. With Cl. Haroche, P. Henry, and M. Pêcheux, "La sémantique et la coupure saussurienne: Langue, langage, discours," *Langages,* no. 24 (December 1971), I see in this fact an indication that such structures are the privileged field of work for ideologies.

30. When a textual element is constitutive of these practices (cf. Hypothesis 8 and the concept of "means of political order").

31. Autogrammatism is possible only where there exists a pluridimensionalism afforded by various writing processes; otherwise oral language will dominate the other forms of writing (cf. what A. Leroi-Gouham calls a "mythogram"; cited by J. Derrida, *Of Grammatology,* trans. G. C. Spivak [Baltimore, 1976], p. 85).

32. The genesis of the forms of economic exchange or circulation has been analyzed by Marx in the first three chapters of *Capital;* what follows here is a very succinct résumé. Cf. the concept of "self-subsistence" (the zero degree of circulation) in Terray, pp. 152–56.

33. E. Mandel, "Initiation à la théorie économique marxiste," *Cahiers du Centre d'études socialistes,* no. 1 (February-March 1964): 9–11, gives several historical examples of how working time is accounted for in relation to exchange.

34. With the development of industry, this class has been able to buy the means of production and become a *capitalist class;* these means of production, once produced, can have an exchange value. Uncultivated soil, on the other hand, has no exchange value; therefore the soil had to be appropriated politically (Asiatic social formation, slave system, feudalism). When land is bought and sold, a juridical fiction assigns it a purely speculative price—which is a political action.

35. This is a function that comes to the fore especially in periods of monetary crisis.

36. J. J. Goux, "Numismatiques," *Tel Quel,* nos. 35 and 36 (1968), reprinted in Goux, *Economie et symbolique* (Paris, 1973), would rather include here the forms of precapitalist State in which the circulation of agents is limited by their belonging to a class; this is not glossed over (any more than is the form of the appropriated surplus); thus there is master and slave, lord and serf. In extreme cases it is not even possible to speak of a State in this kind of political apparatus.

37. The age and experience of the elders (Terray, pp. 130–31), competence in the hunt (p. 122), etc.

38. A like phenomenon occurred in the Roman Empire in the case of citizens, not of slaves: the bourgeoisie recovered its rights.

39. Held by the king: "I am the State."

40. Where there were only peasants, all were equal in *value* as productive agents; this enabled the feudal political relation to become *visible,* since the agents were easily exchangeable, in a kind of "barter."

41. It is this "subjectibility," produced by the juridical ideology, that entails what N. Poulantzas calls "the effect of isolation" (*Pouvoir politique et classes sociales,* p. 230).

42. Whether it be a single agent rebelling, or a group of them, or a significant majority.

43. Thus we find agents of the social formation becoming politically specialized (as

officials, judges, soldiers, etc.) in numbers that increase according to the quantity of surplus economic production.

44. "Signifier" (S) and "signified" (s) are terms that F. de Saussure introduced into modern linguistics. The pair S/s will be isomorphic with the pairs use value/exchange value and body/subject.

45. This analysis depends on Derrida, *Of Grammatology,* by way of J. J. Goux.

46. This concept is defined below, p. 30.

47. Cf. Althusser and Balibar, *Reading Capital,* pp. 52–53, on "mirror recognition" in idealist philosophy.

48. Because of the correspondence between phonemes and letters.

49. Cf. J. P. Vernant, *L'origine de la pensée grecque* (Paris, 1962): "What the *polis* [city-state] system implies is, first of all, an extraordinary preeminence of the word over all the other political instruments of power. It became the political tool par excellence, the key to the entire authority of the state, and the means of commanding and dominating over others" (p. 44).

50. According to de Saussure, the *sign* is the unit resulting from the correlation of S and s.

51. Derrida speaks of logocentrism in both cases, since the functioning of the ideological apparatus is the same, although basically theological in the first case.

52. I do not think that G. Dhoquois, *Pour l'histoire* (Paris, 1971), is right in speaking of "oriental thought" as "basically monist" (p. 104). The text of I. Banu, on which Dhoquois bases his remark, speaks indeed of "the image of the cosmos as a unitary universe" (La formation sociale 'asiatique' dans la perspective de la philosophie orientale antique," in *Sur le mode de production asiatique* [Paris, 1969], p. 288), but only because he fails, in my view, to pay enough attention to the duality god/cosmos as providing the structure for the ideological text (he mentions the duality on p. 291, n. 2); the opposition between state and village communities is to be read, ideologically, in the light of the opposition god/fields, women (cf. pp. 293–94). Cf. also Vernant, pp. 106–9, and my analysis with regard to Palestine below, pp. 60–80.

52a. In Judaism the name is no longer even pronounced.

53. This is why the theme of the (vital) experience of presence plays such an important part in logocentrism, as Derrida has shown. In "I think, therefore I exist," the experience of thought establishes the thinking self as the *measure* of the signifieds that are produced.

54. Althusser's entire critique of the role played in idealist knowledge by evidence and the vision of essences abstracted from existence (cf. *Reading Capital,* pp. 35–41) applies, I think, to this domination that the denominative exercises over the speculative.

55. One aim of the present essay is to raise in a rigorous way the question of the political place of the theological text, and to do so on the basis of the Gospel text itself, specifically the Gospel of Mark. For example, are there structural differences between the theology of the Inquisition and the theology that condemned Jesus to death for blasphemy?

56. I have taken as an example the ideological apparatus that is at work in western gnoseological texts because the epistemological writings of Althusser and Derrida have enabled me to do so. There are perhaps other ideological apparatuses that relate to narratives (later on, we will analyze the role theological ideology plays in obscuring the Markan narrative), rituals, pictographic forms, etc. What relation do these apparatuses have to theocentrism or logocentrism?

57. Cf. the definition of "instance" above, p. 7.

58. Cf. Balibar, pp. 223–24.

59. Cf. Balibar, p. 223; Poulantzas, *Pouvoir politique et classes sociales,* pp. 26, 54 ff.

60. On the concepts of "determination" and "closure," cf. below, pp. 24 ff.

61. Of the Asiatic or of the slave-based type. The case of the European feudal mode of production is different because of the presence of the ecclesiastical apparatus with its Roman heritage.

62. As in Iran (cf. below, pp. 72 ff.).

63. This is what happened in Israel after the Josian Reform; cf. G. von Rad, *Old Testament Theology,* trans. D. M. G. Stalker, 2 vols. (New York, 1962–65), 1:207–10.

64. Vernant offers the Greece of the sixth century B.C. as an example of the transformation of a subasiatic mode of production into a slave-based mode of production. What I have been saying here explains, I think, the appearance "on the periphery of city life, and alongside the public cultus, of associations based on secrecy: sects, confraternities, and mysteries . . . societies of initiates . . . which are active solely in the religious sphere. In relation to the city initiation can provide nothing but a 'spiritual' transformation that is without political impact. . . . The mystery religion acknowledges no privilege of birth or rank, but offers to all who seek initiation the promise of a blessed immortality that was originally an exclusive privilege of kings; it broadcasts to a larger circle of initiates the religious secrets properly reserved to priestly families. . . . Revelation . . . gives the initiates a destiny out of proportion to the condition of the ordinary citizen. Secrecy, in contrast to the public character of the official cultus, thus takes on a special religious importance: it indicates a *religion of personal salvation* that aims at transforming the individual independently of the social order" (Vernant, pp. 52–53). Further on, Vernant shows the parallelism between these religions (or at least the Orphic religions) and the acquisition of political rights in the Greek republic; we cannot but compare the difference *body/citizen,* which law effects, and the *body/soul* difference, which is also present in early philosophy.

65. Bourgeois logocentrism, because of its articulation with the "technical" programs of the industrial productive forces, differs from Greek logocentrism; the Greek logos continues to be "divine," since empirical agriculture is the dominant production.

66. The replacement of god by reason resulted from the long struggle of reason against faith.

67. Here are some important pairs in the apparatus of the ideology of reason: civilized/savage, reason/madness, rational/irrational, real/imaginary (or: rational/illusory), enlightenment/obscurantism, order/disorder, culture/nature: in short, reason/unreason.

68. Cf. L. Althusser, "Idéologie et appareils idéologiques (Notes pour une recherche)," *La Pensée* (June 1970): 19. The first pages of this article explain in a very readable way the question of how the conditions of production are reproduced in capitalism.

69. Ibid., pp. 12 ff.

70. In *Fascisme et dictature: La Troisième Internationale face au fascisme* (Paris, 1970), pp. 332–33. The term "economic apparatus" (*loc. cit.,* note 7; taken over from Bettelheim) designates what I have here called "political apparatus of the economic region," while I use "economic apparatus" to mean the monetary apparatus. The difference between us is not purely verbal; we differ on the Leninist thesis concerning the unity of the state as a "factor in the overall cohesion of the levels of a complex unit

[scil. the social formation]" (Poulantzas, *Pouvoir politique et classes sociales,* pp. 43-44). Does this unity not become a "fetish" if everything (including, for Althusser, the "family") becomes an "apparatus of the state"?

71. Take, for example, the Roman clerical apparatus: it is a *political apparatus* with its functionaries (bishops and priests); it organizes ideological production, the circulation of priests, apostolic movements; it punishes violations, etc.; it collaborates with or resists the political powers (the states or nations). Its principal equivalent is the pope of Rome (the dogma of infallibility marked the beginning of the apparatus's modern centralization). However, what *determines* the political function is the religious ideological production (catechetics, preaching, liturgy, etc.), which is *textually* regulated by the *ideological apparatus* with its dogmatic, ritual, moral, etc., codes, all centered on the principal equivalent, namely, the Catholic god, Jesus Christ. I speak of "determination" because the ideological production assures the functioning of the whole, inasmuch as the ideal relations with the god constitute the agents as the *faithful* (after the manner of "subjects"). If these relations are destroyed (and we have examples of this happening in the last three centuries), then either the clerical apparatus functions in a ghetto or the machinery begins to jam because it loses its specific ideological function (that is, the priests are no longer *read,* in their clerical dress, as representatives of Jesus Christ). The state or the bosses (even if they be among the "faithful") read this clerical dress now as a symbolic representation of the bishop or pope (with whom they lodge protests, for example against a politicized priest); they read it, that is, in terms of a political apparatus.

72. The following sections—pp. 20-26—deal with the articulation of the three instances among themselves.

73. The term is taken from Lacanian psychoanalysis and is used here analogously. In Lacan's theory "demand" is related to the Freudian drive and to desire (cf. A Rifflet-Lemaire, *Jacques Lacan* (Brussels, 1970) pp. 269 ff.). A drive, according to Freud, belongs to the prepsychic realm, although it is erotically qualified, and is present only through the medium of a representation. Desire, according to Lacan, is distinct from a drive, inasmuch as the erotic object defines it as a desire for *this* object; in other words, to a drive there corresponds a plurality of desires.

74. The term is ambiguous because of the biologization latent in it; "need" sounds like something natural rather than historical (cf. Althusser and Balibar, *Reading Capital,* p. 166).

75. Rifflet-Lemaire, p. 270.

76. When a distinction must be made, I will speak of "utopia drive" and "utopia desire" respectively. If "utopia" is used without a qualifying addition, it means "utopia desire."

76a. [The author seems here to be alluding to Bataille's *La part maudite: Essai d' économie générale* (Paris, 1953). —Trans.]

77. Lacan has revived this notion.

78. An extreme example of this is supplied by R. Caillois in his *L'homme et le sacré* 2nd ed. (Paris, 1950), p. 151; cited by Bataille, *Eroticism,* p. 66.

79. On war as festival and display of excess energy before becoming calculated war, cf. Bataille, pp. 76–80.

80. The Asians have provided ritual forms for suicide: hara-kiri, the self-immolation of the Vietnamese bonzes, etc.

81. Bataille, p. 86. Today, novels and films full of violence make it possible to experience the danger vicariously, safe from real danger (ibid., p. 87), by a process of

identification that turns narratives into a form of ideological consumption.

81a. Bataille connects these with erotic fusion.

82. Religious cultus and its temples, its monuments that determine the sites of the festival within the space of the social formation, its products in painting or sculpture, and its myths or "literature," would all have to be analyzed on the analogy of Freudian sublimation, as being the effects of the violence that threatens the social formation, and the release of which is held within bounds by the sacrificial forms. It has been said of art that it is the fruit of passion, that is, of violence and death; art is sacrifical.

83. G. Balandier has studied these societies from the viewpoint of political anthropology (in his book, *Political Anthropology,* trans A. M. Sheridan Smith [New York, 1970]). I am not directly concerned here with classless social formations and therefore have given no references to this book. Nonetheless, I believe that the definition of "political" that I have given and that is more general than that of Poulantzas, is coherent with the chief concepts Balandier employs (cf. especially his third chapter).

84. For the concept of "class interests," cf. Poulantzas, *Pouvoir politique et classes sociales,* pp. 116–20.

85. The principal equivalent of the apparatus of the state is an agent whose body is separated out from among the bodies of the combatants: the king is first and foremost a "hero," a body exceptionally brave in war; compare, with the necessary adjustments, the charismatic leader.

86. The *god,* who is related either to the sacrificial animals or to the ancestors and thus to the slaying of the father (cf. the Freudian myth of the primitive patricide in Freud's *Totem and Taboo*), can become a general equivalent of the ideological apparatus only by reason of this "murder" that has raised the father to his position and made him available for communion by living bodies as an object the consumption of which is lifegiving.

87. I am leaving classless social formations out of consideration.

88. In *Capital,* trans. S. Moore and E. Aveling (New York, 1967), 1:71–84.

89. The theoretical work done by Marx shows in the fact that behind this illusory notion lies a "secret," a "social relation among men" (the relation of the working time they spend producing).

90. The fact that lacuna remain, that theoretical production, in the phase of expansive reproduction, has no terminus and often falls victim once again to idealism, and that the various apparatuses have not yet been dismantled—all this does not prevent us from recognizing that the struggle between materialism and idealism has been going on for about a hundred years. The struggle continues, however, to be too much the task of "intellectual specialists." The workers have still to say their piece in the "concrete analysis of concrete situations" and in the resultant strategy adopted, as a condition for the emancipation of consumption and expenditure, for the order that will permit the erotic and the festive, for the free play of language at the level of bodies, and for a sacrificial activity and a culture that have been revolutionized. An observation: We can speak of *the* idealist site inasmuch as when the site is that of the general equivalent, it is indeed *one* site. On the other hand, we must speak of the *sites* for a materialist reading because here we are dealing with a *plurality,* a multiplicity, namely, the plurality of diverse concrete situations, bodies, products, and writings. This fact shows the importance of analytic and strategic discussions in concrete struggles so as to uncover a common terrain, since no one person possesses *the* right reading.

91. "Restrictive": without augmenting the field of production; "expansive": augmenting the field of production.

92. The distinction cannot be seen in classless social formations in which determination and closure coincide, as they will in a "communist" social formation if one is ever established.

93. Some closures are written in visible form: the walls around "private properties," the frontiers of states, etc. Althusser and Derrida are on opposite sides in an important debate on the question of ideological closure. Althusser sees a Marxist "epistemological break" as clearing the terrain for historical materialism. Derrida, on the contrary, maintains that the "sciences" are still in the grip of logocentric closure: "I do not believe in a decisive break, a single 'epistemological break,' as it is often called today" (*Positions* [Paris, 1972], p. 35). Similarly (in Derrida's view), in order to attain to a radically communist social formation, a series of breaks with the monetary system and the apparatus of the state will be required. If this logic is accepted, I cannot claim that the present text avoids logocentrism.

94. The end of the medieval period saw an excess of workers; at that time, a short-term solution was achieved through extensive slaughter. However, the economic saturation of the productive forces had as a consequence extensive *expenditure* on the part of the lords and merchants; in addition to their luxurious life-style, they did many *good works* (alms given to peasants evicted from their lands by large-scale expropriation and forced into the ranks of the unemployed; gifts to the church for indulgences; Masses for the deceased; churches and abbeys built; etc.). Bataille, following R. H. Tawney (who in turn had taken over Max Weber's well-known thesis on Protestantism and the origins of capitalism), shows how the establishment of the Protestant ideological text, which diverged from the dominant Catholic text and articulated itself around the distinction between faith and works (so that any meriting of salvation was excluded, and salvation was made to depend on "faith alone"), made it possible to stop the enormous expenditure on the privileged unemployed (in the social formations of northern Europe) and to channel the available surplus in the direction of capitalist accumulation; cf. Bataille, *La part maudite,* pp. 163–78.

95. See the next section for the Roman slave system.

96. In his *Pour l'histoire: Essai d'histoire matérialiste comparative* (Paris, 1971), a book that cannot be too highly recommended as a historian's introduction to historical materialism. The first chapter of the book may be skipped.

97. While the atomistic or liberal capitalist mode of production clearly belongs to group S, monopolistic state capitalism is characterized by an increasing identification of private political apparatuses (the monopolies) and the state. The Soviet Union can be classified as a type of "Asiatic capitalism," with a "class-state" and separation S; a "communist" social formation will be an industrial P, in which autoproductivity, as the dominant instance, will determine autogestion and autogrammatism.

98. Dhoquois, p. 132.

99. Cf. Dhoquois, p. 71. There is a different situation in the feudal mode of production, where the slave-based mode of production has broken down the kinship organization of the peasants, and the "contractual bonds" between lord and peasants now take priority over relations of kinship (ibid., p. 141). In Dhoquois' view, we cannot speak of a state in the feudal mode of production. I disagree, and think that the structures of the apparatus of the state, such as we have seen it in its three functions, are present in the feudal mode of production, but reduced to what might be called a

"zero degree of the state."

100. This fact forces us to qualify somewhat the insertion of the Asiatic mode of production in group P, since the peasants do not have complete possession of the means of production, the irrigation works being an essential part of these means. Consequently, the only recourse the peasants have against abuses on the part of the state is *rebellion,* as in China, and an appeal "from an unenlightened to an enlightened despot" (Dhoquois, p. 105, n. 109).

101. Dhoquois, p. 105. To the list he gives I would add early Iran in the time before the great Achaemenid Empire.

102. Cf. Dhoquois, pp. 137–38, for a definition of this social formation.

103. The history of these social formations (like the history of the Asiatic and feudal social formations) is a constant series of wars, lootings, and pillages in which one group wins wealth by destroying others. Marx writes: "Ruined as they were by war and looting, [the peasants under the Germanic mode of production] had to put themselves under the protection of the new aristocracy or the Church, since the royal power was too weak to defend them; but they had to pay dearly for this protection"; cited by M. Godelier, "La notion de 'mode de production' et les schemas marxistes d'évolution des sociétés," in *Sur le "mode de production asiatique"* (Paris, 1969), p. 68.

104. Cf. Dhoquois, pp. 111.

105. Ibid. p. 128.

106. Ibid., p. 129

107. Ibid., p. 123.

108. The Asiatic social formations had already known slavery in its domestic, patriarchal, and state forms.

109. Dhoquois, p. 130.

110. Person: characterized by pronouns *I/you.* Nonperson: characterized by absence of these pronouns and the use of *he.* Cf. E. Benveniste, *Problems in General Linguistics,* trans. M. E. Meek (Coral Gables, Fla., 1971), pp. 217–22.

111. History: "the narration of past events," using the system of the nonperson, and articulating the three tenses of the verb around the *aorist.* Discourse: located in the system of the person (I/you, here and now; use of demonstratives), and articulating the tenses of the verb around the present, to the exclusion of the aorist. Cf. Benveniste, pp. 206–11.

112. Cf. Benveniste, p. 171. See also his analysis (pp. 131–44) of the nominal phrase with its "sententious" character.

113. See below, pp. 92 ff. for the concept of "sequential code."

114. Ibid., p. 208 ("event" refers to "practice").

115. See the definition of "ideological relation," above, p. 10.

116. See above, p. 17.

117. Ibid.

118. Ibid.

119. Cf. n. 81, above, p. 304.

120. This seminal dialectic of the subversive practice explains why there can be a theoretical practice only in connection with subversive practices. It is the latter that by their very break establish the standpoint for the theoretical reading; theory and subversive practices are connected dialectically. Thus, for example, there is no physical science without new technical practices (or experiments), no political science without political struggles, etc.

PART II (INTRODUCTION)

1. G. von Rad, *Old Testament Theology*, trans. D. M. G. Stalker, 2 vols. (Philadelphia, 1962–65), 1: 3–102.

PART II, CHAPTER 1

1. Cf. p. 8 above. Bataille writes: "Eroticism always entails a *breaking down* of established patterns, *the patterns*, I repeat, of the regulated *social order* basic to our discontinuous mode of existences as defined and separate individuals" (*Eroticism*, trans. M. Dalwood (London, 1962), p. 18; italics added). The symbolic field is characterized by a *resolution* that is constantly threatened by dissolution (cf. Bataille's expression, "dissolute life," p. 17).

2. Cf. Hypothesis 4, p. 8.

3. p. 28 above.

4. Cf. the concept of "means of political order," p. 10 above.

5. E. Beaucamp, "Souillure et pureté dans la Bible," in *Souillure et pureté* (Paris, 1972), p. 71. Beaucamp follows these words with a discussion of Hebrew semantics. Cf. also G. von Rad, *Old Testament Theology*, 2 vols., trans. D. M. G. Stalker (New York, 1962–65), 1:262–79.

6. On "social formation," cf. pp. 7 ff.

7. Quotations from the Bible (except for the Gospel of Mark) will be from the *Jerusalem Bible*.

8. Cf. Hypothesis 12, p. 10 above.

9. Cf. *Purity and Danger: An Analysis of the Concepts of Pollution and Taboo* (London, 1966; cited according to the Penguin edition of 1970): "Reflection on dirt involves reflection on the relation of order to disorder, being to non-being, form to formlessness, life to death" (p.5).

10. The term "violence," a theoretical contribution of Bataille, points up one of the lacunae in the book of M. Douglas.

11. Cf. Bataille, pp. 45–47.

12. Cf. "The sphere of the 'proper to' ", p. 21.

13. Cf. R. G. Bratcher and E. A. Nida, *A Translator's Handbook on the Gospel of Mark* (Leiden, 1961), p. 12.

14. Von Rad, 1:263.

15. Cf. below, p. 53.

16. Von Rad, 1:31.

17. As M. Douglas has shown; cf. her chapter 3: "The Abominations of Leviticus."

18. This is a criterion established by tribes of herdsmen.

19. G. Bataille, *La part maudite: Essai d'économie générale* (Paris, 1970, 1953), p. 27.

20. Note on Lev. 18:6.

21. Cf. his *Eroticism*, p. 52.

22. It is the condition for "the space of a clean and tidy house through which move worthy people at once naive and inviolable, tender and inaccessible" (ibid., 217).

23. Cf. ibid., pp. 46–47.

24. Cf. ibid., pp. 57–58.

25. Cf. J. Jeremias, *Jerusalem in the Time of Jesus: An Investigation Into Economic and Social Conditions During the New Testament Period*, trans. F. H. Cave and C. H. Cave

(Philadelphia, 1969), pp. 216–17.

26. For the ancient Hebrews, cf. Exod. 20:26 ("your nakedness," literally "your shameful parts"); 1 Sam. 21:6; Lev. 15:18; Deut. 23:11; 2 Sam. 6:20; 11:11. The references are from G. von Rad, *Old Testament Theology,* trans. D. M. G. Stalker, 2 vols. (Philadelphia, 1962–1965), 1:273.

27. Cf. Exod. 19:21; 33:20; Lev. 19:2; Num. 4:20.

28. Cf. R. de Vaux, *Ancient Israel: Its Life and Institutions,* trans. J. McHugh (New York, 1961), p. 83.

29. The debt system presupposes ownership of an "Asiatic" kind (cf. below, p. 311, n. 5, and p. 67).

30. De Vaux, p. 175.

31. Cf. Bataille, *Eroticism,* pp. 206–7.

32. Ibid., p. 204.

33. On the other hand, a eunuch, that is, "a man whose testicles have been crushed or whose male member has been cut off, is not to be admitted to the assembly of Yahweh" (Deut. 23:2).

34. *Divorce* was practiced and was the object of a special juridical procedure (the husband "has made out a writ of divorce for her"; then "she leaves his home": Deut. 24:1–2). At the same time, however, divorce was also the action of a possessor, since the right to draw up a writ of divorce belonged exclusively to the husband (de Vaux, p. 39).

35. Barrenness was the greatest disgrace for a woman; cf. 1 Sam. 1; Luke 1:25.

36. Unless the act occurred in the open fields where the woman may have cried for help and not been heard; in this case she does not incur the debt. This calls into question the interpretation I offer here.

37. Cf. below, p. 143, commentary on S 35.

38. There was thus no idea of survival in a future life nor any belief in a resurrection of the dead. This latter notion entered the text of the Jewish ideology only during the second century B.C.

39. Cf. von Rad: "It can be shown that, to begin with, the commandment for bidding stealing specifically envisaged kidnapping (cf. Ex. XXI. 16; Deut. XXIV. 7) and that it was only subsequently generalized to arrive at the sense in which we know it now" (1:191).

40. The Jerusalem Bible notes that verses 17–20 form but a single verse in the Septuagint; this fact implies that the translators read the four prohibitions as amounting to a single prohibition.

41. In Deuteronomy the Levites have (from the point of view I am adopting here) the same place as the priests in Leviticus.

42. This provision also relates to the table.

43. Cf. Jeremias, pp. 57, 134.

44. Cf. Bataille, *La part maudite,* pp. 60–62, 79–80.

45. "Cause you to sin against" is literally "cause you to be in debt to."

46. Cf. von Rad, 1:264 and n. 182.

47. We must therefore not oppose visible to invisible, material to spiritual; the narrative also concerns the "visible," inasmuch as Yahweh's power is manifested "visibly."

48. Cf. Lev. 26 and Deut. 28; the latter chapter terminates the so-called Second Discourse of Moses, which occupies the greater part of the book.

49. Under the action of the sun, too, but in these Mediterranean countries the rain is the more precious of the two.

50. Cf. von Rad, 1:224–25.

51. Ibid., 1:36.

52. Ibid., 1:74.

53. Ibid., 1:75.

54. We may call attention here to another idea of Bataille's: bodily strength in combat is related to the desire to run risks: "As far as they are able (it is a quantitative matter of strength), men seek out the greater losses and the greatest dangers" (*Eroticism*, p. 86). Cf. above, Hypothesis 27, p. 20.

55. Here is a passage chosen at random from Isaiah: "His [Yahweh's] land is full of silver and gold and treasures beyond counting; his land is full of horses and chariots without number; his land is full of idols" (2:7-8).

56. Von Rad, 1:219.

57. Translation by von Rad, 1:207.

58. Ibid., 1:265.

59. Ibid., fn. 183.

60. I say "perhaps," because at first sight incest is also connected with "aggressive violence" and thus belongs to the two systems. But such does not seem to be the case, since Deuteronomy, and the Decalogue in particular, do not make this connection.

61. Cf. Lev. 18:27, 29, which uses this term to sum up the list of the most serious forms of sexual pollution.

62. Cf. Beaucamp: "Abomination, the word most frequently used (14 times) to express God's revulsion [and thus to debts]" (p. 65).

63. This to the great astonishment of von Rad, 1:234, n. 101.

64. Cf. von Rad, 2:174, 192.

65. Since the temple was a royal sanctuary, set apart from the other sanctuaries before the Josian reform, its priests were in fact crown officials, according to von Rad, 1:43.

66. Ibid., 1:58–59. Having once set aside "religious considerations," von Rad makes a distinction between "social" and "religious," which shows the bourgeois ideology that is dominant in contemporary exegesis: "There [in the Jotham story] it is a social, and not a religious, bias that holds the kingdom up to such brutal ridicule" (ibid.). This ideology makes it impossible to understand the debt system.

67. Von Rad, 1:323.

68. Von Rad implicitly denies this archaic character, however (1:223).

69. See the citations above, p. 53.

70. Von Rad, "It is remarkable to how very much greater a degree the Book of the Covenant supposes equal rights of all before the law, and the idea of common solidarity" (1:32).

71. Cf. Deut. 17:14–20, and von Rad, 1:75.

72. De Vaux goes so far as to deny the existence of social classes in Israel (p. 108).

73. Cf. von Rad, 1:245, 249.

74. Ibid., 1:74.

75. Cf. above, pp. 23 ff.

76. Von Rad describes the cultus as a gift "for Yahweh," so that he might be mindful (1:241–42) and turn away his wrath from the community (1:250). Pedersen, with whom von Rad disagrees for reasons that seem to be connected with the latter's "Protestant" ideology, "sees as the kernel of the Israelite conception the effort to obtain blessing upon the livestock and the crops" (von Rad, 1:254, fn. 159). Pedersen's view agrees with the analysis we have been proposing.

77. The Levites were substitutes for the firstborn of all the "houses" of Israel, that is, for "those who open the womb, all the first-born" (Num. 8:16), a violent opening that causes all the firstborn to belong to Yahweh (Num. 8:17). If the firstborn were not ransomed (Num. 3:40–51) and replaced by the Levites, they "would have been forfeit to Jahweh" (von Rad, 1:250), and the shedding of their blood would have purified the pollution attaching to birth. This archaic practice was reflected in the animal sacrifices the meaning of which we have been seeing and which were at the heart of the pollution system.

78. Cf. Hypothesis 31, p. 21.

79. Cf. Hypothesis 33, p. 22.

80. Von Rad, 1:71–77.

81. Which corroborates my Hypothesis 36, p. 24.

82. Cf. von Rad, 1:250–51.

83. Ibid., 1:269.

84. The wealthy also claimed legitimacy on the grounds that they were "blessed" by Yahweh: their very wealth was proof of their "righteousness."

85. We may have a reflection of this in von Rad's comment that "the gravest word for sin" "means 'revolt,' 'rebellion'. . . , and originally perhaps 'impeachment of property' (Exod. XXII, 8 [9])" (1:263). For an example of the distortions of the debt system, cf. below, p. 314, fn. 53.

86. Cf. Von Rad, 1:93-102.

87. Does not the bourgeois intelligentsia constantly repeat this ideological gesture of stressing the problematic relating to infrastructural violence, the irreducible facts of death, sexuality, and sickness, or the "problem of evil and suffering," as it used to be called, at the expense of the superstructural contradiction relating to class exploitation, the "social problem," and all that is reducible? That is to say, does the intelligentsia not repeat the gesture of the priestly class at Jerusalem, which allowed the debt system to be hidden by the pollution system? It is enough, for example, to see the importance the intelligentsia attaches to contemporary psychoanalysis, to a type of eroticism, to drugs, to the question of death, etc.—all of which are means of distracting attention from the class struggle, from the "justice" of courts that fill the prisons with the poor and allow the powerful to go about their business, etc. Here again, the irreducible and the metaphysical hide what can be changed.

88. Von Rad, 1:196, fn. 18.

89. Ibid., 1:260–62.

90. Ibid., 1:229.

PART II, CHAPTER 2

1. On the "Asiatic sphere," cf. pp. 26 ff.

2. Cf. G. Dhoquois, *Pour l'histoire* (Paris, 1971), p. 87.

3. Cf. C. Guignebert, *The Jewish World in the Time of Jesus,* trans. S. N. Hooke (London, 1939; reprinted, New Hyde Park, N.Y., 1959), pp. 7–11.

4. There is a vast amount of detailed material in J. Jeremias, *Jerusalem in the Time of Jesus: An Investigation into Economic and Social Conditions during the New Testament Period,* trans. F. H. Cave, and C. H. Cave (Philadelphia, 1969). Jeremias will be cited frequently in the present chapter.

5. See below (this chapter, text with fn. 16) the citation from Baron on the landowner-tenant character of such property; the latter had effects that were political

rather than economic. Marx writes: "In most forms with an Asiatic base, the overarching unit, which is situated above and outside all the small communities, appears as the higher or even the sole owner (in this case, the god), while the real communities are hereditary possessors" (cited by M. Godelier, "La notion de 'mode de production asiatique' et les schémas marxistes d'évolution des sociétés" in *Sur le "mode de production asiatiques"* (Paris, 1969), pp. 63–64. Godelier himself writes elsewhere: "The Asiatic mode of production was to evolve, through the development of its contradiction, toward forms of class societies in which relations at the community level have less and less reality in consequence of the development of private property" (p. 89); in Palestine the last-named development was encouraged by occupation by the Roman slave-based mode of production. Cf. R. de Vaux, *Ancient Israel: Its Life and Institutions,* trans. J. McHugh (New York, 1961), chapter 11; de Vaux, however, does not seem to have fully recognized the "Asiatic" character of ownership in Israel.

6. According to S. W. Baron, *A Social and Religious History of the Jews* (2nd ed., rev. New York, 1952), "we . . . know very little about the relative ratio of the large and small landholdings in ancient Palestine. The country seems never to have witnessed such concentration of landownership in a few hands as characterized the Italian *latifundia.* Hence the small Jewish farmer, and not the slaveholding landlord, remained the backbone of Palestinian culture, indeed of Jewish society at large" (1:277).

7. This is Jeremias's view (pp. 100–08) as against that of Baron (cf. below, p. 81).

8. That is, with the exception of international trade, which was subject to the *publicum* (public treasury) tax.

9. 1 Kings 9:26–10:2 presents Solomon as a great merchant; trade was the business of the state. According to de Vaux, private trade developed after the exile in priestly Judaism (pp. 78–79).

10. In the sense of Engels' remark that "a social function is everywhere the basis of political domination" (cited by Godelier, p. 62).

11. Jeremias analyzes several lists of such occupations (pp. 303–12).

12. Cf. Jeremias, pp. 297–302; the question of inheritance was also involved.

13. Cf. Godelier, p. 55, and my Hypothesis 11, p. 10 above.

14. Cf. my Hypothesis 10, p. 10 above.

15. Cf. de Vaux, pp. 138, 152–53.

16. As we have seen, it was characteristic of the Asiatic social formation that it did not acknowledge the kind of "private ownership" found in the slave-based and capitalist modes of production. In the Asiatic social formation of the Jews, the God of Israel was regarded as lord of the whole country. This fact should, I think, lead to a rereading of the Gospel parables on masters and servants (e.g., Matt. 25:14–30). These are less "parables" than they seem; by this I mean that the underlying logic in them is that of the debt system as extrapolated in an eschatological perspective, and that they are referring to the "bosses" and deployers of political power. The "real boss" will soon be coming for judgment, and those who have not been faithful to the *gift* (gift/debt) will be punished. We usually read these parables through the eyes of western "private property" holders, as though the parables were guarantees of such property!

17. Baron, 1:280–81.

18. Jeremias, p. 228.

19. Cf. my Hypotheses 6 and 31, pp. 9 and 21.

20. "Covenant" is a metaphor based on the political covenants that had been common in the Asiatic social formations of the Near East since the second millennium B.C.

21. According to von Rad, this very ancient narrative preserves the memory of "the founding of the old Israelite Amphictyony" (1:16), that is, the tribal confederation.

22. Cf. von Rad, vol. 2, Part I, chapter G, and Part II, chapter C.

23. A. Tricot, "The Jewish World," in A. Robert and A. Feuillet, eds., *Introduction to the New Testament,* trans. P. W. Skehan et al. (New York, 1965), pp. 58–59.

24. "As a result of the Priestly Document, which may have been brought to Jerusalem by the returned exiles, and its non-eschatological cultic theology, this [eschatological] vision [of the prophets] must have become lost. As time went on, the consolidation of the post-exilic community, which apparently corresponded to the restoration which many of the returned exiles hoped for, had become more and more bound up with an increasingly consistent elimination of eschatological ideas. This does not mean that these ideas were no longer represented: but the ruling priestly aristocracy in Jerusalem tended to push eschatological expectation more and more on one side, and finally forced it into separation" (von Rad, 2:297). The priestly closure thus inverted the narrative/law relation: once fixed in the past, the narrative is dominated by the law.

24a. Jeremias, pp. 233, 235, 237.

25. Cf. A. Paul, "Bulletin de littérature intertestamentaire: L' 'Intertestament,' " *Recherches de science religieuse* 60 (1972): 429.

26. Cf. von Rad, 2:306–8.

27. Cf. above, p. 17.

28. In G. Dumézil, E. Benveniste, A. Dupont-Sommer et al., *La civilisation iranienne* (Paris, 1962). In interpreting the Iranian religions I shall make use of this volume and of G. Widengren, *Les religions de l'Iran* (Paris, 1968; German original, 1965).

29. Zoroastrianism was antiroyal; Widengren shows that the Achaemenid kings did not follow it (pp. 166 ff.).

30. Cf. von Rad, 2:308–15.

31. Ibid., 2:303.

32. Ibid., 2:134.

33. Ibid., 2:299.

34. Regarding Daniel, von Rad says that "without any doubt, the writer of Daniel sides with those who endure persecution rather than with those who take up arms against it" (2:315). But we find a radicalized fraction of the Pharisees—the Zealots, whose interests were rather those of the peasants—leading an armed rebellion against the Romans throughout the first century A.D., and yet also drawing their inspiration from the apocalyptic hope. We may say that this group returned, as it were, to the very source of the apocalyptic texts.

35. "In Dan II and VII, . . . the meaning of the pictorially represented movement [of universal history] is perfectly plain—it indicates a growth of evil. Apocalyptic literature's view of history is therefore pessimistic in the extreme—world history is moving towards an 'abyss' and a 'great destruction' (Enoch LXXXIII. 7)" (von Rad, 2:305).

36. Contrary to Iranian belief, there is here no immortality of the soul. See the argument given in 2 Mac. 12:38–46.

37. The logic of royal justice.

38. Guignebert, pp. 135–38 (italics in the original).

39. Ibid., pp. 90–91.

39a. Ibid., p. 98.

40. Ibid., p. 101.

41. More accurately, the earthly will be transfigured by the heavenly. The heaven/ earth difference will be blurred, and the eschatological closure of Israel's narrative (and of all narratives) will send the reader back to the genesis of every narrative, that is, to the fundamental narrative: "In the beginning God created the heavens and the earth" (Gen. 1:1). *Telos* and *arche,* end and beginning, will be one.

42. A place for the burning of offal; cf. V. Taylor, *The Gospel according to St. Mark* (New York, 1957), p. 411.

43. The *casuistic system* is the text that is symptomatic of a *dislocation* between the old symbolic order and the contemporary symbolic field, and that also attempts to eliminate the dislocation. The dislocation is the result of changes in the social formation and had already been the locus of the struggle between the Deuteronomistic Levites and the prophets.

44. The movement of the Pharisaic communities, whose real problem, as we have seen, was the lack of a specific political force, established an ideological problematic and became an ideological social force; then, since the social formation was one in which the political apparatus of the state was identical with the priestly political apparatus, it became a political social force as well.

45. *The Sacred and the Profane: The Nature of Religion,* trans. W. R. Trask (New York, 1959), p. 43 (italics added).

46. Cited in ibid., pp. 42–43.

47. And of minors.

48. Jeremias, p. 79. [M. Kel. = The Mishnah, Tractate Kelim ("Vessels"); text in H. Danby, *The Mishnah* (London, 1933), pp. 604–49; cf. pp. 605–6.]

49. "We have little evidence of any major technological or organizational advances" (Baron, 1:257).

50. My thesis, then, is that the ideological instance was dominant simply because this was a subasiatic mode of production (illustration: the payment of the double drachma by the Jews of the Diaspora), and that the political instance was dominant because the subasiatic mode of production was integrated into a slave-based mode of production. The latter mode of production determined the former, for, since the subasiatic mode of production had been dominated by foreigners for six centuries, it could assure its internal cohesion only through ideological domination (increased role of the temple; role of the chief priests in the internal apparatus of State; place of apocalyptic eschatology in the Zealot ideology).

51. Cited by Jeremias, p. 25.

52. Our chief source in the first paragraph of this section is Baron's history; cf. 1:250–85; 2:3–59.

53. Baron, 1:279. Here we have a good example of a distortion of the debt system: the sabbatical year, which had been promulgated against the great landowners, had become an intolerable burden for the ordinary peasant!

54. Mark uses the same Greek work, *lēstēs,* for both "bandit" and "terrorists" (Zealot).

55. *Jerusalem Bible: New Testament,* p. 466, col. 2.

56. Those of Herod in Galilee; add those of the temple-state in Judea.

57. Thus, the exclusive importance which the Sadducees attributed to the temple was challenged by the Pharisees who "had to consider world Jewry more than the Sadducees, whose horizon was necessarily confined to the boundaries of Palestine. Hence they [the Pharisees] began to stress those elements in religion and law which

were applicable to Jews outside the country as well" (Baron, 2:45). The sabbath, the synagogue, and the law were some of these elements.

58. A political metaphor based on the Asiatic royal court.

59. But they rallied to the side of the Zealots when war broke out in 66 A.D. (Baron, 2:50–51).

60. But Baron thinks that "the contrast between the more other-worldly character of Pharisaic Judaism and the principally this-world orientation of the prophetic religion is not so great as has been asserted" (2:40).

61. Ibid., pp. 138–39.

62. Guignebert emphasizes "the silence which was preserved by the early Rabbis on the subject of the Messiah's sufferings" (p. 149).

63. Jeremias, p. 119.

64. This was 17 times 10,000 denarii, a denarius being the daily wage of a farm worker (cf. Jeremias, pp. 91, fn. 12, and 120, fn. 1).

65. Ibid., p. 119.

66. P. Prigent, *La fin de Jérusalem* (Neuchâtel, 1969), p. 18, fn. 1.

67. Cf. my Hypothesis 47, p. 28 above.

68. This is total consumption, in Bataille's terminology.

69. Cited in Prigent, p. 43.

70. The last Jewish stronghold to fall to the Romans.

71. Cited in Prigent, pp. 63–65.

72. Cf. Prigent, p. 42, fn. 3.

PART III, CHAPTER 1

1. Cf. Hypothesis 17, p. 14 above.

2. *Elements of Semiology,* trans. A. Lavers and C. Smith (London, 1967), p. 89; *S/Z,* trans. by R. Miller (New York, 1974), p. 7.

3. Cf. above, p.30.

4. R. Barthes, *S/Z,* trans. R. Miller (New York, 1974), p. 8.

5. Ibid., p. 160. Julia Kristeva defines a text as "a translinguistic apparatus that restores the order of the language *(langue)* by establishing a relation between communicative speech *(parole)* that is concerned with information [that is, with denotation, which, "like the phrase belongs to linguistics proper," according to Barthes, "L'analyse structurale du récit, à propos d'Actes X–XI," *Recherches de science religieuse* 58 (1970), p. 8] and different kinds of anterior or synchronous statements *(énoncés)*" ("Le texte clos," in her *Sêmiôtikê: Recherches pour une sémanalyse* [Paris, 1969], p. 113). This "relation" is Barthes's "connotation."

6. Cf. Barthes, *S/Z,* p. 8.

7. Ibid.

8. Kristeva, "Le texte clos," p. 116.

9. Julia Kristeva, *Le texte du roman: Approche sémiologique d'une structure discursive transformationnelle* (The Hague, 1970), p. 25

10. Ibid.

11. Ibid.

12. The term "symbolic," which Kristeva borrows from the American philosopher Willard V. Quine's essay on the reification of universals ("Le texte clos," p. 116), is a term in logic; it has quite a different meaning than in my text where its use is inspired by the writings of Jacques Lacan.

13. Kristeva, "Le texte clos," p. 116.

14. Cf. above, p. 30.

15. Published in *Communications,* no. 8 (1966). We shall refer to this essay as R. B. I.

16. R. B. I, pp. 2–3.

17. R. B. I, p. 5

18. Cf. "narrative communication," R. B. I, p. 18.

19. This is what happens in, for example, the "exercises on short narratives," from the Bible, which G. Vuillod provides in *Langages* (June 1971), pp. 24 ff.

20. Barthes, *S/Z*, pp. 12–13.

21. Ibid., p. 160

22. Ibid., p. 11.

23. Ibid., p. 15.

24. Barthes expressly authorizes such a reading; cf. *S/Z*, p. 16.

25. As is the case with L. Marin in his *Sémiotique de la passion: Topiques et figures* (Paris, 1971).

26. Barthes, *S/Z*, p. 8.

26a. Ibid.

27. R. B. I, p. 6.

28. On the concept of "levels of meaning" in a narrative (a concept borrowed from the linguistic theory of E. Benveniste), cf. R. B. I, pp. 4–6.

29. Ibid., pp. 8–9.

30. Ibid., pp. 9–10.

31. Ibid., p. 13.

32. O. Ducrot and T. Todorov, *Dictionnaire encyclopédique des sciences du langage* (Paris, 1972), p. 379.

33. The term "actants" is suggested by Greimas to show that the analysis is of the "personages" in a narrative "not according to what they *are* but according to what they *do*" (R. B. I, p. 17; italics added). The analysis is of the text, not of "the incident recounted." For this reason, "Jesus" will usually be J, the disciples DD, the adversaries AA, the individual actants I, the "sick" Ic, etc. (cf. the List of Symbols).

34. Cf. above, p. 307, fn. 110–11.

35. As in Barthes *S/Z*, pp. 18, etc.

36. Ibid., p. 19.

37. Ibid. p. 18; cf. also R. B. I, p. 13.

38. R. B. I, p. 10.

39. Cf. above, Hypothesis 12, p. 10.

40. She takes the term from Bakhtine; "Every text is built up as a mosaic of citations; every text absorbs and transforms some other text" ("Le texte clos," p. 146).

41. R. B. I, p. 9, writes: "These two great classes of units, namely functions and indices, should already make possible a classification of narratives. Some narratives are heavily functional (for example, popular tales); at the other extreme, some are heavily indicial (for example, psychological novels)." This, in my view, is a reference back to the mythical/classical typology proposed earlier.

42. Cf. above, p. 300, fn. 13.

43. Cf. below, p. 125.

44. Therefore, with a single exception (Mark 5:40, in S 25g), I accept Aland's choice among variants.

44a. Max Zerwick, *Analysis Philologica Novi Testamenti Graeci* (3rd ed.; Rome, 1966). The first part of this book has been translated: Max Zerwick and Mary Grosvenor, trans., *A Grammatical Analysis of the Greek New Testament* 1: *Gospels–Acts* (Rome, 1974).

45. I shall even keep the definite article with proper names (the Jesus, the Peter, etc.). My reason for this literalness and for departing from the current practice of translators is to emphasize the fact that we are reading a *foreign* text, produced in a social formation quite different from ours. My rejection of "literary style" is therefore a refusal to make the evangelical text "modern," a refusal to treat it "as God's word that speaks to us today." This refusal is, in turn, to be read as a break with a "theology of inspiration" which, in order to lay hold of this "divine word," does away with the text as a production.

46. This is not true of the scenes.

47. Cf. W. G. Kümmel, *Introduction to the New Testament,* trans. H. C. Kee (Nashville, 1975), p. 48.

48. Kümmel, pp. 60-66. Cf. also S. McLoughlin, "Le problème synoptique: Vers la théorie des deux sources. Les accords mineurs," in *De Jésus aux évangiles: Tradition et rédaction dans les évangiles synoptiques* (Gembloux, 1967).

49. Cf. Kümmel, pp. 50–52.

50. An example of this method as applied to Mark may be found in G. Minette de Tillesse, *Le secret messianique dans l'évangile de Marc* (Paris, 1968).

51. E. Trocmé, *The Formation of the Gospel according to Mark,* trans. P. Gaughan (Philadelphia, 1975), is an extreme example of this. See below, p. 332, fn. 6.

52. This and the next two quotations are from Minette de Tillesse, pp. 434–37.

53. For a list of these, cf. Kümmel, pp. 97–98.

54. For example, X. Léon-Dufour says: "Internal criticism adds: *before the year 70*" (in his essay "The Synoptic Gospels," in *Introduction to the New Testament,* ed. A. Robert and A. Feuillet, trans. P. Skehan et al. (New York, 1965), p. 219. The French original is dated 1959. Kümmel's judgment is that "since no overwhelming argument for the years before or after 70 can be adduced, we must content ourselves with saying that Mk was written *ca.* 70" (p. 98).

55. This part of my book was completed before I came upon F. Neirynck's *Duality in Mark: Contributions to the Study of the Markan Redaction* (Louvain, 1972). (It was Neirynck's courses at Louvain, a few years back, that enabled me to plunge into the forest that is the exegesis of the synoptic Gospels.) In his book, Neirynck studies the often noted Markan phenomenon of "double phrases," which N. prefers to speak of as "duality" rather than "pleonasms, redundancies, or repetitions" (p.71). His thesis is that this phenomenon cannot be erected into a general criterion for distinguishing either a "proto-Mark" and "a deutero-Markan recension" (p. 44), or tradition and redaction. Instead, a critical study must be made of each instance (p. 72). Earlier in the book, Neirynck makes the following general observation: "On the whole, the evidence is rather impressive, especially the fact that a kind of general tendency can be perceived in vocabulary and grammar, in individual sayings and in collections of sayings, in the construction of pericopes and larger sections; there is a sort of homogeneity in Mark, from the wording of sentences to the composition of the gospel. After the study of these data one has a strong impression of the unity of the Gospel of Mark. It can be formulated as a methodological principle that the categories we distinguished hold together and that no pericope in Mark can be treated in isolation" (p. 37).

Are we straining if we see this homogenity and unity confirming the rightness of our own methodological option in taking Mark as a *single*, tightly structured text, while regarding the study of synopticity (along the lines of the history of forms and the history of redactions) as subject for a later and secondary analysis?

PART III, CHAPTER 2

1. Cf. O. Cullmann, *The Christology of the New Testament,* rev. ed., trans. S. C. Guthrie and C. A. M. Hall (Philadelphia, 1963): "Jesus-Christ means Jesus-Messiah. . . . We should remember in reading the New Testament that its authors were still at least partly aware of the significance of 'Jesus-Messiah' " (p. 112).

2. Cf. below, p. 233.

3. R. G. Bratcher and E. A. Nida, *A Translator's Handbook on the Gospel of Mark* (Leiden, 1961), p. 12.

4. Cf. above, p. 76.

5. Cf. above, pp. 71–75.

6. From a structural viewpoint the important thing here is the *descent,* not the *dove.* The exegetes have always had trouble in finding a semantic paradigm for situating the dove; cf. V. Taylor, *The Gospel According to Mark* (New York, 1957).

7. Here we have one of the textual snares into which bourgeois exegetical discourse will fall, since it thinks it knows the meaning of the title "son of God" (or "holy one of God"). In point of fact, however, it really produces this meaning by applying either the grill of the later theological discourse (conciliar dogma, for example) or the grill of other biblical texts. It thus condemns itself in advance to a misunderstanding of the ANAL code.

8. Here is another trap into which bourgeois exegetical discourse is constantly falling: it believes that it knows in advance (the mark of ideological knowledge!) what is meant when the word "prayer" occurs.

9. Cf. G. Minette de Tillesse, *Le secret messianique dans l'évangile de Marc* (Paris, 1968), pp. 65–68.

10. Barthes finds a series of contrasts or "antitheses" in Balzac's *Sarrasine* and sees them as belonging to the SYMB code (cf. *S/Z,* pp. 18–24). If I contrast a BAS code with the SOC code (the two are in fact related antithetically, and this reflects back on the SYMB and TOP codes), I do so in order to bring out the fact that the antithesis is the effect (which I call *subversion*) of J's own practice.

11. "Les épis arrachés (Matt. 12, 1–8 et par.)," *Studii Biblici Franciscani Liber Annuus* 13 (1962–63), pp. 76–92. Reprinted in Benoit's *Exégèse et théologie* 3 (Paris, 1968), pp. 228–42.

12. The objection is explicitly aimed only at the DD, but J regards it as implicitly aimed also at him, their teacher.

13. Minette de Tillesse, pp. 137–39, provides a good example of the way in which exegetical erudition misses the meaning of the text. As he sees it, "v. 27 ['the sabbath was made for man's sake, etc.'], placed before v. 28 ['the Son of Man is lord even of the sabbath'], only camouflages somehow what might seem to be the excessive straightforwardness of the latter statement"!

14. Cf. Minette de Tillesse, p. 140.

15. Who are the Herodians? They will be mentioned again in S 40b and S 55f. The answer to the question is not very important for our reading, since the Herodians have but a very minor role in the narrative, and even then are secondary to the Pharisees. I refer the reader to the thoughtful but unprovable thesis expounded by C. Daniel, "Les 'Hérodiens' du Nouveau Testament sont-ils des Esséniens?" *Revue de Qumrân* 6

(1967): 35–53, who thinks that these "Herodians" were Essenes. His conclusions are cited in A. Feuillet, "La controverse sur le jeûne," *Nouvelle revue théologique* 90 (1968): 114, fn. 3.

16. For example, against Lagrange, who is cited in V. Taylor, *The Gospel According to Mark* (New York: 1957), p. 226.

17. Cf. O. Cullmann, *Jesus and the Revolutionaries,* trans. G. Putnam (New York, 1970), pp. 8–9, and J. Jeremias, *The Parables of Jesus,* trans. S. H. Hooke, rev. ed. (New York, 1963), p. 152.

18. Cf. above, p. 76. It is of interest to compare this accusation with the "structural" definition M. Douglas gives of sorcery: "the anti-social psychic power with which persons in relatively unstructured areas of society are credited" (M. Douglas, *Purity and Danger: An Analysis of the Concepts of Pollution and Taboo* (London, 1966), p. 102.

19. Except in S 35c and S 42e; but in this second case, as we shall see, there is no reason for doubting the presence of the actant C.

20. The theological disquisitions on the "mother of Jesus," which have produced well-known results (mariology, the cult of Mary) in ecclesiastical practice, have always run into a stumbling block here. For "mother" is not an individual here; she has no name (though she will have one in S 27). "Mother" is only a function in the SOC, within the category of "house" or kinship. Nonetheless, she is connoted in the incredulity of the kinsfolk when confronted with the narrative of J. In addition, "the brothers" and "sisters" of J call the "virginity of Mary" into question. In the "infancy narratives of Jesus" that are given by Matthew and Luke, the point is not sexual relations or their absence, but the mighty birth of Jesus, in keeping with the Jewish tradition of the election of a newborn child (Isaac, Samuel, John the Baptist). The birth is referred to God, a point made by bringing out the sterility of the mother. According to the New Testament texts, Mary was a virgin at the birth of J, but she was also the nonvirginal mother of other children. In Greek textuality, on the contrary, sex is characterized negatively by the opposition spirit/body; consequently, virginity becomes a matter of abstention from sexual relations and, from the ideological standpoint, includes celibacy as well. In this perspective, Mary will be spoken of as "ever a virgin." Mariology and the connection of the Virgin Mary with ecclesiastical celibacy will perhaps be sites to which a materialist ecclesiology will give preference for the purpose of analyzing the religio-Christian ideological apparatus in its function of repressing the body and sex.

21. S 12a, b is a hybrid structure.

22. Cf. J. Jeremias, *The Parables of Jesus,* trans. S. H. Hooke, rev. ed. (New York, 1963), pp. 13–14, whose analysis has been my guide. However, since his method of reading is that of form history and redaction history (cf. above, p. 96), he concludes that the little passage enshrined in c 2 "is a logion belonging to a wholly independent tradition, which was adapted by Mark to the word *parabolē* (vv. 10–11) and must *therefore* be interpreted without reference to its present context" (p. 14; italics added), as if the narrator were constructing a jigsaw puzzle of detached pieces that are to be read independently each of the other. My method of (textual) reading, on the contrary, endeavors to read Mark as a *fabric*; it therefore supposes that whatever may have been the prehistory of the text, the way in which the whole has been woven together should determine the reading. Cf. also Minette de Tillesse, pp. 166–70.

23. "Satan" = the Adversary. This is why these actants are described as "adversaries" (AA). Like Satan in S 2, they *tempt* J (S 39, S 47, S 55–56).

24. Cf. below, p. 202.

25. This is not the case in Matthew and Luke.

26. Jeremias, *Parables,* p. 151, has given a more adequate interpretation inasmuch as he sees that the usual title for the parable excludes the sower. He proposes as a title "The Parable of the Patient Husbandman," patience being anti-Zelotic. But it is not in terms of patience (or of zeal, for that matter) that J distinguishes himself from the Zealots.

27. Minette de Tillesse remarks that "every time there is mention of a secular kingdom in Mark [S 20d, S 30b, S 58b2], always associated with it is the assertion of a division in it that leads to its destruction" (p. 392).

28. "The Jews so thoroughly identified themselves with Palestine's most representative plants that, in literary metaphor and artistic adornment, the palm tree and the vine became the paramount symbols of Israel" (S. Baron, *A Social and Religious History of the Jews,* 2nd ed., rev. (New York, 1952), 1:252–53).

29. Cf. above, pp. 49 f.

30. Cf. above, pp. 39 f., 61.

31. Cf. J. Starobinski, "The Gerasene Demoniac: A Literary Analysis of Mark 5:1–20," in *Structural Analysis and Biblical Exegesis: Interpretational Essays,* trans. A. M. Johnson, Jr. (Pittsburgh, 1974), pp. 57–84. One cannot fail to be struck, in reading this "structuralist" text, by the work of metaphysical idealism: the distinctions earthly-divine; body/soul; figurative sense (soul of the intended reader)/literal sense; literal, historical/spiritual, etc., determine his theory of the parables in an utterly traditional reading. "Structuralism" does not provide immunity against idealism!

32. Except in S 25d–S 26a–S 25e.

33. Cf. Jeremias, *Jerusalem in the Time of Jesus: An Investigation Into Economic and Social Conditions During the New Testament Period,* trans. F. H. Cave and C. H. Cave (Philadelphia, 1969), p. 365.

34. Cf. pp. 288 ff.

35. Cf. above, p. 41.

36. Cf. Jer. 33:6: "But look, I will hasten their recovery and their cure; I will cure them and let them know peace and security in full measure."

37. Cf. below, pp. 256 ff. For Ricoeur, cf. *Freud and Philosophy: An Essay on Interpretation,* trans. D. Savage (New Haven, Conn.: 1970), pp. 65–114.

38. Cf. above, p. 127. What we may call J's *economic* practice is clearly connected with his *hands.*

39. Cf. above, p. 40 ff.

40. Cf. above, p. 76.

41. Cf. below, 127 ff.

42. Cf. below, 288 ff.

43. Cf. below, 247 ff.

44. This is perhaps the site in the narrative at which the aleatory, or randomness, which is the specifying factor in its play (cf. below, p. 209 and especially pp. 268 ff.), is most marked.

45. The STR of the Z thus becomes a grill for reading the narrative of Mark. Later on we shall discuss the validity of this grill (cf. below, pp. 179 and 234 ff.).

46. The "multiplication" fascinates and prevents the reading of the blessing of filling or satisfaction or repletion. Bourgeois exegetes, who are, in addition, hypnotized by "the Eucharist," do not succeed in reading this major sequence (S 31–S 42 and especially S 40).

47. This is expressly brought out by the parallel narrative of John 6:15: "Jesus, who

could see they were about to come and take him by force and make him king, escaped back to the hills by himself." But we are reading Mark here and must advance slowly.

48. Cf. above, p. 76.

49. Towns, especially during the day (J prays only at night), are dominated by the text of the codes of the SOC in a monotonous, noisy discourse. In capitalist cities, the noise of advertising becomes infernal in the full sense, a pollution of the word.

50. Cf. above, p. 96.

51. Historians discuss the question of these regulations. It seems to be generally accepted that they were instituted by the scribes and adopted especially by the Pharisees and the Essenes (cf. Taylor, pp. 338–39). This explains the expression "tradition of the elders" and the opposition J sets up between this and the "commandment of God," which is attributed to Moses.

52. This reading by J justifies the interpretation we gave earlier of this commandment (cf. p. 46). (Recent?) ecclesiastical tradition has turned it into a "commandment" for children!

53. *Korban* is the sacrificial holocaust (cf. R. de Vaux, *Ancient Israel: Its Life and Institutions,* trans. J. McHugh [New York, 1961], p. 417). What J finds reprehensible, then, is the act of setting aside the debt system and replacing it with the pollution system, as the priestly class did after the exile (cf. above, pp. 56 ff.).

54. Minette de Tillesse, p. 147.

55. Cf. below, pp. 255 ff.

56. As in the case of the servant of the centurion (Matt. 8:5–13); the latter, too, was a pagan.

57. Cf. Taylor, pp. 360–61.

58. In the ANAL code with its constant structure of references to the ACT narrative it is always a question of reading the *manifest text* of the narrative and interpreting it as messianic, and not of looking for some sort of spiritual-signified-hidden-behind-the-material-signifier or the "spirit" hidden behind the "letter," as in traditional theology with its dependence on Greek philosophy. H. de Lubac's defense of the "spiritual sense" in his *The Sources of Revelation,* trans. L. O'Neill (New York, 1968) is unequivocal. Cf. "This spiritualization is simultaneously an interiorization: in saying 'spiritual,' we are also saying 'interior' " (p. 17). "Finally—and here again we have an important point—the spiritual meaning . . . is the meaning which, objectively, leads us to the realities of the spiritual life. . . . The Christian mystery finds its own fullness in being fulfilled within souls" (pp. 20–21). In speaking of the Old Testament, de Lubac urges us "to abandon the seemingly carnal meaning of certain prophecies" (p. 20)—that is, what I called earlier the "earthly viewpoint" of the prophets who are always concerned with material blessings on earth (cf. above, pp. 70 ff.)—but in fact he systematically ignores the "literal [or, rather, textual] sense" of the New Testament. Like the Pharisees, he is unable to read the ACT narrative. The Gospel becomes for him immediately spiritual ("by spiritualizing through an analogous process all the visible data of the work of the Saviour and of his establishment of salvation": p. 41). "Christian tradition recognizes two meanings of Scripture. The most general terminology for them is the 'literal meaning' and the 'spiritual meaning.' These two meanings are related to each other the way the Old and New Testaments are related" (p. 85). In short: installed as he is in the "theological discourse" as we shall define it later on, de Lubac completely ignores "the messianic narrative," for in his eyes everything begins with "the act in which he [Christ] fulfills his mission," that is, "the act of sacrifice, at the hour of his death on the Cross" (p. 109).

59. Cf. below, pp. 235 ff.

60. Cf. Matt. 16:12: "Then they understood that he was telling them to be on their guard, not against the yeast for making bread but against the *teaching* of the Pharisees." Cf. also M. E. Boismard, *Synopse des quatre évangiles en francais* (Paris, 1965), 2:241, regarding the play on words in Aramaic that allows the passage from "leaven" to "word, teaching."

61. Bourgeois exegetes, preoccupied as they are with the history of forms and redaction history, systematically fail to read this sequence, which is such a decisive one. Either the business of the leaven is taken, without qualification, "as a sign to the disciples of the coming of the Kingdom" (Taylor, p. 363), or the commentator finds that "its interpretation offers no difficulty" (Boismard, 2:240), because the clarity of the incident conceals the exegete's inability to read it, or the exegete is interested only in Mark's readers (Minette de Tillesse, pp. 412–13), or, finally (and this is the usual approach), the sequences concerning the loaves refer only to the Eucharist!

62. Cf. above, p. 91.

63. Matt. 16:17–19 brings this out very clearly.

64. Cf. above, p. 98.

65. Cf. above, pp. 74f.

66. Cf. above, pp. 103, 126 f.

67. For example, Cullmann, *Jesus and the Revolutionaries,* where on p. 12 he unwittingly shows the contradiction in his thesis. In addition, his reading of S 42, which he has long espoused (pp. 38–40 refer back to his *Christology of the New Testament),* seems to me to be an obvious forcing of the Markan text, for it is dominated by this opposition of political/spiritual. It is this that explains his distrust of the "title" of Messiah (in his *Christology of the New Testament,* p. 113, he speaks of Jesus' "reserve" toward it).

68. Cf. above, p. 148.

69. This was the subject of Minette de Tillesse's *Le secret messianique,* where the reader will find a survey of the question from Wrede (1901) to 1968.

70. "Messiah" = "the anointed one"; in the Davidic tradition, this personage is the king of Israel (cf. above, p. 84).

70a. Cf. Minette de Tillesse, p. 308.

71. This is Minette de Tillesse's thesis: "In Mark the messianic secret expresses the irrevocable free decision of Jesus to embrace his passion because that is God's will for him" (p. 321). This redaction-history method makes him fail to see that the narrative in the Markan text is continually saying the exact opposite of this!

72. Cf. L. Althusser and E. Balibar, *Reading Capital,* trans. Ben Brewster (New York, 1970), p. 28.

73. Cf. below, pp. 162 f.

74. Cf. above, p. 152.

75. Cf. below, p. 234.

76. Cf. above, p. 82.

77. Cf. above, p. 147.

78. Cf. Cullmann, *Jesus and the Revolutionaries*, p. 39.

79. Cf. E. Benveniste, *Problems in General Linguistics*, trans. M. E. Meek (Coral Gables, Fla., 1971), pp. 217–22.

80. This division of types of Son of Man is found in Bultmann, who, according to Minette de Tillesse (pp. 364–66), points out that the "passages referring to the eschatological Son of Man" do not speak of a "return" or identify Jesus with the Son of

Man, and that the "passages on the paschal Son of Man" are perhaps due to "Mark" himself.

81. Cf. Minette de Tillesse, p. 381.

82. Boismard, 2:405, also reads "ascent" in Dan. 7:13.

83. On Enoch and Elijah, cf. above, p. 77.

84. As illustrated by Acts 1:11: "Jesus who has been taken up from you into heaven, this same Jesus will *come back in the same way* as you have seen him *go there.*"

85. The so-called canonical ending on Mark (cf. below, pp. 233 ff.) will be closed by an "ascent" of J to heaven (Mark 16:19).

86. This is another reason for the introduction of actant C in S 42c.

87. Cf. below, p. 237.

88. Cf. X. Léon-Dufour, *Etudes d'évangile* (Paris, 1965), p. 102.

89. Cf. above, p. 76.

90. Cf. above, p. 74.

91. Cf. below, pp. 277 ff.

92. Cf. below, pp. 289 ff.

93. Cf. above, p. 74.

94. The scribes disappear from the scene after this; we might even say that the text brings them in here only to concretize the "unbelieving generation."

95. Cf. below, pp. 288 f.

96. Cf. A. Chappelle et al., *L'Evangile de saint Marc* (mimeographed text from the July 1959, meeting of the I. E. Th. at Eegenhoven-Louvain), p. 130: the same Aramaic word *talya* is used for both "servant" and "child," thus permitting the articulation of the saying about the servant with the scene involving a child.

97. "To Christ," the Romans would say; cf. Tacitus, *Annals* XV, 44, cited in Ch. Lepelley, *L'empire romain et le christianisme* (Paris, 1969), pp. 89 ff.

98. Cf. below, pp. 221 f.: the problem of the *lapsi* (the "fallen") in the *ekklesiai* of Rome, and the opposition say/do (Peter/Judas). "*Cause* to fall" = betray, denounce a "brother."

99. Cf. above, pp. 127 f.

100. Cf. above, p. 74.

101. Cf. above, pp. 120 f.

102. Cf. above, p. 45 and fn. 34.

103. Cf. de Vaux, p. 39.

104. Ibid., p. 25.

105. Ibid., pp. 35, 40.

106. M. Douglas, who is an ethnologist, writes: "The cases we have considered may throw some light on the exaggerated importance attached to virginity in the early centuries of Christianity. The primitive church of the Acts in its treatment of women was setting a standard of freedom and equality which was against traditional Jewish custom. The barrier of sex in the Middle East at that time was a barrier of oppression, as St. Paul's words imply [Gal 3:28]" (p. 157). After quoting St. Paul, Douglas continues: "in its [Christianity's] effort to create a new society which would be free, unbounded and without coercion or contradiction, it was no doubt necessary to establish a set of positive values. The idea that virginity had a special positive value was bound to fall on good soil in a persecuted minority group. . . . Further, the idea of the high value of virginity would be well-chosen for the project of changing the role of the sexes in marriage and in society at large (Wangermann)" (p. 158).

107. Cf. below, p. 336, fn. 51.

108. Cf. Bratcher and Nida, p. 314, who cite Lagrange. At twelve a girl could marry (cf. S 25). Since "children" here are set over against "adults," we must enlarge the scope of the term to include our "young people."

109. Cf. above, n. 96 for this chapter.

110. As Matt. 23:8–9 says: "You must call no one on earth your father, since you have only one Father, and he is in heaven." Similarly, no one is to be called "Master" or "teacher," because "you are all brothers." In ecclesial life the very imago of the father should be eradicated. In fact, however, the ecclesiastical apparatus has multiplied "fathers" and "teachers" (the magisterium) and has given them the dominant fuction of producing the ideology!

111. It is quite an experience to read the commentary on this sequence in A. Chapelle et al., *L'évangile de Marc,* mimeographed, study session, July 1969 (Eegenhoven-Louvain, 1969). It provides an extreme example of the deformations that the bourgeois ideology in exegesis inflicts on the text by its distinction, so dear to form history and redaction history, between what comes from Jesus (history) and what is the work of the redactors (Luke, Mark).

Here are a few of the more delectable passages. "Let us conclude this discussion: the abandonment of wealth seems to have been required by Jesus only as a means of following him. What the rich man lacks is not the abandonment of wealth but the following of Jesus. The abandonment of wealth, even the giving of it to the poor, matters little" (p. 148). "We must still explain the sadness and departure of the rich man. . . . The departure is usually interpreted as a refusal to follow Jesus. But is this clear from the text? Perhaps he is only obeying the call. After all, Jesus told him, 'Go' " (p. 149). In other words, even the *following* of Jesus is not really *lacking* in him, since he obeys!

The exegesis proceeds as follows. We have a "primitive saying on the difficulty of entering the kingdom of God; this saying makes no mention of wealth" (p. 150). "Mark uses it in a difficult context by introducing the danger of wealth. But wealth is just a specific case" (p. 151). "Because of this, interpreters have *reduced* the original meaning of the text" (p. 152; italics added). As a matter of fact, the flag has already been hoisted: "The sayings on the danger of wealth (Matt. 6:19–24) do not lead to the requirement that wealth be abandoned; that would be a form of legalism and contrary to the *interiorization* that Jesus preaches" (p. 148; italics added). The conclusion: "We can give an answer here to a question that has arisen several times: in the last analysis is the text as a whole really speaking of material possessions? It does not seem so. If we may characterize the pericope as showing the passage from 'having' to 'receiving,' then wealth is simply the material image best adapted to expressing a teaching on a *spiritual attitude* that relates in fact to the whole of human life. In my view, it relates in particular to humanity's *relations with others*" (p. 154; italics added). Here we have the recent form taken by the bourgeois religious ideology, one in which there is a shuttling back and forth between interiority and relations with others. On the next page, "persecutions" are read as "all the worries of family life."

If we take into account the fact that this text was not written by elderly parish priests who had been formed in a prewar theology but by a team of young exegetes who even regard themselves as leaning somewhat to structuralism, the present note becomes all the more interesting. A sequence like S 49 proves to be a good test in reading the narrative of Mark, since what we have in this sequence is a confrontation between the practice of J and his disciples, on the one hand, and the practice of those who belong to the system, on the other. The text calls attention to the ANAL code by means of the emphases we have pointed out, and it multiplies terms that have to do with the economic instance: sell, have (four times), give, poor, treasure, great possessions, riches, rich man. The ANAL code distributes the schemes for reading according to the space in which the readers are situated, as we have seen. The distinctions *interiorization/legalism* and, therefore, interior/exterior and spiritual/material operate in this Jesuit's discourse. In what social site were they produced if not that of the dominant ideology of capitalism?

112. Cf. below, p. 275.

113. " 'To sit' suggests jurisdictional power" (Boismard, 2:316). On the next page, Boismard remarks that "in Dan. 7:13 ff. the Son of Man receives from God power and domination over the nations." As Mark uses the phrase, then, "Son of man" has undergone a partial semantic transformation, in which any overtones borrowed from the Zealotism of James and John has been excluded.

114. The church as "hierarchy," with the "princes of the church" holding the first places. . . .

115. Cf. Cullmann, *Jesus and the Revolutionaries*, p. 43, although his reading of the text differs from mine.

116. W. Vischer, *Die evangelische Gemeinde-Ordnung—Matth 16, 13–20, 28* (Zurich, 1946).

117. G. Crespy, "Recherche sur la signification politique de la mort de Jésus," *Lumière et vie*, no. 101 (January–March 1971), p. 101.

118. Cf. 2 Kings 9:13.

119. Cf. below, pp. 234 f.

120. Cf. above, pp. 81 f., 151–57.

121. Cf. above, pp. 78 ff.

122. Cf. Jer. 8:13.

123. Ibid., p. 55.

124. Cf. above, p. 63.

125. Cf. J. D. Kaestli, *L'eschatologie dans l'oeuvre de Luc* (Geneva, 1969), p. 55, fn. 23: "Cf. the barren fig tree, an image of God's judgment and the desolation of the land in Hos. 2:12; Jl. 1:12; Hag. 3:17; Jer. 8:13; Isa. 34:4. On the other hand, the greening fig tree is the symbol of a new blessing in Jl. 2:22." Cf. also above, p. 124 and fn. 27.

126. Cf. above, pp. 221 f.

127. Cf. Rev. 21:1: when the eschatological time comes, "there was no longer any sea," for Satan will have been conquered for good.

128. Cf. this chapter, fn. 27.

129. Cf. above, p. 311, fn. 5.

130. Cf. below, pp. 208 f.

131. Cf. Matt. 23:29–32.

132. We described the subasiatic Palestinian mode of production as opposing Pharisees/Sadducees at the level of the ideological class struggle, with the Sadducees being connected with the high priests and elders and their scribes. The text, however, turns these ideologically opposed classes into "collaborators," with J as their "common enemy." J's STR threatens all the classes that possess power (SOC). In relation to the C, the Pharisees and their scribes are in a dominant ideological position as compared with the Sadducees. The latter maintain their position only because of the economic-political-ideological role of the temple and their own alliance with the Romans. After 70, when the temple has disappeared, the Pharisaic scribes will gain the upper hand in Judaism.

133. Cf. Luke 23:2.

134. This is also how the exegetes read the text: "Jesus answers with a commonsense observation" (Boismard, 2:345–46). Common sense (that of the ruling classes) is as clear an ideological index as one could want.

135. Cf. above, pp. 45 f.

136. "Materialist" in the sense the word currently has as applied to those who do not believe in an afterlife. The quotation marks are ironical.

137. Cf. above, pp. 72 ff.

138. In this reading I take no sides regarding the statements of the actant J; I shall return to the question at another level of my discourse. Here I am attempting only to restore a reading that has been deformed by the current theological ideology.

139. "Dead" has the same meaning in Luke 9:60: "Leave the *dead* to bury their dead."

140. Cf. above, pp. 55–58.

141. Current exegesis stops here and endeavors to discern the relations between this "pericope" and the Christian communities and their liturgy; it ends by asserting the continuity between the two liturgies. But, if we relate the statement in question to the entire text of Mark by means of its codes, we read a break, not a continuity.

142. Cf. Matt. 6:24; Luke 16:13: "You cannot be the slave both of God and of money."

143. Cf. above, p. 84.

144. This is why Matt. 2:1 ff. and Luke 2:4, in an apparent divergence from Mark, have Jesus being born at Bethlehem of Judah.

145. Cf. above, pp. 157 f. and below, pp. 224 f.

146. In Matt. 23 a sense of great power as well as hot anger mark the teaching and the meeting. Read the discourse in Matthew aloud as if you were an actor, and you will end up red-faced and full of violent feeling. Matthew is showing us a real protest meeting. Let no one try to tell us that Jesus was meek and nonviolent or that he was ignorant of the class struggle!

147. Cf. below, pp. 209 ff.

148. L. Marin, *Semiotique de la passion: Topiques et figures* (Paris, 1971), p. 57.

148a. J. Lamprecht, "La structure de Marc XIII," in *De Jésus aux évangiles: Tradition et rédaction dans les évangiles synoptiques* (Gembloux, 1967). Our reading will be very different from the one he proposes; for example, Lamprecht ignores the words "Let the reader understand!" (b4), which will be one of the focal points in our reading.

149. Cf. above, pp. 71 ff.

150. Cf. below, p. 259.

151. Cf. above, p. 78.

152. Luke 21:24, which is not written according to these codes, relativizes the disaster: "Great misery will descend on the land and wrath on this people."

153. Cf. above, p. 78.

154. As does Matthew. Luke, for his part, breaks the link between the two codes. He is a pagan by origin and lives in the third generation of Christians, some thirty years after the destruction of the temple; for him, therefore, the final narrative is no longer linked to this destruction.

155. Cf. above, pp. 100 f.

156. Cf. above, p. 325, fn. 125.

157. Cf. the MYTH/ACT contradiction, which we identified above (p. 103) and will point out again below (pp. 284 ff.).

158. Cf. Kaestli, p. 107: "The prologue [of Luke's Gospel] shows that Luke is living

in the third generation . . . and we think it preferable to follow H. Conzelmann who dates Luke's works around the year 100."

159. According to the commonly accepted chronology, which places the murder of Jesus in 30 A.D. (cf. *The Jerusalem Bible*, p. 467).

160. Unfortunately, this is what happened when the *ekklesiai* were replaced by the church; the structures of the slave-based mode of production proved to be more effective than any watchfulness.

161. Cf. above, p. 176.

162. Cf. below, p. 331, fn. 5.

163. The Zealots, bent on reform, did not want to change the codes of the SOC but only the "persons" who performed its functions (cf. above, pp. 84 f.).

164. Everyone knows the ideological use people have made of this statement of J, as they "forget" to read what it implies about the structural relation Christians/the poor. They read it as though it "foretold" (theologically) the impossibility of eliminating poverty or, in other words, the eternity of the class system!

165. This hypothesis has been proposed by L. Marin, "The Women at the Tomb: A Structural Analysis Essay of a Gospel Text," in A. M. Johnson, Jr., ed. and tr., *The New Testament and Structuralism* (Pittsburgh, 1976), pp. 93–94.

166. Cf. below, pp. 275 and 277 f.

167. John 12:6 will say that Judas held the money of the group and that he misused it, keeping it from the poor for whom it was meant.

168. As L. Marin indicates in his *Sémiotique de la passion,* p. 146. Marin's analyses are perhaps very fine from a semiotic viewpoint, but when he describes money as "utterly neutral" (p. 156), we are justified in asking whether the capitalist ideology is not betraying its presence here.

169. Cf. above, pp. 158 and 177.

170. Marin, pp. 488 ff. One of the criticisms to be made of his text has to do with his choice of a corpus. (a) When the four accounts of the "passion" are treated as "variants" of a single narrative, the textual *differences,* which are in fact textual *transformations,* disappear from view in a "synoptic vision of the variants." By consciously (p. 235, fn. 150, and also p. 231, fn. 111) ignoring the *two* materialist contributions made by modern exegesis of the Gospels (cf. my remarks above, p. 96), Marin falls into the old trap of "synopticity" into which prescientific exegesis fell. (b) The narrative text which precedes the "passion narrative" and which, as we are in the process of showing here, dominates the reading of the latter—this text and its production in the braid of its codes are cut off from the corpus. How could the reading of it fail to reflect this fact? It will then be necessary to introduce some "pretext" as a reading grill, and this text will be that of the theological ideology that has always dominated exegesis. We shall return to this point.

171. Cf. below, pp. 220 f. and 235 f.

172. This scene, insofar as it relates to Judas, resisted my reading until I found "the secondary working hypothesis" that L. Marin proposes: "There must be a traitor in order that what is, in fact, necessary may be rendered fortuitous and aleatory" (p. 105). Yet how astonishing to read on the next page: "One of the problems raised by the Gospel narratives is this: how can God be made to die? Yet God must die in order that humanity may live. . . . God cannot die; therefore someone must permit this death, make it possible without contradicting or compromising the will or being of God" (p. 106). What contemporary exegete will not be startled to read this? A fourth-century theology is being called on to rescue this brilliant exercise in semiotics!

"It is likewise true that the instrument of the 'solution' will be a mediator and, as such, possessed of two natures: Jesus, who is both man and God" (p. 108). When we read this sort of thing, how can we fail to suspect the entire reading model (which depends on Greimas) that is being used and that, from the Introduction of the book on, is called a reading "of mediation"? "A single problem links the two essays of this book, but it is raised at different levels and at different points in the text. The problem is that of the place, function, and nature of mediation in narrative logic" (p. 9). What complicity may we not expect to find between this model and the most idealist of theologies, between structural mediation and the mediator who is both man and God? Can we not already foresee a whole structural-clerical technocracy hurrying in the wake of this semiotic that is so seductive in appearance? Can we not foresee a new imprisonment of the Gospel in a hermetic discourse proper to a superacademic?

173. Cf. below, pp. 220 ff.

174. For example, when A. Feuillet, *Le discours sur le pain de vie* (new ed.; Paris, 1967), proposes to establish "the connection between the Christ of the synoptics and the Christ of the fourth Gospel," he does not blush to write: "The discourse on the bread of life is filled from one end to the other with the idea that people have another hunger besides material hunger, deplorable though the latter may be [sic!], and that they must look to be filled in a more than physical way" (p. 8). The real question is whether the reading of John's text as a "transformation" of the synoptic texts (and not the other way around) would not make the "second" filling dependent on the "first" and relate the "spiritual" to the "material" so that they become one in the "command-ment of mutual love" of which Feuillet speaks on p. 124.

175. Cf. above, p. 206. This metonymy is expressed with all desirable clarity in Matt. 25:40! "I tell you solemnly, in so far as you did this to one of the least of these brothers of mine, you did it to *me*"; here we have a "eucharistic" discourse if ever there was one.

176. J. Lacan, *Ecrits* (Paris, 1966), p. 259. My reading inverts Lacan's. In the latter, the body of the subject is an archive for the narrative of a lost childhood, for a text that has been suppressed. In my reading, the text-narrative itself is the archive, partially erased, of the body of Jesus, since the Gospel is nothing but the narrative of the practice of the body of J.

176a. Cf. Boismard, 2:390.

177. Cf. above, pp. 101 f.

178. Luke makes this explicit. Luke 22:35–36 contrasts the sending "without purse or haversack" with the need "now" of taking purse and haversack and even of selling a cloak (which stands by metonymy for the body) in order to buy a sword. "Lord, there are two swords here now": "That is enough." After the sequence of the temptation (Luke 22:39–46), which is parallel to this one in Mark, J replies to the disciple who uses the sword: "Leave off, that will do" (Luke 22:49–51). It is, then, the temptation of armed resistance that J has himself overcome. Matt. 26:52 makes the lesson explicit: "All who draw the sword will perish by the sword," for J came not to kill but to save. Bourgeois exegetes, however, are unable to read that J could have been tempted at this level, since their religious ideology immediately puts them at the level of the "superhuman," etc. Boismard, for example, comments on Lk. 22:36: "The mention of the 'sword' to be bought should probably be taken in the metaphorical sense: the courage to enter the struggle against the forces of evil" (2:388). The result is that the Gethsemani sequence, in which J is regarded as "willing his death," is turned into metaphysical theater.

However, John 18:2–19 suggests another possible reading of the erased prepaschal text. In John, as in the three synoptics, the guards who come to arrest J do not know him; but while the other three narratives introduce the kiss of Judas as the sign identifying J, John presents the identification of J by the guards as the result of a dialogue between J and them: "Who are you looking for?/Jesus the Nazarene./I am he." This dialogue, which is emphasized by its repetition, is prolonged by the words: "If I am the one you are looking for, let these others go." The theological discourse, already signaled in verse 4 ("knowing everything that was going to happen to him"), now adds: "This was to fulfill the words he had spoken, 'Not one of those you gave me I have lost.' " In other words, according to John, J lets himself be arrested in order to prevent his disciples from being arrested and killed, as he himself was to be, in a very one-sided struggle, and in order also to permit the work of the BAS circle to continue after his supposed death. In this view, the refusal of armed conflict leads to a kind of negotiation between J and the guards, enabling him to save the lives of the disciples. This would supposedly clarify the meaning of the words at the Supper in John 17:12 ("I have watched over them"—referring to the scene of the temptation in Gethsemani, which John omits—"and not one is lost"), as well as these other words: "This is my commandment: love one another *as I have loved you*. A man can have no greater love than to *lay down his life for his friends*" (John 15:12–13). In handing himself over to arrest and death, J *saves* the life of his friends in a *political* sense that the theology of *salvation* will cause to be forgotten.

179. In this restoration to J of the faith and hope that dogmatics has taken from him by making him the master of all knowledge, we should consult Heb. 5:7–8 and especially Heb. 11:1–12:4, which outlines a theory of hope as wager (STR).

180. Bratcher and Nida, p. 458. The meaning of the word "rebel" is perhaps better brought out today by translating it as "terrorist"; it is evidently the Zealots who are concretely meant here (cf. above, p. 314, fn. 54).

181. This is strongly emphasized in John 18:16: "When Jesus said, 'I am he,' they moved back and fell to the ground."

182. Cf. below, pp. 234 f. and 275.

183. In fact, the chief priests are situated at the three levels.

184. Cf. the diagram below on p. 234.

185. Marin, pp. 164 ff.; Marin's analysis based on Matthew is valid for Mark as well.

186. Ibid., p. 165.

187. Ibid., p. 164.

188. As Minette de Tillesse does, pp. 438 ff., but only for Peter.

189. Cf. Minette de Tillesse, p. 442.

190. Need we point out that this problematic arises today in relation to those who are committed to a political struggle and who, after being arrested and even tortured, have given in and informed on their comrades? And that the criterion say/do can still be valid?

190a. Cf. Boismard, 2:417. For "insurrection," cf. Cullmann, *Jesus and the Revolutionaries*, p. 33.

191. We can only be astounded at the reading given by C. Chabrol, "An Analysis of the 'Text' of the Passion," in *The New Testament and Structuralism* (cf. fn. 165 of this chapter), pp. 145–86. According to Chabrol, Pilate "is not a true representative of Rome," and the sequence represents "the passage to universalism" (p. 183), the universalism, that is, of Roman imperialism! In Marin (p. 61), Pilate becomes, like money, a "neutral term"; in addition, "Pilate = universality" (cf. also p. 74). In this kind of discourse, with its profusion of models, ideology is indeed at work, as can be

seen from the distinction between "religious sphere" and "temporal sphere" (p. 83; cf. pp. 60, 73, etc.), which makes it possible to justify "the religious institution (the clergy)" on the basis of these scriptural texts (p. 81, fn. 8) or even to deduce "the new religious system, as yet 'unnamed,' in which social ritual 'purity' might be replaced by an individual, and no longer social, 'goodness' (?) or 'charity' (?) that would put humanity first of all in a direct relationship with the divinity" (p. 91). The question marks are not placed where they should be, namely, after the individual/social opposition and after the idea of "putting humanity *first of all in a direct relationship* with the divinity." In short, the question to be asked of the Marins and the Chabrols is: what is the ideology of which your models are the carriers?

192. Luke 23:2 makes this explicit: "We found this man inciting our people to revolt, opposing payment of the tribute to Caesar, and claiming to be *Christ, a king.*"

193. John 18:33–38, on the other hand, does find a way of presenting the J/Z distinction to Pilate. It does so by means of the contrast "kingdom of this world/ kingdom not of this world," which has always been travestied by the bourgeois ideology. Admittedly, we would have to read the entire text of John for a full understanding. Let us posit, nonetheless, that "kingdom of this world" refers to the SOC and its codes (therefore a kingdom based on money, the force of arms, and the god of dead men) and that "kingdom not of this world" refers to the BAS and its inversion of the SOC codes. In my view, this means that the statement, "my men would have fought" (John 18:36), is to be read according to the logic of a *subasiatic social formation,* in which the force of arms used by the state determines the class social formation (cf. above, pp. 28 f.). Bourgeois exegetes never fail to read the opposition of the kingdoms in terms of their own ideology (e.g., Cullmann, *Jesus and the Revolutionaries,* p. 46). This ideology, being that of the ruling class, is very much of "this world." The Catalan singer Raimon has read correctly, and I cannot resist quoting him: "We have seen the blood/that creates naught but blood/become the law of the world/we have seen hunger/become the workers' bread;/we have seen imprisoned/men who were right./No!/I say No!/Let us all say No!/*We* are not of this world!"

194. Boismard, 2:417, does not go so far, for how could he connect Jesus with an insurrection? If we must offer a "hypothesis," as he says, it is that various *sicarii,* in keeping with their usual practice, profited by the movement J had roused ("The *Sicarii,* the Daggermen, who in the anonymity of crowds strike down the more important Jewish collaborators with the occupying forces": P. Prigent, p. 13). Nonetheless, Jesus was indeed the principal one "responsible" for this quasi-spontaneous insurrection.

195. Matt. 27:24–25 emphasizes this point with his scene of the "washing of hands" and the subsequent outcry of the C: "His blood be on us and on our children!" Marin, p. 54, has seen clearly that there is in Matthew (and in Mark as well, we may add) a "double condemnation to death: a condemnation of Jesus but also a condemnation of the Jewish people"; the second of these was read after 70, at the narrator/readers level.

196. Cf. below, pp. 254 f.

197. Apropos of the "universality" of the structures cited in the preceding pages: it is as if in a French narrative of the resistance to German occupation at a time when the Nazis controlled a large part of Europe, one were to oppose France/Germany as particular/universal!

198. The scene shows people being unleashed who have been subject to a constricting military discipline, and who now take advantage of a conquered adversary who

might have forced them to fight and possibly even be killed. This sort of thing often shows in the ferocity lower-rank police officials demonstrate when dealing with political prisoners.

199. John would have said "the kings of this world."

200. Cf. above, p. 45.

201. We shall speak again of the importance of this distinction. For the moment, let us observe that while theology has taken this "death" as the privileged object of its discourse, it has almost never asked itself the *reasons* why J was killed. On the other hand, it is noteworthy that in a number of "political" exegeses, from Reimarus to Brandon (discussed in M. Hengel, *Jésus et la violence révolutionnaire* [Paris, 1973], pp. 13–20), this question of the *why* is central.

202. According to the belief of the Zealots: "when reduced to the final extremity, [The Zealots besieged in the Temple by the Romans] awaited with faith the miraculous intervention of the God in whose behalf they were fighting" (Prigent, p. 41). Cullmann is therefore on the wrong track when he contrasts J and the Z in terms of eschatology. He is forced to acknowledge this despite himself, and he gets himself out of his difficulty by a bourgeois reading of "kingdom of this world/kingdom not of this world" (*Jesus and the Revolutionaries*, pp. 12–13 and fn. 18).

203. This second cry is thus the *excess* of life when it expires and meets at last the death that was already at work at the heart of life, as Bataille has shown. May I say that I understood the element of the excessive, the inexhaustible, in this sober narrative, when I read the pages in G. Bataille, *Eroticism,* trans. M. Dalwood (London, 1962) on the cries a woman utters in her orgasm (Part I, chap. 9: "Sexual plethora and death," pp. 94–108)?

204. There is no question here of an "angel," as there is in the parallel passages of Matt. and John. Only the "whiteness," an echo of S 43, connotes the MYTH.

205. This is the reading of W. Marxen, *Der Evangelist Markus: Studien zur Redaktionsgeschichte des Evangeliums*, cited by E. Trocmé, *The Formation of the Gospel According to Mark,* trans. P. Gaughan (Philadelphia, 1975), p. 112 and p. 186, nn. 42–43. Kaestli, p. 52, likewise remarks that "the idea of a gathering of the elect at a particular spot is peculiar to Mark and is omitted by Luke who regards the Parousia as something universal that takes place everywhere simultaneously and cannot be represented in spatial categories."

PART III, CHAPTER 3

1. A. Robert and A. Feuillet, eds., *Introduction to the New Testament,* trans. P. Skehan et al. (New York, 1965), pp. 219–20.

1a. W. G. Kümmel, *Introduction to the New Testament,* rev. ed., trans. H. C. Lee (Nashville, 1975), p. 100.

2. Cf. above, pp. 101 f.

3. This narrative of the circulation of the good news is partially told in the book of the "Acts of the Apostles." The latter breaks off precisely at Rome, some ten years before the writing of Mark.

4. These writings cultivate a deliberate obscurity in order to safeguard clandestinity.

5. Let us reread them. S 20d and S 39c have to do with the judgment upon Israel as seen in, respectively, J's answer to the accusation that he is "possessed" and in his refusal to give a sign to this generation of inept semiologists. S 46d, S 48b, and S 49d

relate to ecclesial practice and to the conditions under which this practice will issue in the eschatological narrative (question of the *lapsi*; acceptance in the manner of children-youth; break with wealth). S 57c and S 60c give a reading of the practices of the two women as lessons in ecclesial economics. Using eschatological imagery, S 54e refers to the destruction of the temple and takes up the question of ecclesial prayer; S 42e and S 58b6 take up the "when" of eschatology: during this generation; S 62b and S 63b enable us to distinguish among the practices of betrayal by the *lapsi*; finally, S 62c posits a postexodic fast of J which, as I have said, I find difficult to read.

6. My reading is thus very different from that proposed by E. Trocmé, although this latter is not lacking in interest. We may sum up his theses on the formation of Mark as follows: (a) Mark 1–13 (S 1–S 58) were written in Palestine around the fifties by a Jewish Christian who spoke Greek, a man of strong anti-Jerusalem and pro-Galilee tendencies; he used two different types of sources, one giving the official ecclesiastical tradition, the other giving popular Galilean narratives; (b) Mark 14–16 (S 59–S 73) were rewritten at Rome after the martyrdom of Peter, on the basis of a document that had originated in the church of Jerusalem; (c) the whole was put together at Rome around 80, which accounts for the explanatory additions (introduced by *ho estin,* which is a Latinism: "that is to say") for the sake of Roman readers (E. Trocmé, *The Formation of the Gospel According to Mark,* trans. P. Gaughan [Philadelphia, 1975], p. 244).

The interest of this thesis, which is not to be rejected *a priori,* resides especially in its confirmation of the "historical" character of the Palestinian codes that are at work in Mark. But my reading supposes that the Markan text is highly structured at the level of its codes and that much more, therefore, must be attributed to the work of the redactor (who is to be located immediately after 70), than Trocmé allows (pp. 244–46). The redactor's work has produced a text that is *unified,* as F. Neirynck, *Duality in Mark: Contributions to the Study of the Markan Redaction* (Louvain, 1972) seems to show conclusively, inasmuch as the thirty kinds of "duality" that Neirynck lists (pp. 75–136) do not seem compatible with a crude division between Mark 1–13 and Mark 14–16, but rather suppose a complete revision of the sources by "Mark."

Once all this has been said, it is self-evident that my reading resists that of Trocmé in many areas: the question of messiahship, the question of the pagans, the question of S 58 (Mark 13, where Trocmé's reading could not be more divergent from mine), etc. We must also add that a debate with this author on details is impossible because he is so much the history-of-forms exegete for whom practically *everything* is to be explained on the narrator/readers level. The narrative itself ends up being completely ignored, and Mark 1–13 becomes a "little ecclesiological treatise" (p. 237)! (Cf. pp. 188–214, where Trocmé gives the main points of his reading of this section.)

The opinion of a theologian friend of mine who consented to read my text gives the tone of the major objection to be raised by exegetes formed under the sway of *Formgeschichte* which has dominated exegesis for the last fifty years: I have written a new "life of Jesus"! Therefore, I shall attempt once again to state exactly what I am doing. My starting point is a new *theory of the text,* which is inevitably a direct challenge to the sway of *Formgeschichte.* The point is not to deny the latter its merits (cf. above, p. 96). It is rather, on the one hand, to unmask the theological ideology which is at work in it (Trocmé, p. 154, fn. 3: "the words *dunamis* . . . and *sōzein.* . . are quite often used in connection with healings, whereas elsewhere in Mark they have a more *religious* sense; it would be impossible to emphasize better *the metaphysical significance* of these acts of Jesus, even though they are concerned with the healing of the body"; italics added) and, on the other, to bring out the aspect of *verisimilitude* and representationality that mark the narratives belonging to the ideologem of the symbol and the sign (cf. above, pp. 89 f.), without therefore falling back into the problematic of the "biography of Jesus" or the "historicity of the signified," as in the older exegesis. In short, my aim is to emphasize the concept of *narrative*. The question thus raised for exegesis by a political reading of Mark implies a revision of the philosophical foundations and the conclusions of exegesis. Has not the history of exegesis from Strauss to Bultmann been marked by shattering breaks in methodology whenever a new (philosophical or semiotic) theory asserts itself?

7. E. Floris, "L'apparition du ressuscité aux apôtres: Etude herméneutique sur Luc 24/36–49," *La Lettre*, nos. 163–64: "Dossier sur la résurrection" (March–April 1972), pp. 17–23.

8. Ibid., pp. 18–19. Floris cites either Old Testament narratives (Gen. 16:7–15; 21:17–20; 18:1–8; Josh. 5:13–15; Judg. 6:11–24; 13:9–20; Dan. 8:15; 9:21–27; Tob. 5:1–8; 18:16–21) or "secular" narratives (*Iliad* 2:22; 2:172; 4:92; 5:800; 2:795; 11:200; 3:130; 3:390; etc.; *Odyssey* 1:105–10 [?]; 2:267–98; 393; 3:371; *Aeneid* 1:314; 2:589; 4:259–80, 554–70; 9:1–15; etc.).

9. Ibid., p. 19–20. He cites Gen. 38; 29:1–14; 45; Tob. 7:1–6; etc., and also *Odyssey* 10:390; 19:39; 21:190; 8:490; 23; 24:320–50; 4:140–50; *Electra* 1090-1230; *Choephorai* 215-22; *Ion* 1370-1445, and Aristotle's theory of these in *Poetics* 11:1–9; 16.

10. Ibid., p. 20.

11. Ibid., p. 19. Floris concludes that in these narratives we are dealing with a "symbolic language proper to epic" (note that epic, according to Kristeva, belongs to the ideologem of symbol; cf. above, pp. 89 f.) and that "the only event [in these narratives] is the experience of the power of the name of Jesus" (p. 21). With such a conclusion Floris slips back into the problem of historicity from which he had previously extricated himself. He also cites with pride his bourgeois ideological "ancestry": Strauss, Feuerbach, Goguel, Bultmann, Ricoeur, and especially J. B. Vico (p. 23).

12. Trocmé concludes that "the church tradition contained no accounts of appearances of the risen Christ" (p. 66).

13. Cf. above, p. 96.

14. We think that the reading proposed here could enable us to restate, in a new textual perspective, the arguments in support of the "two-source" theory, especially at the point where it must account for the convergences of Matt. and Luke against Mark.

15. Cf. M. E. Boismard, *Synopse, des quatre évangiles en français* (Paris, 1965), 1:114.

16. Cf., e.g., the paragraph "In particular" in G. Minette de Tillesse, *Le secret messianique dans l'évangile de Marc* (Paris, 1968) pp. 238–39. My reading is clearly opposed to that of this author. We could derive from the other three Gospels an argument against his thesis, since the theological prediction of the necessity of the death-resurrection of Jesus is much more developed in them than in Mark; at the same time, however, this development is correlative with the playing down of the "messianic secret." If, then, it is this theology that has erased the messianic narrative, it is hard to see how it could be the *goal* of the "messianic secret," as Minette de Tillesse claims.

17. An interesting line of study would be to ask how the insertion of the Q source in the texts of Matthew and Luke has assisted in the subordination of the messianic to the theological.

18. *Myth and Reality,* trans. W. R. Trask (New York, 1963), p. 19.

19. Cf. below, p. 282.

20. *The Sacred and the Profane,* chap. 2 ("Sacred Time and Myths").

PART IV

1. F. Engels, *On the History of Early Christianity* in *Karl Marx and Friedrich Engels on Religion* (New York, 1964), pp. 316–47; A. Casanova, "Le christianisme primitif," in *La naissance des dieux* (Paris, 1966).

2. Cf. below, p. 336, fn. 52, and pp. 280 ff.

3. Cf. A. Aymard and J. Auboyer, *Rome et son empire,* Histoire générale des civilisations 2, 5th ed. (Paris, 1967), pp. 494 ff.

4. L. Althusser, *For Marx,* trans. B. Brewster (London and New York, 1969), pp. 182–93.

5. What Althusser calls "Generality II" (ibid.).

6. Cf. above, pp. 60 ff.

7. Cf. above, p. 127.

8. S 10, S 18, S 26 (four times), S 34, S 37, S 41. Cf. also S 7c, S 25g, S 27b ("works of power are *done by his hands"),* S 28c.

9. Cf. below, pp. 288 ff.

10. Cf. above, p. 139.

11. Cf. above, pp. 172 f.

12. We can even see here a messianic legitimation of "expenditure," in Bataille's sense of the word, but in relation to the filling of the poor, and excluding the luxury attached to wealth.

13. Cf. above, p. 83.

14. Cf. Luke 14:15–24, and Matt. 25:31–46.

15. Cf. above, pp. 52 f.

16. 1 Cor. 13:3, however, seems to offer difficulty here.

17. Cf. above, p. 135.

18. Cf. above, p. 83.

19. Cf. above, p. 331, fn. 205, and p. 237.

20. Cf. John passim, but the term already occurs in Mark S 64.

21. Cf. above, pp. 7–14.

22. If we allow for the changed circumstances, is this not the problem of the petite bourgeoisie and even a part of the proletariat, who, because they save their money, are firmly attached to the banks, those temples of capitalism?

23. "You, however, must not allow yourselves to be called Rabbi, since you have only one Master, and you are all brothers. . . . Neither must you allow yourselves to be called teachers. . . " (Matt. 23:8–10).

24. Cf. above, pp. 93 f.

25. A term that will be justified later on.

26. Cf. above, p. 173.

27. These oppositions: God/money, God/Caesar, God of the living/god of the dead, God/temple, are not to be read as opposing one general equivalent to others (since the God of the living [i.e. human beings] to whom the narrative of J refers is the God who has no image or signifier other than humanity itself; cf. Gen. 1:26–27), but, on the contrary, as opposing the powerful *practice* of J to the general equivalents of the social formation.

28. Cf. above, p. 7.

29. Along the lines of Althusser's "Generality II."

30. It would be interesting, for example, to analyze the relations between the various narratives of revolutionary practice (the French revolution, the Commune, the Russian revolution, the Chinese proletarian cultural revolution, May 1968, etc.) and the ideological discourses (bourgeois, Soviet, etc.) that contain these narratives, and to detect the greater or lesser extent to which the element of subversion has been deleted.

31. Cf. A Rifflet-Lemaire, *Jacques Lacan* (Brussels, 1968), pp. 127ff.

32. Cf. J. Derrida, "Violence et métaphysique: Essai sur la pensée d'Emmanuel Levinas," in his *L'écriture et la différence* (Paris, 1967), p. 169. [Derrida uses *différance* as distinguished from *différence* in French. We can only use the same word in English, or coin a new one.—Trans.]

32a. [Belo writes the French word for "subject" as "(su) je (t)," thus setting off within the word the first personal pronoun *je*. Cf. above, this section, paragraph 2, where Lacan sees the "fractured subject" as "replaced by a 'proper name' and specifically by the pronoun I."—Trans.]

33. Cf. above, pp. 121 ff.

34. Here we have the site for the possibility of a certain expectancy. At the same time, the "mystery," that is, the possibility of subversion, sets limits to the expectancy. In other words, every expectancy can be disavowed by subversion, by the class struggle, by utopia. Who foresaw May 1968?

35. Cf. above, pp. 120, 124 ff.

36. Let us note that it is this indeterminateness that marks ongoing narratives even in the eyes of one whose body is being worked on by the power; it is this mystery that explains, if not the existence of the narratives themselves, then at least the sympathetic magic they exercise on their readers. Why do people read narratives? They are looking for a grill that will enable them to read, even if only through the working of an identification mechanism, their own narrative and destiny. "All human beings, some more, some less, are held in suspense by *narratives* and *novels* that reveal the many-faceted truth of life to them. Only these narratives, read at times in a state of trance, confront them with their destiny" (Bataille, in the preface to his collection of essays, *Le bleu du ciel*).

37. In the phrase "In truth I tell you," the words "in truth" translate the Aramaic *amen*.

38. The verb *exestin* is related to the noun *exousia*, "authority, power."

39. The question of whether Jesus was a Zealot has been raised by S. G. F. Brandon in his *Jesus and the Zealots*, which is cited by M. Hengel, *Jésus et la violence révolutionnaire* (Paris, 1971) p. 16, and by O. Cullmann, *Jesus and the Revolutionaries*, trans. G. Putnam (New York, 1970), p. 7 and fn. 10. The reading of Mark which I have produced dismisses the cases of both the thesis and its contradictors, since failure to define the term "revolutionary" causes the question to be wrongly formulated.

40. Cf. above, p. 28.

41. A revolution is possible only when productive forces are undergoing an intensive process of transformation; this was not the case in Palestine (cf. the citation from S. Baron above, p. 314, fn. 49).

42. Historically, this internationalist element was due to Paul, for the closure of the slave-based mode of production justified him in not attacking either the Caesarian state (Rom. 13:1–7) or even the existence of slavery (Eph. 6:5–9), even while he

exhorted all to communism: "This does not mean that to give relief to others you ought to make things difficult for yourselves; it is a question of balancing [or: of *equality*]" (2 Cor. 8:13). J's STR of passing over to the pagans, as Mark recounts it, is not "historical": a striking illustration of a method of textual analysis that scorns historicity in the historicist sense of word that is current among exegetes.

43. The question is not unrelated to the division among Christians in regard to the Israel/Palestinian problem.

44. Cf. Acts 8:1; 11:19–21.

45. Cf. Acts 13:44–52.

46. As the "theology of inspiration" claims.

47. Cf. above, pp. 51 f.

48. Let us observe in passing that the Essenes had called a halt to the principle of extension. For this reason, the thesis that Christianity is the offspring of Essenism will not hold water.

49. One aim of a communist strategy today will be to displace the proletarian utopia, at the economic level, from money as a fetish to the "bodies" of the products. This shows us the importance of the battle against pollution, in the broad sense of this term. The hippies are a good example in this area.

50. Cf. above, pp. 214 f. and pp. 328 f., fn. 178.

51. A similar process of reasoning would be applicable to questions of marriage, divorce, and sexuality generally. The closuring effect of the subasiatic mode of production is the same in the discussion regarding divorce in S 47 as in the other New Testament texts on woman or sexuality. The problematic of the liberation of bodies in this area is quite different today than it was then, since the subversion of the codes that dominate our symbolic field opens up possibilities that were closured by the subasiatic mode of production.

52. According to my custom, I tried to find some explicit statements either in the "introductions" to the New Testament or in exegetical texts. I did find references here and there to the lower-class background of Christians, but nowhere did I find a chapter or even a section dealing directly and formally with the matter of class membership and with the economic and political situation of the early *ekklesiai*! Whenever the "theme of the poor" has to be handled, what is emphasized is that "the poor are not only a social class but the 'spiritual family' (a very vigorous influence in the Judaism of the day) of the 'clients of God' whose submissive, trusting, joyous faith is summed up in an attitude of religious expectation. This is the basic disposition to which the Beatitude of the poor in Matt. 5:3 refers"(J. Jeremias, *Les paraboles de Jésus* [Lyons, 1962], p. 311). When we realize that all contemporary exegesis is carried on under the aegis of form-history, that is, the method that is concerned to bring out the "vital context" of the Christian communities, then this oversight alone, this ignoring of the economic component in this "context," as though it were not "vital," is enough to justify us in speaking of *bourgeois exegesis*.

53. Cf. below, pp. 280 ff.

54. "Fiction" in Nietzsche's sense of the word; cf. below, p. 270.

55. L. Cerfaux, *The Church in the Theology of St. Paul,* trans. G. Webb and A. Walker (New York, 1959), Book I, chap. 4; Book II, chap. 3; Book III, chap. 3.

56. *Ekklesia* is the singular form of the Greek word, *ekklesiai* the plural.

57. Cerfaux, p. 294.

58. In S 44, where there had been no sending, they are powerless.

59. G. Deleuze, *Nietzsche et la philosophie* (Paris, 1962), p. 3.

60. So too for Marx, every social formation is the effect of a relation of forces, of a class struggle in which, I would add, the utopias of the classes are the "forces" that move them.

61. Deleuze, p. 45.

62. Ibid., pp. 49–50.

63. Ibid., p. 60.

64. Ibid., p. 46. In a social formation, the "reaction" is commanded by what I earlier called the "utopia of order," which is an analogon of the negative will to power. (This analogy would postulate that the negative will to power is equivalent to the Freudian "death drive." Is this legitimate?)

65. Deleuze, p. 48. In a social formation, what I have called "utopia-drive" is the thing that commands activity; it would be the analogon of the will to power as affirmation. We should emphasize that although Deleuze says that power is "power to transform," the terms he uses most often are "production" and, especially, "creation."

66. Ibid., p. 45.

67. Ibid., p. 26.

68. Ibid., p. 53.

69. Ibid., p. 56.

70. Ibid., p. 57.

71. Ibid., p. 60.

72. Cf. ibid., p. 61.

73. Cf. ibid., p. 30.

74. Ibid., p. 28.

75. Cf. ibid., p. 65.

76. Ibid., p. 180.

77. I believe that the same criticism can be directed at the texts of Freud on "culture" and "civilization."

78. For example, the statement that "the idea of representation poisons philosophy" (ibid., p. 92) calls attention to "signs" as symbols of the logocentric ideological apparatus. Another example: the idea that by killing God humanity has retained God's place (cf. ibid., pp. 173–74).

79. L. Althusser and E. Balibar, *Reading Capital*, trans. B. Brewster (New York, 1970), pp. 79–82.

79a. The notion of "labor" becomes, in capitalist bookkeeping, *wages*; the latter are added to the (exchange) value of the means of production in order to form *capital*. To distinguish, as Marx did, between variable capital (wages) and constant capital (the means of production, including raw material) amounts to opening up the analysis of capital and bringing out the idea of *labor power*, just as the consideration of exchange value enabled Marx to bring out the idea of use value. Marx thereby shifted the ground of the problematic: the economic instance was no longer read "through the eyes" of capitalist bookkeeping, of gold capital, but was read from the side of the bodies of either the productive agents or their products. From this materialist site it is possible to interpret the meaning of the relations of production, to evaluate the will to power (*What* is it that wills the liberation of the productive forces? Answer: labor power as an active force), and to elaborate a strategy of liberation. In short, Marx's discourse enables the proletariat to "lay hold of the word"; it assigns to the proletariat the place of the word that has been erased in the bourgeois economic discourse. Nothing could be clearer in this respect than the example of the discussions of LIP.

80. Cf. Deleuze, p. 146: "to deprive the active force of the material conditions

needed for its exercise [I read: the appropriation of the means of production]; to separate it formally from what it can do [I read: by means of fiction fetishization]."

81. One effect of the reaction is the excesses accompanying growth, waste, and the pollution which is being so forcefully denounced today and which will be avoidable only when the proletariat becomes active (autoproductive, autogestional, autogrammatic).

82. Cf. Deleuze, p. 143.

83. Ibid., p. 65.

84. There is an illustration of this point in incidents attendant upon the kidnapping of bosses. See, for example, in Karmitz's film, *Coup pour coup,* the scene in which the kidnapped boss asks for a urinal amid the laughter of the women workers.

85. Nietzsche's use of the term was not accidental: he thought highly of the slavery practiced by the Romans! See his *The Anti-Christ,* no. 18. "Nietzsche uses the terms 'weak' or 'slave' not for the less strong but for the one who, whatever his strength, is separated from what he can do" (Deleuze, p. 69). What feeling was it that led the Deleuze of ten years ago to pass over this Nietzschean contradiction in silence?

86. Ibid., p. 139.

87. Ibid., pp. 138, 205.

88. Ibid., p. 135.

89. Ibid., pp. 158–59.

90. Ibid., pp. 173–74.

91. Ibid., p. 197.

92. Ibid.

93. Ibid., pp. 201–3.

94. Ibid., p. 203.

95. Cf. Rom. 10:15: "How beautiful the *feet* of those who announce good tidings" (literal translation).

96. Cf. above, pp. 235 f.

97. This, it will be recalled, is the erased object of the new teaching given to the disciples in S 42c-e.

98. Negation triumphed over Peter who *denied* the messianic narrative.

99. Cf. Deleuze, p. 93. However, John 18:2–9 allows a different reading as we indicated above, pp. 328 f., fn. 178.

100. It is perhaps this "activity" of J that is connoted by the two proper names, Gethsemani and Golgotha.

101. We may recall the smile which Che Guevara gave the young woman teacher who visited him at a time when he knew he was going to be killed without any possibility of appeal from the sentence (according to *Paris-Match* of that period). We may also recall how the common people said he resembled Christ.

102. The individualization of the collective figure "Son of man" was made possible by a transformation of the strategic absence of J's body, an absence required for the geographical extension of his practice to the world of the pagans where he was to continue the (proclamation of the) messianic practice. That which in the prepaschal narrative was a strategic "absence" became in the postpaschal narrative the definitive absence of the risen J.

103. Cf. above, p. 21.

104. Cf. Deleuze, p. 201.

105. Cf. above, p. 159.

106. Cf. 1 Cor. 15:26.

107. Cf. S 55h.

108. Properly speaking, it is the textual conjunction of "paschal Son of man" and "eschatological Son of man" that produces the idea of the return; the Greek verb *erchomenon* (in S 58b5) can mean either "going" or "coming" (cf. above, p. 160). Boismard, 2:405, makes this point with regard to Dan. 7:13.

109. Cf. F. Nietzsche, *The Anti-Christ,* trans. R. J. Hollingdale (Baltimore, 1968), nos. 29, 32, 34.

110. Ibid., no. 39, p. 151 (italics in Nietzsche).

111. Cf. above, pp. 72 f.

112. Nietzsche, no. 38, p. 150.

113. The discovery in and through writing of what one had not previously been able to read is one of the great pleasures of writing. However, if you reread attentively those passages of my "Reading of Mark" in which there is question of the theological discourse, you will find that space was left open for this affirmation/negation distinction at the narrator/readers level.

114. The two statements: "the elect whom he [the Lord] has chosen" (S 58b4) and "it is for those for whom it has been prepared" (S 50b) do not enable us to advance very far in studying the effects of the theological discourse of predestination on the ecclesial narrative. The references in Paul's letters to the Thessalonians to the idleness of some Christians seem, however, to show that the expectation of an imminent Parousia "halted" the narrative (the practice) of the "elect." When I make "predestination" the matrix of the theological discourse, I am thinking of the relation of this discourse to the narrative. I am not in a position to pass judgment on the role of the theological discourse in the Greek and western gnoseological text. However, the fact that during two periods of accelerated transformation of the codes of the social formation, namely, the two "ends of the world" in the fifth and sixteenth centuries, the theologies of an Augustine and a Calvin made predestination so clear a part of the framework of their respective discourses, is perhaps not unrelated to the thesis I am defending.

115. Cf. above, p. 78.

116. Cf. the canonical ending, Mark 16:19.

117. In S 66c the title "son of the Blessed One," which is connected with the title "Messiah," seems to have no special significance.

118. This is already true in the Pauline texts, which antedate the Markan text.

119. The title "Lord" (a trace of which can be seen in S 52a: "The Lord has need of it") becomes linked with the title "Christ," thus making the establishment clearer still.

120. S 16, S 25, S 26, S 34, S 51, S 71a.

121. S 42e, S 49, S 58b3, b4. Cf. above, pp. 169 and 179.

122. Paul had already developed this discourse. "Jesus our Lord . . . was put to death *for our sins*" (Rom. 4:25); "Christ died *for us* while we were still sinners" (Rom. 5:8); etc. It is noteworthy that this theological metaphorization of the death is connected with the christological establishment.

123. In Paul the absence of the messianic narrative of J is very striking. That narrative is there reduced to a theological summarizing formula about the death and resurrection of J "for our sins."

124. A symptom of this is the words flung at Judas: "Woe to the man. . . . It were better for this man that he had not been born" (S 62b). The words imply predestination!

125. Casanova, "Le christianisme primitif" in *La naissance des dieux* (Paris, 1966), pp.

82–83; the following quotations are from pp. 82–88.

125a. Engels, p. 334.

125b. Ibid.

126. Cf. above, pp. 17 f.

127. Quoted by Casanova, p. 98.

128. The predestination matrix of the theological discourse depends therefore on the MYTH code and was produced in the apocalyptic literature, which was Persian in origin (cf. above, p. 72).

129. Cf. above, pp. 162 f.

130. Cf. above, p. 222.

131. This is a hypothesis that must be verified in the letters of Paul. He too had trouble with questions regarding the unity of the *ekklesiai;* how did his theological discourse relate to these problems?

132. The theological discourse as negation is thus supported by the utopia order.

133. Cf. above, pp. 56 ff.

134. Cf. above, pp. 85 f.

135. Casanova's thesis, which, he claims, "is hard to challenge," that "Essenism is the 'intermediary link' connecting Judaism with Christianity" (p. 125), seems unable in fact to explain the text of Mark; the latter text does challenge the thesis! Casanova bases his thesis solely on some citations from Paul and the Apocalypse; he ignores the Gospels (but he admits this to begin with; p. 79). My entire reading, and especially the decisive role of the fall of the temple, which the Essenes had long regarded as profaned, proves that Mark himself was not an Essene. Moreover, the Qumran texts all bear witness to a closure of these communities; this makes it unlikely that, if Mark were an Essene, the schema of the *road* would dominate the Markan text, as in fact it does. Like the bourgeois exegetes, Casanova is unaware of the "messianic" narrative; for him, the Christian phenomenon is ever-already situated solely at the theological-religious level. It is true, however, as his analysis shows, that the ideologizing theologization of the messianic narrative is determined by the economic and political situation of the *ekklesiai.*

136. Cf. above, pp. 256 f.

137. Cf. above, pp. 72 ff.

138. It is therefore in the logic of the movement of demythologization, as found in Mark, that Luke should break the connection between the two codes and make possible the "postponement" of the eschatological narrative.

139. In this respect the first ecclesial communities differed from the nonrevolutionary communism of the hippie communities, which are closured in marginality.

140. Cf. above, p. 124 and fn. 27, p. 320.

141. Cf. above, p. 159.

142. As it is put in the beautiful Portuguese description of childbirth: *dar à luz uma criança*, "to give a child to the light."

143. This can be easily seen in 1 Thess. 4:17.

144. Allow me to point out here that we must perhaps expect a movement of "defaithfulization" or "delaicization" analogous to the movement of "declericalization." I am thinking of the public "scandalous" statement by several hundred of the laity that they intend not to have their children baptized, in the hope that some day the children will be *converted* in the evangelical sense of this term.

145. Except for the cases of "impure spirit," for the sea (S 23, S 33), and even for the loaves in S 32, in which the MYTH code also is at work.

146. If not in questions of the type, "What was it that really happened?" or "What is the historical element in this narrative?" then at least in questions about the historicity of Jesus' words, his *ipsissima verba*. When the narrative is thus annulled, can we be surprised that bourgeois exegetes should not have discovered the messianic narrative? In all this we are dealing with an undeniable tendency, even though in one or other recent author the tendency is nuanced in many ways.

147. This is quite clear from its predilection for the *logia* of Jesus.

148. This fragmentation, which is due especially to *Formgeschichte* (the "forms" whose history this type of exegesis tries to reconstruct are simply "synoptic fragments"), is an index of an idealist reading. To the latter we have opposed our own reading as a reading of the text in its signifying materiality, a materialist reading that relates the text to the social formation (subasiatic mode of production and slave-based mode of production). While *Formgeschichte* does represent a materialist moment in the history of exegesis (cf. above, p. 96), it has nonetheless been worked on by idealism. In my view, it is only *after* a materialistic reading of the synoptic *texts* as they stand that a study of their prehistory can hope to succeed.

149. Deleuze, p. 44.

150. B. Spinoza, *Ethics,* trans. G. S. (London, 1910), Part III, chap. 2, fn., p. 87.

151. 1 Cor. 2:9.

152. If we must set a "first question" over against this "final question" (which relates to the infrastructural life/death contradiction; cf. above, p. 9), that first question would, according to Mark, be the question of the rich man in S 49: "What shall I *do* so that I may obtain eternal *life*?" Here the word "eternal" establishes the connection with the "final question," according to S 49d.

153. Derrida, "Violence et métaphysique," pp. 118-19.

154. Ibid. Derrida thus introduces an "Essai sur la pensée d'Emmanuel Levinas" in which he compares hellenism and Hebraism. My procedure here, though quite different from that of Levinas, might eventually provide some points for this debate.

155. Cf. above, p. 9.

156. Derrida, p. 142, citing Levinas.

157. Ibid., p. 170.

158. This is one of the major theses of his *Eroticism.*

159. Derrida, "Violence et métaphysique," p. 191. To answer no is to halt the narrative *in advance*; we would still be in the theological discourse.

160. Like philosophy itself, the question of the resurrection is only one *mode* of the "question in general."

161. Cited by Derrida, pp. 223–24.

162. In the Greek gnoseological text the philosophical question is : "What is death? What is life?" In the messianic narrative text the kerygmatic question is rather: "What must I do to have life?"; it is linked with practice, engenders narrative on the basis of narrative, and therefore follows the logic of the eleventh thesis on Feuerbach.

163. The question of the "existence of God," which St. Thomas makes the *first* question in his *Summa theologiae* (I, q. 2, immediately after the introductory question on the status of theology as a "science"), is consequently dependent on the question of the resurrection (though the latter comes toward the end of the *Summa*; cf. *Supplementum,* qq. 75–86). When raised *by itself*, as it is in the western theological discourse, the question is either a tautology ("Does God exist?" "Yes") or nonsense ("Does God exist?" "No"); it continues to be open to the critique made of it by Nicholas of Cusa. It is not an accident that Mark raised the question (in the form of the decisive distinction

"God of living men/god of dead men") only in connection with the *question* of the resurrection.

164. The messianic narrative excludes priests; the theological discourse brought them back, along with the *episkopos*.

165. Deut. 5:11, however, accepted this (cf. Lev. 24:10–23).

166. Has this not escaped the attention of the "leftist Christians" who so readily demythologize the resurrection?

167. Since the last war we have seen a new appreciation of the "resurrection" in the ecclesiastical discourse. This is symptomatic of the fact that, though never explicitly denied, the resurrection had nonetheless been erased from the western ecclesiastical discourse. This is another "history" that deserves analysis.

168. Like Solzhenitsyn, for example.

169. Allow me still another remark about political analysis of the church by revolutionary Christians. These people often attack the church's "possessions, power, and knowledge" (representing the three instances) in an undifferentiated way. The time has come to realize that in the clerical apparatus "possessions" and "power" are at the service of the ideological instance, which is the *dominant function* of the clergy as an apparatus (even if it no longer plays the role of dominant ideology that it did of yore). The decisive criticism must be criticism of this ideological function; it must therefore be first and foremost epistemological (the kind of criticism I have tried to exercise here). The politics of the clergy is not determined by a concern to hold on to their clerical apparatus at any price, as *Eglise, luttes de classes et stratégies politiques* (Paris, 1972), J. Guichard claims pp. 120 ff.), but rather by the relation between their ideological function and the "religious needs" of their clientele (Cf. above, p. 304, fn. 71).

170. Cf. Eph. 2:14.

171. The Gospel is alien to us, and luckily so. To demythologize it is not to bring it closer to us as a "living word" (since a *text* is not a living word) but rather to turn it into a "reading grill." But a grill that is alien prevents any identification with the actant J and better assures the freeplay of our own narratives.

Bibliography

1. VARIOUS THEORETICAL TEXTS

Althusser, L. *For Marx.* Translated by B. Brewster. London and New York, 1969.
———. "Idéologie et appareils idéologiques d'Etat (Notes pour une recherche)." *La Pensée* (June 1970).
——— and Balibar, E. *Reading Capital.* Translated by B. Brewster. New York, 1970.
Banu, I. "La formation sociale 'asiatique' dans la perspective de la philosophie orientale antique." In *Sur le "mode de production asiatique."* Paris, 1969.
Barthes, R. *Elements of Semiology.* Translated by A. Lavers and C. Smith. London, 1967.
———. "Introduction à l'analyse structurale des récits." *Communications* (Paris), no. 8 (1966).
———. "L'analyse structurale du récit, à propos d'Actes X–XI." *Recherches de science religieuse* 58 (1970): 17–38.
———. *S/Z.* Translated by R. Miller. New York, 1974.
Bataille, G. *Eroticism.* Translated by M. Dalwood. London, 1962.
———. *La part maudite: Essai d'économie générale.* Paris, 1970 (1953).
Benveniste, E. *Problems in General Linguistics.* Translated by M. E. Meek. Coral Gables, Fla., 1971.
Casanova, A., "Le christianisme primitif." *La naissance des dieux.* Paris, 1966.
Deleuze, G. *Nietzsche et la philosophie.* Paris, 1962.
Derrida, J. *Of Grammatology.* Translated by G. C. Spivak. Baltimore, 1976.
———. *Positions.* Paris, 1972.
———. "Violence et métaphysique: Essai sur la pensée d'Emmanuel Levinas." In his *L'écriture et la différence.* Paris, 1967.
Dhoquois, G. *Pour l'histoire.* Paris, 1971.
Douglas, M. *Purity and Danger: An Analysis of the Concepts of Pollution and Taboo.* London, 1966.
Eliade, M. *Myth and Reality.* Translated by W. R. Trask. New York, 1963.
———. *The Sacred and the Profane: The Nature of Religion.* Translated by W. R. Trask. New York, 1959.
Engels, F. *On the History of Early Christianity.* In *Karl Marx and Friedrich Engels on Religion.* New York, 1964.
Freud, S. *The Interpretation of Dreams.* Translated by J. Strachey. London, 1961.
———. *Totem and Taboo: Resemblances between the Psychic Lives of Savages and Neurotics.* Translated by A. A. Brill.
Godelier, M. "La notion de 'mode de production asiatique' et les schémas marxistes d'évolution des sociétés." In *Sur le "mode de production asiatique."* Paris, 1969.
Goux, J. J. "Numismatiques," *Tel Quel,* nos. 35 and 36 (1968). Reprinted in Goux, *Economie et symbolique.* Paris, 1973.

Guichard, J. *Eglise, luttes de classes et stratégies politiques.* Paris, 1972.

Herbert, T. "Réflexions sur la situation théorique des sciences sociales et spéciale-ment de la psychologie sociale," *Cahiers pour l'analyse,* no. 2 (1966).

————. "Remarques pour une théorie générale des idéologies." *Cahiers pour l'analyse,* no. 9 (1968).

Kristeva, J. "Le texte clos." In her *Sêmeiôtikê: Recherches pour une sémanalyse.* Paris, 1969.

————. *Le texte du roman: Approche sémiologique d'une structure discursive transfor-mationnelle.* The Hague, 1970.

Lacan, J. *Ecrits.* Paris, 1966.

Mandel, E. "Initiation à la théorie économique marxiste." *Cahiers du Centre d'études socialistes,* no. 1 (February-March, 1964).

Marx, K. *Capital.* Translated by S. Moore and E. Aveling. New York, 1967.

Nietzsche, F. *The Anti-Christ.* Translated by R. J. Hollingdale. Baltimore, 1968.

Poulantzas, N. *Fascisme et dictature: La 3ᵉ Internationale face au fascisme.* Paris, 1970.

————. *Pouvoir politique et classes sociales.* Paris, 1968.

Rifflet-Lemaire, A. *Jacques Lacan.* Brussels, 1970.

Terray, E. *Marxism and "Primitive" Society: Two Studies.* Translated by M. Klopper. New York, 1972.

Vernant, J. P. *L'origine de la pensée grecque.* Paris, 1962.

2. BIBLICAL EXEGESIS

Aland, K. *Synopsis of the Four Gospels: Greek-English Edition.* Stuttgart, 1972.

Baron, S. *A Social and Religious History of the Jews.* 2nd ed., rev. New York, 1952.

Beaucamp, E. "Souillure et pureté dans la Bible," in *Souillure et pureté.* Paris, 1972.

Benoit, P. "Les épis arrachés (Mt. 12, 1–8 et par.)," *Studii Biblici Franciscani Liber Annuus* 13 (1962–63), pp. 76-92; reprinted in his *Exégèse et théologie* 3 (Paris, 1968).

Bratcher, R. G., and Nida, E. A. *A Translator's Handbook on the Gospel of Mark.* Leiden, 1961.

Cerfaux, L. *The Church in the Theology of St. Paul.* Translated by G. Webb and A. Walker. New York, 1959.

Chapelle, A., et al. *L'evangile de saint Marc.* Mimeographed; study session, July 1969. Eegenhoven-Louvain, 1969.

Cullmann, O. *The Christology of the New Testament,* rev. ed. Translated by S. C. Guthrie and C. A. M. Hall. Philadelphia, 1963.

————. *Jesus and the Revolutionaries.* Translated by G. Putnam. New York, 1970.

Dumézil, G., Benveniste, E., Dupont-Sommer, A., et al. *La civilisation iranienne.* Paris, 1952.

Guignebert, C. *The Jewish World in the Time of Jesus.* Translated by S. H. Hooke. London, 1939.

Hengel, M. *Jésus et la violence révolutionnaire.* Translated from German (1971). Paris, 1973.

Huby, J. *L'évangile selon saint Marc.* In *La sainte Bible de Jérusalem* (ed. in fascicles). 3rd ed. rev. by P. Benoit. Paris, 1961.

Jeremias, J. *Jerusalem in the Time of Jesus: An Investigation into Economic and Social Conditions During the New Testament Period.* Translated by F. H. Cave and C. H. Cave. Philadelphia, 1969.

———. *The Parables of Jesus.* Translated by S. H. Hooke, rev. ed. New York, 1963.

Kaestli, J. D. *L'eschatologie dans l'oeuvre de Luc.* Geneva, 1969.

Kümmel, W. G. *Introduction to the New Testament,* rev. ed. Translated from 17th German ed. (1973) by H. C. Kee. Nashville, 1975.

Lambrecht, J. "La structure de Marc XIII." In *De Jésus aux Evangiles: Tradition et rédaction dans les Evangiles synoptiques.* Gembloux, 1967.

Léon-Dufour, X. "The Synoptic Gospels." In *Introduction to the New Testament.* Edited by A. Robert and A. Feuillet. Translated by P. Skehan et al. New York, 1965.

———. "La transfiguration de Jésus." In his *Etudes d'Evangile.* Paris, 1965.

Lubac, H. de. *The Sources of Revelation.* Translated by L. O'Neill. New York, 1968.

Marin, L. *Sémiotique de la passion: Topiques et figures.* Paris, 1971.

Minette de Tillesse, G. *Le secret messianique dans l'évangile de Marc.* Paris, 1968.

McLoughlin, S. "Le problème synoptique: Vers la théorie des deux sources; Les accords mineurs." In *De Jésus aux évangiles: Tradition et rédaction dans les Evangiles synoptiques.* Gembloux, 1967.

The New Testament and Structuralism. A collection of essays by C. Galland, C. Chabrol, G. Vuillod, L. Marin, and E. Haulotte. Edited and translated by A. M. Johnson, Jr., Pittsburgh, 1976. Originally *Langages,* no. 22 (June 1971), entitled *Sémiotique narrative: Récits bibliques.*

Osty, E. *Evangile selon saint Marc.* In his *Le Nouveau Testament.* Paris, 1963.

Paul, A. "Bulletin de littérature intertestamentaire: L' 'Intertestament.' " *Recherches de science religieuse* 60 (1972): 429–58.

Prigent, P. *La fin de Jérusalem.* Neuchâtel, 1969.

Starobinski, J. "The Gerasene Demoniac: A Literary Analysis of Mark 5:1–20." In *Biblical Exegesis: Interpretational Essays.* Edited and translated by A. M. Johnson, Jr., Pittsburgh, 1974. Pp. 57–84.

Taylor, V. *The Gospel According to St. Mark.* New York, 1957.

Tricot, A. "The Jewish World." In *Introduction to the New Testament.* Edited by A. Robert and A. Feuillet. Translated by P. Skehan et al. New York, 1965.

Trocmé, E. *The Formation of the Gospel According to Mark.* Translated by P. Gaughan. Philadelphia, 1975.

Vaux, R. de. *Ancient Israel: Its Life and Institutions.* Translated by J. McHugh. New York, 1961.

Von Rad, G. *Old Testament Theology. 1. The Theology of Israel's Historical Traditions; 2. The Theology of Israel's Prophetic Traditions.* Translated by D. M. G. Stalker. New York, 1962–65.

Widengren, G. *Les Religions d'Iran.* Translated from the German ed. of 1965. Paris, 1968.

Zerwick, M. *Analysis philologica Novi Testamenti graeci.* 3rd ed. Rome, 1953, 1966. The section on the Gospels and Acts has been translated in M. Zerwick and M. Grosvenor, *A Grammatical Analysis of the Greek New Testament.* Rome, 1974.

Contents

Narrative, Key to the Reading of the Great Narrative Text;
The Work of the Seed in S 27; Truth and Error (in Reading);
Practice and the Gospel of the Resurrection of Bodies; The
Murderous Work of Money and Force; The Question of
Power: Life or Death?; The Spirit: Opening of a Field for an
Other, New Society; The Snare into Which Bourgeois Exegetes
Fall: the Heart as Pure Interiority and the Exclusion of the
Body

Their Place in the Narrative; Zealotic Reformism and Nationalism; The Messianic Strategy: Radically Communist, Nonrevolutionary, Internationalist; The Messianic Practice and the
Debt System; Internationalism and the Principle of the Extension of Giving; Pleasure and Utopia, Use Value and Poverty;
"Nonviolence" Is Theological

Narrator/Readers Level: Translation-tradition; The Class Af-
filiation of Mark's Readers; The *Ekklesia*, Space for Reading
and Watchfulness; The *Ekklesia*, Concept of a Practice; *Ekklesia*
in Matthew and Paul; The Question of "Christian Identity" Put
in Terms of Ecclesial Practice

Messianic Narrative and Apostolic Proclamation; Apostolic
Writing; Short Résumé of Nietzsche's Philosophy of the Body
(According to Deleuze); Nietzsche and Marxist Materialism:
Five Remarks; Nietzsche's Strategic Impasse; The Apostolic
Affirmation of the Messianic Narrative; Gethsemani and Gol-
gotha: an "Active" Man Facing Temptation and Death; The
Triple Kerygmatic Movement: Becoming and Being (Jesus Is
the Son of Man), the Many and the One (Sacrificial, Cup,
Baptism), Chance and Necessity ("It Is Written"); Jesus Is the
Messiah; (He) the Son of Man Will Return Soon; Nietzsche
and Christianity

The Question of the Structure of the Theological Discourse;
Predestination as Negation; The Christological Establishment:
Recentering (of Christ) in the Ecclesial Circle; The Soteriolog-

ical Movement: Ransom and the Blood of the Covenant; Christ
as General Equivalent of Christians; The Transformation, by
the Theological Discourse, of Murder into Death: the Reestab-
lishment of the Pollution System in "Christianity"; The
Exploited Classes in the Roman Empire of the First Century,
and Sectarian Religions; Christians: Economically Exploited
and Politically Powerless, the Persecutions of Nero; The
Question of the "When" of Eschatology; The Mythological
Closure of the Theological Discourse; The Question of the
Lapsi and the Unity of the *Ekklesia*; the Episcopal (Sacerdotal)
Site of the Theological Discourse; Recourse to the Codes of
Historical Materialism.

The Messianic Narrative Demythologized; The De-
mythologizing Function of the Scriptures; Remythologization;
Questions for a Materialist Ecclesiology; The Impasse Reached
by Bourgeois Demythologization; Break and Continuity of the
Eschatological Narrative: the Son of Man and Communist
Ecclesiality; After May '68

The Question of the "Miracles" and the Resurrection; The
Difference Between the SYMB and the MYTH Codes in
Mark; The Resurrection Affirmed as a Question; Logocen-
trism and Bourgeois Exegesis; "We Do not Even Know What a
Body's Possibilities Are" (Spinoza); The Resurrection, Final
Question for a Communist Society; The "Question" and the
Finitude of the Horizon; The "Why?" of Golgotha and the
Theological Discourse; The Question Asked by the Christians
of Rome; Mystery and Narrative; Subversion and Resurrec-
tion; Ecclesial Violence and Pollution/Debt; Debate on Power
and Liberation; Insurrection as Site of the Question about
Resurrection

OTHER ORBIS TITLES

ANDERSON, Gerald H.
ASIAN VOICES IN CHRISTIAN THEOLOGY

"Anderson's book is one of the best resource books on the market that deals with the contemporary status of the Christian church in Asia. After an excellent introduction, nine scholars, all well-known Christian leaders, present original papers assessing the theological situation in (and from the viewpoint of) their individual countries. After presenting a brief historical survey of the development of the Christian church in his country, each author discusses 'what is being done by the theologians there to articulate the Christian message in terms that are faithful to the biblical revelation, meaningful to their cultural traditions, and informed concerning the secular movements and ideologies.' An appendix (over 50 pages) includes confessions, creeds, constitutions of the churches in Asia. Acquaintance with these original documents is imperative for anyone interested in contemporary Asian Christian theology." *Choice*

ISBN 0-88344-017-2   *Cloth $15.00*
ISBN 0-88344-016-4   *Paper $7.95*

APPIAH-KUBI, Kofi & Sergio Torres
AFRICAN THEOLOGY EN ROUTE

Papers from the Pan-African Conference of Third World Theologians, Accra, Ghana.

"If you want to know what 17 Africans are thinking theologically today, here is the book to check." *Evangelical Missions Quarterly*

"Gives us a wonderful insight into the religious problems of Africa and therefore is well worth reading." *Best Sellers*

"This collection of presentations made at the 1977 Conference of Third World Theologians reveals not a finished product but, as the title suggests, a process. . . .On the whole, the book is well written and, where necessary, well translated. It adds to a growing literature on the subject and is recommended for libraries seriously concerned with theology in Africa." *Choice*

ISBN 0-88344-010-5   *184pp. Paper $7.95*

BALASURIYA, Tissa
THE EUCHARIST AND HUMAN LIBERATION

"Balasuriya investigates. . .the problem of why people who share the Eucharist also deprive the poor of food, capital, and employment. . . .For inclusive collections." *Library Journal*

"I hope Christians—especially Western Christians—will read this book, despite its blind impatience with historical and ecclesial details and balance, because its central thesis is the gospel truth: eucharistic celebration, like the faith it expresses, has been so domesticated by feudalism, colonialism, capitalism, racism, sexism, that its symbolic action has to penetrate many layers of heavy camouflage before it is free, before it can be felt." *Robert W. Hovda, Editorial Director, The Liturgical Conference*

ISBN 0-88344-118-7   *184pp. Paper $6.95*

BURROWS, William R.
NEW MINISTRIES: THE GLOBAL CONTEXT

"This is an exciting, informed, thoughtful, and ground-breaking book on one of the most vital and threatening issues facing the contemporary church. Father Burrows seeks effectively to show that the older forms of church and clerical life, developed in the West, are both irrelevant and stultifying when transferred *in toto* to the Third World, and that as a consequence, new forms of church and clerical life, forms still within the Catholic heritage to which he belongs and which he affirms, must be developed if the church is long to survive in that new World. Burrows makes crystal clear the need for more open attitudes towards the forms of church and clergy if the newer churches are to become genuinely creative forces in the Third World rather than lingering embassies from the First World. I found the work exceedingly stimulating and the approach fresh and open." *Prof. Langdon Gilkey, University of Chicago Divinity School*

ISBN 0-88344-329-5   *192pp. Paper $7.95*

CABESTRERO, Teofilo
FAITH: CONVERSATIONS WITH CONTEMPORARY THEOLOGIANS

"This book shows what an informed and perceptive journalist can do to make theology understandable, inviting, and demanding. These records of taped interviews with fifteen European and Latin American theologians serve two major purposes: we are allowed to eavesdrop on well-known theologians in spontaneous theological conversation, and we are introduced to new and stimulating minds in the same way."*Prof. D. Campbell Wyckoff, Princeton Theological Seminary*

Conversations include Ladislaus Boros, Georges Casalis, Joseph (José) Comblin, Enrique Dussel, Segundo Galilea, Giulio Girardi, José María González Ruiz, Gustavo Gutiérrez, Hans Küng, Jürgen Moltmann, Karl Rahner, Joseph Ratzinger, Edward Schillebeeckx, Juan Luis Segundo, Jean-Marie Tillard.

ISBN 0-88344-126-8   *208pp. Paper $7.95*

CAMARA, Dom Helder
THE DESERT IS FERTILE

"Dom Helder Camara of Brazil, is a Roman Catholic archbishop whose sense of God's presence breathes through every page. But there is a difference. For Dom Helder has found God's presence in the lives of the poor, in the voices of the oppressed, and he communicates this sense of God's reality very powerfully. He takes us on a spiritual journey that can be utterly transforming if we will risk opening ourselves to him. He is no pessimist; in a world that seems devoid of God's presence, Dom Helder insists that *The Desert Is Fertile*. He does not minimize the 'desert' quality of modern existence: the increasing gap between rich and poor, the insanity of the arms race, and the 'marginalization' of human life, by which he means our tendency to treat the majority of the human family as nonpersons, those who are pushed over to the edges of life and ignored. 'The scandal of this century,' he writes, 'is marginalization.' He reminds us that if to have too little is a problem, so is having too much. 'Poverty makes people subhuman. Excess of wealth makes people inhuman.'" *Christianity and Crisis*

ISBN 0-88344-078-4   *75pp. Cloth $3.95*

CARDENAL, Ernesto
THE GOSPEL IN SOLENTINAME I

"Farmers and fishermen in a remote village in Nicaragua join their priest for dialogues on Bible verses. The dialoguers discover Jesus as the liberator come to deliver *them* from oppression, inequality, and injustice imposed by a rich, exploitive class: they identify Herod as dictator Somoza. Their vision of the Kingdom of God on earth impels them toward political revolution. This is 'Marxian Christianity' not as abstract theory but gropingly, movingly articulated by poor people. Highly recommended to confront the complacent with the stark realities of religious and political consciousness in the Third World." *Library Journal*

ISBN 0-88344-170-5   *Paper $4.95*

THE GOSPEL IN SOLENTINAME II

"Volume 2 follows the pattern of the first volume: villagers in Nicaragua join their priest, Ernesto, in interpreting New Testament verses. These volumes offer a profound challenge to the Christian conscience, and insight into the recent uprisings in Nicaragua. Highly recommended." *Library Journal*

ISBN 0-88344-167-5   *Cloth $6.95*

THE GOSPEL IN SOLENTINAME III

"A continuation of guided discussions on Gospel passages by the peasant folks in the Central American village of Solentiname. Has a most refreshing outlook." *The Priest*
Fortunately, the manuscripts for this and the fourth volume were safely in Orbis' hands before Somoza's soldiers destroyed Solentiname.

ISBN 0-88344-172-1   *320pp. Cloth $7.95*

CARRETTO, Carlo

LETTERS FROM THE DESERT

"Carretto, a very active layman in Catholic Action in Italy for twenty-five years, gave it up at the age of forty-four to become a Little Brother of Jesus. He heard the call to prayer and went into the desert. After a while he began to jot down things. The book was an instant success in Italy where, since its appearance in 1964 it has gone through twenty-four editions. It has been translated into Spanish, French, German, Portugese, Arabic, Japanese, Czech, and now, gracefully enough, into English. I hope it goes into twenty-four more editions. It breathes with life, with fresh insights, with wisdom, with love." *The Thomist*

ISBN 0-88344-280-9   *146pp. Paper $4.95*

LOVE IS FOR LIVING

"This book is truly excellent. Because we are all, indeed, poor, weak and empty, this series of meditations aims right at the human heart and beautifully articulates what goes on there. Some of the chapters are simply brilliant!" *The Cord*

"This book is meant for slow, prayerful pondering—a page or two at a time. It would probably be of help to persons searching for a deeper meaning in daily life, as well as those seeking a better knowledge of the Bible." *Religious Media Today*

ISBN 0-88344-291-4   *158pp. Cloth $6.95*
ISBN 0-88344-293-0   *Paper $4.95*

SUMMONED BY LOVE

"Those of you who treasure Carlo Carretto's books will be pleased by his latest, *Summoned by Love*. The book is a sustained meditation based on a prayer of Charles de Foucauld known as the *Prayer of Abandonment to God*." *Sign*

"Disarmingly simple and direct, Carretto's reflections testify to his familiarity with Scripture, the Church Fathers, and the down-to-earth realities of daily living. For one who is so 'traditional' in his spirituality, many of Carlo Carretto's ideas could be labeled 'liberal.' His writings indicate that he is in the mainstream of what is, and has been, truly vital in the Church universal. This valuable and timely book offers encouragement and challenge for all seeking to live within the changing Church and to find hope and love therein." *Catholic Library World*

ISBN 0-88344-470-4   *143pp. Cloth $7.95*
ISBN 0-88344-472-0   *Paper $4.95*

IN SEARCH OF THE BEYOND

"This little book will spur the reader to find his Beloved in solitary prayer. Creating a desert place for yourself means learning to be self-sufficient, to remain undisturbed with one's own thoughts and prayers. It means shutting oneself up in one's room, remaining alone in an empty church, or setting up an oratory for oneself in an attic in which to localize one's personal contact with God." *Western Michigan Catholic*

" 'To lead others to contemplation is the heart of the apostolate,' according to Carretto. Here are excellent reflections on Scriptural themes, both old and new." *Spiritual Book News*

ISBN 0-88344-208-6   *175pp. Cloth $5.95*

CLAVER, Bishop Francisco F., S.J.

THE STONES WILL CRY OUT
Grassroots Pastorals

"Bishop Claver is the gadfly of the Philippine Catholic hierarchy who persistently buzzes in the ears of President Fernando Marcos and all his toadies. The bishop's book is a collection of fighting pastoral letters to his congregation after martial law closed the diocesan radio station and newspaper." *Occasional Bulletin*

"His gutsy strength has made him a prophet against the repressive regime. Some of his U.S. colleagues could learn from him." *National Catholic Reporter*

ISBN 0-88344-471-2   *196pp. Paper $7.95*

COMBLIN, José

THE CHURCH AND THE NATIONAL SECURITY STATE

"The value of this book is two-fold. It leads the readers to discover the testimony of those Latin American Christians who are striving to be faithful to the gospel in the midst of a most difficult situation characterized by the militarization of society, the consequent suppression of public freedom, and violation of basic human rights. It also invites the readers from other cultural and historical contexts to seek in their own situations the inspiration for a real theology of their own." *Theology Today*

ISBN 0-88344-082-2   *256pp. Paper $8.95*

JESUS OF NAZARETH
Meditations on His Humanity

"This book is not just another pious portrait of Christ. Its deeply religious insights relate the work of Jesus as modern scholarship understands it to the ills of our contemporary world." *Review of Books and Religion*

ISBN 0-88344-239-6   *Paper $4.95*

THE MEANING OF MISSION
Jesus, Christians and the Waytaring Church

"This is a thoughtful and thought-provoking book by a Belgian theologian and social critic, who has lived and taught in Latin America for 20 years. His rich background in evangelization, both in theory and in practice, is evident throughout his book." *Worldmission*

ISBN 0-88344-305-8   *Paper $4.95*

SENT FROM THE FATHER
Meditations on the Fourth Gospel

"In a disarmingly simple and straightforward way that mirrors the Fourth Gospel itself, Comblin leads the reader back to biblical basics and in doing so provides valuable insights for personal and community reflection on what it means to be a disciple of the Lord, to be 'sent' by him." *Sisters Today*

ISBN 0-88344-453-4   *123pp. Paper $3.95*

FABELLA, Virginia, M.M. & Sergio Torres
THE EMERGENT GOSPEL
Theology from the Underside of History

"*The Emergent Gospel*, I believe, is an expression of a powerful and barely noticed movement. It is the report of an ecumenical conference of 22 theologians from Africa, Asia and Latin America, along with one representative of black North America, who met in Dar es Salaam, Tanzania, in August 1976. Their objective was to chart a new course in theology, one that would reflect the view 'from the underside of history,' that is, from the perspective of the poor and marginalized peoples of the world. Precisely this massive shift in Christian consciousness is the key to the historical importance of the meeting. The majority of the essays were written by Africans, a smaller number by Asians and, surprisingly, only three by Latin Americans, who thus far have provided the leadership in theology from the developing world." *America*

ISBN 0-88344-112-8   *Cloth $12.95*

FENTON, Thomas P.
EDUCATION FOR JUSTICE: A RESOURCE MANUAL

"The completeness of the source material on the topic and the adaptability of the methodology—stressing experiential education—to groups at the high school, college, or adult levels make this manual a time and energy saving boon for most anyone having to work up a syllabus on 'justice.' This manual would be a worthwhile addition to any religion and/or social studies curriculum library." *Review for Religious*

"The resource volume is rich in ideas for a methodology of teaching Christian justice, and in identifying the problems. It is also very rich in the quality of the background readings provided. The participant's volume is a catchy workbook with many illustrations. It encourages the student (young or adult) to look at the problems as they are experienced by real live persons." *The Priest*

"Replete with background essays, tested group exercises, course outlines and annotated bibliography, this manual should give any teacher or seminar leader plenty of material to launch a thorough study program—and plenty of strongly stated positions for students to react to." *America*

ISBN 0-88344-154-3   *Resource Manual $7.95*
ISBN 0-88344-120-9   *Participant Workbook $3.95*

GUTIERREZ, Gustavo
A THEOLOGY OF LIBERATION

Selected by the reviewers of *Christian Century* as one of the twelve religious books published in the 1970s which "most deserve to survive."

"Rarely does one find such a happy fusion of gospel content and contemporary relevance." *The Lutheran Standard*

ISBN 0-88344-477-1   *Cloth $7.95*
ISBN 0-88344-478-X   *Paper $4.95*